Understanding

My Life

Backwards

Finding Authentic Faith through Informed Reasoning

Robert A. Voelker, Ph. D., M. Div.

Understanding My Life Backwards: Finding Authentic Faith Through Informed Reasoning
Copyright © 2011 by Robert A Voelker

Printed by Lulu
3101 Hillsborough St.
Raleigh, NC 27607

Printed in the United States of America

ISBN - 978-0-9830410-0-9

Contents

Foreword

Throughout our history, both individually and collectively, we humans have been searching for purpose and meaning in our origin and existence. We have asked ourselves a number of questions, among which are the following: "Who am I?" "Who are we as the human species?" "Are there purpose and meaning to our existence? If so, what are they?" "What is the nature of the powers and forces beyond what our senses can detect and our minds can comprehend – what some have termed god(s) and others have referred to more generically as *Unseen Ultimate Reality* (*UUR*)?" "What is our relationship to *UUR*?"

Through the centuries and the millennia, our cumulative endeavors in philosophy and religion have sought to answer the above questions. As its etymology implies, philosophy loves the wisdom and the knowledge that reflect truths and understandings concerning life's important questions. On the other hand, as its etymology implies, religion attempts repeatedly to tie together the answers to the foregoing questions by situating human existence in a mythical narrative in which humans interact with *UUR* (their gods) and other humans; it is in the decisions and actions of people and their deities in this narrative that the purpose and meaning of human existence are described and depicted.

Through the years many people have found religious frameworks of understanding that have been sufficient for them to navigate through life meaningfully and purposefully. Although there may be times in their lives when specific troublesome questions arise for which their religion does not provide clear and satisfying answers or solutions, they are able to wade through these rough shoals and to remain firmly committed to their faith. For those persons, their religion provides a suitable worldview and a supportive mainstay for living a fulfilling life.

For other people, life unfolds differently. Some find that the beliefs and perspectives of traditional religions are incongruent with their experiences of life, and they therefore choose not to become involved in them. Other people become involved in traditional religions, perhaps through parental influence as they are growing up. For a time their religion seems to serve them well. However, when, in addition to the difficult and challenging problems of everyday living, they experience heartbreaking tragedy, sometimes repeatedly, their religious faith and practices no longer sustain them. The troubled shoals in their lives give way to deeper and rougher waters where the faith supports of their religion are no longer adequate for them to swim and to stay afloat. They must find additional resources in order to survive and then to enable their lives to become meaningful and fulfilling again.

These last two groups of people may still subscribe to a nonmaterial dimension of life and reality, but they are not affiliated with any formal religion. Increasingly over the last half century or so, such people are said to be *spiritual* (or to have *spirituality*) but not to be religious. These persons hold that there is an incorporeal and immaterial dimension to life and existence – that there is *UUR* – but that no present-day religion offers a valid and credible conceptualization of that transcendence. Such people often aggregate an eclectic collection of beliefs and practices from different religious and philosophical sources to form a sort of personal religion that "works" for them.

This book is a recounting of one such spiritual journey – that of my life. My faith journey began in traditional, conservative Lutheran Christianity and wended its way to a nature-centered spirituality. Through a kind of journaling process, in this book I relate the events of my life – particularly the challenges and tragedies – together with my thoughts, feelings and reactions as I attempted to understand and to make sense of them.

Even if no one else were to read this spiritual travelogue, writing it was something that I needed to do for my own benefit – yes, even my own survival. It has helped me to gain perspective on where I have been, and it is helping me to see possibilities for my journey forward.

Through the years I have spoken with many friends and colleagues about what is presented in this book. Many of them have encouraged me to commit these materials to writing for others to read and to consider. At first, I had reservations about publishing these matters at all. After all, this has been just my own personal journey – the events and experiences that I have encountered in my life; my interpretations of them are specific, and perhaps peculiar and particular, to me. Moreover, it is intimidating to write such a book, because disclosure of such intimate details of my spiritual life throws open to the world the struggles of my identity. Using an analogy no longer familiar to most people, in writing such a book I hang all my spiritual laundry out on the clothesline. There for everyone to see are the stains in my shirts and pants and all the rips and tears in my underwear.

When I finally began to write, I envisioned the title to be something pertaining to my journey to authentic faith. However, as I wrote more and reflected further about the contents from a broader perspective, I recognized that I was trying to make sense of what has occurred in my life; that is, I was trying to *understand my life backwards*. Moreover, I concluded that, while the events and conclusions are specific to my life, the *process of finding authentic faith through informed reasoning* is not unique to my situation. That process is a journey that can be undertaken by anyone who desires to do it. Hence, I also included that phrase in the title.

Perhaps some of the specific ideas and perspectives presented in these pages can even help provide insights and perspectives for others, each of whom has her/his own unique journey. It is my hope that others will be emboldened to look backwards at their own journeys in order to discover the truths that will give them the freedom to live forward with new understanding and meaning in their own lives. Finding authentic faith through informed reasoning may not be easy. It was not and still is not for me, but it is ultimately important and well worth the effort.

Undertaking the writing of my first book after age sixty has been a daunting prospect simply from technical and organizational standpoints. But it has also been very difficult from an emotional perspective, because in writing about my life's journey I had to remember and to relive all the disappointments and pains of my life. Excruciating experiences that were distributed over months and years in the more than six decades of my life were compressed and reprocessed in the time that it took to complete the writing about them. That aspect has proven much more difficult than I had anticipated.

One challenge in writing a book such as this is relating the materials in an appropriate tone of expression. While the details were and are important to me and have impacted me greatly, they are only my story. Therefore, I have tried to relate them in a way that is not too presumptuous of their importance to readers. I make no claims that what is true for me should in any way be true for others. At the same time, I wanted to express what I had to say in a strong enough way that enables the reader to grasp the content that I think makes my story worth writing and perhaps relevant to them. I have tried to find an appropriate middle ground. Where I have stepped over the line, I ask for the reader's forgiveness and indulgence.

My processing of the events of my life – *understanding my life backwards* – occurred sequentially, much as recounted in the writing. That process involved much analysis and critical examination of the elements of the Christian tradition in which I was reared. Therefore, those readers who are more or less comfortable embracing most of traditional Judeo-Christianity may conclude early on that I have discarded everything pertaining to that tradition. I encourage them to read on to the end, because those elements of that tradition that still validly inform my life became clear as the examination process was nearing completion.

Because the details of my life necessarily unfolded in the context of the members of my family, I dedicate this book, as appropriate, to their honor and in their memory. My parents Elmer and Helen Voelker birthed me and diligently formed me in the faith that they firmly believed would prepare me for living a faithful Christian life. My first wife Darlene was the first love of my life – a loving, faithful and nurturing companion. With my oldest daughter, Tammy, I first experienced the joy of parenting new life. My second daughter, Cheri, has walked with me and helped me struggle through the difficulties that have occurred during the time that our lives have overlapped. From my youngest daughter, Bethany, I learned that at times I must simply throw caution to the wind and get on with what seems necessary to make the most of life and to try to enjoy it. My second wife, Linda, has been my loving, faithful and supportive companion while I have worked through the many difficulties that occurred in my life prior to my meeting her. I know that it has often been difficult for her, because my processing of my earlier life events has sometimes impeded the development of the greater intimacy that we both desire. Additionally, for much of the time that I was writing this book, she also has been dealing with the declining health of her mother. For Linda's love, patience and courage in giving me the time and space that I needed to work things out, I owe her an immeasurable debt of gratitude. I also owe her many dinners at the restaurants of her choice for spending countless hours as she used her formal training in English language knowledge and writing skills to edit and to modify the manuscript in order to bring it to a publishable form. I hope and trust that I shall be available to her more now that this writing and publishing has been completed.

I also thank innumerable people whose writings and conversations have proved helpful in shepherding me forward along this journey. Those whose writings were seminal in stimulating and informing my thinking will be acknowledged through the course of the book. To those who participated in conversations and discussions that helped sharpen and focus my thinking I also express my sincere gratitude. I thank Millie English and Idania Hutchens for their help in modifying the cover graphics to their final form. Finally, I thank three Catawba College colleagues, Professors Michael Baranski, Steve Coggin and Seth Holtzman for their reading of the manuscript; their critiques and suggestions were most helpful.

Robert A. Voelker
February 17, 2010

Introduction

"The most important quality in a person concerned with religion is absolute devotion to truth."
Albert Schweitzer

Most of the time life is good; sometimes it is very good. We are pleased to be alive. We are glad that we have existence rather than nonexistence. Something within us drives us to keep on going. We seek what fulfillment and pleasure we can find in nurturing ourselves and others and in carrying out our daily activities. Although we might feel that we would like more or better things and we motivate ourselves to acquire or to achieve these better things, we find enough meaning and purpose to continue ordinary life.

Occasionally, we experience special things in life that bring us a greater measure of individual and/or collective satisfaction and fulfillment. We discover a new activity that excites and fulfills us. We enter a new relationship, perhaps one that will ultimately lead us to a lifelong commitment to the well-being of that other person. We celebrate with our mate the birth of a new baby or the achievement of a significant milestone in the lives of our children. We discover and explore a new dimension of our being, perhaps a spiritual dimension.

When we experience life as going well, we do not often reflect deeply on the religious foundations of our life. If we were reared in a religious tradition that emphasizes thanksgiving to God for the blessings that we experience in life, we may regularly offer to God prayers and other expressions of thankfulness. When life is going well, we have little need to examine or question our basic religious tenets. Often, perhaps only subconsciously, we may conclude that life is going well *because* of our religious beliefs and practices. The Christian tradition tells us that God blesses those who love God – those who are obedient to the biblical commandments and instructions. We are thereby conditioned to interpret the good things that we experience in life as blessings from God – God's vindication of the God-pleasing life that we are leading. Indeed, we may even conclude that the very good things that we experience in life are special indications of God's satisfaction with our life.

But life can also be difficult – sometimes very difficult. We are faced with major frustrations in life. We lose a job that has been one of the major sources of support, meaning and fulfillment in life, or we do not get a job that we very much wanted and thought that we were well qualified for. Our marriage or other long-term personal relationship devolves into a bitter separation or divorce. We or a loved one are seriously injured in an auto accident that was the fault of a reckless or drunken driver. A spouse, child or other loved one becomes seriously ill or dies. We ourselves are suddenly faced with serious, perhaps even life-threatening, diseases. At times like these the religious rationale that served to support us when we experienced life as going well is now turned on its head. We now feel the opposite swing of that two-edged sword: if God was especially blessing us because we were living God-pleasing lives, God must now be withholding blessings or, worse yet, punishing us for some present evil in our life. We may then begin to question seriously all aspects of our lives, including the foundations of our faith. What are we doing that is so bad that God is chastising or punishing us? We may turn to our church and clergy to look for answers to our questions, hoping to turn things around and return to the good life of blessings and success.

The foregoing has been written in first

person plural, because my life experience suggests that it is reflective of the way that many Christians deal with life. As one who was reared in a traditional, conservative Christian denomination, I was conditioned to deal with the ups and downs of life in that way.

However, for me at least, this course of events brought no satisfying answers, particularly in dealing with tragedies in my life. The guidance and suggestions of the Church began with the presupposition that the traditional teachings and understandings of the Church were correct, appropriate and sufficient to provide satisfying solutions to the life-shattering, earth-quaking experiences in my life. Ample counsel and guidance were given as to how I might examine my own life for ways to bring it into alignment with God's will for my life. Included were such statements as: "There are some things that we just have to accept and not question in life," or "These types of happenings are just part of the deep mysteries of God that we as mere humans cannot ever hope to understand in this life, but perhaps we'll understand it when we get to heaven," or "God does not promise us a life free of tragedy but to be with us in the midst of tragedy."

My deep frustrations arose as I was forced to deal with losses in my life. As I faced each loss, it became increasingly apparent to me that the traditional Christian approach as I experienced it was inadequate – indeed sometimes counterproductive – for dealing constructively with many issues, both good and bad, in the modern world.

Much of my dissatisfaction with the religious counsel and "support" that I received stemmed from their standing in conflict with or in direct opposition to my experience of the world in which I live. Admittedly, my experience of the world has been strongly conditioned by my career as a research scientist working in biology. Scientific validity depends on rigorous application of logical and rational analysis.

In arriving at the best understanding of a biological phenomenon, I had to ask as many questions as possible. The premise of a scientific approach is that, by asking appropriate questions, one can test and verify those aspects of one's hypothesis that are correct and modify or pare away those that are incorrect. In so doing, one can arrive at the best possible approximation to truth – a robust hypothesis or theory that comprehensively accounts for the phenomenon that one observes in nature as we understand it to operate today.

Yet, the religious counsel that I received suggested just the opposite. Logical analysis and rational critique of the received religious tradition were discouraged or even forbidden. Examination of the historical authenticity of biblical stories and church teachings was deemed inappropriate and a sign of weak faith or of outright unbelief. I was encouraged to *simply accept* tenets that appeared to me illogical and irrational. The truth of my religious tradition was presumed, in spite of whatever spin or distortion might be required to accept it. The interpretations and modern applications of several-thousand-year-old religious writings were and are considered the foundational truths and understandings for dealing with all aspects of modern living. Virtually no suggestions were given or countenanced that would question the validity of these writings or the church's traditional teachings on the actions of God in human life, particularly in human tragedies.

Perhaps an analogy can illustrate the inconsistency as I perceived it. If I were not feeling well and my doctor diagnosed my illness as high blood pressure, I and probably most other people would expect – indeed, would insist – that she/he prescribe a treatment that reflected the best *modern* medical understanding of how to treat high blood pressure. My doctor might well be aware that several hundred years ago a traditional treatment was to attach leeches to one's body to remove excess blood, thereby reducing the high blood pressure. While such a practice made perfect sense according to the medical understanding of high blood pressure at that time, doctors who would use that technique to treat high blood pressure today would lose their medical licenses, and their patients might well die because of their malpractice. Yet, it seems that much present-day traditional Christian counsel and practice does just that. It insists that perspectives that emerged from worldviews of several thousands of years ago remain completely valid, relevant and prescriptive for understanding and making decisions for living today.

Today many people claim that their religion or faith is primary and central to their sense of identity and being. It would seem reasonable that, in this most important realm of their lives, they would have "absolute devotion to truth," as stated in the prior Albert Schweitzer quotation. It would seem that they would use all the best sources of information available to verify, to validate and to corroborate the tenets of their faith life. However, as noted above, the prevailing religious attitude is to accept almost unquestioningly the long-held religious tradition given them by their churches. Thus, it seems ironic and incongruous that, while they claim that their religious faith is the most important component of their lives, they exercise much more rigorous questioning of their doctors in attending to their *physical* health than they do of their pastors and churches in attending to their *spiritual* health.

Why do we think and act in these irrational ways? It may be because from very early in our youth we are taught to accept uncritically and to give traditional, *presumedly correct* answers to questions rather than to use our reasoning capacities to arrive at answers that are valid and verifiable in the context of our understanding of the modern world.

The story is told of a pastor who was delivering the children's message to a group of preschool children who were gathered at his feet during the Christmas Day service. As a lead-in question, the pastor asked, "What has a bushy tail, climbs trees and eats nuts?" After a long pause, five-year-old Bobby raised his hand, and the pastor called on him to answer the question. Bobby said, "My parents told me that, because today is Christmas, the answer to all your questions should be 'Jesus,' but it sure sounds an awfully lot like a squirrel to me." For many of the questions relating to all aspects of our lives, we are conditioned to give the "Jesus" answer, when it has no recognizable connection to the context or circumstances of our questions.

As I began to work through the above thinking, although I was not consciously aware of it, I now realize that I was beginning a journey – a search for authentic faith for my life. My early faith was born of the traditional Christian faith of my upbringing. As I grew up and moved out into the world, that formative faith was further molded by the experiences of my professional development and of my career as a scientist. It was severely tested by my life experiences as a husband and father. It continues to be an examined faith – one that is daily tested for its adequacy to orient me toward the fullest possible life in the world that I live in today.

As one birthed from and nurtured by a traditional Lutheran faith for much of my life, it has not been easy to undertake the critique of my faith that I shall describe in these pages. Church leaders and fellow congregational members were almost universally averse to such considerations, because close and critical examination of church teachings and practices was deemed disruptive and "rocked the boat." I suspect that asking difficult questions made many uncomfortable and was threatening to their concept of a life of faith. Yet my spirit drove me to continue that journey, in spite of whatever resistance that I encountered. This personal need to find answers to the questions of my life led to growing alienation from congregations where I was a

4

member. This was painful, because my needs to know and to question came at the expense of feeling excluded from the congregation's communal life – something that was very supportive of me as I experienced tragedies in my life. However, I came to realize more and more that my personal pain and dissatisfaction of not pursuing that journey were greater than the discomfort of whatever resistance and alienation I faced while on that journey. I had to face this journey of inquiry with honesty and integrity. In Albert Schweitzer's words, I needed to proceed with *an absolute devotion to truth*. I could not refuse to continue my journey or to turn away from what appear the best ascertainments of truth available to me just because I faced resistance and rejection from leaders and members of the Church.

At some point, I began to look for examples of courage and boldness of others who appeared to have undertaken spiritual journeys in the face of opposition and rejection. I found that through the centuries many other persons had questions similar to mine – some in the face of adversity, others as part of their quest for purpose and meaning in their lives. When appropriate, I will refer to the witness and testimony of others who helped illumine my pathway to authentic faith.

My writing about my search for authentic faith has given me an opportunity to retrace my own journey. It is something that has been happening within me for many years, and it is continuing. It was necessary and important for me to reflect and to write it out in order to realize where I have been and where I am going. Thus far, I have found

what is an effective and meaningful perspective for my experiencing and dealing with life in its ups and particularly in its downs. However, even during the past few months and years I have recognized significant changes in my thinking and perspectives; surely and hopefully, additional changes will continue to unfold. In this book I describe what I recall as the most formative experiences in that journey.

It is also my hope that my telling of my story will permit – even empower and embolden – others to have the courage and commitment to ask the necessary and important questions that will enable them to develop authentic faith for their lives. At the present time conservative, fundamentalistic groups are appearing in all forms of religion. Evangelical Protestantism and Roman Catholicism have swung strongly to the right. Fanatical elements of Islam are creating division and raising havoc in the Muslim world. Seemingly, all faiths are placing increasing emphasis on acceding to traditional church authority and practices and in literalistic interpretations of their respective Scriptures. In the face of this tide toward acceptance and application of unquestioned traditional understandings, courage is required to examine the tenets of one's religious belief structure methodically and critically for the purpose of deriving authentic faith. Following Albert Schweitzer's exhortation, we must proceed with *absolute devotion to truth*, whatever truth's origin and source might be. Hopefully, this book will facilitate the travel for those who find it important, even necessary, to make that journey.

Chapter 1

New Life and Frozen Eggs

The births of famous people are often associated with celestial happenings and grand announcements. As one reared in a traditional Christian home, I am most familiar with the birth story of Jesus. The gospel of Luke narrates that angels notified shepherds and sang in the skies to announce his birth. The gospel of Matthew tells of a star that appeared and guided the Magi to Jesus' birthplace.

No such celestial fanfare surrounded my birth. Rather, my parents were confronted with the mundane and daunting challenge of getting my mother to the hospital so that she could be under her doctor's care for the birth of their first child. At the time – January, 1943 – my parents lived out in the country on a farm in southern Washington County, Kansas. They were planning for me to be born in Clay County Hospital – the nearest hospital, yet located in Clay Center, Kansas, some fifteen miles from their home. This was a significant distance to travel under the best of circumstances, but this trip could potentially be complicated by the fact that all this would have to occur in January in rural Kansas. The roads from my parents' house to the nearest gravel-paved road consisted of five miles of unpaved, dirt roads, which in the winter time could become muddy and then deeply rutted as cars traveled on them. Then, zero and sub-zero temperatures could freeze those deeply scarred roads. Whether muddy or frozen, these roads could become nearly impassable for my parents in their 1939 Chevy.

Contemplating having to deal with these conditions, my parents planned a two-step process to get my mother to the hospital. They would use my grandparents' Model A Ford to traverse the five miles of rugged, unpaved roads from my parents' house to my grandparents' house, located on the gravel-paved highway. Then they would use their own Chevy to travel the remaining ten miles on the gravel-paved highway from my grandparents' house to the hospital.

When my mother went into labor early on the morning of January 24, 1943, my father implemented those plans to get her to the hospital. He then returned home to get some sleep, because in a few hours he would have to arise to do the morning farm chores. And doing those chores was no small task, because their farm had no electrical power; everything had to be done manually – "by hand," as they expressed it. He would have to feed the cattle and the pigs, milk the cows, gather the eggs and feed the chickens in the henhouse. Some of the eggs would be eaten; the remainder, along with cream separated from the cows' milk, would be sold to generate some cash with which to buy food staples that could not be grown on their farm.

As he returned to the house with the bucketful of eggs, he heard the telephone ringing; he set down the eggs on the porch and went inside to answer the phone. The call was from the hospital, informing him that at 7:23 AM his wife had given birth to their first child, a son. Anxious to see his new-born son, he hurriedly began to wash up and to dress, in preparation for going to the hospital. Later that day when he returned home from the hospital, he discovered that, in his haste and excitement, he had left the bucketful of eggs on the porch. Since this was January 24th and the place was Kansas, the temperature on the unheated porch was very cold – frigid enough to have frozen all the eggs in the bucket. He knew that frozen eggs could not be sold, but his upbringing also told him that good food is never thrown away. Therefore, for the next week or more, until the entire bucketful of about 120 frozen eggs had been eaten, he had to think of as many ways as possible in which frozen eggs could be used to make meals for himself and for my mother, after she returned home.

In recalling the details surrounding my birth, this story is most vividly remembered by my parents. Thus, my birth was not associated with a guiding star or other celestial event. Even the announcement of my birth to my father resulted in a bucketful of frozen eggs. Perhaps my parents' remembrance of this story was an omen that seeing humor in an otherwise unfortunate or even tragic situation would be important in my life. Making the best of that frozen egg incident would also turn out to be an ironic metaphor for my life.

One week later on Sunday, January 31st, I was baptized at home. Normally, this would have been done at church, but the weather in Kansas can be brutally cold in January, and my parents did not wish to risk the life or health of their newborn son, who was especially precious to them because my mother's first pregnancy had miscarried. Moreover, as devoutly Lutheran parents, it was important to them that their son be baptized as soon as possible, because parents should not delay baptism. If a child were to die before being baptized, his or her eternal fate was in doubt, and they would carry the unbearable responsibility of having had the opportunity but having failed to have their child baptized. Although, of course, I do not recall it, undoubtedly I was christened "Robert Allen Felker" rather than Voelker; "Felker" is the only pronunciation of Voelker that I ever recall from Rev. George Lehenbauer, the German-speaking pastor of St. John's Lutheran Church, Palmer, Kansas, who baptized me. My godparents, or baptismal sponsors as they were called, were my two grandfathers, William H. P. Voelker and August F. Moddelmog, and my uncle, Edward Moddelmog, who was my mother's youngest brother.

That I would be baptized as a Missouri Synod Lutheran was seemingly preordained. When later in life I became interested in family history and genealogy, I learned that all eight of my second generation ancestors came to the US from what is present-day Germany or what were parts of Prussian Empires. The family names were: Voelker (Völker), Proehl (Pröhl), Tewes, Killman, Moddelmog, Schwanke, Kessler and Licking (Lücking). Upon settling in the United States, all had become affiliated with congregations that would become or were already a part of the Lutheran Church – Missouri Synod. To my family, there was only one true church – The Lutheran Church – Missouri Synod (LCMS).

In order to understand how I was reared, it is necessary to know something of my parents and their experiences as they were growing up. My father, Elmer Walter Voelker, was born in 1919 in Washington County, KS, the second of three children born to William and Marie Tewes Voelker, devout Christians who reared their children in the strict traditions of conservative Lutheranism. His formal education ended with the eighth grade, with all except one year of his schooling having been received at St. John's Lutheran School. He was a young teenager at the time of the Great Depression. He often related that during that time he worked twelve-hour days on a neighboring farm for 75 cents per day and took his own lunch – and he felt fortunate and thankful to have a job. On some of the more difficult days that he recalled, he would split dry hedge (Osage orange) logs all day for firewood – very hard, physical labor.

His sense of obedience to his parents is illustrated by his career choice. After graduating from the eighth grade, he expressed to his parents his desire to go to high school and then to trade school to learn to be a machinist. Their response was that his older brother William had become a farmer after finishing elementary school and that he should do the same. My father unquestioningly obeyed, and he was a very good farmer for 45 years. However, his machinist interests persisted through all his years of farming. He maintained a small blacksmith shop on the farm in which he could repair farm machinery and tinker with mechanical devices. Significantly, after he retired from farming at age 65, he got a job as a machinist at a factory in nearby Linn, the small town to which my parents had moved. He worked there until age 79 – afraid to miss a day of work lest he lose his beloved job. As he expressed it at age 72, "you do the best work when you have a job that you enjoy doing." Through finding and holding this job, his life became more fulfilled emotionally and spiritually than it had ever been: he was finally able to do what he had always wanted to do.

My mother, Helen Delia Moddelmog, was born in 1920 in Lyon County, KS, the ninth of ten children of August and Caroline Kessler Moddelmog. At about age eight her family moved to Washington County, KS, so that she and her siblings could attend St. John's Lutheran School. There she met and became friends with my father, although more than ten years would pass before they became romantically interested in each other. Like my father, she was a young teen-ager at the time of the Great Depression and was indelibly imprinted by the hardships of life without sufficient water, a problem that recurred in the early 1950s in a drought on the farm on which our family was living.

One story illustrates the effect that it had on her. In the late 1950s my father surprised her with the gift of an automatic washing machine. Although my father assured her that it was not necessary, in order to conserve water she would wash and rinse two loads of clothes using the water of only one wash cycle and one rinse cycle. As the first wash cycle was nearing completion, she would stop the washer before the spin cycle began, wring out the water from the first load of clothes by hand and set them aside. Then she would put in a second load of clothes, reset the control to the beginning of the wash cycle and wash it in the same water. Upon completion of the second wash load, she allowed the washer to complete the post-wash spin cycle. The rinse water then filled the washer and rinsed the second load. As the second load was nearing completion of the rinse cycle, she would again stop the washer before the post-rinse spin cycle, wring out the second (rinsed) load by hand and set them aside. She would then put the first wash load in and reset the control to the beginning of the rinse cycle so that it could be rinsed. When that rinse was completed, she allowed the washer to complete the post-rinse spin cycle. The irony was that, when my mother got an automatic clothes washer, washing became more of a job for her than when she was previously using a wringer-type washing machine. Given that frugal attitude towards the use of water, it is little wonder that my parents had been unwilling to throw away any of the frozen eggs at the time of my birth – or anything else that was still usable.

Another story gives an indication of the strict, parochial conservatism of my mother's family. When the first wife of their pastor, Rev. William Miessler, died, my maternal grandfather was on the board of elders, the governing council of St. John's Lutheran congregation. When Rev. Miessler subsequently dated and became engaged to a *Baptist* woman, the board of elders, including my grandfather, felt it necessary to examine her Christian beliefs in order to determine whether she was suitable to be their *Lutheran* pastor's wife. All such concern apparently was for naught, because she turned out to be as loving and caring a Christian woman and pastor's wife as the congregation could have hoped for.

Having introduced my parents with these almost-caricatured thumbnail sketches, I must now credit them fully for being the loving, responsible and caring parents that they were. In addition to me, they had four other children: Richard ("Dick," b. 1944), Howard (b. 1947), Gerald ("Gary," b. 1950) and Joyce (b. 1959). We children were reared in the strict, conservative Lutheran tradition that my parents were taught was the proper and loving way to rear children. That included strict discipline (including spankings) for wrong-doing. A sense of love and caring was rarely expressed in words or hugs; rather it was manifested in providing for our physical needs and ensuring that our spiritual welfare was attended to by religious instruction at home and at school and worship and Sunday school at church. I do not recall our family's ever lacking food for meals or clean clothes or shoes to wear, although the food was never fancy and the clothes and shoes were purchased not because of their stylishness but because of their durability and functionality. Our house was always comfortably warm and as clean as an otherwise busy farm housewife could keep it with five active, growing children living in it. While my parents occasionally argued and became angry with each other over differences of opinion, to my knowledge there was never any physical abuse or infidelity. Marital fidelity was simply the right and expected thing to do. Period.

In this home setting I received valuable training for life. I learned the value of money and the willingness to do hard work in order to earn it. I learned to live with a minimum of "stuff" in my life. I learned to take responsibility for my actions, even when that sometimes meant being punished for a wrong choice that I had made. I learned to share. I learned that responsible people stand by their words and promises to other people. I learned the importance of religious influences in the formation of values and resiliency in my being.

This modest, if sometimes austere, setting of my home and family conditioned me to view life as essentially serious. Life is about solemn attention and obedience to religious rules and expectations. Life is about solving problems to make life better. Life is about work; the saying that "A farmer's work is never done" seemed all too true. That outlook led to my having a sense of guilt if I stopped to relax and to enjoy myself when there was still useful work to do.

Yet, as I look back on life, it is not only the seriousness and the hardships that I remember. Rather, for whatever reasons, my most vivid memories are of light and often humorous incidents. The earliest ones precede my active memory and were related to me by my parents; the nature of these stories suggest that, although life may have been serious and hard, it was necessary and appropriate to find levity and light-heartedness amid the challenges and difficulties of life. I now relate a few of those stories.

When I was learning to talk, I could not pronounce Robert, so I referred to myself as "Bobbo," and my parents then also began addressing me by that nickname. As a toddler learning to walk, I had lots of energy and was constantly on the go. When the time came for potty training, my parents would put me on the potty-chair and tell me, "Now, Bobbo, sit still!" Then they would turn their attention to other matters. No sooner would they leave me than they would hear me say to myself, "Now, Bobbo, dit doo! (my version of 'Sit still.')" and off I would run to do whatever I found more interesting than potty training. I've been "on the go" ever since.

As the wife of a farmer, my mother almost always helped with the morning and evening chores. This necessitated leaving Richard (my younger brother by fifteen months) and me alone in the house for varying lengths of time. My mother recalled that, before she entered the house, she would say a silent prayer, never being quite sure what she might find. The following two incidents are representative of what she found.

As my mother took care of Richard, I was observant of things that she did for him. One time when he had a cold, I had observed that my mother gave him some cough syrup. Wanting to be helpful because Richard was coughing while my mother was outside doing chores, I took matters into my own hands. I poured cough syrup into a teaspoon and gave it to Richard. Fortunately, the cough syrup was in the kitchen, and Richard's crib was several rooms away. I poured a spoonful of cough syrup in the kitchen, but by the time I reached Richard's crib, I had spilled nearly all the cough syrup, as evidenced by the many drops on the floor. Thus, Richard was spared of any harmful effects of a potential overdose of cough syrup.

When Richard reached the age of liking to bang things together, I had observed my mother's giving him toys to bang together to make noise. Wanting to make my brother happy, I also gave him things to play with. However, my choice of toys for Richard was not so wise. I found several glass Mason fruit jars in the kitchen and took them to Richard to play with in his crib. Fortunately, my mother came back into the house before Richard had broken any of the jars and hurt himself.

When Richard and I grew to three and four years of age, respectively, we formed a dynamic duo, which sometimes included getting ourselves into situations with undesired consequences. We both liked to eat raisins, and from time to time we would sneak into the kitchen, get Mom's box of raisins from the cupboard, and go off to hide and to eat them. One particular spring day while Mom was washing clothes, her supervision of us was less attentive than she usually found necessary. Richard and I got the box of raisins from the kitchen cupboard and sneaked out behind the henhouse to enjoy our raisins. The chickens had been let out of the henhouse to forage for food, and for reasons unknown, Richard and I had caught a hen. Wearing bib overalls, we were sitting on the ground, leaning against the back wall of the henhouse; Richard was holding the box of raisins from which we were eating, and I was holding the chicken. Then unexpectedly, the chicken defecated on the bib of my overalls. To our dismay, the chicken defecation looked just like the raisins that we were eating. Needless to say, our raisin-eating party was over. It would be many years before Richard and I could look at – let alone, eat – raisins again!

At birth I weighed 8 pounds and nine ounces, a rather good-sized baby. However, fifteen months later Richard was born and weighed 9 pounds and 15 ounces – a really big baby. Later, at age fifty my mother commented that she was still recovering from those two events in close succession. And she probably was, because raising Richard and me was no small challenge.

Richard's large size at birth resulted in an unusual relationship between him and me. By the age of three or four he was already bigger than I was. As oftentimes occurs in families of modest means, younger children wear *hand-me-downs*, clothing that their older siblings have outgrown. From the time that he outgrew me until I was able to buy clothes for myself, I wore many – from my perspective – "hand-me-ups." I was older, but I wore clothes that my younger brother had outgrown.

Usually, birth sequence establishes a sort of *pecking order* among the children in a family. The difference in age is reflected by a difference in size that continues until the children grow up and learn to relate to each other in mature ways. Because Richard and I were of similar size, there seemed to be near parity between us. Although I was a little older, he was a little bigger. That relationship meant that neither of us could "lord it over" or "get our way with" the other; we somehow had to work things out. We never tried to resolve that superiority issue, especially in terms of physical strength. Deep down, I think that each of us feared that the other might win, if we were to try to determine who really was the *strongest*. It was better to live with that unresolved tension than to live with a resolved situation that the other had won. I think that relationship contributed strongly towards my desire to seek *a priori* equality relationships with others in life rather than to have the need to establish ranked relationships through forceful confrontation. Later in life in both education and competitive sports, I exerted much effort to do well and to succeed, but I received no satisfaction in winning at the expense of others or in seeing others lose.

One experience arises from my memory from about age four, probably because of the pain associated with it – even though it was a good experience. One Sunday afternoon my Uncle Ed, my baptismal sponsor and a very good baseball player, came out to our house. He had gotten a new baseball glove, so he gave me his old glove and a baseball. We played pitch-and-catch for a while, until he had to leave, probably for an evening baseball game. The glove might have been an old one, but it was new to me, and it came from someone whom I greatly admired and respected. After Uncle Ed left, I wanted to continue to play and to learn to use the glove better, so I improvised. I threw the ball up into the air as high as I could and caught it when it came down. This went fine for a while, until the ball missed my glove when it came down – and hit me squarely on the nose. I do not remember whether I got a nosebleed or not, but I very much remember the pain of the ball's hitting me on the nose.

As I look back, I wish that my father had spent more time with me playing baseball and just having fun. Skill-wise he could have done so, because he was a very good softball pitcher. His "out pitch" was a riser or "upshoot," as he called it. He was among the best pitchers in the area, and I remember going to his softball games during my early youth. Playing softball was something that he had done prior to getting married to my mother and that he continued to do well into my youth. I've rationalized his lack of *fun* time with my brothers and me by recognizing that, as a farmer, his long days and nights (during harvest or other busy times) were filled with necessary farm work, after which he was very tired. And there simply were not enough hours in a day to do everything.

Early in life I learned that it was important to relate well to adults, especially on my father's side of the family. My father, Uncle Bill, Aunt Dorothy (who never married but lived with my grandparents and helped with the farm work) and Grandpa Voelker helped each other in their farming activities. Although each had their own farms, they jointly owned expensive farm machinery such as harvesting and hay-baling equipment, and they moved from farm to farm to do those farming operations. Thus, they were frequently at our farm, and I learned to interact successfully with them. As a first-born in my family of origin, I was an only child for 15 months, and I related only to my parents. At the time, on my father's side of the family I had only one cousin, Jean, who was less than a year older then I was. Therefore, from early in life I learned that, to get along successfully, I had to do the things necessary to please adults. That ability has continued to serve me well throughout life, although I learned later in life that pleasing others can come at a cost.

Until I was four years old, my family continued to live on the same farm, which was owned by my Voelker grandparents. Then in 1947 my parents purchased their own farm with the help of my father's parents. It was an exciting time for our family for at least two reasons. First, this farm was theirs; they would work to improve it and to pay for it with money that they earned. Second, the Rural Electrification Administration was building electrical power lines in the countryside, and electrical power was being installed at the time that our family moved to the new farm. The availability of electrical power opened up all sorts of new possibilities and conveniences in life. My parents could then use electrical power for doing farm chores and for carrying out farming operations; they no longer had to do everything "by hand."

But tragedy followed only two years later in July 1949, when fire destroyed all the farm buildings except the house and the garage. Much hay and stored grain and all the chickens were lost in the fire. It was a serious financial hardship for our family, but, having faced the adversities of growing up during the Great Depression, my parents resolved to overcome the adversity and did so. They were aided by much help from my family and the people in our community, especially other members of their congregation, St. John's Lutheran Church.

Another reason that the new farm was desirable was that it was only 1¾ miles from St. John's Lutheran School, the elementary school that my parents had attended and that I would be attending. The school was started within a few years of the founding of St. John's Lutheran Church, Palmer, Kansas, in 1878. For many years it had existed as a two-room school, with kindergarten through grades four in the lower room and grades five through eight in the upper room, with each room's students' being taught by one teacher. Its establishment and operation stemmed from the strong belief of congregations of the Lutheran Church-Missouri Synod that only an education that combined the learning of secular subjects with Christian instruction properly reared children for Christian living. During the final six weeks of the 1948-49 school year, I attended six weeks of kindergarten, which was considered a preparation for enrolling in the first grade the following fall. I then attended that school for eight years, graduating from the eighth grade in 1957.

The daily schedule followed an ordering of subjects that reflected the priority and rationale for attending a Lutheran parochial school. Every day began at 9:00 AM with a devotional time, followed by either study of Bible stories or instruction in the doctrines of the Lutheran Church, using Luther's Small Catechism. The secular subjects were then studied in perceived order of importance. English and arithmetic followed religious instruction and were generally completed by lunch time. After lunch came reading, social studies (geography and history), spelling, and, if there was time, science, health and

occasionally art. With four grades of students to be taught by each teacher, English and arithmetic often extended well past their scheduled times, but that was considered allowable, because science and health, particularly, were considered less essential to one's education than English, arithmetic, reading, social studies and spelling. Just before the end of the school day at 4:00 PM, a closing devotion was held, after which students were dismissed to go home.

From the beginning I was a good student, always contending for the top of my class of from 10-15 students. Being in a classroom with three other grades meant that the teacher had relatively little time for each grade; therefore, we students often had to learn on our own. I was able to do that well, and that experience trained me well for life, enabling me to take personal responsibility and to work independently.

Several memories stand out from those years, probably because they contributed to my developing into a *responsible* person. The first event occurred when I was in the third grade. When I took my report card home, I had done well in subject matter, but the teacher, Miss Suhr, had written a note: "Robert could do better work if he did less talking in the classroom." When my father read that, I got a spanking, and, of course, I did less talking in the classroom thereafter.

The second event happened towards the end of the same year. Learning spelling consisted of assigning a list of words that were to be spelled correctly and used appropriately in sentences. A preliminary dictation of the list of words would occur on Wednesday and final dictation occurred on Friday. One Friday, Miss Suhr was dictating the list, which included the word "pretty." When I looked around, I noticed that the word "pretty" was included in one sentence that was written on the chalkboard. I raised my hand, and, when Miss Suhr acknowledged me, I said, "Ha, Ha, Miss Suhr. The word "pretty" is written on the chalkboard." She said, "Then everybody ought to get that one correct." I then proceeded to write the word on my paper – except that I spelled it "preety." It was the only word that I missed on spelling tests that whole year, and it taught me an important lesson about the consequences of being a cocksure smart aleck.

The third event happened during the fall, when I was in the fourth grade, as my brother Richard and I were walking home after school one day with some friends. On our way we passed a farmstead that had several apple trees behind the house, and from the road the apples looked ready to eat. So several of us went over to the trees, and each picked an apple and began to eat it. We continued walking about fifty yards down the road and passed the farmhouse. As we came to the driveway to the farmhouse, the wife of the farmer, who had also been my first and second grade teacher, stepped out of the driveway in front of us. She had seen us picking her apples, and said, "I'll take my apples, please. And I'll thank you not to pick any more of them. I'll be contacting your parents about this incident." Needless to say, we were frightened and gave her the apples. Worse yet, as we proceeded on home, we knew that the real time of reckoning was yet to come. When we got home that evening, our parents had already been contacted by telephone. When they asked us about what had happened, we knew that it was better to own up to what we had done rather than to deny it or to try to blame someone else. After all, the expected punishment for two wrongs was worse than for just one wrong. Then, as was usual for such major wrong-doings, my brother and I both got spankings that evening. As years went by, I began to look back on that incident as my Garden of Eden experience – picking the forbidden fruit, getting caught and being punished for my sin – although it certainly was not my first sin.

My attending St. John's Lutheran School achieved what my parents intended it to accomplish. I received a good education in secular subjects and a very thorough indoctrination into Missouri-Synod Lutheranism. The content and substance of that religious instruction can be summarized in the following narrative. Human beings were created perfect by God but fell into sin through the Fall – the disobedience of Adam and Eve, which caused all subsequent humanity to be sinful and in need of a savior. The restoration of a saving relationship with God occurs by God's grace through faith in the atoning work of Jesus Christ's sacrificial death on the cross, the knowledge of which comes alone from the Bible. Salvation comes to people by grace alone through faith alone as revealed through Scripture alone. (The sophisticated Latin terms were – and we used them: *sola gratia*, *sola fide* and *sola scriptura*.) Following the warnings of Martin Luther, the role of good works in life was regarded with suspicion; while it was important to do good works, one must be cautious about thinking that they were, in fact, good, because that might be considered works-righteousness – a mortal sin for Lutherans.

The biblical narrative was presumed to be fully historical. While instruction in grades 1-4 consisted of studying Bible *stories*, students in grades 5-8 studied Bible *history*. When there were apparent disagreements in attempts to integrate the biblical stories into secular history or into the context of modern understanding, the Bible was presumed to be correct, and the secular perspective was declared to be in error or was somehow harmonized with the biblical view.

One part of my Lutheran education was being taught what to believe in order to have a saving relationship with God, as noted above. A second part, almost equally important, was how I and others were taught to regard anyone who was not a Missouri-Synod Lutheran. The presumption was that Missouri-Synod Lutheranism has gotten it all right. Even other Lutherans were in one way or another deficient or defective. Non-

Lutherans were hardly Christian, and non-Christians were hopelessly lost pagans and heathens.

I look back and reflect on this formative period of my life with a mixed assessment. First, I received a good education that enabled me to go on and to succeed in high school, college, graduate school and in several careers in life. I received a religious and spiritual formation that enabled me to orient myself positively in the world as I perceived it at the time. My faith understanding sustained me. From both my parents' and my own perspectives, I was maturing into an individual who could live a responsible Christian life and carry forward the Missouri-Synod Lutheran tradition with commitment and self-confidence.

However, I now also recognize less satisfying dimensions of my early formation. In the parochial Lutheran setting there was little need or opportunity to question anything that I had been taught and, as a diligent student, had learned. For the most part, the curriculum contained only internally consistent elements of a closed system, and I was largely sheltered from different and sometimes conflicting views held by others in the outside world. The views towards people of other faiths fostered by this education were exceedingly arrogant. Rather than learning to see different perspectives as opportunities to expand my own understanding, I was encouraged to insist on the correctness of the Missouri-Synod Lutheran tradition that had been engrained in me.

I was confirmed in my faith on April 14, 1957; as for other Lutherans, this was a right-of-passage event in my life, a time when I confessed and professed for myself my belief in and commitment to the Missouri Synod Lutheran understanding of Christian faith and when I could begin receiving Holy Communion with the adults of the congregation. One month later I was graduated from St. John's Lutheran School; in May 1957, life was going well for me. I was growing up confidently and responsibly. My parents and I were satisfied with my progress and development both in the spiritual and the secular dimensions of my life; and St. John's Lutheran Church and School, together with my family, were largely to be credited for my progress and success.

Chapter 2

Early Questions

In the fall of 1957 I enrolled in Linn Rural High School, as it was known then. It consisted of 140-150 students in grades 9-12. It was a community public high school located in Linn, Kansas, a town of 400-500 residents. Although a public high school, it was located in a community where there were four strong LCMS (Lutheran Church-Missouri Synod) congregations, three of which had Lutheran elementary schools. Consequently, 80-85 per cent of the students were LCMS Lutherans. The other 15-20 per cent were a mixture of mostly non-LCMS Lutherans and a few Methodist and still fewer Roman Catholic students. The students were in general rather well-behaved and respectful of teachers and other students in school. Most students were diligent; some like me were highly motivated. Discipline problems in school were rare and usually minor. Among the students, there were a few who became involved in underage drinking during nonschool hours, but, to my knowledge, illegal use of drugs was almost nonexistent.

On the other hand, of the approximately ten teachers on the faculty, none were LCMS Lutherans, although most were members of other Christian denominations. Perhaps half of the teachers had been there ten years or more; some had been there between 20 and 30 years. This was a reflection of the fact that most teachers liked to teach at Linn Rural High School. The salaries were satisfactory, the teaching atmosphere was conducive to learning, and most teachers could integrate into the community rather easily.

The Christian but non-Lutheran church affiliation of the staff had several important consequences for me. The strongly controlled *Lutheran* curriculum of my previous eight years of school was replaced by one that was more open, although still reflective of a generally conservative, *Christian* rural setting. Those of us who had been taught to believe that Lutherans, particularly LCMS Lutherans, were the only really true Christians were now exposed to teachers and other students who were genuinely good people, although not even Lutheran. These subconscious experiences helped open my mind to at least the possibility that goodness and truth also existed outside my parochial church and home settings.

One of the first inconsistencies between the "history" that I had been taught in elementary school and other possible understandings of history occurred in my world history class. There I learned that several ancient world religions had preceded Judaism and Christianity in the present-day Middle East. Indeed, it seemed that the Ten Commandments of Judaism and later Christianity had been adapted from or at least had incorporated parts of other secular, even pagan, moral codes. The biblical Creation and Flood stories appeared to be specific monotheistic adaptations of preexisting creation and flood myths that circulated throughout other cultures in the Ancient Near East.

However, the greatest conflict between my religious indoctrination and other views of the world emerged in science classes. In general science, notions of the origin of the solar system and planet earth through *the big bang theory* were presented. In biology, I encountered the concept of biological evolution – the notion that the origin and diversity of living organisms occurred through processes and forces inherent in nature rather than through some external special creation by God, as described in the biblical Genesis account. My general science and biology teacher, Mr. Pritchard, was sensitive to the conflicts that these different ideas created for me and others; apparently, he had had to deal with them himself as he grew up as a non-LCMS Lutheran. When I and others would confront him, perhaps even belligerently, with what we had been taught as the "true origin" of the physical universe, he did not belittle or dismiss us. Rather, he insisted that he was presenting what scientific studies indicated was the best understanding of the origin and operation of the natural world.

Thinking back on those interactions with Mr. Pritchard, I realize that he used good tactical teaching skills, engaging and encouraging us to use our logical and analytical thinking skills to sort out the conflict for ourselves. He was respectful of us, while at the same time challenging us to grow to new levels of understanding. He appreciated how that approach had worked in his own life and had led him to his particular perspective. Yet, he did not insist that we simply accept his viewpoint; he knew that we would have to work through it ourselves.

I recall that dealing with those issues was problematic for me. I realize now that I was beginning to discover for myself what constitutes valid and reliable authority for me to accept an idea as a premise for my life. The knowledge that I was acquiring and understanding through science seemed to "ring true"; it seemed consistent with the world that I experienced in everyday living. It made sense to me.

However, my religious training did not stop with my graduation from St. John's Lutheran Elementary School. While attending high school, LCMS students were expected to participate in Walther League, a youth organization that combined continued Lutheran religious instruction and counsel with social activities. Its purpose was to provide students a continuing LCMS Lutheran perspective from which to deal with questions and challenges of adolescence and young adulthood. Included were topical and Bible studies on such issues as smoking, proper use of alcohol, dating and appropriate sexual behavior, and conflicts between science and religion.

By this time St. John's congregation had a different pastor, Rev. Ed Schade. I had looked forward to Pastor Schade's coming to St. John's, because he had a son, Edward, Jr., who was my age. I anticipated that he would have an interactive and engaging approach to dealing with questions and challenges of teenage youth. I was especially interested in his perspective on science and religion, because by this time I had become quite interested in science and was considering pursuing some aspect of it as a career.

When our youth group studied the topic of creation and evolution, I discovered that both the study guide and Pastor Schade held the view that the biblical creation account in Genesis was to be taken as literal history. According to this understanding, the earth and everything in it were created by the spoken word of God in six 24-hour days. The authority for accepting that account as the final word of truth on the matter was that the Bible is the inspired, inerrant Word of God on all matters of faith and life – including science. To question the truth of the Bible on any matter is to open the door to all sorts of doubt that can lead down the slippery slope to eternal damnation.

It was in this context that I heard for the first of many times an important and necessary corollary to buttress the notion of biblical inerrancy and absolute authority: "There are some things that you can not understand; you should simply accept them on faith because the Bible says they are true; you should not try to understand them or question them." Already at that time in my life that assertion seemed at most a half-truth. Yes, it did seem true that there were indeed things in life that I did not, and might never, understand. But to accept an idea or understanding from the Bible as being the final word and immune to critical thinking in light of modern understanding seemed illogical and unreasonable. It was already becoming apparent to me that the way that humans understand almost everything in life has changed and continues to change through time. Why should that not also be true for religious matters and understandings?

The science-religion conflict was framed clearly for me. From the Church's perspective, either I accepted the Church's literal, biblical understanding completely and thereby remained on the straight and narrow path to eternal salvation, or I accepted what science had determined to be the best understanding of the natural world – and risked eternal damnation of my soul for that apostasy.

It was not an enviable dilemma for a teenager who was facing all the other problems of sexual maturation and identity, dating relationships and growing independence from my parents. It would be a long time before a satisfactory resolution would occur. At the time I was not willing to give up my commitment to either the teachings of my church or to my growing appreciation of science as a genuinely good and reliable source of information with which to understand and to orient my life.

In trying to resolve these science-religion conflicts in my own life, I read the writings of others who had dealt with these issues, and I resolved them in much the same way that these writers had. They had concluded that Scriptures and nature were two different sources of knowledge, both authoritative. Scriptures provided so-called "revealed knowledge of God," which was primarily concerned with my eternal salvation and how to live my life in a God-pleasing way but also authoritative when it spoke on matters of nature and how the world was created and continues to function. So-called "natural knowledge of God" was what could be learned from what God instilled and integrated into nature at the time of creation. This natural knowledge of God was understood to be an imperfect knowledge of God, veiled by defects in humans' understanding and analytical ability introduced by The Fall.

That perspective was an early form of what today has been called NOMA – non-overlapping magisteria. Science and religion are two totally different areas of human endeavor and understanding; they cannot – and perhaps should not – be integrated with each other. While this was not a very satisfying resolution for me, it seemed the best available. That it had been adopted by others struggling with the same tensions that I was experiencing seemed valid grounds for my accepting it – at least provisionally.

However, at that point I was moving toward several conclusions. One was that a scientific approach to understanding life could provide answers that were intellectually satisfying and likely to be consistent with the world that I lived in and experienced. A second was that unquestioned authority – even that of the Bible – sometimes was troublesome, causing me to deny or to disregard ideas and understandings that my life experiences attested to me as being most certainly true. Viewed from the perspective of my parents and the members of my church, I had started down the slippery slope – but it was a place that I needed to go.

In spite of the underlying science-religion conflict, the academic aspects of my high school education were going very well. I was consistently on the high honor roll. Socially, I "kept my nose clean," as the saying went. I was involved in athletics, where I competed successfully and lettered in football, basketball and track, the only team sports available. I sang in the choral group, which was known as the Glee Club. I also participated in drama activities; each year our school had an entry in area and regional drama competitions, and during my last three years I was selected to be in the casts of those plays.

It was in the context of those plays and my classes that I was influenced by Mr. Gaylord Ukena, who taught English and world history and was the director of the drama activities. He saw in me potential that I had not seen in myself. Growing up in rural Kansas I had acquired the local speech vernacular, including many grammatical improprieties and careless speaking habits. One day at an appropriate time and setting he said to me, "Bob, you are intelligent and have possibilities to go far in education and in life; you would do well to learn to speak in a way that reflects your intelligence and education." While at first his comment stunned me, I soon recognized its importance and adopted it as a motivating pep talk for my life. I began cleaning up my speech and vowed to try to learn to speak as correctly as I could. In my adult life I have often looked back on that conversation as a pivotal springboard in my personal development.

His assessment of my intelligence also served to affirm my mental abilities, including what I had been thinking in the area of the religion-science conflict in my life. If Mr. Ukena, whom I highly respected, said that my thinking abilities were sound, then the conclusions that I was reaching in thinking about God and science might well also have some merit and validity. This encouraged me to continue struggling with this conflict in my life.

I earlier indicated that, for the most part, I followed the straight and narrow path in my social life. To my knowledge, hallucinogenic and other drugs were not easily available; even if they were, I had no desire to experiment with them. Fewer than a half dozen times in my high school years did I drink beer illegally. Because the legal age for drinking beer in Kansas was 18 and I reached that age in January of my senior year, I could legally drink during the last several months of high school. I did not date a lot, and, when I did, I scrupulously followed the guidelines received in my religious training with respect to what could and should be done in interacting with girls – which meant that almost nothing happened. I obeyed the adage: "If you keep both feet on the floorboard of the car when you are parked with a girl, nothing bad is likely to happen."

Lest the reader think that my school mates and I never tested the boundaries of appropriate behavior, I recall two incidents that happened during my sophomore year that I now relate with some embarrassment mixed with a certain amount of glee. Miss Beatrice Jones, a new English teacher, had been hired to teach the freshman and sophomore English classes. Miss Jones was of medium height and slender build with a meek, almost submissive, disposition. Moreover, she had the medical condition called St. Vitus dance, which causes affected persons to walk with a hesitating and unsteady gait. This combination of characteristics caused her to project a very unimposing figure, such as could result in a distinct lack of command and control in classroom situations. As I recall, this may also have been her first teaching job; even if not, she was relatively inexperienced, and maintaining class order was not her strong suit. Consequently, during my sophomore year, the freshman class of about forty students, the largest in the history of the school and including a number of particularly mischievous boys, had managed to turn freshman English into chaos. The restoration of discipline to the mutinous ship became the task of the aforementioned Mr. Ukena. Not counting the probationary penalties that were imposed, order was restored in one day: Mr. Ukena did not mess around.

Through all the above turmoil the freshman class had given Miss Jones the nickname "Peaches." How or why I do not recall, if I ever knew. However, with that moniker came a certain amount of subtle ridicule and her being the target of practical jokes. One Friday evening there was a school-wide activity in the gymnasium-auditorium, perhaps a dance or drama. Roger, a sophomore classmate, and I decided that we would put an auto bomb on Miss Jones' 1953 Dodge. After installing the device, we hid behind other cars in the parking lot to await Miss Jones' reaction when she came out to her car. When she got into the car and turned the ignition to start the car, the characteristic siren sound of an auto bomb screamed and smoke came rolling out from under the hood. Nearly in panic, Miss Jones hurriedly clambered out of her car and in her characteristic gait scrambled into the high school office to tell our principal, Mr. Elmer Hart, that there was some problem with her car. As Roger and I watched from a discreet distance, Mr. Hart walked out to Miss Jones' car and got into it. When he turned the ignition switch, a second siren sound followed and smoke again bellowed out from under the hood. What Roger and I did not know was that two other students had decided on the same project on the same night. A veteran (and perhaps perpetrator) of similar pranks himself as a youngster, Mr. Hart immediately recognized what had gone on. He opened the hood of her car, jerked out the remnants of the two auto bombs, and closed the hood again. Returning to the office, he assured Miss Jones that there was not a serious problem with her car and that everything would be okay.

The next week when I was in the high school office, Mr. Hart was relating to others – it seemed with a certain amount of pleasure that suggested that he wished that he had been part of it – what had been done to Miss Jones' car the previous Friday night. Not being a habitual participant in such activities, I'm sure that I appeared very uneasy as I heard him repeat the story. I often wondered if my reactions there signaled to Mr. Hart that I had been involved in that mischievous prank. If he suspected my involvement, he never did directly ask me. Perhaps he thought it beneath my dignity to have been involved. Perhaps he did not want to put me on the spot of having to admit to the dastardly deed. Needless to say, I never volunteered the information regarding my involvement.

I think that the following characterizes how I was regarded by my fellow students. I was respected, but perhaps not admired, for my academic achievements. Especially during my last three years, if I was nominated by fellow students for an office, it was much more likely to be for a National Honor Society office than for a class office. As a serious and dedicated student, I was not very fun-loving and social; and, because I did not date very much, I would have been positioned toward the nerdy end of the scale. But I was comfortable with that, because, while the goals of most other students were to stay in the community and to farm or to go to technical, secretarial or beauty school, I had decided that I wanted to go to college. In

doing so, I would be among the first to do so on both sides of my family.

My parents were also trying to influence my choice of career. From their perspective, it would have been ideal for me to become an LCMS pastor. As their first-born son, my going into pastoral ministry would have been consistent with their obedience to the biblical exhortation of "giving the first-fruits to the Lord." From a more sectarian perspective, they would have liked me to enter the primary profession in which one could be a proponent of an LCMS understanding of Christian faith and thereby bring eternal salvation to others. While they may have had those hopes and dreams for me, I am thankful that they were not overbearingly insistent on my fulfilling their desires.

Becoming a Lutheran pastor was not something that attracted me, for reasons that are not altogether clear to me. Perhaps it was just an emerging expression of my teenage independence. Perhaps it was my determination that I did not want to enter a profession that caused people to become like my pastor – dismissive and rejecting of the incorporation of modern scientific findings into one's understanding of life.

I gradually settled on what I considered a compromise. I would become a Lutheran high school science teacher. That choice was *Lutheran* enough to satisfy my parents, and it was *scientific* enough to satisfy my own interests, desires and needs. I learned that I could get such an education at Concordia Teachers College, Seward, Nebraska, as it was then called, and I began applying for admission and scholarship aid to go there. By the second semester of my senior year, I had been accepted for admission at Concordia and had been offered enough scholarship aid that, together with what I could earn, I could afford to attend; I committed to enroll there in the fall of 1961.

The remainder of my high school education was then directed towards that goal. I worked hard academically to learn as much as I could and to achieve the highest possible grade point average. The result was that I was named valedictorian of my senior class, which included giving an address at commencement ceremonies.

My senior class had chosen as its motto the King James Bible verse Proverbs 4:7: "Wisdom is the principal thing; therefore get wisdom: and with all thy getting get understanding." (New Revised Standard Version: "The beginning of wisdom is this: Get wisdom, and whatever else you get, get understanding.") I decided to use this as the theme for my valedictory address.

I prepared for that address with a great deal of apprehension, because public speaking was not easy for me. Although I had been a cast member in dramas, the valedictory address would be up to me alone. Moreover, I still had vivid memories of forgetting the words when trying to sing a solo during high school and having experienced stage fright.

I worked hard to prepare the address and was helped considerably by Mr. Ukena, who constantly assured me that I could do it well. He not only helped me with the grammatical aspects of my preparation but had also introduced me to the poem "If" by Rudyard Kipling in our senior English class. As part of the address, I read the entire poem, and it has remained deeply influential throughout my life. I quote it, followed by my own commentary on its impact on my life.

If you can keep your head when all about you
Are losing theirs and blaming it on you,
If you can trust yourself when all men doubt you
But make allowance for their doubting too,
If you can wait and not be tired by waiting,
Or being lied about, don't deal in lies,
Or being hated, don't give way to hating,
And yet don't look too good, nor talk too wise:
If you can dream--and not make dreams your master,
If you can think--and not make thoughts your aim;
If you can meet with Triumph and Disaster
And treat those two impostors just the same;
If you can bear to hear the truth you've spoken
Twisted by knaves to make a trap for fools,
Or watch the things you gave your life to, broken,
And stoop and build 'em up with worn-out tools:

If you can make one heap of all your winnings
And risk it all on one turn of pitch-and-toss,
And lose, and start again at your beginnings
And never breath a word about your loss;
If you can force your heart and nerve and sinew
To serve your turn long after they are gone,
And so hold on when there is nothing in you
Except the Will which says to them: "Hold on!"
If you can talk with crowds and keep your virtue,
Or walk with kings--nor lose the common touch,
If neither foes nor loving friends can hurt you;
If all men count with you, but none too much,
If you can fill the unforgiving minute
With sixty seconds' worth of distance run,
Yours is the Earth and everything that's in it,
And--which is more--you'll be a Man, my son!

This poem communicated with my soul. In doing so, it did several important things to broaden my perspective and to empower me. First, the source of this profound inspiration was *secular* – nonbiblical. This ran counter to the perspective that I was receiving in the indoctrination of my parochial religious education, which assumed that the particular LCMS Lutheran perspective on all issues was both correct and the final word. It reinforced my growing suspicions and awareness that the non-Lutheran world "out there" really did have genuinely good and valid input for my life – perhaps in some cases better than the religious perspective that I was receiving.

Second, this source of inspiration was also *nonscientific*, which helped me realize that, as valuable as scientifically-derived knowledge and understanding are, that is not all there is to productive and meaningful living. Third, it reinforced the importance of seeking and adopting high ideals in life – something I considered myself already trying to do. Finally, it contended that one can measure one's motives and actions against high ideals, whether biblical or not, and that, if one finds them consistent, one can and should act with courage, confidence, conviction and determination. As I was processing the conflicting science-religion issues in my own mind, this assurance gave me permission and the confidence to proceed – even if it meant going in directions where the religious counsel that I was receiving tried to inhibit me from going.

My valedictory address went well during commencement exercises. I felt a sense of accomplishment and a great sense of relief. Although the success of that address did not completely erase the memory of my earlier stage fright, it did much to restore my confidence in my public speaking ability. It seemed a fitting conclusion to my high school experience.

When I was graduated from Linn Rural High School on May 19, 1961, I was still very much a product of my LCMS upbringing. I still held very traditional Lutheran views on matters of sin and salvation. However, new doors had been opened in my life. I had become aware of secular sources of truth and in some cases had begun to drink freely from those springs to enrich my life. My parents and I were pleased and even proud – if Lutherans could properly use that word and feel that emotion. I was now bound for college and an endeavor that very few in my extended family had experienced.

In the fall of 1961, I enrolled at Concordia Teachers College (CTC). At the time, its curriculum was strongly oriented towards preparing teachers for elementary and high schools in the LCMS. Because I wanted to become a Lutheran high school science teacher, I looked forward to my education there. My interest was science, although I had not yet decided whether it would be biology or chemistry.

My decision to major in biology was influenced by an event that occurred during my freshman year while I was taking my first biology class, which included a Monday evening lecture. As the class was meeting one Monday evening in the building that housed all the sciences, there was a loud explosion that rocked the building. An investigation of the cause of the explosion determined that two upper classmen had been conducting unauthorized "experiments" in the chemistry lab. Neither had life-threatening injuries, but one had lost three fingers on his left hand. My interests had already been leaning towards biology; the occurrence of the explosion in the chemistry lab served to further convince me that biology would be the better major for me.

Included as part of the required curriculum of all students were courses in Old and New Testament History and in Christian Doctrine. The perspectives of these religion courses were a continuation of what I had been taught in my previous Lutheran indoctrination. The authority of the Bible was not to be challenged. If there were perceived conflicts between traditional LCMS Lutheran teachings – which were presumed to be *the* correct biblical interpretation – and views posited by modern science, social science, or even other Christian perspectives, the LCMS position was to be given deference. Some faculty members contended that these variant non-LCMS interpretations were, after all, simply misguided efforts to disprove the Bible and should be dismissed on that basis. Others who were more open to the input of historical investigations had to walk a thin line between openness and loyalty to the Church, because there was afoot in the LCMS a conservative movement to oust persons who acknowledged any authority but the Bible in understanding matters of faith and life. In the late 1960s that would lead to the expulsion of so-called "moderates and liberals" from Concordia Theological Seminary in St. Louis, Missouri, the flagship seminary for the training of LCMS pastors. Faculty members at CTC who kept their ear to the ground on such matters were fully aware of the consequences to their careers if they were somehow to acquire the reputation of being moderate or liberal on any biblical or theological issues.

My response to this authoritarian perspective was to accept it for what it appeared to me to be – one religious perspective. I was continuing to move toward the conclusion that it was not, and could never be, my own personal perspective. That other students on campus whom I considered intelligent and reasonable reached the same conclusions confirmed my assessment of the overall religious environment.

Meanwhile, I had decided to major in biology and was scheduling as many courses in biology as possible. During the course of my studies, the biology staff consisted of four members, three of whom played significant roles in my professional formation: Prof. Carl Brandhorst, Prof. Wilbert Rusch, and Prof. Paul Tucker. Dr. Brandhorst, the only biology professor with an earned doctorate, was an excellent teacher and scientist who was nearing retirement. I think that he fully accepted the notion of biological evolution; he presented it as the best explanation that modern science had concluded was responsible for the origin and diversity of living organisms. At the same time, he was aware of the consequences of an overt endorsement and an "in your face" manner of presenting the concept in his classes: students would be deprived of making up their own minds on the issue, and a lot of turmoil could be caused in the school and the wider church. Overall, he encouraged his students to observe nature, to study it carefully and to reach and to accept the conclusions that such scientific analyses provided.

Prof. Rusch left after my second year at Concordia. My exposure to his perspective on evolution was limited. However, I learned that he was actively involved in the Creation Research Society and other groups that were intent on establishing the validity of the literal biblical account as the correct understanding of nature and the origin and diversity of life. When he left CTC, he joined the faculty of a sister LCMS college in Ann Arbor, Michigan, where Dr. Paul Zimmerman, another ardent proponent of biblical creationism, was president. While I did not share the perspective of Prof. Rusch and his ideological colleagues, I did read their writings – especially their critiques of evolution – in order to determine for myself whether they seemed intellectually honest and scientifically valid. I had some serious doubts and skepticism about their claims as I read their writings, and, as my biological education continued, these doubts led me to discount entirely their goals and objectives.

Although I had few courses under Dr. Brandhorst, his approach made much more sense to me than that of Prof. Rusch. Therefore, I modeled my philosophical approach to biology and to science in general after that of Dr. Brandhorst. His perspective "rang true" to my experience of life. At any point in life, we think and act on the basis of the *best* knowledge and understanding available to us. With the passage of time that *best* is replaced by still better knowledge and understanding. Responsible, productive and fulfilling living requires that we always draw on the best that is available. The notion that ancient writers could have known and anticipated modern conditions, situations and problems and have written counsel to address them seemed simply absurd.

Prof. Paul Tucker influenced me in a different way. In the second semester of my junior year I was taking genetics under Prof. Tucker. One day he commented to me that he sensed that I had unusual aptitude in biology, and he thought that I should consider pursuing an advanced degree in some area of biology rather than teaching in high school after graduation. By that time, I had accelerated my course scheduling so that I was planning to graduate at the end of the first semester of my fourth year. In subsequent discussions we agreed that perhaps I should first pursue a master's degree, and, if that went well, I could continue on in a doctoral program. Because I was quite interested in genetics, we decided to explore opportunities available in that area.

After several telephone calls, we arranged a meeting with Prof. Dwight Miller, an evolutionary geneticist at the University of Nebraska in Lincoln. He expressed interest in my working with him as a graduate student and suggested that I submit application materials for admission upon graduation from CTC. I did so and was accepted.

Meanwhile, extracurricular life on campus continued much as it had in high school. I did not play football my freshman year. I was still nursing ankle injuries from my senior-year athletics in high school, and I wanted to get off to a good academic start in college – a much higher priority for me than athletic involvement. My football career during my sophomore, junior and senior years as a running back-wide receiver was quite successful. During one game I was credited with 272 rushing yards, a record that stood for many years. I played junior varsity basketball for one year. During my freshman, sophomore and junior years I was a sprinter on the track team; my times of 10.0 and 22.4 seconds in the 100- and 220-yard (not meter!) dashes, respectively, stood as school records for a number of years. During the spring of my senior year, I played baseball, where I was an outfielder-relief pitcher. I was not very successful, but I had wanted to try my hand at it before I left college.

It was during this time of my life that my attitudes towards athletics and professional sports in general were developing. Participation in athletics seemed indeed to offer opportunities to learn useful lessons for life, such as cooperation, teamwork, working hard to achieve a desired goal, winning and succeeding graciously, and losing gracefully. However, winning at great expense to the winners often also meant losing at disproportionately greater expense to the losers both in money and loss of status. The great emphasis on winning often resulted in the losers' feeling a sense of having accomplished nothing, though in reality they might be the second best team in the world. Moreover, the practical and pragmatic side of me asked the question: even if a person or team is the best in the world at football, basketball, baseball, golf or whatever sport, what has becoming the best at that sport contributed to the well-being of humankind or the world situation? People spend huge amounts of time, energy and money to become great athletes and to become voyeurs of great athletes. But in the end is the world really any better off? I never discovered a perspective from which to see positive answers to those questions. Consequently, pursuing whatever opportunities I might have had in professional sports never became a priority for me.

During the first several years of college my social life also continued much as it had in high school. While I dated a number of girls, some as often as a dozen times, I did not develop a serious relationship with any of them. Even though I thought that I might find a life's mate while in college, perhaps I was so focused on academic achievement and involvement in varsity sports that I did not attend to the details of developing extended dating relationships. But I was not particularly concerned, because college was, after all, first about getting the best possible education.

All that changed as I entered my last semester in the fall of 1964. My college education was nearly completed, my grade-point-average qualified me for graduation with high distinction (CTC's equivalent of *magna cum laude*) and things were falling into place for me to attend graduate school. The world's possibilities seemed at my doorstep.

During cheerleading tryouts that fall, I noticed a pretty young girl who was competing to become a member of the cheerleading squad. Actually, there were two of them – she was one of a set of identical twins whose surname was Worthy – Darlene and Marlene, or Dar and Mar, as they referred to each other. The embarrassing part for me was that they were so identical that I could not tell them apart. How should I go about asking one for a date when I did not know which one I was asking? And how should I act when I met one after asking for a date, not knowing whether she was the one I had asked for a date or her sister? This was a sensitive, high-stakes situation, and I did not want to make a mistake; after all, I could never make a first impression a second time. I cautiously put myself into situations where I could learn to distinguish between them, with the intention of then asking out whichever one most caught my fancy. During the course of this investigation, I discovered a subtle difference that became a short-term lifesaver for me. Marlene had a small mole beside her mouth that Darlene did not have: "<u>M</u>ar has a <u>m</u>ole by her <u>m</u>outh." MMM became my alliterative reminder of who was Mar and who was Dar.

As it turned out, the cheerleading tryout results also provided an aid to my distinguishing between them, because Darlene was selected for the cheerleading squad but Marlene was not. From that point on for a short period of time, if I met one of them with the other cheerleaders, I was confident that it was Darlene. Because her schedule of cheerleading practice coincided with my football practice schedule, there were more opportunities for chance meetings for us. After an appropriately short period of time for me to plan my coup, I asked her for a date and she accepted!

Darlene was a junior transfer from a sister Concordia College in Portland, Oregon. Her major was sociology, and she had come to CTC to complete her final two years, in preparation for teaching in a Lutheran elementary school. While at Portland she had dated another guy, but that relationship had ended. She was also still grieving the death of her father, who had unexpectedly died of a heart attack only four months earlier.

After several dates we started going steady, often on double dates. As the fall progressed, I realized that Dar was very special to me, and I began to think of the possibilities of her being my life's partner. By Christmas break we were serious enough that I went with her to her home in Seaside, Oregon, to meet her mother, Letha, and younger sister, Sharon. That 1900 mile December trip from Seward, Nebraska, to Seaside, Oregon, was unforgettable. There were six of us students and all our luggage in my 1961 Ford Falcon; we went through every imaginable kind of temperature and precipitation as we traveled to her house and then returned for the two weeks of classes that remained in the fall semester.

I was graduated from CTC on January 27, 1965 and in February began work on my master's degree with Prof. Dwight Miller in the Department of Zoology and Physiology at the University of Nebraska in Lincoln. On Valentine's Day I proposed to Dar, and she accepted; we began planning for our wedding the next August at her home church.

As I began taking coursework in genetics and evolution at the University of Nebraska, I became aware that the scientific world took for granted a completely different perspective of the origin and diversity of life than the "Lutheranized" version that I had been taught, the latter largely tailored to consistency with literal interpretations of the Bible. I soon recognized that, if I were to be taken seriously as a scientist, I would have to regurgitate almost all of what I had been taught as "Lutheran" science and then integrate what I was now learning into a credible new religious perspective. I was unwilling to give up the core notions of God and personal salvation, but I recognized that this new religious perspective would be very different from anything I had earlier imagined.

During my second semester in graduate school I was offered and accepted the opportunity to work as a graduate assistant in Prof. Miller's laboratory, where he was studying the evolutionary relationships between different species of fruit flies in the *Drosophila affinis* subgroup. Flies of this group of species appear physically and morphologically identical to the untrained eye. Yet they are different species, because they do not naturally interbreed with each other in nature, just as tigers and lions do not naturally interbreed. By studying the sequences of the salivary gland chromosomes of these flies, one can deduce how the present-day species have all been derived from a common ancestor in the distant past. These studies, as well as similar studies done by others on other Drosophila species, presented irrefutable evidence before my very eyes that biological evolution both had occurred in the past and continues to occur in the present. These experiments and experiences convinced me that those who deny the reality of biological evolution can only do so if they are ignorant of what is happening in nature around them and/or they have an ideological presupposition that prevents them from seeing what is patently obvious to those who objectively study nature.

Darlene and I were married on August 22, 1965, at her home congregation, Faith Lutheran Church, Seaside, Oregon by Rev. Rudolph Weiser, who because of his suggestive surname had acquired the nickname "Bud." Our honeymoon consisted of a leisurely trip through the states of Washington, Idaho, Montana and Wyoming on our way back to our CTC dorm counselor apartment at Seward, Nebraska, where we lived during her last year of school. I car pooled to Lincoln to continue work on my master's degree, and she continued attending classes at CTC. She completed her degree in May 1966 and accepted a teaching position at Calvary Lutheran elementary school in Lincoln, not far from the University of Nebraska campus. Her salary and my research assistantship stipend provided sufficient income for us to live comfortably. In addition, we received help from my parents in the form of meats and garden produce from their farm. As I was nearing completion of my master's degree, I knew that it would be necessary for me to complete a doctoral degree if I wanted to continue to study in what had become for me the fascinating area of population genetics and evolution. As a supportive wife who saw that happiness and fulfillment in our marriage related to my personal fulfillment, Darlene agreed to continue to teach until I completed a doctorate. We agreed that we would postpone having a family until the completion of my doctorate and that she would use birth control pills until such time as we wanted to become pregnant.

Early in 1967 with Prof. Miller's help in selecting them, I applied to four schools at which I could carry out doctoral work in evolutionary genetics. I was accepted at and received scholarship offers from all four. Part of our application process included inquiries about the possibilities for teaching employment for Darlene. While all four graduate study opportunities seemed equally good for me, the only firm teaching opportunity for Darlene was in Austin, Texas. So I accepted the offer from the University of Texas (UT).

After receiving my master's degree in May 1967, Darlene and I moved to Austin in August, where my studies began in September. My advisor was Prof. Wilson Stone, a prominent Drosophila evolutionary geneticist who was nearing retirement. Because my first year consisted almost exclusively of taking necessary coursework for later research work, I did not seriously look for a research project on which to base my dissertation. As matters unfolded in the spring of 1968, Prof. Stone became ill with a bleeding ulcer and very unexpectedly died. This necessitated either my changing schools or finding another mentor in the Zoology Department at UT. Fortunately, Prof. Ken-ichi Kojima, a quantitative population geneticist, agreed to work with me as his graduate student, and I was able to continue my studies there. In the end this turned out to be fortuitous, because it gave me an opportunity to get experience and training in another dimension of population genetics and evolution.

The research on which my doctoral dissertation was based involved determining the relative genetic and biological fitness of *Drosophila affinis* males that carried different-sized Y chromosomes or no Y chromosome. The experiments enabled me to observe natural selection firsthand in laboratory populations of these fruit flies, as males with either large or small Y chromosomes systematically displaced males that lacked Y chromosomes, thereby demonstrating that they had greater fitness. To the reader this may seem rather esoteric research, but in a biological context it represented a clear demonstration that natural selection, the force that acts to mold the direction of evolution, could be observed and studied in a specific context in a laboratory setting. It demonstrated to me conclusively that evolution by natural selection is a real phenomenon acting in animal populations. Whatever its underlying causes might be, through this research biological evolution became a permanent part of my understanding of the world, and no claimed religious or other authority could any longer minimize its importance as a force in the biological world.

It is common practice that persons receiving a doctoral degree undertake one or several years of postdoctoral work before moving into a faculty position at a college or university or to a principal investigator position at a research institution. Consequently, during my last year of graduate work, I applied for and received a National Science Foundation Fellowship to do postdoctoral work at the University of Oregon, Eugene, with Prof. Edward Novitski as my mentor. Those studies were scheduled to begin in August 1970.

Thus, as I received my doctoral degree in May 1970, my educational and life experiences had absolutely convinced me of the operational reality of biological evolution in nature. Evolution has happened throughout the existence of life on earth, and it continues to happen today in all living species – including humans. Anyone who chooses to deny its existence is ignorant of what is going on in the biological world; anything else they might say about real-world biology becomes immediately suspect and of questionable validity.

Although I was perceiving serious incongruities between my religious/spiritual and professional aspects of my life, I was attempting to do what professional acquaintances were doing – proceed on the assumption that those two dimensions of my life could be kept separate, albeit in tension. On the other hand, my worship life as a member of the LCMS was continuing. Thus, during my Austin graduate school years I was worshipping weekly at Hope Lutheran Church, where Darlene was teaching second and third grades in their newly started Lutheran elementary school. I considered Rev. Keith Fox, the pastor, to be an insightful and forward-looking person, who recognized that, if the Church was to be a viable and continuing influence in American society, it would have to undergo at least minor evolutionary change and most likely also major revolutionary change. Although I had completely dismissed the validity of what the Church was contending to be the proper understanding of the biological world, I was still attempting to hold onto as much as I could of what it said about the spiritual dimension of human existence – sin, faith, salvation, and the nature of God as portrayed by the Lutheran Christian tradition.

Chapter 3

Shattered Dreams – and New Hopes and Concerns

As winter yielded to spring in 1970, the world seemed full of promise for Darlene and me. The research on which my doctoral dissertation would be based was completed, and most of the analysis of the data was done. I had already written a good deal of my dissertation, and everything was on schedule for me to receive my doctoral degree in the May graduation exercises. My application for a National Science Foundation fellowship for postdoctoral research had been successful, and I would be starting work on that at the University of Oregon, Eugene, in the following September. If all went well, during the coming year or so, I would be appointed to a faculty position at some college or university, and we would finally be able to settle down in a community that we could call home.

Darlene was also excited. My postdoctoral work in Oregon meant that she would have more frequent opportunities to see family and friends from her earlier days, most of whom lived in the beautiful Northwest. Moreover, because we had reached the point where the end of my schooling was in sight, we were ready to think about having a family. Early in the spring she had gone off birth control pills, and by early May we knew that she was pregnant, with the expected arrival of our first child sometime in December. It seemed to us as if Christmas had arrived very early that year.

Because graduation exercises were not a big deal to me, I did not "walk" to receive my degree. Much more important to me than any pomp and ritual associated with receiving the Ph. D. degree were the doors that it opened for me. Rather, Darlene and I were looking ahead and finalizing our plans for our move to Eugene, Oregon. In order for Darlene to experience as little stress and trauma as possible during the move, we made arrangements for her to fly from Austin to Portland, where she would stay with her sister Marlene. I drove our loaded U-Haul truck, towing our 1967 Ford Fairlane car behind. The trip through west Texas, New Mexico, Colorado, Utah, Idaho and Oregon was scenic, but I had several breakdowns with the truck that caused the trip to last three or four days longer than it would have otherwise taken. But I arrived in Eugene safely, ready to get settled and to begin my research project.

Time flew by quickly that fall. We were busy getting settled in and preparing for the arrival of our first baby. As time permitted, we were visiting some of Darlene's relatives and friends whom she had not seen for some years. Before we knew it, December had arrived, and we were finalizing plans at Sacred Heart Hospital in Eugene for our baby's birth.

Through the day on December 10 Darlene felt increasingly stronger labor pains. Early the next morning she was admitted to the hospital. At the time fathers were not permitted in the delivery room of Sacred Heart Hospital, so we knew from the outset that I would stay with her during labor but that in the delivery room she would be attended to only by Dr. Hoskins, her obstetrician, and his nurse. Even though Darlene was a rather petite woman, labor went without complications, and on Friday, December 11, at 12:44 PM, Tamara Diane Voelker was born. With dark blue eyes and dark brown hair, she weighed five pounds and was 18½ inches long – not a large baby but large enough, given Darlene's small size.

After a several-day stay in the hospital, Darlene and Tammy, as we decided to call her, came home. Because it was nearing Christmas break at the University of Oregon, I was able to take time off so that our new family could settle in together. Darlene and I were beginning to live the dream that we had looked forward to through the previous six years of my graduate work.

Soon after relocating in Eugene, Darlene and I had affiliated with Grace Lutheran Church. A member of the LCMS, it was a congregation with moderate to open views on most issues. A number of its members were associated with the University of Oregon, which no doubt contributed to the intellectual openness of the congregation.

On January 17, 1971, Tammy was baptized at Grace Lutheran Church. As parents, Darlene and I agreed on the importance of this rite, signifying Tammy's incorporation into the Christian community. We were committed and prepared to raise and to nurture our beloved daughter in a life of obedience and service to God. Our delaying her baptism for about five weeks permitted her to grow a little and become stronger, and it also allowed us to select a date when Darlene's family could arrange to be present for that special celebrative event.

About that time I began applying for faculty positions in population genetics. In mid-February 1971, I traveled to St. Louis, Missouri, for an interview at Washington University. Because my airplane trip would take us almost directly over Kansas, where my parents lived, we thought that it would be an ideal opportunity for my parents and the rest of my family to see Tammy, my parents' first grandchild. So Darlene and Tammy went with me. Although I did not get the job for which I interviewed and the weather was bitterly cold in Kansas, we had a very nice visit with my family.

February warmed into March in Eugene. Tammy appeared to us to be progressing normally, considering her birth size and weight. She had periodic bouts of crying, but Dr. Berryhill, her pediatrician, and we attributed them to colic, a not uncommon occurrence in newborns. She would likely soon outgrow it.

One sunny and warm but quite breezy Sunday afternoon in late March, Darlene and I took Tammy for a stroll through our Eugene neighborhood in her baby carriage. After a short while we looked into the carriage to see how she was enjoying our little outing. What we saw terrified both of us. Tammy was almost blue in the face and did not appear to be breathing normally. We quickly returned to our duplex apartment and immediately took her to the Sacred Heart Emergency Room. By the time that we arrived at the hospital, she was again breathing normally, and her typical facial coloration had returned. The emergency room doctor could find no problem with her and suggested that we take her home and keep a close eye on her. We noticed no further problems and considered things to be going well enough that we drove to Darlene's mother's house in Seaside, Oregon, to celebrate Easter with Darlene's family on April 11.

When Darlene took Tammy to her next scheduled pediatric appointment, Dr. Berryhill indicated that he was concerned that Tammy's development was no longer progressing normally but that he was at a loss as to what might be the reason. He suggested that he see her again in several weeks in order to reassess her situation.

Darlene and I were by then quite concerned, so both of us went to her next appointment. Dr. Berryhill told us that he had been doing some literature research but still had no definite idea what was causing Tammy not to develop normally. He had come across a number of possibilities, some of which could be minor but others of which could be quite serious. He wanted to do further tests which could eliminate some of the possibilities. Of course, we agreed to have the tests done as soon as he could schedule them.

When the results of those tests were in, we scheduled a consultation with Dr. Berryhill. The test results had eliminated all the simple and transient possibilities. Whatever was affecting Tammy was potentially serious, possibly life-threatening, and she might not survive. When I heard those words, I was so shocked that I became very light-headed. To keep from fainting, I lay down on my back on the floor of the patient room and propped my feet up against the counter. I remember looking at Tammy and thinking that it was just not possible that Darlene and I could lose our precious daughter.

We took Tammy home and treasured our time with her, not knowing how long that might be. We were now becoming increasingly aware that she was losing full muscular control of her legs and, to a lesser extent, her arms. She was having increasing difficulty eating and clearly was not thriving. By early May her condition had deteriorated to the point that Dr. Berryhill suggested that we admit her to the University of Oregon Medical School in Portland in the hopes that they could diagnose her condition and hopefully provide treatment. He arranged for her admission there.

By now desperately seeking any treatment that could save our daughter, we took Tammy to Portland, where she was admitted to Dornbecker Hospital. The doctors there were able to carry out a number of additional tests in order to reach a diagnosis of her condition. After completing these tests, they informed us that the results of all those tests were negative. The remaining possibilities were very serious, untreatable and likely fatal. If she indeed had one of those conditions, it could be definitively diagnosed only by an autopsy. All that could be done was to keep her comfortable as her condition worsened.

During the subsequent weeks Tammy's condition continued to deteriorate, reaching the point that she was unable to breathe on her own. We were told by her doctors that, in order to remain alive, she would need a tracheotomy that would allow her to breathe with the aid of a breathing machine. Because the doctors' diagnosis was not definitive, we agreed to the procedure. We continued to hope and to pray that perhaps there had been some misdiagnosis – perhaps they had overlooked something – and that there would be some kind of miraculous turnaround.

Except for occasional sporadic and almost spastic movements, Tammy's arms and legs were by that time almost motionless. Darlene and/or I stayed with her nearly around the clock, perhaps more out of our own needs and peace of mind than it was of benefit to Tammy. On one occasion, while neither her nurses nor Darlene or I were by her bedside, Tammy's hand managed to tug on the breathing tube and detach it. By the time that the nurses discovered what had happened, she had been without sufficient oxygen for an unknown length of time. She was still alive, but her brain had suffered significant damage. She was comatose and there was no longer any indication that she was aware of our presence.

Darlene and I were now painfully overcome by the realization that Tammy would not recover; we were going to lose her; she was going to die. We were now in the difficult situation of having to decide if we would remove the breathing tube and let her die. We decided that we would leave the hospital in Portland, drive down to our apartment in Eugene and stay there overnight. During the sixty mile trip down and back we could talk about and decide what we would do about Tammy. While in Eugene that night, we called the hospital in Portland and learned that Tammy's condition was about the same as when we had left her.

We started back to Portland about mid-morning the next day, still not sure what decision we should make. Our hearts very much wanted to hold on to Tammy, but our minds told us that life for her was no longer meaningful and that we should allow the doctors to disconnect her from the life support system that was keeping her alive.

Darlene and I did not have to make that decision. When we arrived at the hospital late that morning, we were told that Tammy had died within the previous hour. Her struggle was over, but the most difficult part of our struggle – life without our precious daughter – was now intensifying. Her death on June 3, 1971 – at the tender age of 5 months and 22 days – would forever change our lives.

We made arrangements for her funeral and burial. The service on Saturday, June 5, was held at Hillside Chapel in the Portland suburb of Oregon City, near the home of Darlene's sister Marlene and her husband, Tom Moeller, with whom we had been staying during Tammy's hospital stay. The service was conducted by the Rev. Don Jerke, assistant pastor at Grace Lutheran Church in Eugene. Pastor Jerke, or Don as he wanted us to address him, was about our age and had provided us a listening ear during the ordeal of Tammy's illness; now he offered what words of consolation and hope he could as we said our final goodbye to her. The weather was rainy that Saturday of her funeral, so her burial in Riverview Cemetery, Portland, was delayed until Monday, June 7. Perhaps because our grief was too intense, Darlene and I decided not to be present as her small casket was laid into its final resting place. Her funeral on Saturday had provided a measure of closure; and because there would be no service associated with her burial, it seemed to us better not to be there.

In addition to the medical aspects of Tammy's illness and the emotional impact of her death, there was also the religious dimension of that ordeal on our lives. From the time that we first learned of Tammy's potential health problems through her death and into our grief process, Darlene and I prayed fervently and repeatedly, individually and together, that God would heal Tammy and give us the wisdom, insight and strength to be what Tammy needed from us as parents. Our immediate family was lifted up in prayer by our extended families, by many friends and by the congregations of our families and friends. That support was extremely important to us; had we not received it, Darlene and I sometimes wondered if we would have survived the loss of our dear Tammy. Typical of such expressions of sympathy was the following note in the Sunday bulletin of the congregation of one of our family members.

Little Tammy Voelker, baby daughter of Mr. & Mrs. Robert Voelker of Eugene, left for her heavenly home Thursday afternoon. We regret she had to leave us but rejoice for her sake for now she is with Jesus. Funeral was Saturday in Oregon City. Memorials may be made to the Dornbecker Hospital, Children's Dept., U. of O. School of Medicine in Portland.

Yet, when all prayers had been offered to God and all that was deemed possible was done, Tammy had died; we had lost a beloved member of our family. Our religious communities tried as best they could to comfort and to support us. Included were comments intended to make us feel better such as: "God also needs little angels in heaven" or "God chooses the best among us and takes them to himself." Such platitudes would better have been left unspoken, for they did nothing to assuage our sense of loss or to provide any satisfying rationale for Tammy's illness and death or for the role and actions of God in this tragedy.

Although Darlene may have felt differently, for me the whole superstructure of my religious understanding had been put to the test and seemed to be inadequate. While I could not put my finger on the specifics of why it was inadequate, the notions of a permissive God who would allow such a tragedy as the death of a beautiful infant – my daughter – seemed unworthy of the title *God*, especially of a benevolent and loving God. Yet I continued to try to salvage elements of my traditional faith to sustain me, although it was becoming increasingly difficult.

Meanwhile, coping with the physical and emotional aspects of Tammy's illness and death had had a devastating effect on my search for a faculty position. Those attempts were put on complete hold until after her death in early June, by which time most openings for positions beginning in the fall were already filled by most colleges and universities. Moreover, another tragedy impacted my job search. In seeking faculty appointments, the awareness of positions and the recommendations of one's doctoral mentor are extremely important in being considered and hired for a position. Earlier that year, Prof. Ken-ichi Kojima, my doctoral advisor and mentor at the University of Texas, had been killed in an auto accident. Thus, he was no longer there to act as an advocate and proponent in my seeking a position, and I was on my own in trying to secure a position.

The openings still available consisted mostly of further postdoctoral work, and I began applying for them. One of those openings was in the Quantitative Genetics Program at North Carolina State University in Raleigh, North Carolina. I applied for a position and was invited for an interview in early August; within a week I was offered and accepted the position. Emotionally, Darlene and I were ready to leave the setting where we had experienced so much pain and heartache. Perhaps our moving to a new area and having a fresh start would give our lives a much-needed lift, although we knew that we were moving to a place where neither of us had family or friends as a support system. But because it was the only job opportunity that appeared, we decided that we would go and make the best of it. Packing our belongings into a U-Haul truck, Darlene and I moved to Raleigh in late August to begin my work there. Our trip took us through Kansas, where we stopped for several days to visit my family. Our stay there provided us much-needed emotional support and a respite in the 3100 mile move from Eugene to Raleigh.

Upon Tammy's death, with our permission the doctors had taken the necessary tissue samples to be able to verify what they suspected was the cause of her death. The findings were sent to the University of North Carolina in Chapel Hill, and an appointment was set up for us to go there and discuss the results with a genetic counselor. The report verified what the doctors at the University of Oregon Medical School had suspected – that Tammy had had Werdnig-Hoffman disease, a form of infantile spinal-muscular atrophy. It is characterized by the progressive atrophy or degeneration of the anterior horn of the nerves from the spinal cord that provide the stimuli for activating all the skeletal muscles of the body. When these nerves degenerate, the muscles that should be activated by them also degenerate, leading to the loss of movement that we had observed in Tammy. The typical onset of the infantile form of the disease is between birth and six months of age, with death usually occurring by nine months of age – the course that it had taken with Tammy. There was not, nor is there now, a cure or treatment to halt the progression of the disease. While that was certainly not good news, Darlene and I were relieved to know that all had been done for Tammy that could have been done; nothing further could have prevented her ultimate death from the disease.

But there were also further unsettling implications of this report because of the consequences of this diagnosis for any future children that we might have. Werdnig-Hoffman disease is caused by a type of mutation known as an autosomal recessive gene. To understand the cause and transmission of this type of genetic condition, it is important to know that each of us has twenty-three pairs of chromosomes; one member of each pair is inherited from our mother and the other from our father. In most people each member of a pair of chromosomes carries two normal genes, and they have normal health. However, rare individuals in the population, like Darlene and me, carry a normal gene on one member of the chromosome pair and a defective gene on the other member of the pair. Both Darlene and I were nevertheless normal, because the normal gene is dominant to the defective gene. On the other hand, Tammy had gotten two copies of this defective gene – one from Darlene and one from me.

Because each fertilization of an egg by a sperm is a random combination event, this meant that one-fourth of the fertilized eggs produced by Darlene and me would be expected to have two defective (mutant) genes. Thus, twenty-five percent of any future children born to us would be expected to share Tammy's fate. Yes, three-fourths of the children would be expected to be normal, but one-fourth would be affected. Was this a risk that we were willing to take? Could we emotionally survive another child's death? What would be the emotional impact on us, even if our next child lived?

Were there any alternatives to taking this risk? In 1971, as we were facing this decision, the only realistic alternative to taking this risk was a reproductive technique known as artificial insemination by donor (AID). In the use of this technique, sperm would be collected from a medical student; a doctor would then use a catheter or other device to introduce the sperm into the vagina of the woman hoping to become pregnant. From that point the sperm would move through the uterus and fallopian tubes to fertilize her egg. Because the vast majority of persons in the population carry two normal copies of a gene, the chance that any medical student sperm donor would carry one normal and one defective gene (like me) is almost zero. Therefore, if we used AID in conceiving subsequent children, the risk of our having another child with Werdnig-Hoffman disease would be virtually zero.

I think that from the outset Darlene was leaning towards the AID option, but she had one concern: how would I feel about our having children who were biologically hers but not mine? At first, I did not know how I felt. It would be a disappointment not to

have children of my own; I thought about it a little while and realized that it must be similar to the experience of a friend of mine, who with his wife had adopted two children because they could not have children of their own. When I talked with him, he said that, while he was fully cognizant that their children were not biologically theirs, it had no effect of which he was aware on his interactions with his children, who were then a two-year-old boy and a newborn girl. I trusted his judgment and, considering myself quite accepting of nontraditional things, told Darlene that I felt that I was ready to proceed with her becoming pregnant using AID. In late 1971 we made plans for that to begin.

When Darlene went in for her physical examination to ensure that all was in order to begin AID, she experienced much more discomfort during the pelvic examination than was usual for her. The doctors decided to hold off on the procedure to see if something "was going on" with her. At the next examination she experienced even more pain, and her doctors suspected that something was indeed amiss. Further exploration revealed a large mass of unknown origin in the region of her right ovary. When her doctors surgically explored the matter, they found that she had a cyst on her right ovary that had become infected. Their only option was to remove her right ovary and a part of her right fallopian tube, which had also become infected. They assured us that her remaining left ovary and fallopian tube should allow her to conceive and carry a fetus through pregnancy. She recovered quickly after the surgery.

About two months later, Darlene began AID and soon become pregnant. Time seemed to pass quickly as we awaited the arrival of our next baby. Still feeling the painful loss of Tammy almost two years earlier, we were looking forward to this new source of joy in our life. Her due date was January 24 – my birthday, meaning that I could possibly have a present for my thirtieth birthday!

Her pregnancy was uneventful. Although it was monitored closely, we chose not to learn the gender of our new baby. Darlene and I took a Lamaze course, a requirement for me to be in the delivery room with her. A week or so before the due date, the fetus dropped into the appropriate position for birth. On Monday, Darlene began to experience minor labor contractions. By Tuesday morning, January 23, the contractions were becoming stronger, and we were advised to come to North Carolina Memorial Hospital in Chapel Hill, where the delivery would occur. We arrived shortly after noon, Darlene was prepped for delivery, and we were put in a labor room to wait, wondering if delivery would wait until after midnight – and my birthday. Labor progress was followed throughout the day by monitoring cervical dilation. By early evening her cervix was fully dilated, and it was apparent that delivery would occur before midnight. About 6:30 PM her obstetrician checked her and said, "Let's go have a baby."

As is often the case at medical school hospitals where students and interns are training, the delivery room seemed like Grand Central Station. Besides Darlene and me, there were the obstetrician, his nurse and an intern. There were the pediatrician, his nurse and an intern. I sat on a stool next to Darlene's head and held her hand as she pushed as the doctors instructed her. At 6:52 PM, January 23, 1973, our second child, another daughter, was born. The name that we had selected for a baby girl was Cheri Renee. Cheri is derived from the French "cher' or "dear one," because she was very dear to Darlene and me. She weighed 6 pounds and 14 ounces and was 20½ inches long. The pediatricians examined her carefully and found her to be in excellent health. Darlene and I were elated.

But our elation would soon be tempered. A not uncommon medical condition called Rh incompatibility occurs when a mother has Rh-negative blood and her fetus is Rh-positive – which can occur only if the father is Rh-positive. Darlene's being Rh-negative and my being Rh-positive meant that this was a potential problem for us. But, because Rh incompatibility never occurs if both the mother and the father are Rh-negative, Darlene's doctors had chosen Rh-negative medical students as sperm donors for AID in order to completely avoid this problem. Darlene was fully aware of the genetic control both of Rh incompatibility and of Werdnig-Hoffman disease. Therefore, she expected that the sperm donor would have contributed genes that would have caused Cheri to be both Rh-negative and normal with respect to Werdnig-Hoffman disease.

The nurses in the newborn baby care section of the hospital had not been apprised of the details of Cheri's conception and birth with respect to either Werdnig-Hoffman disease or Rh incompatibility. On the day after Cheri was born, one of the nurses came into Darlene's room to report the results of Cheri's blood analysis. She reported that all the chemical analyses were normal and that her blood type was "A-positive, just like her father's." When Darlene heard "A-positive", she immediately realized that Cheri was *not a product of AID* but of one of her eggs' having been fertilized by one of *my* sperm. Consequently, this also meant that there was a twenty-five per cent chance that Cheri could have inherited the mutant genes that cause Werdnig-Hoffman disease.

When Darlene heard "A-positive, just like her father's," her jaw dropped, and she looked very shocked. The nurse, who was expecting that Darlene would be pleased to hear all of the results as good news, saw the disappointment on Darlene's face and said, "Is there something wrong?" Not wanting to explain everything to the nurse and to deal with her own emotions at the same time, Darlene simply said, "No, I was just surprised to hear that."

So our carefully made plans to prevent the recurrence of the disease that had taken Tammy's life seemed to have been frustrated. During the early weeks and months after Cheri came home from the hospital, Darlene and I lived with very mixed emotions. She and I experienced them somewhat differently, but the following were factors in our dealing with our awareness that Cheri was our biological child. On the one hand, we wanted to be everything that we could be as parents and emotionally bond to Cheri. On the other hand, the awareness that Cheri could possibly die if she had Werdnig-Hoffman disease caused us to maintain an emotional safe distance, because both of us were not sure that we could personally survive the loss of Cheri, emotionally re-experiencing our loss of Tammy.

As Cheri grew and developed, we were fearfully on the lookout for any signs that she might have Werdnig-Hoffman disease. Anything unusual in her behavior or development was likely to raise a red flag in our consciousnesses. The way that she was positioned in the uterus before birth caused several carryover effects after birth. First, for some time she had an asymmetric smile, and her facial appearance was asymmetrical when she cried. Second, her feet both pointed slightly to the left rather than each pointing slightly toward the outside of her body, a condition that was corrected by her wearing foot braces from about two to five months of age. Seeing these were potential omens of things to come.

However, Cheri continued to achieve the normal developmental milestones, and by nine months we were increasingly optimistic that she did not have Werdnig-Hoffman disease. While she did not crawl a lot, her crawling was completely normal when she did. As she was nearing a year, she began to crawl to and to pull herself up next to chairs or tables and stand there, figuring out how she could get to the next object without crawling there. But she was not willing to risk falling, while trying to walk there. Finally, on January 23, 1974 – her first birthday, she walked a distance of about four feet from a chair to a coffee table – without falling. It was an important milestone for her, but it was even bigger for Darlene and

me; we were becoming more and more convinced that she was indeed free of Werdnig-Hoffman disease. As she continued to develop normally, we became more relaxed and were able to enjoy life more fully once again.

Following our move to Raleigh in August 1971, Darlene and I had joined Our Savior Lutheran Church, an LCMS congregation. We had both become increasingly uncomfortable with the strong conservative swing in the LCMS, particularly in the Midwest, and had decided that we would find a congregation that was more moderately oriented in its doctrinal positions. If that church happened to be an LCMS congregation, we would join it; if not, we were prepared to join another denomination. Our Savior congregation and its pastor had chosen not to become embroiled in the larger liberal-versus-conservative denominational conflict and therefore were able to maintain an openness that was unusual for LCMS congregations at the time. It met our criteria, welcomed us and served our needs, and so we joined in late 1971.

On February 25, 1973, Cheri was baptized at Our Savior Lutheran Church. Our family became very active members, joining Sunday School and Bible Class and rarely missing worship services. Over the course of the 22 years (1971-93) that I lived in Raleigh, I was elected to many of the major offices in the congregation. Compared with my formative LCMS experience in elementary school and college, Our Savior congregation was "a breath of fresh air"; it provided an atmosphere for us to explore the questions of our spiritual and doctrinal lives. Darlene and I felt that we were an integrated part of the congregational community.

During that time I continued reflecting on several matters of the science-faith intersection in my life. As a population geneticist I was aware of the probability of persons' being genetic carriers (having one normal and one defective gene) of rare genetic conditions such as Werdnig-Hoffman disease. People who are related to each other have a much greater chance of both carrying the same defective gene and therefore of having an affected child; completely unrelated people have the lowest probability of having affected children. Darlene's ancestry was a mixture of English and Native American; my ancestry was totally Germanic. Statistically, the chance that we would have married and had an affected child was about as close to zero as one could get. Yet, exactly that had happened to us, and we had lost Tammy.

Moreover, from my perspective, the idea that God had somehow "allowed" that to happen was absurd. The notion that God was somehow involved in rolling the genetic dice and permitting some people to have children afflicted with fatal diseases – perhaps in order to test their faith – was insulting to my notion of God. The occurrence of genetic diseases in populations is governed by the laws of probability, not by a God who somehow "controls" things by tweaking the system. It was increasingly becoming apparent to me that traditional notions of God's acting in nature were inadequate for – and perhaps even destructive of – a nurturing and supportive faith.

Another doctrinal matter concerned the issue of death itself. Traditional Lutheran (and other Reformation) Church doctrine holds that physical death is the result of The Fall – Adam's and Eve's sins in the Garden of Eden. Before The Fall humans and presumably all other creatures were perfect and did not die – they lived forever. With The Fall came sin and the consequences of sin, including corruption of nature and genetic mutations that cause human disease and death.

An informed, modern understanding of nature finds serious problems with the above perspective. First, nature could not sustain itself long-term if organisms, including humans, did not die and decompose into materials usable by subsequent living organisms. Without death, soon all the resources of the earth would be tied up in living organisms;

there would be nothing left to give rise to new organisms. Considered from a biological perspective, from the time that life originated, death also had to exist. Death did not somehow or sometime come onto the scene later.

Second, the notion that mutations are an evil consequence of sin is absurd from a biological perspective. To be sure, some mutations, perhaps even most, are detrimental under some conditions to the organisms that possess them. But from a biological perspective, mutations occur naturally and are the raw materials needed for evolution to occur. It would have been impossible for life to arise and to evolve into the many forms that exist today without the occurrence of mutations. Nature's logic (if one can call it that) requires the continuous generation of mutations for life to adapt to the changing conditions on our planet. From our human perspective, mutations are a two-edged sword: some have contributed to increasing human intelligence and disease resistance; others cause fatal diseases like Werdnig-Hoffman disease. Some mutations give rise to a more beautiful rose; others result in susceptibility to rose leaf blight. From nature's perspective, you cannot have one without the other.

Tammy's birth and death had given to Darlene and me a most fulfilling dream, only to be followed by an unimaginable calamity. During and after the nightmare of her illness and death, I found that my mostly traditional faith was not sustaining me while trying to come to grips with this tragedy; rather, it was requiring me to ignore, to distort or to completely deny a number of my understandings of what is going on in the real world – the world in which my senses and understandings orient me. This troubled me no small amount; yet, sustained by the people in my community of faith, I was attempting to hold onto as many of the elements of my traditional faith as I could, especially in what I deemed *spiritual* matters. Already I was beginning to sense that the struggle would only become more difficult.

Chapter 4

If God Exists, What's Going On?

By the time that Cheri reached six months of age late in the summer of 1973, Darlene and I were becoming more and more confident that she was free of Werdnig-Hoffman disease and that, barring an accident or other unexpected illness, she would remain a part of our family. Before we had any children, we had talked about having a family of at least two children, possibly two or three years apart so that they might together share many experiences of growing up. Thus, we began to make plans to utilize AID for Darlene to again become pregnant – this time using appropriate contraceptive measures to ensure that our next child would be a product of AID.

Professionally, I also had reason to be very pleased by how things seemed to be going in life. I was teaching and doing research as a visiting assistant professor in the Department of Genetics at NCSU, a position with a reasonable promise of becoming permanent. However, all was not well with me emotionally; something was working beneath my consciousness that from time to time prevented me from functioning normally. When I consulted my physician, he ordered a number of scans and blood-work analyses. The results on all were the same: they were all normal. He said that, physically, I was "as healthy as a horse." He suggested that perhaps I should see a psychologist or psychiatrist to see if my distress was mentally or emotionally based.

Very much wanting to feel better, I made an appointment to see a psychiatrist as soon as I could. After perhaps a half-dozen visits, his diagnosis of my situation was anxiety-depression. The likely contributing factors were my failure to process in a constructive way my emotions relating to two issues: my grief associated with Tammy's illness and death and my anxiety surrounding the possibility that Cheri might have Werdnig-Hoffman disease. Although it was daunting to learn that I was not emotionally well, it was at the same relieving to know that there were indeed reasons why I was not feeling well. Knowing the devils in my life did not get rid of them, but at least it helped me know that I was dealing with something; it raised the possibility that I could work through this anxiety-depression and once again feel a sense of well-being.

Later looking back on those years, I realize that moving from Oregon to North Carolina only two months after Tammy's death contributed to my not properly grieving her death. Consciously, my mind was ready to leave the scene of the intense emotional pain surrounding Tammy's illness and death. I reasoned that I could simply move to a new geographical area and have a fresh start, and all would be well. That awful experience was out of sight and therefore out of my mind. But my subconscious mind did not work that way. Even today, more than thirty-five years after Tammy's death, my subconscious mind reminds me each June 3rd of my having lost her. Once I consciously acknowledge that event, my subconscious mind allows me to move on again with life. If I fail to consciously acknowledge that loss, my subconscious mind continues to haunt me until I do. It is one of the mandatory rituals in my life.

I can now also better appreciate the deep-seated fear that the potential loss of Cheri had on me. It was not just a fear; it was a terror – a rational fear based on my knowledge of the one-fourth genetic probability of her having Werdnig-Hoffman disease combined with what I considered the strong possibility that, if she did, I would not be able to deal with it emotionally and that such a loss would destroy me. Carrying the emotional freight of those issues finally was reaching the point of being the straw that broke the camel's back in terms of my well-being.

But I was determined that these two issues be challenges that made me a stronger person rather than barriers that stopped me in my tracks. Again, I was buoyed up by workplace friends and my church community. Through all this, the doctrinal tenets of my traditional faith did little to support and to sustain me. Gradually, however, my emotional resilience returned, and I was again able to cope with life successfully.

And good news always helps. Several months after beginning AID, in late 1975 we learned that Darlene was pregnant, with our new baby's expected arrival in May 1976. This time we were confident that the pregnancy was a product of AID. Time passed quickly as her pregnancy progressed; before we knew it, May had arrived. After induced labor on Monday, May 24, 1976, at 1:59 PM, our third daughter was born, and we named her Bethany Anne. She weighed 7 lb. 10 oz. and was 19½ inches long. She was Rh-negative, which reassured us that she was a product of AID. On June 6 she too was baptized at Our Savior Lutheran Church, and she also became an active participant of the congregation with Cheri, Darlene and me.

Already as a young child Bethany was a free spirit. If there was something that she thought might be interesting and fun, she would give it a try, sometimes to her parents' chagrin and dismay. She and Cheri became close friends as well as mutually adoring sisters. By the time she was nearing three years of age, Bethany had become the emotional sparkplug of our family. She injected energy, levity and spontaneity into our family life, which had previously been quite solemn and serious from having had to deal with our previous adversities.

In 1976 I had relocated to the National Institute of Environmental Sciences (NIEHS) in Research Triangle Park, NC, where I was a research geneticist. By 1979, my research interests had shifted from population genetics to developmental genetics of the fruit fly (*Drosophila melanogaster*). I was well on the way towards tenure, and my professional future looked bright and secure.

Darlene had also been able to return to teaching; she had found new fulfillment as a preschool teacher at Western Boulevard Presbyterian Preschool, where she was an excellent teacher and was being courted to replace the retiring director. She felt that being a solo director would take her away from her beloved classroom too much, and she finally agreed to work as co-director. Cheri had attended that preschool, and Bethany would be enrolling in the three-year old preschool class in the fall. With that schedule, Darlene had a fulfilling involvement outside our home, and she could always be home when the girls were home, an important consideration for both Darlene and me.

In the spring of 1979 Cheri was about to complete kindergarten. She loved school and was an eager "teacher" to her "student" Bethany, as they played school at home. They were realizing the full benefits of being similar enough in age to play together well, yet different enough to each have their own identity and to proceed through their developmental stages individually. Our dream of family was finally returning for Darlene and me.

On Saturday morning, March 31, 1979, our family was eating breakfast in our eat-in kitchen. Darlene and I were seated across from each other at the long ends of the oblong kitchen table. Cheri, to my left, and Bethany, to my right, were seated across from each other at the sides of the table. As we were eating, I looked at Bethany and noticed a small lump under her left ear in the place where lymph glands swell when a person has mumps. As we examined her more closely, it was clear that she had a lump only on her left side. We looked at the lump closely for indications that it might be an insect bite or sting but found none. We decided that, if it persisted, we would have her pediatrician, Dr. Anne P. Askew, examine her.

The lump persisted into the next week and Darlene took Bethany to be examined by Dr. Askew. Analysis of the blood sample that was taken showed everything to be normal. Dr. Askew was puzzled by Bethany's symptoms but reassured us that, because all the blood analyses were normal, it was not likely to be anything serious. Because the lump was a swollen lymph node, perhaps Bethany had a mild case of mumps; if so, it was unusual. First, it was present only in the lymph node on one side of her neck. Second, she had received her immunization against mumps, which is virtually completely effective in preventing mumps. Dr. Askew suggested that she see Bethany again in two weeks, unless she became noticeably ill.

During the next week, Bethany began running a slight fever and was becoming restless and clingy, wanting to be held or to sit on Darlene's lap much more than usual. As the week progressed, she was eating less and clearly was not feeling well. When Darlene contacted Dr. Askew's office to report the new symptoms, she was told to bring Bethany in for another examination.

This time the results of the blood work analyses were not normal. Whereas most healthy persons have a white blood cell count of 6,000-10,000 per milliliter of blood, Bethany's count was in the 80,000 to 100,000 range; because even persons whose immune systems are fighting bacterial or viral infections usually have counts in the 20,000 to 40,000 range, this clearly indicated that something was seriously wrong, and Dr. Askew immediately referred us to North Carolina Memorial Hospital (NCMH) in Chapel Hill, where there was a pediatric hematology/oncology unit.

When we checked into NCMH several days later, Bethany's white blood cell count had reached the 150,000-200,000 range. After being checked in by admission personnel, she was seen by Dr. Campbell McMillan, a pediatric hematologist-oncologist in his sixties. After examining Bethany and getting the results of her blood-work analyses, he informed us that she had acute lymphocytic leukemia or childhood leukemia, so-called because it rarely occurs in people over twenty years of age. It was a disease that could be effectively treated, and some types had cure rates as high as 80 percent. Further analyses indicated that Bethany had T-cell leukemia, for which the cure rate was about 50 percent.

Darlene and I were again devastated, but hopeful. A 50 percent chance of cure was not great, but we felt that, with Dr. McMillan's expertise and care and our providing everything that we could, Bethany would be cured. The treatment regimen began immediately, with Bethany remaining in the hospital for somewhat over a week to receive the initial chemotherapy and radiation treatments. Many of the diagnostic tests involved recovering bone marrow or spinal fluid samples. Despite the use of anesthetics, these were painful procedures for Bethany. But they were also very emotionally difficult for Darlene and me, because one or the other of us usually held and/or restrained Bethany as these procedures were being done.

Following her release from NCMH before her third birthday, May 24th, the outpatient phase of treatment began. It involved a sequence of six different treatments of radiation or chemotherapy administered over a six-week cycle, with one type of treatment being received each week. Each Monday morning Darlene would take Bethany to NCMH in our 1977 Volkswagen Rabbit for a mid-to-late morning appointment. Darlene later recalled and related that Bethany, then just over three years of age, would talk to herself as she sat in the infant seat in the back of the car, trying to "psych" herself up for the pain and discomfort that she anticipated would be involved in the treatment. She faced the treatments reluctantly but saying that "if I'm going to get better, I have to do this."

By July and August of 1979, several cycles of treatments had brought her leukemia into remission, and she was put on a maintenance therapy schedule, which involved monthly visits to NCMH for treatment. Bethany had tolerated the treatments remarkably well. She had lost all her hair, but she had a little hat that she faithfully wore whenever she was outside or in public. She came to accept it fully, and it became part of her identity.

Some of the chemotherapy treatments caused her to become quite nauseated, but she found a way to cope with that also: her "little green bucket." It was a small green plastic pail, perhaps a gallon in size, into which she would vomit when she became nauseated. After she returned home from a treatment, she would sit on the floor playing with her toys, her little green bucket beside her. If she became nauseated, she would grab the bucket, vomit into it, wipe off her mouth with a nearby piece of cloth or Kleenex and resume playing. She was not going to let a little nausea interfere with her experience of life.

Facing all the pain and discomfort of her therapy treatments also caused her spirit to mature much beyond her three-plus years of age. I recall one particular Monday on which she had received a treatment that often made her nauseous into the late afternoon or evening, after which she would usually fall asleep. I had a meeting at the church that evening. Before I left, Darlene and I had decided that, when I came home after the meeting late in the evening, I would awaken Bethany and give her some fruit juice to drink and some soda crackers to eat. When I got home, I went to Bethany's bedroom, gently awakened her and asked her if she would like something to eat and drink. Half-awake, she nodded "yes"; so I picked her up and carried her into the kitchen and set her down in her little booster seat at the table, while I went to get the juice and crackers. As I returned to the table, Bethany was rubbing her eyes, trying to wake up. She looked at

me and said, "Daddy, did you have a good time tonight?" I was stunned by her statement. After experiencing all the pain of her chemotherapy treatment and all the nausea and vomiting through the afternoon and evening, her first consideration was to ask *me* if *I* had had a good time. This was no ordinary child!

Other than losing her hair and experiencing nausea, the primary side effect of her treatments was her susceptibility to infections and illnesses. Because her treatments suppressed her immune system, any bacterial or viral infection that Darlene, Cheri and I could successfully fight off could prove devastating or even fatal to Bethany. In spite of this, we were encouraged to let her experience as much of life as possible, taking the necessary precautions not to expose her to infectious diseases. Thus, when September of 1979 came, we enrolled Bethany in the Tuesday and Thursday morning three-year-old preschool, where Darlene was co-director. Darlene was able to be vigilant about possible communicable diseases, and, if there was any question of a student's being sick, we kept Bethany out of preschool until the threat had passed. This plan worked well, and Bethany was able to attend almost every class.

As we moved into January and February, 1980, everything seemed to be going well in Bethany's treatment and recovery. Her immune system was returning to normal, and her hair was growing again – a brown color now, in contrast to the blond hair that she had lost because of the chemotherapy and radiation treatments for leukemia. Her stamina was returning, and the fun-loving aspects of her personality were reappearing. We were looking forward to celebrating Easter and to all the fun and excitement which that would bring for seven-year-old Cheri and soon-to-be-four-year-old Bethany.

On Palm Sunday, March 30, we attended the early worship service. Later in the morning we were told that Bethany had had an unusual spell during her Sunday School class. As she came to us after class, she appeared normal, except that, when she smiled, her smile was asymmetric – one side of her mouth drooped somewhat.

We immediately called Dr. McMillan; he had given us permission to call him any time we had questions or serious concerns about Bethany's health. He told us to bring Bethany to NCMH, and he would meet us there. We arrived shortly after noon and were taken to an examination room, where Dr. Mc-Millan soon joined us. As he walked in and looked at Bethany, I saw tears well up in his eyes. I knew at that moment that the prognosis for Bethany's recovery was not good. He said that he suspected that leukemic cells were again dividing in her cerebrospinal fluid, which in turn had caused the spell and her asymmetric smile. He ordered a spinal fluid tap, and it confirmed his suspicion.

The treatment plan was to inject drugs into the spinal fluid that could kill the leukemic cells and retard their further growth there. The devastating realization was that the leukemic cells were there because they had become resistant to methotrexate, which had been one of the primary drugs in the earlier chemotherapy regimens. Monitoring the number of leukemic cells in her spinal fluid soon confirmed that they were continuing to multiply, despite using the highest doses of methotrexate deemed safe for therapeutic use. Late in April, with great disappointment and personal pain, Dr. McMillan told us that there were no further medical options available to treat Bethany. Barring some miracle, we could only hope to keep her as comfortable as possible as the leukemia ran its course.

Darlene and I were again devastated. Our immediate concern was to make the remainder of Bethany's life as comfortable as possible, while also attending to the needs of Cheri. At age seven, she was aware that Bethany was very ill and would not live, but all that seemed to have relatively little meaning for her, except that Bethany would no longer be with us.

With all possible conventional medical possibilities having been exhausted, well-meaning people suggested that we go to Mexico or other such places to seek medical cures that were said to be effective, but which the US Food and Drug Administration had not yet approved for use in this country. Dr. McMillan and others assured us that, if such treatments in fact existed, they would be in use or in the process of being tested for use in this country. Such promises of foreign miracle cures only play on the emotions of desperate people, who in the end do not acquire the cures they seek and lose countless sums of money in the process. Consequently, we rejected all such false promises of hope. If there were to be a cure, it would be effected by God's healing work in and through Bethany's body.

Meanwhile, we were intent on making Bethany's final days and months with us as comfortable as possible. At the time, Hospice of Wake County NC was being established. It had cared for fewer than a dozen patients, none of them infants or children. When we inquired whether they would consider a ministry to Bethany and our family, they said "yes" and within several days were working with us.

The Hospice team, a nurse and a volunteer, provided our family a wonderful and supportive ministry under the most difficult of circumstances. The nurse monitored Bethany's medical condition and, together with the supervising doctor, saw to it that everything medically possible was done to keep Bethany comfortable.

The volunteer was a young woman, known to her friends as Tiddly. In late April, when she first came to our house to see Bethany, Tiddly asked, "Bethany, can I come to visit you?" Not feeling very well, Bethany responded, "No." Tiddly said, "I'm going to come to see you anyway." Bethany responded, "Then I'll throw you out." Tiddly said, "I want to visit you, so I'll come back in." Bethany responded, "Then I'll throw you out again."

Tiddly came, often bearing candy and small gifts, and Bethany soon accepted her. Tiddly's almost daily visits allowed Darlene to leave our house to go shopping, to run errands and to just plain get away. Tiddly would often read books to Bethany, and they played games together. A special relationship developed between them. One day when Darlene was out of the house, Bethany and Tiddly were there alone, playing a game. At one point Bethany stopped, looked directly into Tiddly's eyes and said, "Tiddly, will you be my friend forever?"

Although Bethany's condition was getting worse in early May, she kept talking about what she wanted to do for her fourth birthday party, which would be Saturday, May 24th. We began to doubt that she would live that long. She was sleeping for longer and longer periods of time, often not even waking to eat. From Monday, May 19th, until Friday, May 23rd, she hardly awakened at all.

To our great surprise, she awakened early on Saturday morning, her birthday, and said, "What are we going to do today for my birthday?" Not expecting her to be in any condition to celebrate her birthday, we were unprepared and scrambled to put something together. With Tiddly's and some other friends' help, we contacted several persons. A local woman who played the character Guppy the Clown for children's birthday parties agreed to come. Another man, a member of our congregation who hosted the "Uncle Paul" children's show on a local TV station, also was pleased to come and entertain. Both agreed to drop by for a 10:00 AM birthday party for Bethany. It was a party as wonderful as we could make for Bethany, knowing full well that it would be her last. By 11:30 AM Bethany was very tired, and the party ended. But Darlene and I were comforted by knowing that she had experienced at least some pleasure on her birthday.

Her birthday having passed, Bethany had little else to live for. One of her few remaining highlights was a visit to our house by Dr. McMillan, her pediatric oncologist from NCMH. He had driven the 30 or so miles from Chapel Hill for one final visit to his special little patient. Bethany had touched him as she had touched all of us.

As he stepped outside our house after visiting Bethany, I thanked him for all that he had done for her and for our family. I then said. "Dr. McMillan, I do not know how you can continue to work with patients like Bethany, knowing that so many of them will end up dying. How are you able to do it?" He replied, "Yes, many, perhaps most, of my patients do die. But some live, and that sustains me. And for those who die, I find fulfillment in knowing that I have helped extend their lives for some time and given them comfort and support in dealing with their disease."

Bethany continued to weaken, and about 7:30 AM, Monday, June 16, she died a peaceful death. When representatives of the funeral home came to pick up her body, the attendants were having a difficult time maneuvering the gurney down the hallway to her bedroom where she had died, so I told them that I would carry her body to the front door, and they could take her from there. Although doing that was emotionally very difficult, it seemed like the last act of love that I could do for her in our house.

Her funeral was held at Our Savior Lutheran Church on Wednesday, June 18, in an overflowing church that included many health care workers who had worked with her. Bethany had touched many lives, and all needed to say a fitting goodbye to her. Her death was not just a loss to our family but also to the entire community. She was buried not far from a shade tree in Raleigh Memorial Park, along Glenwood Avenue (Highway 70) northwest of Raleigh.

Darlene and I were again engulfed in deep grief. But this time, in addition to attending to our own survival, we had to attempt to be nurturing parents to Cheri, who was dealing with the loss of her sister, best friend and playmate. Therefore, we arranged for her to meet regularly for some months with a children's grief counselor, who helped Cheri process her thoughts and feelings relating to Bethany's death.

Recognizing that we, too, needed support in dealing with Bethany's death, Darlene and I became involved in Compassionate Friends, a support group for parents whose children of any age have died. The Raleigh chapter was getting organized in 1980, and we were invited to become part of the founding group. Our participation was invaluable to us. We recognized that other people with similar losses were feeling the same intensity and depth of grief and pain that we were feeling. As weekly gatherings stretched into months, we saw each other beginning to work through the grief process and to recover. As parents with more recent losses than ours joined the group, we were able to model the recovery process for and with them. During the several years that Darlene and I worked with that group, I realized that I was dealing not only with Bethany's death but also with Tammy's death. Many of the feelings that I had suppressed after Tammy's death were then being brought out and dealt with in ways that facilitated healing, rather than the continuing festering that had led to my earlier bout with anxiety-depression. Probably no such healing is ever complete, but Compassionate Friends helped Darlene and me take important steps along the way towards healing from the losses of Tammy and Bethany.

Having dealt with the medical, personal and emotional aspects of my family's coping with Bethany's illness and death, I now summarily address the religious and spiritual dimensions. Our friends and church community again provided immeasurable support and encouragement in whatever ways they could throughout the ordeal of Bethany's illness and death. From the beginning, we as a family prayed together and individually with each other and for each other. Because we had become very integrated into Our Savior congregation, our losses and pains were their losses and pains. We and our needs were incessantly lifted up before God in prayer. If during Tammy's illness people had knocked loudly on heaven's doors on our behalf, during Bethany's illness they had used battering rams and jarred open heaven's doors on our behalf. No spiritual stone was left unturned for us in terms of personal self-examination and consideration that somehow God could be speaking to us or specifically to me through these tragedies. But I still found no satisfactory answers to my questions concerning how a loving, caring and providing God could "permit" such tragedies in the lives of people who tried to faithfully serve him.

By now I had concluded that my church's teachings on matters of science and nature were uninformed by modern understanding and should not be taken seriously, no matter how much biblical authority was invoked to support those teachings. However, I was still struggling to hold on to those church teachings that addressed *spiritual* matters. God as the creator of the world seemed plausible, recognizing that God has used and continues to use the evolutionary process to bring about emerging nature. The presence of sin in the world – as evidenced by human's destruction of nature, including other humans – provides ample evidence that people need to repent and conform their lives to laws that support and sustain God's creation. The notion of Jesus' death as a sacrifice to reconcile humans with God, although unusual from a modern perspective, made a certain amount of theological sense. Perhaps there was still salvation in traditional Lutheran theology and teaching after all.

However, my experience with Compassionate Friends also had provided an important *spiritual* insight. A requirement of involvement in this grief group was (and still is) that participants not attempt to impose their particular religious perspective on others in the group. It is implicitly recognized and explicitly stated that, while a particular religious perspective may be important in helping some people deal with their grief and loss, a different religious or nonreligious perspective may be important, even necessary, for others. My Lutheran training and counseling from Lutheran pastors was quite emphatic that "real" solutions to spiritual problems come only from Christian, and preferably Lutheran, sources. The specific content of that advice was that, if one drew near to God by drawing on one's traditional resources, one would gain the necessary strength and consolation to deal with the problems at hand. Yet, here my experience was that I was drawing much more solace, consolation, strength and healing from a *secular* source than I was from my traditional Lutheran faith resources. Not surprisingly, my confidence that my traditional Lutheran perspective was an adequate resource in dealing with even the spiritual crises of my life was seriously waning.

There was a certain, perhaps theological, irony in Cheri's living and in Bethany's dying. In Cheri's case Darlene and I had attempted to use modern medical approaches to prevent our having a second child afflicted with a fatal genetic disease. Our use of artificial insemination by donor, a modern medical technology, failed; yet Cheri survived. In Bethany's case, the use of modern medical technology had worked to prevent her having the genetically fatal disease; she escaped that disease, only to die of a completely different – and equally fatal – disease.

What was going on? What, if anything, did those happenings have to say about how God acts in the world? Was God perhaps indicating that it was the divine will that Tammy and Bethany were supposed to die, no matter what Darlene and I did? Was God "having his way," no matter what we tried? Was God revealing to us that it was wrong to use our best judgment and modern technology to influence the laws of nature? Simple answers to these questions seemed to trivialize the divinity and dignity of God. These and other questions cried out to me for satisfactory answers; despite my seeking for but not finding them, I still tried to hold on to as much as I could of my traditional faith.

Chapter 5

What in Hell Is Going On, God?

Even with our participation in Compassionate Friends, recovering from our loss of Bethany (and, belatedly, Tammy) was difficult and took a number of years. By the mid 1980s Darlene and I had each found fulfilling opportunities in which to invest ourselves. For a time Darlene continued her position as co-director of Western Boulevard Preschool, which was growing both in terms of reputation and numbers of students. The school was located not far from NC State University, and graduate students, in particular, competed to enroll their children in the school. After some years the other co-director left to teach in the North Carolina public schools, and Darlene then became the sole director, although she always insisted on teaching at least one class. It was remarkable to me that she, at five feet and one inch in height and barely one hundred pounds in weight, could use her soft voice to command the respect and attention of her classes of ten to fifteen energetic three- and four-year-olds. Her caring ways elicited a like response from her students. I think that being a very effective preschool teacher was a way to invest her maternal nurturing abilities; perhaps she subconsciously saw her students as surrogates for Tammy and Bethany.

My career at the National Institute of Environmental Health Sciences was well established. I had a tenured position as a research geneticist, directing a staff of usually about six people, which included postdoctoral fellows, technicians and students from nearby universities. My research on a significant problem in Drosophila gene control was resulting in numerous publications per year, including some in the most prestigious scientific journals. My salary provided a comfortable living for our family of three, which allowed Darlene to teach in a situation that provided a meager salary but brought her much fulfillment. I poured myself into my work, probably for several reasons. While I enjoyed my work very much and found it fulfilling, intense focus on my work also probably kept me from dwelling on the painful reminders of the losses of my two daughters.

Before we had any children, Darlene and I had thought that we would like a family of two or three children. After Tammy's illness and death and the decision that we would use AID in the conception of any other children, we decided that we would settle for two children. Thus, when Cheri was old enough to be sure that she did not have Werdnig-Hoffman disease and when we knew that Bethany was a product of AID, our desire for two healthy children was met, and we decided that Darlene would have a tubal ligation. That permanent form of birth control would prevent us from having an unintended pregnancy, in which case we would again be confronted with all the anxieties of possibly having a child with Werdnig-Hoffman disease. In addition, we were both over thirty and ready to get on with life beyond diapers. Bethany's death did not cause us to rethink our decision. Cheri was already seven, and a new baby would not be a pal and playmate for her as Bethany had been. As far as our family was concerned, Darlene and I would focus on making the best possible world for Cheri.

By the mid 1980s Cheri had moved on through elementary and middle school and was about to enter senior high school. She had gone through some counseling to help her deal with Bethany's death. In addition she was fortunate to be one of a group of five girls who had begun preschool together and had stayed together in the same schools as they moved through the grades. Several of them were like sisters to Cheri, and they probably played important surrogate roles for Bethany, her sister and best friend whom she had lost. Cheri began playing a trumpet and, after several years, was good enough to be first chair in her school band. During her freshman year of high school our family hosted Steffi, a German exchange student; for at least one year Cheri had a "sister," albeit three years older than she was, rather than three years younger as Bethany had been.

Cheri, Darlene and I also remained very active in Our Savior Lutheran congregation. As Cheri moved into high school, Darlene and I thought it a worthwhile growth experience for Cheri to go with us to a Youth Servant Event – an organized week-to-ten-day experience in which church youths under adult leadership and supervision would go to a community to help build or restore houses for poor and elderly persons. Cheri was not convinced that she wanted to go; she would be the only youth from our congregation, and, as a high school freshman, it was pretty "yucky" to go with one's parents – especially to a place where there were lots of other teenagers without their parents. But she finally agreed, reluctantly. On the evening of our first day at camp, we sat around the campfire as each person introduced her/himself and explained why s/he had come to camp. When Cheri's turn came, she was bluntly honest: "My parents were coming, and I did not have any place else to stay. So I came with them." She ended up having a great experience that week. Over the next few years she attended a number of other similar events – some with and some without her parents.

One particular memory of that Servant Event stands out. One of the community-building activities involved being what was called a "Secret Servant/Secret Pal." At the campfire closing on the first night, each person's name was written on a small piece of paper, and they were all put into a small box. Each person then drew out a piece of paper, and during our time together she/he was to be a Secret Servant to the Secret Pal whose name was on that paper. Being a Secret Servant involved doing small deeds of kindness – a piece of candy or gum under the pillow, a friendship card – for the Secret Pal *without* the recipient's identifying her/his Secret Servant. Around the campfire on the final evening, each person would guess who had been her/his Secret Servant, and then the Secret Servant would reveal her/himself.

During the week I had noticed that, as a typical fourteen-year-old girl, Cheri was admiring some of the boys who were there. About the middle of the week she came to me and asked if I would give her some more money. When I asked her what she had done with the money that we had given her when she came to camp – an amount that she had agreed would be enough, she said, "I want to buy something for my Secret Pal." I said, "But you do not have to spend a lot of money to do that." She said, "But this person is special." Trying to imagine which of the young boys she was trying to impress, I gave her some money – five or ten dollars, with the fatherly advice and admonition, "Spend it wisely, because you'll not get any more." The rest of the week went by, and she asked for no more money.

As we sat in a ring around the campfire that last evening together, the time came for each of us to learn the identity of our Secret Servant. Each person would close her/his eyes and name the person whom they thought had been her/his Secret Servant. Then the Secret Servant would get up, walk over and stand in front of the person whom they had been serving. The recipient would then open her/his eyes and learn the identity of her/his Secret Servant. When it came my turn to guess who had been my Secret Servant, I closed my eyes and acknowledged that I had no idea who had been my Secret Servant. That person had done some very nice things for me and had done them very discreetly. My eyes still closed, I heard some tittering sounds as someone got up and walked over to stand in front of me. I opened my eyes: it was Cheri. She was my Secret Servant. I was that *special one* for whom she needed some more money to buy something. That experience remains one of life's extra special memories of interactions between Cheri and me. It was a very humbling experience for me.

We still missed our dear Bethany, but we were doing the best that we could to move on with our lives. If there was one lesson that Bethany would have wanted to teach us, it would have been to enjoy life whenever possible, because you do not know how long you will have it. As difficult as it seemed for us to enjoy life, we were trying – with some success at times.

Darlene and I were also attempting to explore new dimensions of our spiritual lives. During the 1980s, Our Savior congregation began using the Bethel Bible Series in order to enhance knowledge of biblical content among its members. Both Darlene and I enrolled in and completed the program. As a follow-up extension, the Crossways Bible study series was then chosen to accomplish the same goal from another perspective. Both of these programs treated the biblical narrative as essentially historical, although they attempted to draw out the theological content rather than emphasizing the historical aspects of the events. This was particularly true of their dealing with the Genesis creation story, where the emphasis was on God's involvement in creation rather than on the specific details of how creation occurred. This presumably reflected the realization by the authors of those studies that any literal understanding of those stories was no longer tenable. The overriding theme of both of these Bible study series was that God's activity was directly responsible for the unfolding of, first, the Hebrew narrative and its literature (Old Testament), and, second, the Christian narrative and its literature (New Testament). Not surprisingly, because these studies were written by Christian authors, the presuppositions were that the

true and final culmination of God's story was Jesus the Christ and that the Christian Church was founded on the basis of Jesus' teachings and those of his followers.

While the biblical narrative presented a coherent and internally consistent story, at least as presented from the perspective of the authors of the biblical studies, some troublesome questions were more frequently occurring in my mind. Is not the biblical story just what one would expect, if it were told from a "truth in the mind of the teller" perspective? In my professional work life, the truth of a concept was based on being able to demonstrate the general accuracy, reliability and validity of its content. How could one know which, if any, of the details of the biblical narrative were historical, especially if they were "events" that are not part of recorded history or of our experience in today's world? Even if events could be demonstrated to be historical, how could one be sure that they were *God's* acting in the world?

Traditional worship was also becoming increasingly stale and unsatisfying for Darlene and me. When in the fall of 1985 we heard of a group of Lutherans who were holding weekend retreats called *Cursillos*, (Spanish for "little course" and modeled after the Roman Catholic movement), we decided to attend. The Thursday evening through Sunday evening retreats were very intense and introspective experiences that helped one examine all aspects of one's Christian life in the context of strong community formation. The music was contemporary and informal, using mostly guitar accompaniment. My interest in the group prompted me to resume guitar playing, something I had felt pressured to give up when I went to Concordia Teachers College in Seward, where guitar accompaniment had not been considered appropriate for the dignity of Lutheran hymns and songs. Playing guitar while accompanying contemporary Christian songs in this new setting gave me new purpose in life, while at the same time trying to revitalize a Christian doctrinal content that was becoming passé and irrelevant to my life.

Darlene and I felt nurtured and uplifted by our participation in the group and remained involved as its Lutheran form adopted the name *Via de Cristo (Way of Christ)*. We invited others in Our Savior congregation to participate, and some 20-30 of its members did. By the late 1980s there was sufficient interest in Our Savior congregation that a contemporary worship service was introduced into the life of the congregation. At first, it was offered only at one of the two morning services on the last Sunday of months that had five Sundays – which meant that three or four services were held per year. From the outset there was limited support from the pastor, and there was strong resistance from traditionalists, who mockingly referred to it as the "Honky-Tonk" or "Hee-Haw" service. A group of us, for whom I was the most vocal spokesman, contended that offering a contemporary service provided additional variety for interested persons within the congregation and extended an outreach to others in the community who did not come from and, therefore, did not identify with traditional Lutheran backgrounds. Moreover, no one would be deprived of traditional worship, because the other service on Sundays when there was a contemporary service was always a traditional service. Enough congregation leaders approved, if only reluctantly, and the contemporary service became a regular inclusion in the worship life of the congregation. However, through the experience of getting approval to have it, I had learned that even at Our Savior, which I had considered rather open to new ideas and practices, there was a core of staunchly traditional Lutherans. Many of these were members who had moved to Raleigh and the Research Triangle Park area from the Midwest; they had brought with them those ideas, attitudes and practices of the Lutheran Church-Missouri Synod that no longer spoke to my life.

As we entered 1990, Darlene and I were looking ahead to our 25th wedding anniversary in August. At least some of those years had been very difficult for us. Although statistics showed that a majority of marriages that had suffered the death of even a single child ended in separation and divorce, we were determined that ours would survive. In May 1991, Cheri would be graduated from high school and go away to college; her leaving home would free us for new possibilities. While we were more and more disillusioned with the rightward drift of our congregation and denomination, we were still convinced of the merits of a Christian life lived in community and in service to others. We tossed around several ideas about how we would spend the remainder of lives, one of which involved going to a foreign land where she could teach in a school or preschool-kindergarten and I could teach in a college. Perhaps we could explore opportunities to do that in the future.

By 1990, our involvement with *Via de Cristo* had become a very significant component of our spiritual lives. Darlene and I had each served as team members to plan and to work on a number of weekend retreats. I had been elected president of the Eastern North Carolina *Via de Cristo* leadership team, the group that was responsible for selecting the leaders for the weekend retreats. At the April 1990 meeting of the leadership team, when Darlene's name was suggested as a potential leader for a retreat, I thought it inappropriate as her husband to participate in those deliberations and dismissed myself, although I thought that she would be an excellent leader. She was unanimously selected to be the leader of the weekend retreat that was planned for November 1990. When she was asked whether she would be willing to serve as the team leader, she accepted; in being asked, she felt both honored and humbled. She had come to recognize and accept her own abilities and skills in working with small children, but she had always had reservations about leading adults. This would be her opportunity to prove to herself and others that she could effectively lead and coordinate adult activities, and she diligently began the process of selecting the approximately forty members of the team to work with her. The organizational team meeting was scheduled for Saturday, June 2.

Although Darlene was feeling well, she had noticed that small red spots were beginning to appear on her skin. At first she ignored them; as they became more numerous, she thought that perhaps she had some type of rash or skin infection, and she made an appointment to see a dermatologist. Because the dermatologist did not recognize the spots as typical of any skin lesions, he took biopsies of several of the spots to see what additional information analyses of these could provide. When the results of the biopsy analyses came back, Darlene was told that the red spots contained suspicious cells and that she should consult with an oncologist for further work. We immediately recognized that the reference to see an oncologist meant that there was an ominous suspicion that some type of cancer was involved. She made an appointment at a local oncology group practice, where she was scheduled to see Dr. Kenneth Zeitler.

When Darlene and I met with Dr. Zeitler, he told us that the abnormal cells in the skin were cancerous but that further tests would be necessary to determine the specific type. He took a bone marrow biopsy, and, after receiving the results of its analysis, scheduled another appointment. At that meeting he told us that Darlene had acute myelocytic leukemia (AML), an aggressive form of leukemia for which the cure rate was in the range of 50 percent. He said that the disease was still in the early stages and that she had the best chances for successful treatment and cure if treatment were begun while she was still strong and otherwise healthy. He suggested that she begin chemotherapy as soon as she could work it into her schedule.

This shocking news put everything else in our lives on hold. Darlene knew that she would be unable to be the team leader for the November retreat and informed the appropriate people. Dr. Zeitler estimated that we should plan for a month to six weeks of hospitalization for Darlene, because treatment for AML involved quite aggressive chemotherapy. As we worked out our schedule, we decided that, while I would be with her at particularly critical times, I would try to continue my working schedule as much as possible. We did not know how much time I might need to take off later. Although Cheri was 17, we also needed to make arrangements for her care.

We were able to put things into place so that Darlene could be admitted to Rex Hospital in late June to begin treatment. The chemotherapy involved a series of treatments that lasted several weeks. At first, she tolerated it quite well, although she soon had frequent episodes of nausea and lost her appetite. It was a struggle for her to eat and to drink and to keep anything in her stomach. Her team of doctors, including Dr. Zeitler, turned to one medication after another to control the nausea. Eventually, it was necessary to give her nutrition through intravenous infusion. After the first round of chemotherapy, her bone marrow was checked, and it was decided that she needed another round of treatment. Because chemotherapy suppressed and destroyed her bone marrow, red blood cells and blood platelets had to be provided as necessary by transfusion to keep her alive. After a number of transfusions, her body developed a reaction that resulted in the collecting of fluid in her lungs and around her heart, which resulted in her being moved to intensive care for a period of time. At that point there was some question whether she would survive, so her identical twin sister Marlene from Oregon flew to Raleigh to be with her. Marlene's coming also provided a medical benefit: because they were genetically identical, Marlene could provide blood platelets and other blood products that Darlene's body would not reject, as it was attempting to do with blood products from other persons.

Humorous situations sometimes occur that lend some levity to otherwise very serious and tragic situations. When Darlene was taken to intensive care, the nurses and other personnel in the oncology unit knew that she was very seriously ill and that her life was hanging in the balance. As stated above, Marlene came to be with Darlene within a day or two of her being taken to intensive care. About a day after Marlene's arrival, I asked her if she wanted to go with me to the oncology unit and meet some of the people who had been taking care of Darlene. As Marlene and I came walking down the hallway towards the nurses station in that unit, I noticed the extremely shocked look on their faces. I then realized that they were unaware that Darlene had an identical twin, Marlene, whom the casual observer could easily mistake for Darlene. The first impression of the people at the nurses' station was that Darlene had made a miraculous recovery in the intensive care unit and was returning to the oncology unit to resume her chemotherapy treatments.

Unfortunately, no such quick recovery was in store. Rather, things got worse. During the second round of chemotherapy, a systemic yeast infection had become established in Darlene's body. The only available treatment was a drug called Amphotericin; the side effects of its intravenous infusion were so drastic that those who administered it referred to it as "amphoterrible." But there was no alternative drug, and it had to be used.

The second round of therapy had ended, and Darlene could go home, as soon as she went 48 hours without a fever. But day after day she continued to run fevers that spiked to 102-104 degrees Fahrenheit, an indication that her immune system was recovering and attempting to fight off the systemic yeast infection. The end of July passed, and the middle of August came; the fevers persisted. August 22 would be our 25th wedding anniversary, and we had hoped that she could go home by then; still the fevers persisted. With Dr. Zeitler's permission I asked if I could bring a little wine that we could share at a make-shift anniversary dinner in her hospital room on the evening of August 22. He agreed, and I brought a little of her favorite wine. However, the combination of chemotherapy treatments had so altered her taste buds that she could not recognize the taste; as she tried to taste it, she again experienced nausea, and we abandoned our attempt at a celebration dinner.

Finally, in early September, after more than ten weeks in the hospital, Darlene was permitted to come home. Her fevers persisted, but her doctors decided that the medical infusions could be continued at home. Perhaps more important, a return to her home environment would provide an atmosphere more emotionally conducive to her recovery. When she entered the hospital, she had weighed 100 pounds and was in robust health. When she returned home, she weighed 74 pounds; all her ribs were starkly visible, and she did not have enough strength to walk the fifteen feet from our bed to the bathroom by herself.

While the home health care staff took care of her medical needs, I was responsible for the rest of her care. My biggest concern was to get her to eat and to drink enough not only to maintain her weight but to help her regain both weight and strength. Almost nothing tasted good to her, and she still had frequent bouts of nausea. After trying many different kinds of food, we finally arrived at a "balanced" diet: fresh cantaloupe, butterscotch pudding made with Ensure Plus instead of milk, and O'Doul's alcohol-free beer. These tasted good to her, so I was more than happy to have available all that she would eat and drink.

Because Darlene was home, we were able to sleep together in the same bed again. We both treasured the physical proximity of being able to sleep together again, although she was, of course, too weak and frail for us to experience sexual intimacy. She was not the same vibrant person who had gone to the hospital nearly ten weeks earlier; neither was I the same person who had taken her to the hospital. She still had fever spikes, when her body felt as though it was burning up. Those spikes were followed by periods of time when her body temperature, particularly in her extremities, was much below normal. One night, while she was sleeping very soundly and I could not hear her breathing, I reached over to touch her. Her arms felt so cold that I wondered if she was still alive. She was, but for one dreadful moment I thought that she had died.

All of this was very difficult for both of us, but we were determined that we were going to do everything possible for her to get well again. By early October her appetite had increased somewhat, and she was able to walk around in the house. By the end of October her diet was still almost only cantaloupe, butterscotch pudding and O'Doul's; but she was up to about 80 pounds and her walk was getting stronger. By mid-November she was strong enough for the car ride and an evening visit to the weekend retreat for which she had originally been chosen to be the leader. By late November her weight had reached 85 pounds, and she and I were going on short walks through the neighborhood. Her hair, which had been a graying brown before she lost it due to chemotherapy, was growing back; it was about a half inch long, thick and very black. She was becoming well enough to return to worship services at church.

December came and with it Christmas. We celebrated it as happily as we could, not knowing what the future would bring. By that time Darlene had reached nearly 90 pounds, and we were going on regular 2-3 mile strolls through our neighborhood, sometimes walking quite briskly.

Medically, her situation had improved considerably. Her doctors continued to monitor her blood, and there were no signs of recurrent leukemic cells. While there were still indications of residual yeast infection in her liver, her body appeared to be successfully overcoming it. The long-term strategy was for her to continue to gain strength. By perhaps April or May she would hopefully still be leukemia-free and the yeast infection would be largely overcome, at which time she would receive a bone marrow transplant from Marlene. Because Marlene was her identical twin sister, this would be a perfect bone marrow match, and there should be no problems with tissue rejection. We were optimistic that all would go well.

Unfortunately, things did not continue that way. When her February blood work analysis was done, leukemic cells were found. Her doctors felt that, if they were to try to bring the leukemia into remission again, neither of the two most likely outcomes was favorable. First, they might well not be able to bring the leukemia into remission again; it had been difficult the first time, and the recurrent cells may well be ones that were resistant to the drugs used in the chemotherapy treatments. The second possibility was that she might not physically survive the rigors of the treatments that would be needed to get rid of the leukemic cells. The fact that Darlene had an identical twin sister who would be a perfect match donor provided the option of proceeding with a bone marrow transplant, but they recognized and informed us that it would be a very risky procedure – at best. When her doctors explored the bone marrow transplant centers for a place to carry out this procedure, most refused; they considered it too risky to commit their facilities and resources to Darlene's case, when they already had waiting lists of other patients whose chances for a successful outcome were much greater than Darlene's. Moreover, because their reputations as transplant centers depended on their success rate, they were extremely reluctant to accept a patient whose outcome was in doubt from the start.

Finally, her doctors succeeded in getting Darlene accepted for treatment at the Fred Hutchinson Cancer Research Center (FHCRC) in Seattle, Washington. Treatments could begin as soon as arrangements could be made to get Darlene to Seattle. We hastily arranged for air ambulance service, and on Wednesday, February 27, a Learjet ambulance plane transported us from Raleigh to Seattle. On board were the pilot, a nurse, Darlene and I. After refueling stops in Iowa and Idaho, we arrived in Seattle in the late afternoon, where we were met by relatives who took us to FHCRC, where Darlene was admitted to Swedish Hospital. After several days of initial testing, they were ready to begin the transplant procedure. We were apprised of the risks involved in any bone marrow transplant procedure and that the risks in Darlene's case were even greater because of her having active leukemia. We understood the risks; whatever the risks and odds were, we were going to proceed, because it was Darlene's only chance for survival.

Darlene's bone marrow transplant procedure was typical. First, over a course of about a week, she received heavy doses of chemotherapy and the maximum tolerable amount of whole body radiation in order to completely destroy all her bone marrow cells, healthy as well as cancerous. Then healthy bone marrow stem cells that had been taken from Marlene were given to her in what seemed very much like an ordinary blood transfusion. Remarkably, the stem cells "know" that they should travel to and settle into the interior of the bones where the diseased stem cells have been destroyed. There they become established and begin dividing and differentiating into the various cells produced by bone marrow stem cells – red blood cells for carrying oxygen and carbon dioxide, blood platelets for normal blood clotting, and various types of white blood cells which provide the body immunity to infections and diseases. During the ten days to two weeks between the transfusion of the bone marrow stem cells and the first appearance of newly produced red blood cells, platelets and white blood cells, Darlene was vulnerable to any type of infection. Although I was able to see her and to spend significant amounts of time with her during that time, I had to wear surgical garb

and a face mask to ensure that I did not transmit anything harmful to her. There were numerous other devastating side effects to the chemotherapy and whole body radiation that necessitated her being on a morphine drip during that time in order to tolerate the pain. As had been the case during her chemotherapy in Raleigh, Marlene was also able to donate platelets and red blood cells that were completely compatible with Darlene's body because of their genetic identity.

Then began the wait for two hoped-for results: the reappearance of new white blood cells to indicate that the transplanted stem cells had become established and the lack of reappearance of any leukemic cells. During this waiting period the debilitating side effects of the radiation and chemotherapy gradually waned, and Darlene was weaned off the morphine. As her body began healing, there was a transition from the intravenous feeding that had sustained her during the transplant to feeding by mouth again. In order for her to regain strength and to stimulate her appetite, she was encouraged to begin minimal exercise as soon as possible and to progress to walking in the hallways of the transplant unit as soon as feasible.

By the end of May Darlene had made remarkable progress. Her white blood cell count had increased so that she was less susceptible to disease and infection. The early analyses of her bone marrow had shown no recurrent leukemic cells. Her appetite was returning, and she was regaining strength, mostly through walking. The hallways in the transplant center formed a square, with each side being about one hundred feet in length; a lap around the hallway was thus about 400 feet. By now Darlene and I were walking about twenty laps once or twice each day, and her walking speed had earned her the nickname "The Charger." She was scheduled to continue this routine until the middle of June, and, if all went well, she could go home.

When Darlene and I went to Seattle for Darlene's transplant, Cheri had remained in

Raleigh, where she was staying with the family of Donna, one of her five classmate friends mentioned earlier. They lived close to Athens Drive High School, where both would be graduated in May 1991. Darlene and I kept in close touch with Cheri through phone calls, more frequently after Darlene had begun recovering from the transplant. Our greatest disappointment was not being able to be present for her high school graduation in mid-May. She was graduated in the top ten percent of her class. She had applied for acceptance at a handful of schools and had been accepted at the University of North Carolina at Chapel Hill (UNC-CH) – her first choice. Even better, her four close friends had all applied there and had been accepted, too. The circle of friends that had begun in preschool would continue on to college. As difficult as it was for Cheri not to be with her family, she was dealing quite well with things in her personal life, and Darlene and I were very pleased with and very proud of her.

The red letter day on the calendar in Darlene's room was Wednesday, June 19. On that day they would take another bone marrow sample; if no leukemic cells were found, she would be able to go home. She was getting stronger and continuing to feel better, so we were optimistic that she would get a good report. Wednesday came and the bone marrow sample was taken. On Thursday, the transplant team of doctors came into Darlene's room to discuss the results with us. As they came into her room, we noticed that they all had quite serious facial expressions – an ominous sign. Then they gave us the bad news: there was no doubt; there were many leukemic cells in her bone marrow again. Because it had been necessary to transplant her while she had active leukemia, not all leukemic cells were killed by the chemotherapy and whole body radiation. Some had survived, and the leukemia had returned. We asked what, if anything, could be done? They said that it would not be possible to try another transplant because Darlene would not survive it. There was no further treatment that they could offer. They suggested that we make arrangements to return home as soon as possible. Because Darlene was feeling reasonably good, we should take advantage of that as long as it would last.

Through the generosity of friends' donations of frequent flyer points, we were able to schedule a return to Raleigh on Friday, June 21. Our flight took us through Dallas-Fort Worth airport, where changing concourses between flights can involve a good deal of walking. It seemed ironic that Darlene and I were strongly walking at a brisk and strong pace to catch our flight to Raleigh, even while knowing that in her bones lay the seeds of what was likely to kill her in the not-too-distant future. When we arrived at the Raleigh-Durham Airport in the late afternoon, we were picked up by friends and driven home. Cheri had come with them to meet us at this most disappointing homecoming.

Early during the week of June 24, we had an appointment with Dr. Zeitler. Darlene and I had many questions about what her life expectancy might be. He said that, while it was not possible to know for sure, it would likely be a few months at most. What would her death be like? He went on to assure us that it would be possible to control her pain and that she likely would not suffer great discomfort. He suggested that we put our legal and any other matters in order as soon as possible, because it was not possible to predict the course of her disease. During the next few days, we tried to anticipate everything that would need to be updated and took care of them.

During the next several weeks, Darlene began to say her goodbyes. She, Cheri and I did what we could together to fill the time with what we hoped would be meaningful – if also painful – memories for Cheri and me. As I write these lines, it was only fourteen years ago that those things happened; however, I must honestly say that I do not remember many of the things that we did. Perhaps there is still too much pain associated with those memories for me to recall them freely. Perhaps the high anxiety and apprehension of her impending death caused those experiences to not even register in my memory. My memory of specific details surrounding her last weeks of life resume when she became so ill and weak that she had to be admitted to Rex Hospital on Monday, July 15.

We knew then that she would not live long. Not wanting to be away from her at all, I requested and received a cot from the hospital so that I could stay overnight with her in her room. We talked about many things, but mostly we both just wanted to spend her remaining time together. Darlene expressed her deep disappointment about not being able to be present for Cheri's future college graduation, marriage and seeing Cheri's children. On Tuesday, as we were alone in her room, she commented, "It's awful sitting around waiting to die. I feel so useless."

Her breathing was becoming more labored, as Dr. Zeitler had said might happen in her final days. By Wednesday morning enough fluid had collected in her lungs that she was experiencing breathing anxiety – the feeling that she was out of breath and unable to breathe deeply to get enough oxygen. Sensing that she might not have much longer to live, she requested that our pastor come to offer our family Holy Communion. He did, and Darlene, Cheri, Marlene (who had come to be with her sister) and I celebrated Holy Communion together one final time.

By early afternoon her inability to breathe deeply had reached the point of panic – much as one feels when one has one's breath knocked out. Dr. Zeitler was called and said that it was time to begin a morphine drip to ease her anxiety. He said that it was now important for us to communicate to each other all that we wanted to say, because Darlene would lose consciousness as the dosage of the morphine drip increased and further communication would be impossible.

It was time to say goodbye. Darlene sat up, her feet dangling off her bed. She, Cheri and I wrapped our arms around each other and embraced; we thanked each other for all that we had meant to each other in life. I looked into Darlene's eyes and saw what I interpreted as terror. She was not afraid to die, but she now realized fully that her death would come soon, and her eyes expressed the agony of having to accept it.

She lay back down, and the nurses connected the morphine drip to her permanently installed catheter tubing. I held her hand as the drip began, and I could feel her beginning to relax. Although I would have given anything to continue to communicate with her, I now accepted that that was impossible, and her comfort in her last days and hours was of greatest importance. She gradually lapsed into subconsciousness.

In the following, I recount what happened in her final days and my interpretations of those events. Although she could no longer communicate, Darlene's mission was not yet completed. Throughout the week countless people were coming in to visit. They were saying goodbye to her and expressing their support to each other and to Cheri and me. If there was an overriding theme to Darlene's life, it was that, when people come together under appropriate circumstances, good things happen. Bridges are built between people, and a stronger sense of community is developed. Despite her not being actively involved, her remaining alive was doing just that – bringing people together for positive things to happen. Even after she lapsed into the morphine-induced subconsciousness on Wednesday, people continued to drop by for visits on Thursday and Friday. Because her room frequently could not accommodate all the visitors, another room in the hospital was set up as a hospitality room. Pizza was ordered for people to eat, either as they waited to visit her or when they talked with others after having visited her. She still had purpose in life; her impending death was still bringing people together.

54

On Saturday morning, Dr. Zeitler dropped by to check on her condition. As we were gathered around her bed, he shared his assessment of her situation. He said that she could remain in her present state for hours, days, even perhaps weeks. We could be in this situation for the long haul. Our family should make plans for someone to remain with her, but that others needed to get away – for their own health and well-being. After he left, we began to talk about how we might work out such a schedule.

I think that in her subconscious state Darlene heard that conversation. From her perspective her continuing to live was becoming a problem for family and friends. She was no longer an agent for bringing people together for positive things to occur; she was now becoming a burden on people's lives. It was now time to let go; she had done all the good that she could in her life's mission. By late Saturday afternoon her breathing became more and more labored. By early evening her breathing pattern indicated that she would not live much longer. Finally, mercifully, shortly after 9 PM, Saturday, July 20, 1991, she drew her last breath and died.

The pain and agony of her death were unspeakable; but, in a strange way, the relief that her long and painful struggle was over helped us to accept her death. Yet, our family, the church, and the larger community still needed to say goodbye to her. To permit family and friends from a distance to attend, we scheduled her funeral for Wednesday afternoon, July 24. The church was over-flowing, with people standing in the entry way and out into the street.

The service included a mixture of hymns and scriptural readings from traditional Lutheran liturgies as well as the playing of tape recordings of contemporary songs that expressed particularly Cheri's and my feelings about Darlene's life and death. Cheri, remembering her mother's role as an encour-ager, supporter and sustainer, chose to in-clude "Wind Beneath My Wings" (written by Larry Henley and Jeff Silbar and sung by Bette Midler). Having been at Darlene's side through our loss of Tammy and Bethany and through her illness and death, I included "The Great Storm is Over" (words and music by Bob Franke, sung by John McCutcheon). As Tammy's and Bethany's father, I had experienced great anguish and pain in their loss; I can only imagine that it must have been greatly amplified and intensified for Darlene, who as their always-available mother was integrally involved in all aspects of their lives. However, I could experience her illness and death only as someone who walked closely with her through her pains and struggles; I could not possibly know it from her perspective. For Darlene the great storms of life were indeed now over. Her legacy would be carried forward by the countless people whose lives she touched, including Cheri's and mine.

Following the emotionally wrenching funeral, Darlene's body was laid to rest in Raleigh Memorial Park, under the same tree that shaded Bethany's grave. While Cheri and I had hoped to find a plot beside Beth-any's grave, the closest available touched Bethany's plot only on one corner. Cheri and I were sure that Darlene would have been pleased to lie close to a child, especially her own daughter; in death, even as in life, she was most fulfilled when children were gathered around her.

Again, I have not detailed all the reli-gious and spiritual aspects surrounding Darlene's illness and death, except to include those that were necessary details of the story. From the time of Darlene's first diagnosis with leukemia until she drew her last breath, prayers for her healing and the well-being of our family were sent to God from countless people in countless places at countless times. If prayers on Tammy's behalf could be symbolized by hard knocking on the heav-en's door, and if prayers on Bethany's behalf could be symbolized by knocking open heaven's doors with battering rams, the pray-ers on Darlene's behalf could only be characterized as obliterating heaven's doors and walls and storming the halls of heaven. Prayer services and healing services were held; every imaginable way to get God's attention to heal this special woman was invoked. Yet, she, like Tammy and Bethany before her, had died. From a medical perspective, Tammy's death was inevitable; no cures were (or still are) available. For Bethany and Darlene, however, cures are commonplace; half or more are cured. Yet Bethany and Darlene – these two genuinely good and important people, were not healed by God. If these huge amounts of supplication do not influence the mind of God, is it possible to influence God at all? Is God deaf? Does God even exist? These questions would continue to challenge my thinking.

Following Darlene's death in the latter part of July, Cheri and I returned to what seemed like an almost empty house. The occupants of one and one-half of the three bedrooms in our house were no longer alive and with us. What had only ten years ago been the home to our family of four was now just the two of us – and that would change soon. Cheri had been accepted at UNC-CH, and classes would begin there in late August. She and I discussed the possibility of her waiting a year and then enrolling, giving her some time to adjust and the two of us some time to grieve together the loss of Darlene. Her choice was to enroll during the next month. She would be on campus with her four close friends who had also been accepted there, and school work and associated activities would give her something on which to focus, other than the loss of her mother. I agreed to support her decision, and we made plans for her to enroll in the university.

She enrolled at UNC-CH, and by her own assessment the first year was pretty much a disaster; yet, that may still have been better than if she had stayed at home. As had happened for me in moving to Raleigh after Tammy's death, Cheri's being away at school enabled her to attempt to not deal with the grief issues surrounding Darlene's death. Cheri could not focus on academics, and consequently was not succeeding in her coursework in her usual way; emotionally, she became depressed and began working with a counselor in order to deal with her grief. By the end of her first year she had not flunked out, but neither had she succeeded in any significant academic sense. Yet, I think that simply surviving the death of her mother, her closest friend and confidante in life, was a successful outcome for her – and for me. I had learned that mere survival of the loss of a close loved one was sometimes the most that one could hope for. Processing that loss and growing from it could only come after the passage of time allowed one some distance from which to see it in perspective.

Chapter 6

Trying to Move On

How does one live on in the shadow of tragedies in one's life? As I looked at my situation in September 1991, I saw a house that could potentially have contained a family of five but now contained only one – me. Tammy's death was 20 years in the past; Bethany's death was 11 years in the past; Darlene's death was only two months in the past. Cheri had gone off to school, and I was living alone. Our three-bed-room house had now become my three bedroom house. Or was it a prison? Where does one go to find the courage and strength to live forwards at a time like that?

Most people would probably turn to their religion – their faith – to seek support. But my confidence in God for providing healing, strength and support in my life was shattered. When I had turned to the God of my traditional Lutheran upbringing to provide healing for my daughters and wife, I could only interpret God's response as having ignored or turned a deaf ear to my pleas for help. Moreover, the myriad prayers and supplications that had bombarded God from my family, friends and doctrinally-correct Lutheran church community had similarly gone unanswered. To me at that time, my needs were unlikely to be met in the continuing understanding and practice of the traditional Lutheranism of my upbringing. As a youngster playing baseball, I had learned that "after three strikes, you're out;" my traditional religious approach had struck out with respect to its adequacy in sustaining me in the crises of life. Later in life I came across someone's definition of insanity: trying to do something the same way for the eleventh time expecting better results when it has not worked the first ten times. I might end up going insane, but it would not be in continuing religious practices that were not

supportive of my dealing with the issues of my life.

Following Bethany's death, Darlene and I had found consolation, strength and support in Compassionate Friends, a group in which people who had lost children to death drew help and healing from shared community, whether or not that was accompanied by religious resources. So after Darlene's death I sought and found a community support group that included others like me – persons who had lost their spouses. Over several months, the six or seven of us who met regularly told and listened to each others' stories of pain and loss. Although hearing about the deep, heart-felt pain of the other members did not take away my pain, it did help me understand that I was not alone in experiencing those horrible feelings. One of the terrors of my grief processes, particularly with the losses of Tammy and Bethany, had been the feeling that the intense agony and hurt that I had felt was so bad, so intense, that no one else could possibly feel that bad. In these two support groups I learned that others were feeling the same intense agony and hurt. Not only was I not alone in my feelings; what I was experiencing was "normal" for a person who had suffered such a great loss. The intensity of the pain was an indication of the magnitude of my loss. As the group moved forward together, we could see each other progress and learn from the modeling of recovery by others in the group.

Physically, life was also challenging. I had difficulty sleeping; when I did get to sleep, my dreams were often haunted by the look in Darlene's eyes just before she had begun the morphine drip in my last communication with her. As time passed, I discovered that walking three to five miles every evening helped me to get rid of the tension in my body and to ready me for sound sleep. As more time passed, the recurring dream of the look in her eyes became less frequent. At present, I see it only if I intentionally recall it.

Periodically, I would get the feeling of a slight burning in my stomach, much like I thought an ulcer might feel. I stumbled onto a solution for dealing with that. The funeral service for Darlene had been tape-recorded, and I was given a copy. Perhaps a month after her death, when I had that feeling in my stomach, I sat down to listen to that tape. As I listened, I began to cry and cry. I cried until I could cry no more. But by the time that I had listened to the entire tape, the feeling in my stomach was gone – if only for a week or so. Then I would listen again and repeat my crying ritual. Gradually, the length of time increased until I got that feeling in my stomach again – a few weeks, then a month, then two months. By about six or seven months after her death, I needed my crying ritual only very occasionally.

For me the grief process this time around was rather different. Having already grieved the losses of Tammy and Bethany, I was aware of the steps or phases in the grief process (shock, denial, anger and guilt, depression, acceptance, empowerment) and how they were likely to affect me. That is not to say that they were not painful; rather, they were no longer terrifying, because I was able to recognize them for what they were. While the listed order corresponded to the approximate chronological sequence in which I was likely to experience them, their sequence of occurrence was really likely to be more mixed up. If I were to express my emotional state using weather analogies, the first three to four months were pretty uniformly cloudy, gloomy and stormy. The four to six months following that were still quite cloudy days, with the sun occasionally peeking through the clouds. That was followed by six months to a year of partly cloudy days. By the end of that period I had reached a "new normal," by no means the same as before Darlene's death, but a period

of stable functionality in her absence.

Despite being able to say that I have worked through the grief process in dealing with the losses of Tammy, Bethany and Darlene, I have come to regard the grief process as a life-long experience, in some respects similar to the recovery of a person from alcohol or other substance abuse. It is something that "keeps on keeping on," as the saying goes. Each time an anniversary date in the life, illness or death of one of my lost family members occurs, my subconscious mind requires that I acknowledge and re-process that event, before it allows me to move on freely with life. Recalling and remembering the events associated with the illnesses and deaths of my three loved ones for the purpose of writing this book took about two weeks' time. That process was so unsettling for me that I experienced chest pains and symptoms suggestive of a heart attack. I went to the emergency room and was admitted to a local hospital for diagnostic tests to determine whether I had experienced a mild heart attack. All tests were negative; I had not experienced a heart attack nor did I appear to be in danger of having one. When I related to the doctors who treated me, including my personal physician, that I had been writing about these painful experiences, they concluded that the mental and emotional processing of those painful events in that compressed time frame was most likely responsible for evoking in me those symptoms. I realize now that I will continue to live with the fallout from my losses for the rest of my life.

It has been said that when people's parents die, they lose their past; when their spouse dies, they lose their present; and when their children die, they lose their future. In my experience, the loss of my children was more devastating. Perhaps it was because they were my children, and I was losing my future; perhaps it was because I was experiencing the deaths of close loved ones for the first time. Because Darlene's death was my third experience, it may be that it was less devastating because I had already gone through the grief experience two times. Even so, it was still a life-wrenching loss.

The unfolding of my life has been counterintuitive. My expected sequence of life occurrences was the deaths of my parents, followed significantly later by either my spouse's or my death, followed many years later by the deaths of my children. In my life that sequence of events has been largely reversed. The deaths of my children, Tammy and Bethany, at ages 6 months and 4 years, respectively, were followed by the deaths of my wife, Darlene, at age 46, and of my mother, Helen, at age 85. As I write these lines at age 63, my father, Elmer, is still alive; at age 86 he is healthy enough not to need any medication except an occasional aspirin for pain. The full significance of these deaths for my life will require more reflection. At least, I have come to realize the importance of trying to live life fully in the present; there is no guaranteed extended future for anyone!

Life has to be lived forwards. By whatever means and resources necessary, I was able to do that. From the outset, however, I had resolved that I would not resort to the use of alcohol or drugs to numb myself from the pains of my losses and grief. Because I had not previously been inclined to use or abuse of either drugs or alcohol in my life, I did not experience any lure to resort to either of them. Given the emphasis on being "responsible" during my upbringing, such a solution was simply not an option for me.

As I was working through the grief process, I was considering what I would do with my future. Professionally, my career was still moving forward successfully. Although I had been physically gone from my laboratory at the National Institute of Environmental Health Sciences for more than three months during Darlene's bone marrow transplant in Seattle, through the modern conveniences of telephone and electronic communications I was able to continue directing the research work. Following Darlene's death, getting back to my office and to the work that was intellectually stimulating and challenging for me provided a focused concentration on matters other than my family losses. Falling back into a familiar routine was both stabilizing and therapeutic for me.

Socially, other than with coworkers and members of my church, my contacts were with the support group mentioned earlier. Some months after that group dissolved, I began to want female companionship again. In our support group we had discussed the hazards of jumping into another relationship too soon after the death of one's spouse. In doing so there was the possibility of trying to replace one's lost spouse – to fill the void in one's life – rather than being able to freely relate to and to accept the new companion. Cognizant of that advice, I prepared myself to begin dating again.

As noted earlier, participation in the *Via de Cristo* (*VdC*) movement had been an important component of Darlene's and my spiritual lives. After first attending one of the intense three-day weekends, *VdC* participants get together some weeks later at what are termed *ultreyas* – three-to-four hour gatherings at which people renew their friendships and deepen their relationships. In March 1992, I attended an *ultreya* in Greensboro. There I again met Linda Hopkins, who had worked with and had become a good friend of Darlene while working together in *VdC* activities. Darlene had introduced Linda to me at an *ultreya* three years earlier. Meanwhile, Linda, a divorcee of about two years, had found new direction for her life through *VdC* and had enrolled at Lutheran Theological Southern Seminary in Columbia, South Carolina, preparing to become a Lutheran pastor.

Of our conversation that evening, Linda would later say that she felt "grilled." I kept asking pointed questions about seminary and seminary life. She had no way of knowing that I had been considering the possibility of going to seminary. I was reaching the point in my life that I needed to do some serious theological delving and processing. What better place to do it than at a seminary? I thought that my having lost three family members to death had provided me with valuable experience to be a pastor who could walk with others in loss and grief. I had already decided that, if I were to go to seminary, it would have to be at a seminary of the Evangelical Lutheran Church in America (ELCA), a sister Lutheran denomination of the LCMS, but which was theologically more open than the LCMS. When I asked Linda for a date so that I could get to know her and so that we could talk about seminary some more, she accepted.

We continued dating through the summer and into the fall of 1992, and our relationship deepened. When I went to visit her at the seminary in mid-November 1992, I proposed, she accepted, and we set our wedding date for February 13, 1993. We selected that date for several reasons. It was close to Linda's birthday on February 16 and Valentines Day, February 14. Additionally, we were both planning to go on a seminary-sponsored trip to the Taizé community in France during spring break in early March; that trip could serve as a honeymoon of sorts, despite the fact that about ten "chaperones" would be going with us. We were married in the chapel at LTSS, went on the trip to the Taizé community and had a good time, despite getting lost in Paris the day before flying back home.

Some students of the grief process consider the last stage of the grief process to be empowerment – a commitment to some purpose or cause, in which one can expend positive energies derived from the grief process. For me that purpose came out of my theological struggles and what I perceived to be inadequacies of my traditional LCMS religious resources. It was clear to me that those resources were not helpful and were in many ways hindrances to my understanding the natural world and my place in it. Thus far, I had given the benefit of the doubt to the Church's traditional teachings on spirit-

ual matters, such as God, sin, salvation, the person and work of Jesus, prayer, the Trinity, etc. With respect to those matters, I had held onto what Martin Luther called "a coal miner's faith" – "I believe whatever the Church believes." Luther's description was not disparaging of miners; indeed, his father had been a miner. Rather, he meant that coal miners of his time accepted the Church's teachings without questioning them too much – perhaps not as much as they should. For me, it was now time to delve into those matters to see whether there was warrant to continue to hold onto them. If the Church's teaching was so wrong on matters of science, on which it claimed to have authority, could it also be misleading or even wrong on *spiritual* matters, on which it claimed even greater and ultimate authority?

Having gotten hold of a reasonable handle on living life forwards again, it was time to begin understanding life backwards more fully – not just my life, but the life of my Lutheran tradition and the life of Christianity. And where better to do that than at a seminary – a Lutheran seminary because of my religious heritage. So I decided to resign from my research scientist position and to enroll at Lutheran Theological Southern Seminary in Columbia, South Carolina, where my new wife Linda was completing her second year. There I could pursue the teachings of Lutheran Christianity to their core and to their roots and explore for myself whether those teachings were founded on sufficient truths for me to anchor my faith and life.

Why did I do it? Why did I leave a position that was tenured and secure for the rest of my career for a life of uncertainty and the unknown? I think my decision was influenced by my perception of the role that change plays in my life. When I perceive that life is going well, I am not inclined to see any need for change. I am free to change, if I so choose. Change is voluntary. When I perceive that life is difficult, I tend to draw on my religious and spiritual resources to deal with the difficulties. I hang onto those resources, because I have found or others have told me that those resources are useful and adequate to deal with difficulty and adversity. I resist changing those resources, because I fear that changing them would lessen their efficacy in helping me deal with my difficulties.

However, the consequences of this philosophy of life are that, the longer that I hang onto my old resources as they continue to be inadequate in helping deal with my adversities, the more pain I experience. This can continue until the pain of not changing becomes greater than the pain of changing. I had reached the point in my life at which the well of my traditional Lutheran Christianity had run dry. Somehow I had to find deeper waters in that tradition or look to other wells to quench the thirsts of my life.

While my understanding life backwards had started before then, its pace accelerated with my enrollment in seminary. It continues to the present and presumably and hopefully will continue as long as I live. That process of understanding has not occurred linearly but rather developed and grew as a large river that has been fed by many streams, creeks and smaller rivers. I will try to present that development systematically later, but first I want to describe the biographical setting in which that theological evolution occurred.

I enrolled in Lutheran Theological Southern Seminary, Columbia, South Carolina, in the fall of 1993. As I took the introductory Old and New Testament History courses, I became aware that these courses were concerned with how the Old and New Testaments came into existence, rather than with treating all their contents as "history." While there were certainly historical events in the biblical books that could be documented in secular history, not all the events in the biblical narrative should be regarded as historical. In addition to the required courses for a Master of Divinity, I took as many courses as I could that

explored the interface of science and religion and that recounted the development of specific theological doctrines such as the Trinity, Jesus the Christ as God, and other counterintuitive Judeo-Christian concepts. With each successive course I learned that Christianity was a much more diverse collection of interpretations of who Jesus was and of the meaning and purpose of his life and ministry than I had been taught by my church. The distilled version of early Christianity that had been passed on to me as "the" biblically correct Lutheran tradition was only one of many possible perspectives – and not always the perspective which seemed to me to follow from careful biblical consideration or the known historical context.

At seminary, I gained a deep appreciation and respect for what has been termed the *historical-critical* method of biblical study and interpretation. The basic supposition of that methodology is that the most enlightened understandings of biblical writings can be obtained if all possible information about the time, place, author, and political, religious, linguistic and other influences can be determined. A comprehensive understanding of the worldview from which it came and what it meant when it was written can assist in assessing what, if anything, that particular writing might contribute to understanding and influencing life today. It was then that I realized why the historical-critical methodology was much more readily accepted within the Evangelical Lutheran Church in America (ELCA) than in the LCMS. Such studies frequently raise serious challenges to or disallow some of the strongly literalistic interpretations held within the LCMS. As theological and doctrinal perspectives of non-Lutheran Christian churches were also studied, it became apparent to me that there was much more plasticity and breathing room in Christianity than is included in Lutheranism, even within the ELCA.

A surprising – but perhaps in some ways

anticipated – discovery for me was that the historical-critical approach to the study of the biblical writings and times was not something new. Its roots date back to the Reformation, and by the early eighteenth century it was being more commonly used. Soon after careful analyses revealed that the sun, not the earth, is the center of our solar system, questioning minds began to carefully scrutinize all facets of human culture, including religion. They discovered that elements of the received biblical tradition in many areas of life did not stand the tests of critical examination in light of expanding seventeenth, eighteenth and nineteenth century knowledge and understandings. The larger picture that was forming for me was the following. While scientists, historians and even many biblical scholars accepted the new understandings and incorporated them into the emerging new world view, churches and other religious institutions for the most part steadfastly chose to ignore or to resist these new views and understandings, for reasons that will be explored later. Not surprisingly, Church leaders and members increasingly found themselves living in a world that was perceived very differently than the way it was viewed by persons outside the Church who accepted these new findings. That incongruity between traditional Church views and informed secular views of the world has reached an impasse, only one aspect of which is the science-religion conflict, with which I was already so familiar. Its larger dimension is the *Church's refusal to accept and to integrate into its doctrines and church practices anything that contradicts long-held Church traditions*, even when new understandings have been derived by careful and thorough studies of early Judaism and early Christianity. Thus, *the difficulty and conflict lie not in what is known but rather in the Church's refusal to accept into its life what is known.* That realization prepared me for many later discoveries.

During a year of solo internship in a small congregation, I had the opportunity to discover and to explore how my being and personality could facilitate effective congregational ministry. I learned that sermons that I prepared and delivered from the pulpit from an outline before me were not effective; if I almost fell asleep in delivering them, I could only imagine what the listeners were experiencing. Effective preaching for me involved a quite different approach. During the course of a week, I would prepare a carefully-thought-out, written sermon to help me thoroughly organize the contents for delivery, but on Sunday morning I would extemporaneously deliver the sermon from between the two front pews, having only the briefest of notes, in case I should forget important transitions. I also discovered that, for me, effective preaching was effective teaching. Important in sermon delivery were questions that invited the listener into active thinking about the sermon content. Not surprisingly, from where I was moving in my own theological journey, I also invited the listeners to at least feel free to ask questions about some of the "sacred cows" of Lutheran doctrine and practice.

Linda was graduated from seminary in 1995, while I was not graduated until 1997. During my last two years of seminary Linda took a position as a hospital chaplain at Richland Memorial Hospital in Columbia, SC. Shortly before my graduation we entered what is known in Lutheran circles as "the call process." It includes the completion of informational forms by persons seeking calls and by congregations seeking to call a pastor. The intent is to find a good "match" between the talents and abilities of the person(s) seeking a call and the needs and opportunities in a congregation. Linda and I had decided that we would seek a joint call – the two of us each filling one-half of a full-time position in a congregation. That way we could minister together. We could share one full-time salary, because our two daughters (Cheri and Millie, her daughter from her first marriage) had already completed college, and we did not have large, pressing financial needs. If opportunities for separate ministry were to arise later, we would consider them. Moreover, in the other "half-time" of our lives, each of us would be free to pursue other interests.

The call process soon led us into conversation and to an interview with Wittenberg Lutheran Church in Granite Quarry, North Carolina. Our early meetings with the six-person call committee went well. The possibility of a husband-wife pastoral team suggested to them possibilities for new and more fully developed ministries in their congregation. From Linda's and my perspectives, there were exciting possibilities for our ministry together as well as individual opportunities for each of us; it looked like a good match. After we had met with the entire congregation, we were issued a call; we accepted their call and began our ministry there on July 1, 1997.

We experienced all the benefits of the "honeymoon" that most pastors relish during their first year or two of ministry in a congregation. The congregation accepted our leadership in continuing those ministries that were going well and in implementing many of the changes that a congregational self-study had indicated were needed in the congregation. The combination of Linda's more traditional Lutheran approaches to ministry and my invitations to inquiry and ecumenical inclusiveness provided a smorgasbord of opportunities for congregational members and to the unchurched in the community.

From Linda's and my perspectives, one inviting aspect of ministry opportunities at Wittenberg that emerged early in our conversations with the call committee was the desire of some members of the congregation for a contemporary or informal service. When they learned of my abilities to play the guitar and to lead contemporary and so-called praise songs and Linda's gifted singing voice, those interested in such a service became strong proponents for calling us.

Soon after beginning our pastoral ministry at Wittenberg, those desires for a contemporary/informal service arose and became part of the congregational discussion. From my earlier experience at Our Savior in Raleigh and from discussions with other congregations who had introduced such services into their worship offerings, we had received the counsel to go slowly – even very slowly – in introducing such services. It is necessary to lay the proper groundwork and to prepare people for the changes that can accompany the introduction of a second service, particularly in a congregation such as Wittenberg, with an average worship attendance of 100-125 per Sunday morning. The reasons for adding the service were two-fold. It added a greater variety of worship opportunities for existing members, some of whom were particularly attracted to more contemporary worship experiences. Second, it would be an outreach to the community to invite others into the Wittenberg experience of "sharing God's love," as the theme of their ministry came to be called. The traditional service would remain at the same time, 10:30 AM, so persons who preferred that would lose nothing; the new service would be offered at 8:30 AM, which also would not require a change in the 9:30-10:15 Sunday School hour. Even those who regarded a contemporary/informal service with suspicion or disdain conceded that they would stand to lose nothing; with the support of those who wanted such a service and the reluctant concession of those who did not want it, a contemporary/informal service was initiated in the summer of 1998.

At first the attendance at the new service was small – perhaps 20-30; most of those who attended were members of the congregation who had expressed an interest in such a service. As word spread through the community that a Lutheran church was holding an early contemporary/informal service, other Lutherans came, either because of the nature of the service or because of the hour at which it was offered. Non-Lutherans and people in the community looking for a home church began attending. The attendance began to increase – first to 40, then 60, then 80.

The success of the new service foreshadowed its own doom. As attendance at the early service continued to rise, attendance at the traditional service correspondingly declined. On the Sunday morning when attendance at the new service reached 105, the attendance at the later traditional service was only about 30. For people whose allegiance was to the traditional service, dissatisfaction and fear became a more common Sunday morning experience than meaningful and fulfilling worship. Some long-standing traditional members began worshiping at and then transferred their membership to other churches. Some simply stopped worshiping at Wittenberg. Those who were elated by their sense of fulfillment from and the success of the early service stood in stark contrast to those who were disappointed and disgruntled by what was happening to the traditional service. A great division had formed in the congregation.

Through all this developing turmoil, Linda's more traditional approach to ministry continued to be well-received. However, in Bible and topical studies I was proceeding in what seemed to me the only honest and beneficial way to learn – presenting Lutheran and biblical perspectives of doctrine and faith while inviting open inquiry in all matters, with intentional attentiveness to the perspectives of other Christian denominations and open ears to possible contributions to faith understandings by non-Christian religions and secular sources. Many in the congregation found that approach to be enlightening and conducive to their spiritual growth. Others, often those whose strong preference was for the traditional service, found such invitations to openness and inquiry improper and threatening or even blasphemous.

Just as a coach is the easiest person to get rid of when a team is not playing well, the pastor is the easiest person to get rid of when things are not going well in a congregation.

Among the dissatisfied, there arose a momentum for the need to get rid of the pastors, particularly Pastor Bob. Encouraged by the significant proportion of the congregation who felt that my presence was leading the congregation in the right direction, I resisted the movement to get rid of me. When I consulted with the leadership of the North Carolina Synod of the ELCA, I was counseled that the disgruntled people at Wittenberg Lutheran Church were seeking to be consoled and comforted – not challenged.

As I reflected further on the situation, it became apparent to me that neither the totality of Wittenberg congregation nor I was any longer feeling much sense of fulfillment, growth and ministry. From my perspective, I was frustrated because my efforts to introduce views and perspectives that seemed to me important for faith and life were not only rejected by some members but were deemed by many of those same members as inappropriate views and perspectives for *me* to embrace. I also tried to reflect on my contributions to the negative congregational situation, however well-meaning my intent. I began to reexamine some of my reasons for thinking that I was being called into congregational pastoral ministry. My ability to minister to one family whose adult son died of cancer affirmed my pastoral ability to walk with people in pain and grief – one of the primary reasons for my having felt called into pastoral ministry. The content of my preaching and manner of delivery were well-received and generally considered edifying to members' lives. I assessed that I was perceived as a strong leader and that my leadership style invited appropriate participation and input by all members of project teams. Yes, it seemed to me that I did possess abilities to be an effective pastor, but not at Wittenberg Lutheran Church in Granite Quarry, North Carolina.

I am not a quitter by nature, and, although I was reluctant to do it, I resigned as pastor of Wittenberg Lutheran Church on December 31, 2001, after four and one-half years of pastoral ministry. Linda was put in the very difficult situation of continuing as solo pastor, dealing with the turmoil and difficulties that were mostly attributable to me. She continued for about five months, while the congregation decided on its future direction. While I think that the congregation appreciated her abilities and effective ministry and would have liked to keep her, it ultimately decided to go in a direction unencumbered by attachment to the struggles of my ministry. She began pastoral ministry at another congregation in September 2002, where she continues to serve until the present.

Reflecting back, the decision for Linda and me to share a joint call probably was not a good one for several reasons. First, the outcome described above – a congregation's finding fault with my ministry, but accepting hers – meant that she ended up having to leave a situation where she might otherwise have served well indefinitely, if she had been a solo pastor.

Second, during our ministry we were together and we were in ministry 24 hours a day, seven days a week. A marital relationship survives and thrives best when husband and wife are able to spend time apart from each other. They have breathing room, separation and the opportunity to develop a yearning for each other. When they spend too much time together, the question "How can I miss you when you never go away?" becomes apropos. In the busy modern world most couples find it necessary to schedule time together; Linda and I ended up having to schedule time apart from each other.

Moreover, when we were together, we were nearly always talking about matters relating to congregational ministry – when we went out to eat, when were traveling, whenever. We finally had to make rules like the following for ourselves: it is off-limits to talk about church matters after 9 PM in the bedroom. We had to get over our misguided notion that, if sixteen hours of ministry per day is good ministry, eighteen or twenty hours per day is better ministry. I think that,

overall, our relationship during the early part of our marriage was stifled by our decision to share a call in ministry.

Meanwhile, in the nonpastoral ministry half-time of my life I had become involved in two activities. The first was family history. In my last year of coursework at seminary, one course assignment was to profile the life and history of a congregation. I chose my congregation of origin – St. John's Lutheran, Palmer, Kansas. As I worked on that project, I had become aware of the close intertwining of the congregation's history and my Voelker family history. As I pursued strands of my family history, I became, as genealogists would say, "hooked" – fascinated with my family's history and feeling a need to find out as much about it as I could. After exhausting resources on the Voelker family history, I pursued the other seven of my two-generations-back ancestors: Proehl, Tewes, Killman, Moddelmog, Schwanke, Kessler and Licking – all German Lutherans. Linda and/or I made nearly a half-dozen trips to Germany to gather from the church books and civil records whatever we could learn about these families.

Having learned what I could about my ancestry, I realized why it was inevitable that I would be baptized and grow up as a member of the Lutheran Church-Missouri Synod. All of my German Lutheran ancestors joined congregations that were part of or would become part of that Lutheran church body. Reflecting on that history as I was becoming increasingly disillusioned with the teachings and practices of the LCMS, I began to visualize that upbringing as the religious cocoon in which I had developed and been formed. While it was an important requisite for my religious and spiritual development, to become an adult butterfly and fly on my own I had to leave that cocoon and fly to places that my spiritual antenna sensed were important places in life. That understanding helped me give myself first the freedom and then the courage and confidence to wander out onto the slippery slopes that my biblical literalist Lutheran trainers had warned me to avoid.

Although my years of pastoral ministry at Wittenberg Lutheran Church included painful experiences, particularly near the end, I nevertheless learned a great deal there. It helped me realize that, from my perspective, Lutheran and other denominational forms of Christianity often are ill-suited and even detrimental as forms of religion in the modern world. Rather than facilitating people's living in the world as we understand it today, modern Christianity, for the most part, transports people back to the world views of the New Testament and earlier times. In working through my grief following the loss of pastoral ministry, I reached the stage of empowerment – having the courage and energy to try to do something to change that situation.

The second nonpastoral involvement for me was college teaching. I had always known that I loved teaching. I found some of my greatest fulfillment in the teaching aspects of pastoral ministry. Soon after beginning pastoral ministry in 1997, I inquired about the opportunities for teaching at Catawba College in Salisbury, located about five miles from my home. Soon, as an adjunct professor I was able to teach a day program, undergraduate course for non-science majors entitled "Concepts of Genetics," which deals with the many different ways that genetics impacts people's lives – including genetic diseases, human development, gene cloning and DNA sequencing, human cloning, stem cell research and the like. Teaching this course allowed me to keep abreast of developments in my pre-seminary career and to do what I dearly loved – teaching. As the course developed and evolved, it became a respected and appreciated course; the word on campus was: "You'll have to work 'your butt off,' but you'll learn a lot of very interesting stuff." I was pleased with that assessment.

Later, after resigning from pastoral ministry, I was able to teach more courses at Catawba College, including religion courses in the night, adult-learning program. In preparation for teaching "Introduction to the New Testament" and "Christian Beliefs," I was able to survey and investigate the breadth and depth of academic knowledge in these two areas. My discoveries further informed my growing awareness that views held by Lutherans as the only true and orthodox positions were only one small corner of Christianity – and, from my perspective, not necessarily the most reflective of careful biblical interpretation, let alone consideration of relevant secular information.

I had begun to understand life backwards more fully and, in doing so, had gained insights on changes that were necessary for me to live forwards. I now turn to an examination of those spiritual tenets of Christianity to which I had continued to give deferential authority as I dealt with the illnesses and deaths of Tammy, Bethany, and Darlene, but which seemed increasingly inadequate to support and to sustain me in those times of crises. Those deliberations were destined to lead, even to drive, me in new directions.

Chapter 7

Examining Scriptural Content and Origins: The Hebrew Bible/Old Testament

Earlier I used a medical analogy to illustrate what seems to me a significant inconsistency: while modern Christians insist on using the best and most modern knowledge and understandings in dealing with matters of medicine and their health, they seem quite satisfied to accept ages-old, incomplete and even erroneous knowledge and understandings in matters of their religion and spirituality – which they deem the most important dimension of their lives.

At the root of this inconsistency lies the issue of *authority*. Definitions of authority include the following: "the power or right to give orders or make decisions," "an expert whose views are taken as definitive," "assurance; freedom from doubt," "official permission or approval," "the right to control or direct the actions of others, legitimized by law, morality, custom or consent," and "an accepted source of expert information." Authority – the right to control or direct the actions of others – may be asserted or claimed by a person or by an institution, perhaps even at the threat of some negative consequences or punishment for ignoring or disobeying those who wish to exert that claimed authority. *Ultimately, however, authority is granted to those who exercise it by the consent of those over whom it is exercised.*

Why is it that many people accept the best modern understandings as being authoritative in secular matters but accept only understandings of ancient writings as being authoritative in the religious matters of their lives? It is because they have somehow consented to be influenced or controlled by these two different authorities.

I now turn to an examination of whether consent and concession to these two respective authorities are warranted. If people are to grant authority over their lives to persons or institutions, they expect them to be trustworthy – valid and reliable. They expect that the ways in which authority is exerted over them are in their interest and for their well-being. They expect that the premises used in exercising authority over them be rooted in goodness and based on truth.

Like Pontius Pilate, people could ask, "What is truth?" Definitions of truth include such words and phrases as: "actual state of a matter," "conformity with fact or reality," "a verified or indisputable fact, proposition or principle," and "actuality or actual existence." Truth involves honesty, integrity, veracity and verifiability. When capitalized, Truth can sometimes refer to an idealized or fundamental reality apart from and transcending experience. While people might subscribe to the existence of "Truth," its veracity, validity and reliability can only be assessed or verified by their experience of the implications and of the consequences of that Truth for their lives.

What about the "truth" of modern scientific information as a basis for accepting it as authority in such matters as medical technology? The methodology of the discovery and formulation of scientific information ensures that it is verifiable; it is not accepted as an established principle unless it is repeatedly and reliably demonstrable. Those findings that become laws of nature and principles of understanding are consistent with people's experience of the world. They actually exist; they have repeatable reality; they have positive consequences for people's lives (although, of course, scientific information and technology can be used to the detriment of humans and of their environment). For example, when people appropriately use medicine or medical technology that is rooted in solid scientific understanding, they are healed and cured of disease. Because there is a basis in and a consistency with reality, they can rely on these understandings as they formulate their view of the world and orient themselves in it. The scientific principles have utility in supporting, sustaining and bringing fulfillment to people's lives.

It may be argued that there is more to life than what people can observe, measure and comprehend – that there are unseen, spiritual realities, undetectable by people's physical senses (what I have previously termed *Unseen Ultimate Reality*); that may also be true, and I shall deal with that issue later. For the present, however, I have attempted to establish that through modern scientific methodology humans have arrived at the best understandings of the functioning world that have existed in the history of humankind. And most people implicitly recognize that – by explicitly utilizing the medical advances and all the other technological advances in modern society. In many ways people regard that authority as being true enough for them that they construct their view of the world around those understandings, even entrusting their lives to it in their dependence on modern medicine.

Why, then, is it important that *religious* authority be examined? It is because some pretty preposterous claims for people's lives today are made on the basis of that authority – persons, places and events entirely inconsistent with people's experiences of life today. The biblical narrative takes for granted that God talks to and communicates directly with humans. The New Testament relates accounts of Jesus' virgin birth, miracles, resurrection from death, and eternal life with God in heaven. The biblical writings speak of sick persons' praying to God or Jesus and being healed; they also relate that dead persons were brought back to life.

The early Christian writings and creeds present Jesus as both God and human. Moreover, the New Testament writings not only make claims for Jesus and his followers of their time; they assure that, in the present time, believers in Jesus and his message have access to those same wonderful resources of healing and wholeness; they promise that everyone who believes that Jesus is their savior will have eternal life in heaven after their physical deaths. They promise healing to people who are persistent in prayer as were people in the New Testament narrative. To subscribe to these claims "through faith" has huge importance and many implications for people's lives – sometimes including outright denial of what their life experiences tell them is real in the world today – and they suspect may also have been the real situation in biblical times.

Yes, these claims are so illogical and inconsistent with people's modern experience that they have a right – yes, even the duty – to ask whether these presumptions and claims are true. Are they based on reality? Is there sufficient evidence to conclude that they happened historically and, therefore, that they are a reasonable basis for similar expectations for people's lives today? If these seeming improbabilities and impossibilities can be substantiated, they can be accepted as viable truths for orienting people's lives today, as they were for their adherents at the time when they were written. If, however, they cannot be verified as being real events in people's lives – if those stories and beliefs were somehow peculiar to the worldviews and religious settings of ancient times, then modern people are forced to reassess their perception of the biblical and church authorities that derive from them and what importance, if any, those biblical claims have for people's lives in the modern world.

In previous chapters I recounted that during and following the tragedies of my life I had attempted to retain my traditional Lutheran faith as a support for my spiritual life. It was with the foregoing questions and considerations that I began my inquiry to determine whether the Bible and the Christian faith that emanated from it still possessed the validity and reliability to remain the foundation of my spiritual life.

As I began and continued that examination, I reminded myself of the statement of Albert Schweitzer quoted earlier: "The most important quality in a person concerned with religion is *absolute devotion to truth*." Although Schweitzer's statement does not indicate what truth is or connote that absolute truth can be found, it implies that the best determinations of what really and actually occurred should be the truth that informs my present-day understanding of the biblical narrative. After learning the best assessment of truth about the Bible, I must assess whether that truth has sufficient merit to be deemed the ultimate and absolute authority for my faith. This latter stage is likely to be the most difficult and threatening to my sense of spiritual security, because it is likely to challenge some of my most deeply-held and most cherished core beliefs. But no matter the discomfort and perhaps even pain, I must absolutely commit myself to seeking the truth – wherever that may lead me.

As I search for the reasons why the Bible/Holy Scriptures have such great authority, two broad questions can guide my investigation. First, I ask whether there was something in the origin or formation of the biblical writings that warrants this authority and high esteem. Second, I ask if the Bible has always been granted this absolute degree of authority by the Church or whether it acquired this elevated status sometime after its formation. In this and subsequent chapters I shall address these questions.

In investigating the origins of the Bible, I will want to use the best tools available for historical research, just as I would if were investigating some more recent topic, such as the American Revolution or the War Between the States. For biblical studies the combination of the best investigative tools has been termed the *historical-critical* meth-

od of study. It draws on all possible sources of information – including especially sources *independent* of the Bible itself – that can be used to ascertain the historicity and circumstances of details in the biblical writings. The term *critical* in this context does not mean "to find fault with," as it commonly does in everyday language; rather, it means to ask those discerning questions that are most likely to ferret out the truth concerning the biblical writings. An analogy would be a news reporter's covering some event; that reporter is expected to ask the "critical" questions that are likely to provide the true details relating to that event.

Application of historical-critical methodologies seeks to answer questions about authorship, date of writing, place of writing, purpose of writing, language in which the document was written, worldview of the author, sociological and cultural setting, how the document was used at the time of writing, comparison with contemporary religious writings, archeological and anthropological data and anything else that can provide insight into an understanding of the biblical documents. If the individual biblical books and the Bible in its entirety are to merit authority, it is reasonable to expect answers to the above questions to substantiate that authority.

As I begin to investigate, however, I face several large challenges. First, the biblical narrative is long and complex; indeed, most of the sixty-six books of the Bible contribute to that narrative in one way or another. Consequently, I cannot hope to examine meaningfully all aspects of the entire narrative. Second, hundreds, probably even thousands, of books have been written detailing the findings of various historical-critical studies of the biblical writings. Thus, I am forced to select and to summarize. My selective screen will be to look most closely at issues that relate to my using the biblical writings as an authoritative basis for my faith foundations and for expectations in my life today. While there are in some cases diversities of opinions, on the issues that I will address here there are generally strong consensuses. Interested readers are encouraged to consult biblical concordances and commentaries and other writings to verify conclusions that are used here. In this chapter I will focus on the Hebrew Bible, the Christian Old Testament.

Before I begin, I note briefly the time frame in which historical-critical methodologies have been used to study the biblical writings. They began in Europe, primarily Germany, in the seventeenth and eighteenth centuries and reached full maturity in the nineteenth and twentieth centuries. Thus, nearly all of these discoveries and conclusions have been known for some time; nearly all are more than 50 years old; many, perhaps most, are as old as 150-200 or more years. Later, I shall consider why there has been much hesitancy and unwillingness of theologians and church leaders to embrace and to incorporate these findings into the dogmas and worship practices of Christian churches.

My approach will begin by tracing the biblical narrative roughly as it unfolds in the sequence of the books of the Hebrew Bible, the Christian Old Testament. As details appear in the narrative, I shall examine them more closely to see whether they merit the authority for me that has been attributed to them by Church tradition.

The first part of the biblical narrative is found in Genesis 1-11. Its stories detail creation, The Fall, the initial populating of the earth, the Noahic Flood and the subsequent repopulating of the earth, including the genealogy of the ancestors of Abraham. Some biblical scholars have referred to this part of the narrative as "prehistory," implying perhaps that it pertained to real people, events and places that existed before there were written historical accounts. More appropriate characterizing terms used by other scholars are "ahistorical" or "nonhistorical," because the people, events and places in these legendary stories had no actual his-

torical existence. Rather, biblical scholars have categorized these stories as "myths," invoking a very different meaning than our general use of the word *myth* today, which implies pure fiction or fantasy. Rather, biblical myths are stories that reflect the deep cultural self-understandings of a people – in this particular case, the Hebrews. In the worldview in which the myths arose, they reflected plausible and credible accounts for all aspects and elements of human life and existence. The Hebrew myths answered the questions of the origin of humans, of how the world came into existence and why it existed as they understood it, of how the Hebrew people came to be and to live where they did. All ancient cultures had their own respective myths. Indeed, all cultures, ancient and modern, have mythical self-understandings that are situated in their respective worldviews. Some of the Hebrew myths, notably the flood myth, are quite likely adapted versions of myths from older neighboring nations and civilizations. Although these myths may quite accurately portray human characteristics and behaviors and teach us lessons about ourselves, because they involve no actual persons, places or events, they provide no authoritative basis for expectations, understandings or conclusions about the actual world of today. This is especially true *vis-à-vis* any use of details of these myths pertaining to the origin and operation of the natural world to contradict carefully derived, modern scientific understandings.

The second segment of the biblical narrative is related in chapters of the Old Testament from Genesis 12 to the end of the book of Judges. It begins with the "call" of Abraham, regarded by the Hebrews as the founding event of their status as Yahweh's chosen people and continues until the Israelites entered and occupied the Promised Land. Included in this part of the narrative are the stories about Abraham, Isaac, Jacob, Joseph, the enslavement in Egypt, Moses, Aaron and the Exodus, Joshua and Caleb, and the judges, including Gideon and Sampson.

Many Old Testament scholars question the historicity of many of these persons, events and places; some even doubt whether there is any historical basis at all to this part of the narrative for the following reasons. First, although not entirely unexpected, there are no references to these persons or events in the written histories and records of the surrounding nations mentioned in this part of the narrative. Second and more importantly, attempts to situate these people, events and places historically are fraught with a serious difficulty that relates to the origin and development of written Hebrew language. While early elements of the Hebrew language existed in written form as early as 1200-1300 BCE (Before the Common Era = BC – Before Christ), the earliest scattered written anecdotes that ultimately became part of the Hebrew Bible were most likely written somewhere around 1100 BCE. Moreover, there was no systematic writing of the Hebrew narrative that became part of the Hebrew Bible until around 1000 BCE, one or two centuries after the last of the persons and events related in this section of the biblical narrative (if they were, in fact, historical).

Those biblical scholars who maintain some historical basis for this segment of the narrative have situated Abraham, Isaac and Jacob somewhere in the 1800-1600 BCE interval, although some have placed them one or two centuries earlier. Those same scholars have divided opinions in placing the events of Moses' life and of the Exodus several hundreds of years later, either in the 1450-1400 or the 1250-1200 BCE time period, with the latter being preferred. After the Israelites' entrance into the Promised Land (Land of Canaan), they probably completed its conquest and settlement by around 1100 BCE.

Thus, assuming that they were historical, all the stories about Abraham, Isaac, Jacob, Joseph, Moses and Aaron, Joshua, Gideon and Sampson were transmitted *only orally*

for several to many hundreds of years before being written down. Biblical scholars call such accounts sagas and legends. Embedded within them are perhaps historical people and occurrences, but because of the extensive modifications in details and in interpretations that occur during oral transmission, it is impossible to know which are historical details and which are changes and accretions added in oral transmission or in interpretation, even after they were written down. Thus, it cannot be known whether the following well-known people and events were historical: Abraham, Isaac, Jacob, Joseph, the birth of Moses, the call of Moses, the Exodus from Egypt and Moses' role in it; God's giving the ten commandments to Moses on Mt. Sinai; Joshua's leading the Israelites into the Promised Land; and the Fall of Jericho. Whatever historical events lay behind these stories may have been altered and embellished considerably while being orally transmitted for generations of Hebrews over hundreds of years. It is perhaps little wonder that many of these persons and events appear "larger than life." As with the earlier mentioned myths, it is possible, even likely, that some of the "persons" and "events" in these sagas and legends were imported from surrounding nations and cultures and adapted for the Hebrew setting.

Because of the high degree of uncertainty about the historicity of the persons and the events in this part of the biblical narrative, there surely is no evidence to claim that, because these people and events are related by the biblical narrative, therefore they are true and can be used as authoritative examples of what actually happened historically then and of what can be expected to happen in people's lives today.

The third and last segment of the Old Testament narrative extends from about 1050 to 300 BCE. This portion of the biblical narrative can much more readily be corroborated with historical people and events of the other nations in the Ancient Near East. The biblical narrative and written historical documents of neighboring nations recount diplomatic interactions and military battles with the armies of the Kingdom of Israel and/or the Kingdom of Judah, albeit usually with a favorable perspective of the nation whose history was being written. Nevertheless, the accounts in the writings of the surrounding nations are clearly referring to the same historical events related in the biblical narrative.

Perhaps because this portion of the biblical narrative is more closely tied to documentable written history from nonbiblical sources, there appear fewer "larger than life," fanciful people and events in this segment than in earlier completely or largely nonhistorical segments of the biblical narrative, although some still occur. Notable among them are the David and Goliath story and stories from the ministries of Elijah (encounter with the prophets of Baal; interactions with the widow of Zarephath; the fiery chariot) and Elisha (retrieval of the floating ax head from the Jordan River), and many of the episodes in the book of Daniel (actually probably completed about 164 BCE).

It should be noted, however, that although this portion of the biblical narrative contains many people and events that can be documented and verified from nonbiblical sources of history, the *interpretations* of the events and assessments of the people are reflective of a particular Hebrew point of view. Because most of the Old Testament writings were authored by people from the Kingdom of Judah (Southern Kingdom), not surprisingly, that nation and its leaders are usually cast in a much more favorable light than are those of the Kingdom of Israel (Northern Kingdom) and of the surrounding pagan nations. Thus, although this portion of the biblical narrative contains historical events, its presentation of them often reflects strongly theologically, nationalistically-conditioned, and even biased points of view.

Because it was during this period of the biblical narrative that many Hebrew religious, governmental and social institutions developed to the forms that would later influence Christianity, some aspects of these institutions will be more closely examined.

The most important of these was the Hebrew notion of a monotheistic deity, the concept and name of which changed during the course of development of the Hebrew religion. In the prehistorical and early historical periods, the name of the Hebrew deity was apparently designated by the four Hebrew letters YHWH (called the tetragrammaton), the meaning of which is "I am who I am" or "I will be who I will be." This unspeakable name of God was later transliterated as Yahweh (Jehovah) and designated in later English Bible translations as LORD (all capital letters). Following the Hebrew's contact with the Canaanite peoples, whose pagan religions were polytheistic, the name El was added to names of the Hebrew deity. The name El alone historically referred to the father of the Canaanite gods; in combination with other words it could designate particular deities: El Shaddai – God of the mountains, El Elyon – God the exalted one, El Olam – God the everlasting one, etc. More common in the Hebrew Scriptures was the plural Elohim, which implied that Yahweh was the God above all the gods. The *syncretism* (attempted combining) of early Hebrew and Canaanitic names for deities led to frequent reference to God as the LORD God. After the Exile (586 BCE) many Hebrew writings designated God's name as Adon – meaning "a revered master or superior." So as not to unintentionally profane God's name by speaking it when reading the Scriptures, the familiar form "Adonai" ("my lord, my master") was spoken when the Hebrew terms for Yahweh or the LORD God appeared in the text. While this brief summary omits large amounts of information about the names and characteristics of the Hebrew deity, it illustrates the *continuously evolving status during Hebrew history of the name and concept of God*. Thus, it is erroneous to conclude that there was an *unchangeable* name and concept of God in the Old Testament.

Moreover, there is a kind of paradox involving the Hebrews' dealing with the name and concept of God. First, as noted above, Yahweh's name was unspeakable. Second, there was also a strict prohibition against making any "graven image" to represent Yahweh. Yet, throughout the Hebrew biblical narrative Yahweh is almost invariably referred to in anthropomorphic terms; although regarded as a deity who was holy – set apart and totally other, Yahweh is depicted and described as having thoroughly human thoughts and as acting in thoroughly human ways: Yahweh "spoke," Yahweh "saw," and Yahweh "heard." Yahweh "formed man from the dust of the ground." Yahweh was "walking in the garden," Yahweh "cursed the serpent," and Yahweh "drove the man and the woman from the garden." Most of Yahweh's activities are narrated in terms of human activities. The apparent intent of this way of relating Yahweh's activities in the Old Testament narrative was to show his purpose for and involvement in the lives of his chosen people, Israel. Yet, it is rather peculiar that their "so holy and other" Yahweh was associated with thoughts and actions that were so thoroughly human.

Like contemporary neighboring nations with their pagan religions, the Hebrews also instituted specific offices to administer their religious and governmental functions. Among the earliest acts of worship was sacrifice, the burning of animal or plant materials upon an altar as an offering to a deity. Also a common practice among the Canaanites as well as other surrounding pagan religions, the ahistorical segment of the biblical narrative (Genesis 1-12) recounts frequent offerings of sacrifice to Yahweh. The Hebrews' understanding of their being Yahweh's chosen people in return for their obedience to and worship of him alone began with Abraham and further developed among his descendant wandering clans and tribes. Abraham, Isaac and Jacob personally offered their own sacrifices to Yahweh as a form of worship. Among their descendants, the first specialized religious office to emerge was that of the *priest*, whose duty it was to offer sacrifices to Yahweh. The sacrifices were for thanksgiving for blessings received as well as for atonement for the sins of the people. In addition to sacrifice, priests were also consulted as sources of divine revelation concerning various matters in life. Regarded as sources of divine counsel, priests had a considerable amount of authority and respect among the people. It is noteworthy that the pagan religions of surrounding nations also had priesthoods that carried out similar functions.

According to the biblical narrative, when the Hebrews had been slaves in Egypt for a long time, they became a numerous people, and God determined to free them from slavery. He then instituted a second religious office – that of *prophet* – when he "called" Moses to be his spokesman to the Egyptian pharaoh in order to secure their release. Moses was considered by many Israelites to be the first and greatest of the Hebrew prophets because of his role in the Exodus, the formative and founding event of the nation of Israel, as the Hebrew nation came to be called. Like prophets (sometimes also known as seers or oracles) in surrounding pagan nations, the Israelite prophets were deemed to receive revelations from and to know the will of the gods. Their most prevalent function was "speaking forth" to the people the word of the gods rather than predicting events of the future. Often this word from the gods was one of harsh judgment and condemnation; prophets were frequently depicted as being reluctant to speak forth their message because they knew that it would not be well received. At other times the counsel of prophets was sought by leaders to learn what course of action the god or gods desired. From the time of Moses (ca. 1300 BCE, if he was in fact historical) until the time of Malachi (ca. 300 BCE), prophets appeared periodically on the scene. Included among them were Samuel, Elijah, Elisha and Nathan, as well as Isaiah, Jeremiah, Ezekiel and the Minor Prophets, with the latter prophets being known from the biblical books bearing their respective names.

According to the biblical narrative, at the time of Moses the prophetic and priestly functions were separated, when the descendants of Moses' brother Aaron were designated as the priestly family (although in later times nondescendants of Aaron also held the priestly office). The priests' duties and instructions for carrying out the ceremonial laws of the Hebrew religion were part of the Sinai revelation from God to Moses and were codified and written in the book of Leviticus. From that time until the destruction of Herod's Temple by the Romans in 70 CE, priests were the officials who could preside over sacrifices and other rites and rituals in the Hebrew temples.

If one concludes that the earlier discussed second segment of the biblical narrative had some historical basis, then for about 200 years (1250-1050 BCE) the Israelites existed in the Promised Land as a loose confederation of tribes. During that time the earliest political leaders among the tribes of Israel were judges such as Gideon and Samson. These were men who were often renowned for their wisdom and/or leadership in battles as the tribes sought to conquer and to wrest the land from the native Canaanite inhabitants. Judges were not necessarily noted for their special access to Yahweh's words and will but were nevertheless deemed to be sent by Yahweh to help his chosen people, the Israelites, conquer and settle the land.

The last of the judges, Samuel, was also a prophet. His name meant "name of God" or "his name is God," indicative of the authority that he commanded and the respect with which he was held in Israelite society. According to the biblical narrative, Yahweh communicated his will for his people to and through Samuel, including details of how to conduct the wars of conquest. From the time of Moses to Samuel, Israel existed as a theocracy – government by Yahweh's will and words, as communicated to the Hebrews through Yahweh's chosen leaders, such as Moses, Joshua and Samuel.

During Samuel's tenure as judge/prophet, Israel was engaged in wars with neighboring Canaanite nations, most notably the Philistines. Noting the greater success in battles of those neighboring peoples who were governed by kings, the Israelites demanded that Samuel appoint for them a king. According to 1 Samuel 8, Samuel perceived this request as a rejection of Yahweh's rule and perhaps his own leadership and sought counsel from Yahweh over the matter. Yahweh instructed Samuel to apprise them of the demands and burdens that would afflict them under the leadership of a king but to accede to their demands if the Israelites still wanted a king. In spite of these warnings, the Israelites insisted that they wanted a king. Samuel then anointed Saul as Israel's first king, whose reign was ultimately judged by the biblical narrative to be a failure. Samuel then anointed David as the second king, whose reign was judged by the biblical narrative to be the zenith of power and glory of Israel as a nation. King David politically unified the disparate tribes that had settled in the Promised Land, conquered Jerusalem and established it as the capital city of the kingdom. He made plans to build a temple in Jerusalem that would also make it the religious center of the kingdom, thereby using religious unity to enhance and to solidify the political unity.

When Samuel, under Yahweh's directions, anointed first Saul and later David to be Israel's kings, the power and authority of Yahweh became vested in the king. While several subsequent kings were also anointed by later prophets, later kings were generally anointed by priests, the visible representatives of Yahweh for the Israelite religion. The symbolism of the priestly anointing of the king can hardly be overstated. Through anointing, the virtually absolute authority that had been seen to have been vested only in Yahweh, symbolized by the priest, had been bestowed upon the king. The Hebrew term *Messiah*, (Greek *Christ*, later used to designate Jesus of Nazareth) meant "the anointed one" or "Yahweh's anointed one." The actions and words of the king were considered to emanate from Yahweh himself. This relationship of holding and transferring governing power that developed between the priests and the monarch served to mutually ensure their respective statuses and authorities. Religious anointing thus became the vehicle which authorized and buttressed the political power of the king and his government, in order to carry out whatever he deemed appropriate for the kingdom.

In the nations surrounding Israel, the kings were often regarded as gods. Kings won wars and killed enemies; kings provided security and peace; kings exercised absolute power; kings were the visible symbol of divine power and authority. The feats of kings were incorporated into and celebrated in the religious rites and rituals of the nation; the kings had harems that included any and all the women in the land that the king desired. These god-kings fathered children with human women, and their children were regarded as "sons of god." When the god-king died or was killed and one of his sons became king, that "son of god" was then elevated to the status of a "god." Although this seems quite alien to the modern mind, it was an understood and an accepted part of the societal order of many ancient cultures.

As indicated by the consternation of the prophets, priests and other religious leaders in their writing of the biblical narrative, this view of kings as gods permeated Israel's society as well. The Israelite religion explicitly forbad that any person or thing be regarded as "god" instead of Yahweh. Yet, examination of the etymology of the names of the kings (Table 7.1) gives clues as to what actually happened historically among the Israelites. The meanings of the names of the first three kings (Saul, David and

Solomon) suggest that they were not yet perceived as gods but as designated rulers by Yahweh in service to Yahweh and to his people.

However, after Solomon's death (ca. 922 BCE) the kingdom split into the Kingdom of Judah (Southern Kingdom; tribes of Judah and Benjamin; later origin of term *Jews* from Judah) and the Kingdom of Israel (Northern Kingdom, The Ten Northern Tribes). Examination of the meanings of the names of most of Judah's and Israel's kings indicates that they were closely identified with God, in that names that began with "Jeh" or ended in "ah" included the Hebrew syllables that denoted *Yahweh*. Thus, the king's actions were seen as Yahweh's actions, perhaps to the point of merging the identities of Yahweh and the king. It is little wonder, then, that the Hebrew people looked at their visible king and began to adore and to worship him rather than the invisible Yahweh.

While such an exalted state may have provided political authority for the king and his government, it provided much "heartburn" for the prophets and religious leaders who were trying to uphold the unique holiness of Yahweh. From the time of the division of the Kingdom in 922 BCE until the Northern Kingdom was carried into captivity by Assyria in 721 BCE and the Southern Kingdom was carried into captivity by Babylon in 586 BCE, the primary role of the prophets became that of critique of the kings and of the priests who were in collusion with them in ways that the prophets considered contrary to the will of Yahweh. The prophets and the later writers of the Old Testament narrative interpreted the final destructions of the two kingdoms as Yahweh's punishing judgment for their failure to fulfill their part of Yahweh's covenant with them: "I will be your God, and you shall be my people."

However, if the monarchial rule of the United, the Northern and the Southern Kingdoms are assessed in the context of their day, they mirrored quite typically what was happening in surrounding nations. They

Table 7.1. Names of Israel's kings, dates of reign (BCE), and their meanings.

King's Name	Meaning of King's Name
United Kingdom	
Saul (1020-1000)	"Asked for," "Requested" or "Prayed for"
David (1000-961)	"Beloved"
Solomon (961-922)	"Peace" or "Prosperity"
Kingdom of Judah (Southern Kingdom)	
Rehoboam (922-915)	"May the people expand."
Abijah (915-913)	"My father is Yah(weh)"
Asa (913-873)	Probably a contraction of "God or Yahweh has given."
Jehoshaphat (873-849)	"Yahweh judges" or "Yahweh has judged."
Jehoram/Joram (849-842)	"Yahweh is high."
Ahaziah (842)	"Yahweh has seized."
Athaliah (Queen) (842-837)	"Yahweh is great."
Joash/Jehoash (837-800)	"Yahweh gives" or "Yahweh has given."
Amaziah (800-783)	"Yahweh is strong."
Uzziah (coregency) (783-742)	"Yahweh is my strength."
Jotham (coregency) (750-735)	"May Yahweh complete."
Ahaz (735-715)	A contraction of "Yahweh has seized."
Hezekiah (715-687)	"Yahweh is my strength."
Manasseh (687-642)	"One who causes to forget."
Amon (642-640)	"Trustworthy, reliable, faithful."
Josiah (640-609)	"Let (or may) Jahweh live."
Jehoahaz (609)	"Yahweh has grasped" or "Yahweh has taken hold of."
Jehoiakim (609-598)	"Yahweh raises up."
Jehoiachin (Jehoiakin) (597)	"Yahweh establishes."
Zedekiah (puppet king) (597-587)	"Yahweh (is my) righteousness."
Kingdom of Israel (Northern Kingdom)	
Jeroboam I (922-901)	"May the people grow numerously."
Nadab (901-900)	"Yahweh is willing" or "Yahweh is liberal."
Omri (coregency) (876-869)	"Worshiper of Yahweh."
Ahab (869-850)	"Father's brother"
Ahaziah (850-849)	A contraction of "Yahweh has seized."
Jehoram (849-842)	"Yahweh is high."
Jehu (842-815)	"He is Yahweh."
Jehoahaz (815-801)	"Yahweh has grasped" or "Yahweh has taken hold of."
Joash (801-786)	"Yahweh gives" or "Yahweh has given."
Jeroboam II (786-746)	"May the people grow numerously."
Zechariah (746-745)	"Yahweh has remembered."
Shallum (745)	"Retribution"
Menahem (745-736)	"One who comforts."
Pekahiah (736-735)	"Yahweh has opened (the eyes.)"
Pekah (735-732)	"He (Yahweh) has opened (the eyes.)"
Hoshea (732-722)	"May Yahweh save."

illustrate how religious and governmental institutions developed to form a collusive authority to rule societies, as human societies were evolving successively from nomadic clans and tribes to agrarian communities, villages, towns and cities, and nations. There is nothing unique about what happened in the history of the Hebrew people.

After being conquered and taken into captivity by the Assyrians in 722 BCE, the Kingdom of Israel was never again reconstituted as a nation and has therefore been referred to as the "Ten Lost Tribes of Israel." The residual inhabitants who remained in that geographical area were the ancestors of the Samaritans, whom the later Jews despised or looked on with contempt.

After the conquest of the Kingdom of

Judah by the Babylonians in 586 BCE, it never again achieved status as a prominent nation. After approximately seventy years of captivity in Babylon, it was subsequently ruled by the Persians (538-331 BCE) and the Greeks (331-142 BCE). Although the Jewish people had political independence from 142-63 BCE, they were not a strong nation politically, and the strategic location of their land frequently made it a military highway when more powerful surrounding nations went to war with one another. Finally, the Jewish people were conquered by Pompey of Rome in 63 BCE and remained under Roman rule until 135 CE.

Thus, an overview of the Old Testament narrative has been completed. The first segment was a completely ahistorical segment, the story line of which extended from Creation to the immediate ancestors of Abraham. The historicity of the second segment, extending from the call of Abraham until the time of the judges, is very difficult to document and to assess, because its contents were transmitted only orally for a period of a few hundred to perhaps a thousand years. Therefore, it is impossible to determine which people and events in this segment were historical and which reflect "greater-than-life" details that accrued as these legends and sagas were told and retold with reinterpretation through the generations and centuries. Finally, the third segment of the narrative, extending from the time of Samuel to the end of the Old Testament, contains much independently verifiable history. Many of the persons and events of this segment are documented in the written histories of surrounding nations. Because the biblical narrative was written by Israelite authors, perhaps often commissioned by their kings, it often reflects much more favorably on the Israelite nations than do the corresponding written accounts of the surrounding nations.

Before looking more closely at the writing of the books of the Old Testament and their being collected to form the Hebrew Bible, two concepts will be examined that are basic to understanding the Old Testament narrative: the presumed structure and organization of the universe and the meaning of sacrifice.

One aspect of the worldview of the Ancient Near East, which included the Israelite people and all the surrounding nations, was the so-called "three-story universe." With slight modifications the same understanding is well documented from the Hebrew Bible, as well as from contemporary Egyptian and Babylonian records. According to that understanding, the universe consisted of three stories or tiers – much like a modern domed stadium. The lower story – the rooms under the playing field – was the place of the dead (Hebrew *Sheol*), where people existed after death as shadowy figures, although it was not associated with reward or punishment for thoughts or actions in life. Supported by pillars above the lower story was the middle story, the more or less flat earth – the playing field – where people and other organisms lived and life took place. Supported by mountains at the ends or edges of the more or less flat earth was the third story – the sky or heavens, the dome – from which were suspended the sun, the moon and the stars. When the "windows of heaven opened," rain or snow fell. Above the dome in the Hebrew understanding was located Yahweh, the LORD God, who through his word and will controlled the movement of the celestial bodies in the dome and looked down on the earth and directed its activities, much as a puppeteer controls marionettes.

It is important to recognize that the three-story universe was assumed by all biblical writers of both Old and New Testaments. As biblical writers penned their manuscripts, they presented everything as happening in the three-story universe, because it was the only one they knew. Today, all advanced societies accept a very different model of the universe – heliocentric, with the earth and other planets revolving around the sun, with moons revolving around planets and with distant stars in our and in other solar systems.

In evaluating the biblical writings, it is necessary to ask whether the three-story universe is the way that the universe was organized at the time of the biblical writings and whether the operation of the universe has changed between then and now. Or has the universe always been functioning more or less as it is understood to operate today? Is it that the ancients interpreted its operation differently, based on the information and understandings available to them? Without much reflection it is reasonable to conclude that the universe has always been organized and has always functioned essentially as it is understood today (although there is still much that is not known about it).

What then does that mean for the authority of biblical writings for today, when they talk about God's being in the heavens or Jesus' ascent to heaven? Is it necessary to adopt the view of the universe of biblical times? Or is it necessary to question what was really happening in ancient times, with respect to people and events involving the heavens and other elements of that worldview? Is it possible that the biblical narrative is so peculiar to that ancient worldview that it has little or no authoritative relevance for today? I conclude that the answer to this latter question is "Yes," which means that extreme caution must be exercised in drawing any conclusions from parts of the biblical narrative which presuppose that worldview.

The Hebrew/Israelite practice of sacrifice was integral to its religious life. Animal sacrifice was not unique to the Israelites; it was known in the religions of many ancient cultures. Although not found among the Hebrew/Israelite people and considered an abomination by them, the religious practices of some of the surrounding nations also included human sacrifice. My interest in sacrifice as part of the Israelite religion stems from the later Christian interpretation that the death of Jesus was a sacrifice for human sin. There were many kinds of Israelite sacrifice, but the most solemn and significant involved sacrifice for the atonement to God for sins against God or other humans. Such sacrifices involved offering the blood of an animal – sheep, goat, bull, or certain birds. The scent of the burning blood was deemed pleasing to God, causing God to forgive or to blot out the sins of those for whom the sacrifice was offered.

My first reaction might be to recoil in disgust at the thought that the stench of burning blood could be "pleasing to God." If the smell was not good, what was so important about sacrificing *blood*? The early Hebrews and later Israelites were nomadic herders; their source of meat was their sheep, goats and cattle, which had to be slaughtered by bleeding the animal in a religiously prescribed (*kosher*) way. Once the animal's throat had been cut, it began to bleed. As more and more of its blood was lost, the animal became weaker, dying as it lost the last of its blood. From the Hebrews' perspective, if an animal with all of its blood was fully alive and an animal that had lost all its blood was dead, *it was reasonable to conclude that the life force of animals resided in their blood.* Indeed, that understanding is explicitly detailed in Leviticus 17:11: "For the life of a creature is in its blood," and 17:14: "for the life of every creature is its blood." The consequence of that reverence for blood was that no *blood* – no *life* – of any kind could be eaten by Hebrews. Moreover, because life was considered to reside in the blood, sacrificing the life (blood) of the animal could atone for or buy back the life of the human for whom the sacrifice was offered. Without the sacrifice, the human stood condemned to death before God; but with the life in the blood of the animal atoning for the sins of the human, the human's life was atoned for and redeemed.

That life resided in the blood of an animal or human seemed an altogether reasonable conclusion for people of biblical times, but it does not seem at all reasonable

Table 7.2. Comparison of the organization of the Hebrew Bible and of the Old Testament of the Christian Bible.

Hebrew Bible (24 books)	Christian Old Testament (39 books)
The Law (Torah) (5 books)	Genesis
Genesis	Exodus
Exodus	Leviticus
Leviticus	Numbers
Numbers	Deuteronomy
Deuteronomy	Joshua
The Prophets (8 books)	Judges
Former:	Ruth
Joshua	1 Samuel
Judges	2 Samuel
Samuel (1 & 2)	1 Kings
Kings (1 & 2)	2 Kings
Latter:	1 Chronicles
Isaiah	2 Chronicles
Jeremiah	Ezra
Ezekiel	Nehemiah
The Twelve:	Esther
Hosea	Job
Joel	Psalms
Amos	Proverbs
Obadiah	Ecclesiastes
Jonah	Song of Solomon
Micah	Isaiah
Nahum	Jeremiah
Habakkuk	Lamentations
Zephaniah	Ezekiel
Haggai	Daniel
Zechariah	Hosea
Malachi	Joel
The Writings (11 books)	Amos
Psalms	Obadiah
Proverbs	Jonah
Job	Micah
Song of Solomon	Nahum
Ruth	Habakkuk
Lamentations	Zephaniah
Ecclesiastes	Haggai
Esther	Zechariah
Daniel	Malachi
Ezra-Nehemiah	
Chronicles (1 & 2)	

today. Modern knowledge indicates that the basis of life is much more complex than that. But the more basic question is about sacrifice: Did the sacrifice of animal blood really bring about the atonement for sin? Did it somehow restore relationships between people or between people and God because that was the ancient understanding of the importance of blood? A more realistic understanding is that, while the sacrifice of animal blood was very important to Hebrew religious life, it was a "symbolic" importance that had nothing at all to do with anything that was happening physically and biologically. That realization has huge implications not only for modern understanding of ancient Hebrew animal sacrifice but also for the Christian understanding of the blood of

Jesus' sacrifice on the cross as an atonement for human sin. That notion will be examined further in the next chapter.

Having looked at a thumbnail sketch of the Hebrew biblical narrative and at the importance of some of Israel's religious and social institutions, I turn to a consideration of the composition and writing of the Hebrew Bible, the Christian Old Testament. In this and subsequent chapters, the term *canon* will be used frequently to designate the set of sacred writings that is officially recognized as authoritative by a religious body. In the present context that refers, respectively, to the canons of the Hebrew Bible and later of the Christian Bible.

Although they have the same textual content, an examination of Table 7.2 shows that the Hebrew Bible was organized quite differently than the Old Testament of the Christian Bible. The Hebrew canon was divided into three large subdivisions: The Law (Torah), The Prophets, and The Writings. The Law and The Prophets had the highest and equal authority in governing the lives of the Hebrew people; their commands and requirements were always important and required obedience. The Writings, on the other hand, had much less authority; their counsel and admonition were considered spiritually edifying and educational, but usually not mandatory. If there was disagreement between the contents of The Law or The Prophets, on one hand, and The Writings, on the other hand, The Law and The Prophets always had greater authority than The Writings. By contrast, when these same books became part of the Old Testament of the Christian Bible, all thirty-nine books were regarded by the Christian Church as having equal authority.

As determined by the use of *historical-critical* studies, the authorship of the books of these three subdivisions is shown in Table 7.3. *The Law* (*Torah*) or the Pentateuch consists of Genesis, Exodus, Leviticus, Numbers and Deuteronomy. While its narrative relates a continuous story that begins with Creation (ahistorical) and ends

with Israel's entering the Promised Land under the leadership of Joshua (prehistoric), its literary content is quite diverse. Included were the myths, sagas and legends noted earlier. As to its authorship, although often called "the five books of Moses," clearly no part of them was written by Moses (who, if he was a historical person, lived earlier than 1200 BCE), because the earliest written parts of the Pentateuch were probably written about 1000-950 BCE. Scholars have found within the Pentateuch four prominent literary sources: J (Yahwist; ca. 1000-922 BCE), E (Elohist; ca. 900-722 BCE), D (Deuteronomist; ca. 621 BCE) and P (Priestly; ca. 587-539 BCE). Rather than being individual writers, these sources probably represent "schools of thought." Thus, the Pentateuch appears to have been "written and edited by committees" over a period of nearly 500 years. Beginning about 1000 BCE, it was composed, modified and edited by anonymous religious leaders, who continued to adapt the content and their interpretations of it to meet their understandings of what Yahweh did for and expected of his chosen people over that period of time.

The second major subdivision of the Hebrew Bible is *The Prophets* (Joshua through Malachi in Table 7.3), which was further subdivided into two groups: the Former or Nonwriting Prophets included Joshua, Judges, Samuel and Kings, the latter two of which were not subdivided in the Hebrew Bible. These four books consist of narrative *about* rather than sermons and/or writings *of* the prophets contained therein. Like the Pentateuch, these narratives were likely derived from skeletal J, E, P and D core sources and stories that were continually modified, reinterpreted, edited and added to over a 400-500 year period by anonymous religious leaders.

The Latter or Writing Prophets include the Major Prophets: Isaiah, Jeremiah, and Ezekiel; and The Twelve (Minor Prophets): Hosea, Joel, Amos, Obadiah, Jonah, Micah, Nahum, Habakkuk, Zephaniah, Haggai, Zechariah and Malachi. It should be noted

Table 7.3. Books of the Hebrew Bible: Authors and Dates of Writing

	Book	Date of Writing (BCE)	Author
The Law (Torah)	Genesis	1000-450	Multiple anonymous J^1, E^2, P^3 & D^4 writers and editors
	Exodus	1000-450	Multiple anonymous J, E, P & D writers and editors
	Leviticus	600-450	Multiple anonymous mostly P writers and editors
	Numbers	1000-450	Multiple anonymous J, E, P &?D writers and editors
	Deuteronomy	640-550	Multiple anonymous D writers and editors
The Prophets	Joshua	1000-540	Multiple anonymous J^1, E, P & D writers and editors
	Judges	750-550	Multiple anonymous writers and editors
	Samuel (1 & 2)	1000-540	Multiple anonymous J, E, P & D writers and editors
	Kings (1 & 2)	1000-540	Multiple anonymous J, E, P & D writers and editors
	Isaiah		
	First Isaiah	782-647	Isaiah and disciple-editors
	Second Isaiah	587-538	Anonymous student/disciple of Isaiah and editors
	Third Isaiah	538-500	Anonymous student of 2nd Isaiah and editors
	Jeremiah	627-580	Jeremiah and editors
	Ezekiel	593-571	Ezekiel and editors
	Hosea	750-720	Hosea and editors
	Joel	~350	Joel and editors
	Amos	786-746	Amos and editors
	Obadiah	580-400	Obadiah and editors
	Jonah	500-400	Anonymous
	Micah	742-698	Micah and disciple-editors
	Nahum	630-600	Nahum and editors
	Habakkuk	609-598	Habakkuk and editors
	Zephaniah	640-609	Zephaniah and editors
	Haggai	520	Haggai and editors
	Zechariah	520-400	Zechariah, later writers and editors
	Malachi	486-465	Anonymous
The Writings	Psalms	1000-300	Multiple anonymous authors and editors
	Proverbs	100-500	Anonymous, including foreign sources
	Job	?580-500	Anonymous sage
	Song of Songs (Solomon)	950-500	Anonymous
	Ruth	?500-400	Anonymous (?woman)
	Lamentations	587-550	Anonymous (?Jeremiah)
	Ecclesiastes	300-200	Anonymous (Qohelet = The Preacher)
	Esther	After 465	Anonymous
	Daniel	167-164	Anonymous
	Ezra-Nehemiah	538-333	Anonymous
	Chronicles (1 & 2)	~400	Anonymous

[1] The Yahwist (J) was a tenth or ninth-century BCE history, composed either during the united monarchy of David and Solomon (1000-922 BCE) or in the Southern Kingdom of Judah shortly after the split of the kingdoms (922 BCE).
[2] The Elohist (E) was an eighth-century BCE history, written for the Northern Kingdom of Israel (922-722 BCE).
[3] The book of Deuteronomy (D) is a seventh-century BCE document associated with the reform of Josiah in 621 BCE.
[4] The Priestly (P) history was written in the sixth century BCE in the wake of the Babylonian Exile (587-539 BCE).
Source: *The New Interpreter's Bible.* Vol. II, p. 5.

that the Christian Old Testament (Table 7.2) rather freely intermingles the Hebrew prophetic books with the third Hebrew subdivision, *The Writings*.

If they do in fact relate historical events, Joshua and Judges cover the approximate time from 1200-1100 BCE, still well before the actual writing of any of the books of the Hebrew Bible. Therefore, their contents also contain materials, including legends and sagas, which had been transmitted orally for several hundreds of years. Beginning with the book of Samuel, the stories and accounts may have been committed to writing not too long after their occurrences. However, even these writings contain illustrative, non-historical vignettes. The stories of Samuel's birth and being "called by God" in the night are reminiscent of the boyhood stories of religious heroes in other cultures of the time.

The prophetic books of the Hebrew Bible were written between about 1000 BCE, the time of King David, and 400 BCE, the time of the prophets Obadiah and Zechariah. Although the prophetic writings include actual historical events, they also contain much interpretive coloring of the historical events. For example, most of these books were written by persons in the Kingdom of Judah (Southern Kingdom) rather than by persons in the Kingdom of Israel (Northern Kingdom). Thus, in these writings, actions and kings of the Southern Kingdom are presented much more positively than events and kings in the Northern Kingdom. Moreover, because the writers, particularly of the so-called "histories," may have been commissioned or in some fashion been authorized by the king, they were likely to interpret the actions of that king in a favorable perspective. These possible influences necessitate caution in drawing conclusions about the accuracy of "historical" reporting in these writings.

Favorable interpretation and treatment of the king, some priests and of the Israelite people was not the case, however, for most of the books named after specific prophets. Hebrew prophets, like prophets in nearly all ancient religions, were deemed to "speak forth" the words of a deity concerning people and events in the world. Hebrew prophecies were often words of harsh judgment, criticizing kings, priests or citizens, because of the prophet's perception that they were failing to follow the laws and ordinances of Yahweh. In various ways prophets felt "called" or "sent" by God, often involuntarily, to utter their oracles and words of judgment. Sometimes in the context of these words of judgment, they would issue predictions of disaster or doom that would follow if their warnings were not heeded. Much less common was the straightforward prediction of some future event

Although it cannot be known with certainty, as shown in Table 7.3, the prophetic books were in most cases probably not written by the prophets themselves.

Rather, the core of the book may have originated with oral and/or written prophecies by the named prophet; through the decades and, in some cases, centuries, that core message was elaborated and modified by disciples and students of the prophets. Most notable among the examples of the latter is the book of Isaiah. Much of chapters 1-39 is quite possibly attributable to the prophet Isaiah himself (First Isaiah) around 720 BCE; chapters 40-55 were probably written by disciples of Isaiah (Second Isaiah) around the time of the Babylonian captivity from 586-538 BCE; chapters 56-66 were quite probably written after 538 BCE by still later students of Isaiah (Third Isaiah), after the Babylonian captivity. The content and tone of these three sections allow a determination of when they were written. Yet, because all 66 chapters reflected the Isaiah "school of thought," they were combined into a single document – the book of Isaiah. Such examples of pseudonymity – writing under the name of a prominent person – were accepted literary practices in the ancient world. Pseudonymity often served to honor and to show theological continuity with the named person, as well as probably giving greater authority to the later writings.

As shown in Table 7.3, the third subdivision of the Hebrew Bible was *The Writings*: Psalms, Job, Proverbs, Ruth, Song of Solomon (Songs), Ecclesiastes, Lamentations, Esther, Daniel, Ezra-Nehemiah and Chronicles. The Writings were a miscellaneous collection: Psalms was the hymn/prayer book of the Hebrews; Proverbs contained adages and wisdom sayings for life, many of which were adopted and adapted from the wisdom literature of surrounding nations. Song of Songs celebrated love and marriage. Ecclesiastes was a reflection on the incomprehensibility of life; Ruth, Job and Esther were inspirational stories that illustrated God's blessings of the faithful; that the book of Esther includes no mention of God may indicate that, although it narrates the origin of the Feast of Purim, its core may have derived from a legend from a neighboring pagan country. The latter part of the book of Daniel relates to the Maccabean Revolt and rededication of the Temple, celebrated at Hanukkah, the Feast of Dedication. (The book of Daniel is unique, in that parts of it were originally written in Aramaic, unlike the entire rest of the Hebrew Bible, which was written in Hebrew.) Lamentations recounts the deep grief and loss, purportedly of Jeremiah, after the Babylonians captured and destroyed Jerusalem in 586 BCE. Chronicles and Ezra-Nehemiah are religious-political commentary, recounting and celebrating Israel's status as Yahweh's chosen people after the return from the Babylonian Captivity. As indicated earlier, The Writings were considered important spiritual writings for the Hebrews but mostly as complementary and supportive material for The Law and The Prophets, the acknowledged scriptural authorities.

The writing, editing and revising of the documents that would later become the Hebrew Bible began around 1000 BCE and continued at least until the writing of Daniel at about 164 BCE. However, agreement on which writings should be included in the Hebrew Bible canon occurred over an approximately five hundred year period that overlapped the most recent end of that interval. The Pentateuch (Torah) reached canonical status about 400 BCE, meaning that from that time forward Israelites regarded it as having full religious authority to guide and direct their lives. The Prophets became canonical about 200 BCE. Agreement on which books should be canonically included in The Writings did not occur until perhaps as late as the period between 150 BCE and 100 CE. However, even after there was agreement on the canonicity of The Writings, they had considerably less authority than The Law and The Prophets.

The foregoing section has considered the writing and editing of those documents that ultimately became part of the Hebrew Bible.

However, those documents were not the only writings that were considered for inclusion in the Hebrew Bible. This section presents from a historical perspective a consideration of a number of writings that were ultimately excluded from the Hebrew canon.

In order to consolidate the political power and authority of his newly conquered lands, before his death in 323 BCE Alexander the Great instituted Greek as the *lingua franca*, the official language of the Hellenistic Empire. That meant that, although people usually continued to speak their native language locally, in the broader empire the ability to communicate in Greek became important and even necessary. Therefore, as time passed, Greek became more and more the spoken and written language also among Jews, particularly those educated Jews who lived outside Palestine in the learning centers of the Hellenistic Empire. Jewish Scriptures, originally written and still only available in Hebrew, were becoming less accessible to Greek-speaking Jews. To address that situation, the Jewish religious leaders of Alexandria, Egypt, undertook the translation of their Scriptures into Greek. This project began about 250 BCE with the translation of the Pentateuch and continued until all of the Scriptures had been translated into Greek. The resulting translated work was termed the *Septuagint*, "seventy" in Greek. It was so-called because, according to a tradition preserved in the *Letter of Aretas*, seventy-two Hebrew scholars (twelve groups of six members each) labored for seventy-two days to translate the Hebrew Scriptures into Greek. When the twelve groups compared their independently produced translations, they found them to be identical, signifying that divine guidance had directed their translations. While this account was surely a legend, it did serve to attribute mystery and to give divine authority to the *Septuagint*.

What is more important, however, is the composition of the *Septuagint*. Table 7.4 lists those writings that were considered for

Table 7.4. Writings included in the *Septuagint* that are not included in the canon of the Hebrew Bible. Variations in the names and titles of these writings are indicated in parentheses.

1 Esdras
Tobit
Judith
The Rest of the Chapters of (Additions to) the Book of Esther
The Wisdom of Solomon
Ecclesiasticus, or the Wisdom of Jesus Son of Sirach
Baruch
The (A) Letter of Jeremiah
The Prayer of Azariah and The Song of the Three Jews (The Song of the Three)
(Daniel and) Susanna
Daniel, Bel, and the Snake (Bel and the Dragon)
The Prayer of Manasseh
1 Maccabees
2 Maccabees

inclusion in the previously described Hebrew canon but were ultimately excluded.

The contents of some of these writings add to or are related to writings that are included in the Hebrew Bible. Like many of the writings that were included in the Hebrew canon, the authorship and date of writing for most of these documents are unknown. What they share in common is that Jewish religious leaders decided not even to include them in The Writings, the lesser authoritative set of books in the Hebrew Bible. In that respect, they represent a snapshot of what happened during the canonization process of the Hebrew Bible; more writings were considered for inclusion than were ultimately selected. Nevertheless, these writings were regarded as edifying Jewish religious literature. However, for reasons to be detailed later, these writings were included as the Apocrypha in the biblical canons of the Roman Catholic and Orthodox Churches. They are often referred to as Deuterocanonical books, because they comprise a second and additional canon that is not included in the Hebrew or Protestant Bibles.

In addition to the Hebrew canon and the Deuterocanonical books, there were numerous other Jewish writings (not listed here) that appeared between 300 BCE and 100 CE (Common Era = AD, *anno Domini*). They were apparently not ever considered by Jewish religious leaders to be appropriately significant and authoritative for inclusion in the Hebrew Bible. Collectively, they have been termed Pseudepigrapha ("writings with false superscriptions"). Like the Deuterocanonical books, however, they were also deemed edifying religious documents,

A consideration of the totality of available information about the Hebrew canon, the Deuterocanonical books and the Pseudepigrapha reveals that the decision-making by Jewish religious leaders as to which writings would and would not be included in the Hebrew canon was an ongoing process that lasted many centuries. It was long thought that at the Council of Jamnia in 90 CE the Hebrew canon was declared closed – no more writings could be added. Even if recent evidence suggesting that the canon was closed as early as 150 BCE is correct, the canonization process still lasted several centuries.

What is known about the actual writing of the documents that came to be included in the canon of the Hebrew Bible? Despite writings' being named after or in honor of specific people, the authorship of most writings is unknown. Most were probably written by leaders of the Hebrew religious community. Those included priests, prophets and probably writers commissioned by the kings, especially of Judah.

There is no evidence that individual writers penned their words as they were being "inspired" from some extrinsic or external source. Rather, they were expressing their own thoughts and judgments as they presented and interpreted their religious narratives. They used accepted writing standards of their time, one of which will be examined shortly. They related the details of the stories as happening in the worldview (the German biblical scholars called it the *Weltanschauung*) of their times. That included their conceptions of the physical universe as well as of the political, sociological, cultural and religious (their own and those of the surrounding nations) settings of their times. They wrote as responsible religious leaders in their world setting. While present-day readers might have a much different worldview today and therefore find it necessary to critically reexamine their writings, the ancient writers ought not be criticized for placing their narratives as thoroughly as possible in the contexts of their times; their own honesty and integrity and the credibility of their writings to the readers and hearers depended on their setting their writings as thoroughly and accurately as possible in their contemporary contexts.

To use a current analogy, writers purporting to present valid and credible accounts and interpretations of happenings today must relate the details of those accounts in the context of the worldview of 2000 CE. In 2500 CE, someone reading those accounts written in 2000 CE might have a very different worldview than that of the present, which would quite probably require them to critically examine them and quite possibly to arrive at very different understandings than those of the authors in 2000 CE. Would the authors in 2000 CE have been wrong or dishonest? Certainly not. They were writing for the people of their time,

using their best understandings of the realities and actualities of their world context.

This analogy also extrapolates relevance for the present considerations. If the worldview of today is drastically different from that of the time of the biblical writings, do the conclusions reached by the authors of the biblical writings have authoritative relevance for the present time? Or is it the case that, while those writings may have been relevant and valid and have had tremendous significance for the people of the time of their writing (and perhaps even for many succeeding generations for as long as the worldview remained the same), they have little or no relevance, let alone authority, for today? The best evidences and assessments of modern biblical scholarship indicate that such is the case, especially pertaining to modern understandings of history and of the natural world. That is not to say that the modern understandings are the final word. To the extent that further knowledge necessitates, future understandings will be modifications of present ones. The overarching principle, however, is that the most correct understanding at any given time is based on the most valid and reliable truths at the time when those understandings are formulated.

A commonly used device in ancient religious writings was the literary technique of having gods speak directly to or with their followers. Like the authors of pagan religious writings of nearly all cultures surrounding ancient Israel and Judah, the authors of the Hebrew biblical writings used that same literary device of having Yahweh speak directly with his chosen people. As noted earlier in this chapter, in the biblical narrative Yahweh's activities in relation to Israel were related anthropomorphically – in terms of human thoughts and actions. Thus, it was considered believable to expect that Yahweh could make known his words and will to his people through oral and even written communication.

In reflecting on that phenomenon, it is appropriate to ask how and why it is credible that Yahweh spoke directly to the Hebrews in ancient times but does not speak directly with his followers today. Or if it is credible that the LORD God spoke directly to people of the Hebrew faith, is it perhaps also true that the gods of the religions of the surrounding nations spoke directly to their followers as well? Or is it that believers of the Judeo-Christian tradition have been indoctrinated by their churches to believe that God's speaking directly with people actually happened in the instances related to their God in their Scriptures, but that such accounts are mere pagan fictional stories when gods of other religions spoke to their adherents? The historical reality seems rather to be that the writers of Hebrew Scriptures were simply following accepted literary practices and customs of all religious writing of their time. The most reasonable conclusion that I reach from all of these considerations is that God or gods have never spoken directly to people in pagan religions or in Judeo-Christianity then or now.

Why would ancient religious writers use the literary technique of having gods communicate with their adherents through speaking and writing? Perhaps one example from the Hebrew Bible serves as an appropriate illustration. Exodus 20 relates the LORD God's giving of the Ten Commandments to Moses to be transmitted to the Israelites. The Ten Commandments were important rules for the orderly organization and operation of Hebrew religious and communal life. The first several commandments are particular to the Hebrew religion, prescribing a proper relationship between the Hebrew people and Yahweh. On the other hand, it has long been recognized that the remainder of the commandments pertaining to honoring parents, not killing other humans, not stealing the property of others, not slandering others and not coveting others' wives or property are similar to, and quite likely derivative from, moral and ethical codes of older surrounding nations, such as the Code of Hammurabi. By writing an account in which the LORD God explicitly wrote the Ten Commandments in stone, the religious leaders gave these rules absolute and enduring authority in the communal lives of the Hebrew people. Numerous other examples could be cited, in which the words spoken by the LORD God became foundational to the religious and communal lives of the Hebrew people. By using the literary technique of having Yahweh speak or write directives, the religious leaders gave authority to the commandments and directives that far transcended any authority that those same words would have possessed had they or even the king issued them.

Many other features of the historical roots and writing of the documents that were later collected to comprise the Hebrew Bible could be examined. My interest, however, has been to determine whether there was anything in the writing or collecting of these books that warrants their being given special status and authority for the present time. The writers appear to have been religious leaders of one kind or another, perhaps most often priests or prophets. Their literary techniques, styles, methods and the contents of their writing were typical of religious, including pagan, writings of their times. The peculiarity of the Hebrew religion was its monotheism – worship of a single deity – Yahweh – rather than the polytheism of its neighboring nations. That factor alone, however, makes the Hebrew writings unique but not more authoritative. The authors' attitudes and the content of their writings indicate that they were addressing serious questions and problems of their particular times. While the writers apparently hoped and expected the immediate readers/hearers of their respective times to respond to their messages, there is no indication that they had any sense or consciousness that they were somehow being inspired to write some unchanged eternal message – authoritative truths for all times. Rather, as subsequent religious leaders considered the growing collection of writings, they quite frequently found it necessary to modify and to amend them in order for them to be appropriate witnesses to their religion and to merit authority for contemporary use. Over time those writings were considered holy – set apart as the Hebrew canon – and given special status as authoritative instructional materials and deemed of critical importance to faithfully propagate the Hebrew religion. In short, it was use of the literary technique of gods' communicating commands and orders directly to people within the writings combined with the collective decision of religious leaders concerning which documents were of most importance for the life of the community that ultimately granted authority to the written documents that became the Hebrew Bible.

Thus, I can understand and appreciate how and why the Hebrew Bible came into existence and why it was given great authority in forming and informing the religious lives of the Israelite people. At the same time, I recognize that the worldview and the styles of religious writings of ancient times are so different from their counterparts of the twenty-first century that many of those writings have little direct relevance for me today; indeed, it is difficult or even impossible to try to understand many of them in the context of the present worldview. While I may be able to derive useful insights from some of them for life today, in no way can or should they be given overarching and absolute authority over my life.

Chapter 8

Examining Scriptural Content and Origins: The New Testament

Based on results of historical-critical methods of investigation, in the previous chapter I concluded that those characteristics of the narrative of the Hebrew Bible/Old Testament which lie outside the experience of modern reality were results of the worldview of the time and of the nature of religious writing within that context. That is, things that do not happen today did not actually occur then either, but rather were incorporated into Hebrew religious writings just as they were used in the writings of pagan religions of the time. The authority of the Hebrew Bible derived from two principal sources. First, the literary technique of having Yahweh speak or write commands and ordinances gave the authority of Yahweh to those specific contents. Second, the selection of sets of documents by Israel's religious leaders to be included in The Law, The Prophets and The Writings gave those sets of writings authority for guiding the lives of the people of Israel. Concerning the authority of the Old Testament writings for today, while they may still provide some useful insights for life, they lack comprehensive authority for ordering and orienting lives in the modern world. Consequently, a literal use of Old Testament writings cannot be used as an authority for me to derive understandings and expectations in my life today.

While such a conclusion concerning the authority of the Hebrew Bible (Old Testament) might at first seem threatening, it has to some degree already been assumed by most Christians, who consider themselves a people of a new covenant, the New Testament. The ceremonial and religious laws of Judaism are no longer considered author-itatively binding for Christians, because they have been superseded by those beliefs and practices that emanate from the belief that Jesus is the Christ, the anointed one of God. The overall consequence is that most Christians selectively ignore and disregard any tenets of the Old Testament that conflict with teachings and dogmas of the New Testament.

I now turn to an examination of the development of the New Testament – what it says and the nature and authority of its writings. Because these writings appeared more recently than the history and the writing of the Old Testament Scriptures, more and better sources of information are available for consideration. Moreover, whereas the presumed time frame of the Old Testament was from about 1800 BCE until 4 BCE (the nominal date for the birth of Jesus), the happenings in and the writing of the New Testament documents occurred between 4 BCE and 150 CE, a much shorter and more recent time frame. In this chapter all dates will be assumed to be CE, unless otherwise noted.

Beginning this investigation, I again remind myself of the counsel of Albert Schweitzer to dedicate my efforts to seeking the truth. As in the case of the Hebrew Bible, I will utilize knowledge and information that biblical scholars have derived through use of the historical-critical study approach, which draws especially on extrabiblical sources to assess and to evaluate the veracity and validity of details of the New Testament narrative. Applying what I can best assess to be the truth may prove even more challenging in the case of the New Testament, because it contains the core foundational bases for the Christian Church, including the Lutheran tradition that spiritually formed and informed me.

Sketching a mental time line of the New Testament era helps place the events of its narrative in perspective. There is consensus that Jesus was born about 4 BCE, when Augustus Caesar was the Roman Emperor and Herod the Great was governor of Galilee. If Jesus began his ministry at about 30 years of age (Luke 3:23), his ministry began about 27, when Tiberius (ruled 14-37) was the Roman Emperor and Pontius Pilate (ruled 26-36) was procurator or governor of the province of Judea. Although the gospels of Matthew, Mark and Luke suggest a ministry lasting about one year, the gospel of John suggests a ministry lasting about three years; all four gospels agree that his ministry ended with his crucifixion and death. There is consensus among New Testament scholars that Jesus' crucifixion and death occurred about 30. His Jewish followers, at first located in Jerusalem and surrounding Palestine, believed that he was the Christ, the anointed one of Yahweh, whose coming had been anticipated in certain Hebrew Bible references: "The LORD your God will raise up for you a prophet." (Deuteronomy 18:15). For about 50-60 years, those believers comprised a sect of Judaism; other than their believing that Jesus was the Christ and the implications of that, they continued all the practices of Judaism – circumcision, sacrifice, observance of purity laws, obedience to Torah, pilgrimages to Jerusalem, etc.

Beginning perhaps about 35-40, the apostle Paul carried the Christian gospel to both Jews and non-Jews in Asia Minor and later to present-day Greece. The congregations that he started included many Gentiles, who had previously been members of pagan religions of the day. Guided and directed by Paul's teachings and interpretations concerning the life and ministry of Jesus, those congregations were exempted from many of the requirements of strict Judaism. Paul continued his ministry until the early 60s,

when he was imprisoned. Tradition holds that he was executed in Rome around 65.

The relationship between the followers of Jesus who continued to strictly observe Jewish practices and those who did not was a contentious one. The apostle Paul championed freedom for Jesus' followers from obligatory observance of Jewish religious practices, particularly circumcision. The apostle James, the brother of the Lord and the foremost leader of Jesus' followers in Jerusalem, led the group who insisted on strict adherence to Jewish religious practices such as circumcision. The apostle Peter apparently vacillated back and forth in this struggle, perhaps trying to find a peaceful middle ground but ending up angering both sides. This conflict between the *Jewish* Christians and the *free* Christians persisted for about fifty years in the early Christian Church.

Equally important, particularly in Palestine, was the conflict between the Jews who accepted Jesus as the Christ and those who did not; both of these groups of Jews were continuing all the practices of strict Jewish observance. Males were circumcised. They worshiped and sacrificed together at the Temple until its destruction in 70. They continued to observe the Jewish purification rites and practices. They gathered together in synagogues. Finally, sometime around 90-100 the acrimony between these two groups of Jews reached the point that the Christians, those who believed that Jesus was the Christ, were expelled from the synagogues, a situation alluded to in the gospel of John (12:42; 16:2). From that point forward the Christian Church and Judaism followed separate and largely independent courses.

Also important in understanding the New Testament narrative is knowledge of the time frame of the writing of those documents that came to be included in the New Testament, shown in Table 8.1.

A first important observation is that there is almost no correlation between the commonly listed order (column 4) of the books

Table 8.1. New Testament Writings: Consensus on Authors and Dates of Writing. The writings are ordered according to their consensus dates of writing. Dates and names in parentheses indicate significant minority opinions

"Book"	**Date of Writing**	**Author**	**Sequence in NT**
1 Thessalonians	51-52	Paul	13
1 Corinthians	54-55	Paul	7
2 Corinthians	55-56	Paul	8
Galatians	51-54	Paul	9
Philippians	56-58	Paul	11
Philemon	54-56, 56-60	Paul	18
Romans	56	Paul	6
Colossians	60s-70s (54-58)	Anonymous disciple of Paul (Paul)	12
Mark	~70	Anonymous	2
Luke/Acts	75-85	Anonymous	3, 5
Ephesians	85-90	Anonymous disciple of Paul	10
Matthew	80-85	Anonymous	1
2 Thessalonians	70-90 (51-52)	Anonymous disciple of Paul (Paul)	14
James	~90	Anonymous (An unidentified James)	20
Hebrews	~95	Anonymous	19
John	90-100 (75-85)	Anonymous	4
1 Peter	95-100 (60s)	Anonymous (Peter)	21
1, 2 & 3 John	90-100	Anonymous "Elder"	23, 24, 25
Revelation	95-100	John of Patmos or Anonymous	27
1 & 2 Timothy	100-110	Pseudonymous disciple of Paul	15, 16
Titus	100-110	Pseudonymous disciple of Paul	17
Jude	130-140	Unknown "Judas, brother of James"	26
2 Peter	100-150	Anonymous	22

in the New Testament and the chronological sequence in which they were written (column 2). Even the consensus writings of Paul and the larger Pauline corpus (see below) are ordered according to the lengths of the books rather than according to chronological sequence in which they were written. Although this observation might initially seem unimportant, its implications for present-day reading and interpretation of the New Testament writings will be discussed later.

There is consensus that the apostle Paul's writings were the earliest; he wrote letters to the various congregations that he had founded in present-day Asia Minor and Greece, some apparently answering questions in letters written to him from the congregations, others containing his counsel and exhortations on theological issues and on congregational conflicts and practices. First Thessalonians was probably written about 51-52. It was followed by the writings to the Corinthians (54-56); although now present in the New Testament as 1 & 2 Corinthians,

those two books are probably composites of as many as four or five separate letters that were later edited together. The letter to the Galatians was written in the 50s, although there is disagreement whether it was early or later in that decade. By the early 60s, he had also written Philippians, Philemon and Romans; as mentioned earlier, tradition holds that Paul was executed in Rome about 65 under Emperor Nero (ruled 54-68).

A common practice in New Testament times, also noted earlier for Isaiah in the Hebrew Bible, was *pseudonymity* – writing in the name of an earlier, revered and authoritative person who had died. Most biblical scholars conclude that, although written in the name of Paul, the books of 2 Thessalonians (70-90), Colossians (60-70) and Ephesians (85-90) were written by his disciples or followers. There is strong consensus that 1 and 2 Timothy and Titus, also written in the name of Paul, were written by disciples of Paul, as late as 100-110, or perhaps even later. This group of books is called the *Pauline corpus* because they were either written by Paul himself or by his disciples, who purport to express extensions of Paul's theology and thinking on many issues.

The only writings of the New Testament that contain significant information about Jesus' life and ministry are the gospels, about which there is again strong consensus about their authorships and times of writing. Although the gospels are named for important New Testament personalities, the earliest available manuscripts of all four gospels are *anonymous* – no authors are identified. Sometime after being written, their being named after important people – disciples of Jesus or their associates – gave them connection to Jesus. This association gave the writings authority in ways similar to earlier-mentioned pseudonymity.

Although the specific purposes for writing are not given in each of the gospels, for the gospel of John it appears to be quite explicitly stated in John 20:30-31: "Now Jesus did many other signs in the presence of his disciples, which are not written in this book. But *these are written so that you may come to believe that Jesus is the Messiah, the Son of God, and that through believing you may have life in his name*" (New Revised Standard Version: NRSV). Thus, the gospel of John was written explicitly to persuade people that "Jesus is the Messiah, the Son of God," so that they might believe in Jesus. It is worth noting that neither the gospel of John nor any of the other three gospels claims to be anything like a comprehensive biography or history of Jesus' life. Judging from the tone and content of all four gospels, they are rather more like testimonials. They probably were written and used in order to recount the Jesus story in various early Christian communities; they may also have been efforts to convince others to become followers of Jesus, much as propaganda and advertisements attempt to induce people to join organizations and to buy products today. Comparisons with contemporary non-Chris-

tian writings show that the gospel writers used the same literary techniques and styles of writing that were utilized by writers espousing other religions of New Testament times. To be sure the early Christians would have regarded these other religions and writings as pagan; conversely, the adherents of the pagan religions would have held their own religions and writings to be true rather than early Christianity and its writings.

The first gospel to be written was Mark, apparently written around the time of the fall of Jerusalem in 70. Matthew was probably written about 80-85. Luke-Acts was written about 75-85, or perhaps somewhat later, and John was most likely written about 90-100. At this point, it should be noted that Mark and John, the earliest and latest gospels, were written about 40 years and 65 years, respectively, after the end of Jesus' ministry (30). Although occasionally people lived to be quite old, the average life expectancy at that time may have been 40-50 years at most; thus, it is likely that none of the gospels were written by eyewitnesses of Jesus' life and ministry, and some writers may have been second and perhaps even third generation followers of Jesus. During the period (40-65 years) between Jesus' death and the writing of the gospels, the accounts of Jesus' life and ministry most likely circulated exclusively as oral stories. Because of the absence of eyewitnesses and because of the oral circulation of the Jesus stories, it is perhaps little wonder that the gospels were later associated with the names of people who were Jesus' disciples or their associates; it should also come as no surprise that differences in details about Jesus' life and ministry arose and accrued during this period of oral transmission.

Judging from statements in the earliest Christian writings – *i. e.*, Paul's letters, Jesus' early followers apparently expected him to return physically to their midst within their lifetimes (1 Thessalonians 4:9-18; written about 51-52). With the passage of forty years or more and with Jesus' failure to return, the gospels were likely written in various cities around the Roman Empire to formalize the story of Jesus' life and ministry for his followers in each of those communities, who for two or three generations had related the stories about Jesus through oral transmission. The different details and emphases of the four gospels reflect the divergent understandings of the significance of his life and ministry that had already arisen through 40-65 years of oral transmission after his life on earth.

Scholars have long noted the similarities between the gospels of Matthew, Mark and Luke; they have been termed the *synoptic* (*syn* – "together," *optic* – "to see") gospels, because they understand and present the life and ministry of Jesus similarly, although each paints a different picture in telling the story. Most scholars believe that the writers of Matthew (written 80-85) and Luke (written 75-85) drew primarily on the gospel of Mark (written about 70), adding materials from a so-called *Q source* (a hypothesized document consisting mostly of sayings of Jesus) and from their own individual sources to emphasize the details of Jesus' life and ministry that they deemed most important.

The gospel of John, on the other hand, probably originated independently of the other three. Jesus as pictured by the writer of John is hardly a human being. He is not born; he came into existence when "the Word became flesh." He knows what God knows; he sees into the hearts of people. He is fully in control of all situations, even at his trial and crucifixion. Clearly, the community where this gospel was written already had an understanding of a different and more mystical Jesus than those communities where the other three gospels were written and read.

About 40-50 years after Jesus' followers started what would become the Christian Church, the Acts of the Apostles (written about 75-85) presents the writer's understanding of the origin and early dispersal of Christianity. While the writer purports to recount many details in the life and teachings of the apostle Paul, biblical scholars have noted numerous discrepancies between details in the narrative of Acts and what Paul teaches and says about himself in his own writings. The amount of time (perhaps 50-60 years) between the beginning of the Jesus cult shortly after his death and the writing of Acts, together with the author's acknowledgment of not being a witness to those events, has led many biblical scholars to conclude that the writer of Acts wrote a *theological rather than a historical account*, adding rather freely and creatively to the accessible historical information in order to produce a quality writing of the time.

The remainder of the New Testament is a collection of miscellaneous writings. Hebrews (written about 95) presents one early Christian community's understanding of Jesus' life and ministry as the ultimate fulfillment of various tenets of Judaism – Jesus as sacrifice, prophet, priest, etc. James (about 90) emphasizes the importance of works and deeds that are consistent with faith claims of Jesus' followers. 1, 2 and 3 John (90-100) deal with doctrinal disputes that arose in the community for whom the gospel of John was written. 1 Peter (85-100), 2 Peter (about 100-150) and Jude (130-140) were written for early Christians who were being persecuted and/or were dealing with what their writers considered false teachings in their communities.

Perhaps the New Testament writing about which the greatest controversy exists is the last book, The Revelation of St John, or simply Revelation (singular). While there is agreement that it was probably written about 95-100 for Christians who were being persecuted by Emperor Domitian (ruled 81-96) and the Roman government, diverse opinions abound about many other matters. The most thorough historical studies suggest that the writer, John of Patmos (unless the author is anonymous), is not to be identified with any John in the New Testament narrative or the writers of the gospel of John, or of 1, 2 and 3 John, but rather a later Christian named John, who apparently resided on the island of Patmos off the coast of Asia

Minor.

Revelation is a translation of the Greek *apokalypsis* – "that which is revealed". But what is being revealed? Revelation was obviously written in a coded and symbolic language, so that it was understandable only to those who knew the key to the code – early Christians who were being persecuted – and not to those who were being criticized and castigated in its writings – the Roman government and its agents. Examples of the symbolism include references to Rome as *Babylon* and to the caesars as *monster beasts*. For centuries biblical scholars have debated whether the language contains specific encoded meanings for times future to its writing. Those church bodies which hold that future meanings were intended have derived doctrines such as premillennialism, postmillennialism and amillennialism from those interpretations. The conclusions of the historical-critical study approach are the least speculative: Revelation was written for early Christians who were being persecuted in the Roman Empire; while it may have provided assurance and consolation to later Christians who were also being persecuted, perhaps continuing to do so even today, it contains no specific or intended meanings for times future to its writing. Irrespective of those questions, Revelation provides an appropriate bookend to the Christian narrative, complementing the Bible's origin bookend – Genesis.

One of the claims for the authority of the New Testament writings is that they were "inspired" by God, specifically by the Holy Spirit. Therefore, it is appropriate to ask whether any evidence for "special inspiration" in the writing of these documents has been discovered. The writers apparently had a sense of inspiration – importance and purpose, sometimes even of urgency – in the writing of their respective documents. The tones and emphases of their writings often suggest that they considered their writings advisory and even exhortative towards living in their particular communities as faithful

believers in God and followers of Jesus. Particularly in the gospels, the writers also used the literary device of God's directly revealing himself to and through a person – Jesus, who later came to be regarded as one person of the Holy Trinity and equal to God the Father. As will be discussed in the next chapter, it was only long after they were written that these writings came to be regarded as advisory for the empire-wide Christian Church. All the writings were set firmly in the worldviews (three-story universe, etc.) and understandings of their scattered communities in the Roman Empire. As will be noted later, they contain elements comparable to those included in contemporary religious writings that early Christians would have considered pagan. Continuing the emphases of the writings of the Hebrew Bible, they were singularly devoted to their God Yahweh, but they differed in that they regarded Jesus as the Christ, God's Messiah or anointed one anticipated by many in the Hebrew tradition. The authors were writing to deal with issues and challenges of their own times, with little or no apparent sense or awareness that they were somehow writing truths for the far or even the near future. Thus, while they may have been considered important and authoritative for their particular communities, there is no indication that these writings were composed under special circumstances, or that they were intended for any purposes other than the times and communities of their respective origins.

As was the case for the writings of the Hebrew Bible, the writers of the documents that came to comprise the New Testament also used the literary device of having God communicate directly with his followers. In the New Testament, God's revelation was often presented as coming through the person of Jesus, who, particularly in the gospel of John, knew rather completely and perfectly the mind and the will of God, his Father. Another mechanism was God's revealing a course of action or a correct understanding to people through dreams, as was the case for Jesus' father, Joseph, in the gospel of Matthew and for Simon Peter in the Acts of the Apostles. It might be asked whether the writers of these documents were being honest and truthful when they presented these revelations as the words and actions of God. The answer is "yes." In religious writings of the time, both pagan and Christian, it was commonplace that gods were said to speak and to reveal themselves directly to people. Those styles and literary techniques of expression were primary vehicles whereby the religious leaders (Christian, Jewish, and pagan) gave authority to their understanding of the desire or command of their deity for their religious community. Being stated as *the word of god*, these teachings and religious practices were given authority and respect in the community. Thus, the writers of the Christian documents were not being dishonest. They were simply using styles and literary techniques typical of religious writings of the day.

Despite knowing those details about ancient religious writing practices, it is not uncommon for Christian adherents to believe and to claim that their deity *really did speak* the words attributed to God in the Scriptures, because their deity is the *true* god – the *real* God – and therefore was really capable of communications of that sort. Pagan gods, on the other hand, were *false* and *nonexistent* and, therefore, incapable of such communication. While such claims and beliefs give Christians a deep sense of confidence and certitude in the validity and authority of their religion, such views completely fail to take into account the nature of religious writings at the times when these documents were written.

Because the central character is Jesus, whom his followers claimed to be the Christ, the New Testament writings will be examined carefully to determine what they say about him and how those writings should be interpreted in light of the worldview at the time in which they were written.

His name was Jesus – or if his town of origin is included – Jesus of Nazareth. He was born a Jew, he lived all his life according to Jewish religious beliefs and practices, and he was crucified and died as a member of the Jewish faith. His name is defined functionally in Matthew 1:21, "and you are to name him 'Jesus,' for he will save his people from their sins" (NRSV). The name *Jesus* is related to the Aramaic *Jeshua* and the Hebrew *Joshua* which mean "Yahweh is salvation."

Jesus (of Nazareth) was his *name*, not Jesus *Christ* or *Christ* Jesus. Any designations other than Jesus (of Nazareth) were *titles* that were ascribed to him by his followers; modern day parallel associations of titles and surnames would be *President* Bush, *Governor* Easley, *Pastor* Smith, or *Doctor* Jones; the designations *president*, *governor*, *pastor*, and *doctor* are *titles* that have been affixed to the surname, *not names* in themselves. These titles will now be more closely examined: 1. Messiah (Hebrew) or Christ (Greek); 2. Son of God; 3. Son of Man; 4. Lord; 5. Master; 6. Teacher; 7. Rabbi; 8. Son of David.

The most prominent title applied to Jesus was *Christ* or *The Christ*. The documents that became books of the New Testament were written in Greek and therefore used *christos*, whereas the Old Testament books, written in Hebrew, had used *messiah*. Because both meant "anointed" or "the anointed one," the titles Christ and Messiah will be used interchangeably in the following discussion. It should be noted that the original Hebrew and Greek languages in which the Old and New Testament documents were written consisted only of what we today would call capital letters; thus, there was no distinction between what we today refer to as proper nouns (capitalized) and common nouns (noncapitalized).

The rite of anointing was practiced in many nations and cultures of the Ancient Near East. Among the Hebrews, the title *messiah* referred to someone whom Yahweh had anointed or designated for an office. Kings, priests and prophets were anointed, which symbolized that they were set apart by the application of oil to their heads for their specific offices in the community. Because of their having been anointed, all of these were messiahs – anointed ones of God. Isaiah 45:1 even denotes Cyrus, the pagan king of Persia, as being Yahweh's anointed one (*messiah* in Hebrew), because of the role that Cyrus played in allowing the Israelites to return to their homeland after the Babylonian captivity. Thus, it is important to note that, although the title Messiah was appropriately applied to many people of various offices in the Hebrew Bible, the title Christ was uniquely applied to Jesus by his followers in the New Testament writings.

Through the time of the later Old Testament period, various notions and expectations had become associated with The Messiah. Among the most prominent was the belief and fervent hope that The Messiah would have the power and authority to overthrow the hated Roman government and to restore the Israelite kingdom to its former greatness at the times of King David and of King Solomon in the distant past. According to Acts 1:6, after his crucifixion and just before his ascension, Jesus was asked by his disciples, "Lord, is this the time when you will restore the kingdom to Israel?" (NRSV). This suggests that even some of Jesus' disciples, after spending his entire ministry with him, may still have harbored those expectations of him.

Given the teachings and actions of Jesus' life and ministry as presented in the gospels, it might be asked why the great majority of Jews did not accept Jesus as The Messiah. Contemporary nonbiblical writings relate that, in the years prior to Jesus' life, many Hebrews had either claimed to be or were thought by their followers to be The Messiah. All of them had been captured by the Romans and executed and therefore had been proven to be frauds. Jesus' fate turned out to be very much the same: he was captured and executed by the Romans as a political criminal. In addition, the Jewish Messianic expectations excluded any possibility that The Messiah could be a convicted criminal and executed by the most shameful of deaths – crucifixion. Such a death meant that a man was accursed, and The Messiah surely could not have been an accursed man. Nevertheless, Jesus' followers during his lifetime and after his death regarded him to be the promised Hebrew Messiah and therefore applied that title to him.

A second title applied to Jesus was *Son of God*. Equivalent titles were *Son of the Blessed One*, *Son of the Most High*, and *God's Son*. Many people who hear *Son of God* tend to think that *Son of God* equals *God*. However, such was not the case in biblical times. Saintly humans were regarded as sons and daughters of God, not because they were God, but because they seemed to have a special relationship with God and/or their lives were deemed to be clear examples of obedience to God's laws.

Perhaps even more influential to people's thinking about sons of gods was their experience as subjects in Roman society. In the Imperial Roman Cult, emperors were designated as "gods" by the Roman Senate and subsequently worshiped. Statues of emperors were erected to be adored and worshiped. During the latter half of Jesus' life, when Tiberius (ruled 14-37) was emperor, the silver Roman *denar* coin contained the inscription: "Tiberius Caesar, son of the divine Augustus." Augustus (ruled 27 BCE - 14 CE), Tiberius' father and the emperor at the time of Jesus' birth, had been declared divine by the Roman Senate after his death; therefore Emperor Tiberius was known as "son of god." The same was true for other emperors; some of the more eccentric and deluded emperors even declared themselves to be gods and demanded adoration and worship while they were still alive. On a humorous note relating to that practice, as Emperor Vespasian (ruled 69-79) recognized that he was about to die, he said to one of those attending him, "I suppose I am becoming a god." When an emperor was declared a god, it was the civil expectation that subjects of the empire revere, honor and worship him appropriately. The persecutions that early Christians experienced were often because of their refusal to worship and to offer sacrifices to emperor gods as part of the Imperial Cult.

If a deceased emperor had been declared divine and his son was the ruling emperor, the son was considered a "son of god" – but usually not a god. Nevertheless, a ruling emperor "son of god" commanded the reverence, adoration and obedience of his subjects.   When Christians committed themselves to the rule of Jesus the Christ, they were declaring that he, not the Roman emperor, was their "son of god" (*Son of God*) and the ruler of their lives.

Thus, Jesus' being declared to be the *Son of God* would have been justifiable to his followers on both grounds. As the human example of one having a special relationship with Yahweh and living most fully according to God's laws, Jesus was regarded as their Son of God. As the ruler of their religious lives, he was also their Son of God – their spiritual emperor. But the confession of these early followers of Jesus that he was Son of God was not an assertion that he was God.

A more enigmatic title of Jesus was *Son of Man*. It is peculiar because in the gospels it is used only by Jesus to refer to himself. He used it in alluding to his role as a revealer of the truths of God in his ministry, to his impending suffering and death, and to his role as judge at the end of time. While its use had no implications of Jesus' being God, it did imply that Jesus was fulfilling a special role given to him by God – he was a messiah, anointed to carry out these functions.

The titles *teacher, rabbi, master* and *lord* can be considered as a group. All were titles of courtesy and respect used in addressing one's human superiors, similar to the modern "sir." *Teacher* and *rabbi* would have been used by someone to address a person from whom one had learned truths and insights of great importance. The term *master* would have implied the right or authority of the person being addressed to command and give orders to the speaker – perhaps a slave addressing her/his master.

The term *lord* is more ambiguous. Both Greek and English have a single word for *lord*. The Greek "ὁ κύριος" (transliterated to the English *kyrios*) and the English *lord* have the same meaning – "a person who has dominion over others; a master, chief or ruler." When the Hebrew LORD (Yahweh) was translated to Greek, it was translated as *kyrios*. When the Hebrew term for God (*Adon* or *Adonai*), a slave-master or other human superior, was translated, it, too, was translated *kyrios*. The predominant use of the term *lord* in New Testament times would have implied a human superior-subject relationship. Almost only in citations of the translation of the Hebrew Bible into Greek (the Septuagint) would *lord* have referred to the Hebrew LORD (Yahweh). This appears to have been a fortuitous and convenient ambiguity, however, as Jesus' followers addressed him as *lord*. At first, it was a term of human respect; as Jesus' status grew among his followers during and after his lifetime, users may have conflated the meanings of *lord* and of LORD. Among some followers, Jesus as *lord* and Jesus as LORD became one and the same. Jesus was then *both master and God*.

Addressing Jesus as *son of David* was an affirmation of his qualifications for being The Messiah. One Hebrew expectation was that The Messiah would come from the descendants of King David, to whom Yahweh had promised in 2 Samuel 11 that his descendants would sit on the throne forever. The genealogy in Matthew 1 and references to Jesus' birth in Bethlehem, the city of David, were other evidences presented by New Testament writers to bolster their claim that Jesus was indeed The Messiah.

Another designation that exalted the

status of Jesus was identifying him with the Greek term "ὁ λογος" (transliterated "ho logos) – commonly translated into English as *the Word*. Most prominently, in an early Christian hymn in the first chapter of the gospel of John, *the Word* starts out as an impersonal entity: "the Word was with God, and the Word was God." The Word then becomes that which was spoken by God at creation, through which all created things came into existence. Later in v. 14, "the Word became flesh"; *the Word* had then become human, implying but not naming Jesus. Later in vs. 18, in some early manuscripts Jesus Christ was identified as *an only Son*, *the only Son*, and even *God*. Through this early Christian hymn, a connection, connoting equality, was established between Jesus Christ, Son of God, The Word, and God. Through this clever manipulation of Greek words the Word was God and, ultimately, Jesus was equated with God.

To summarize, although Jesus (of Nazareth) was his name, he was given many titles by his disciples and later followers. However, when those titles are examined more closely, none of them assert that he was generally regarded by his followers as God – Yahweh. Perhaps that should not be surprising. His early followers were Jews, believers who held the unassailable belief that *Yahweh alone* was God. The Apostle Paul, an extremely devout Jew, repeatedly championed Jesus as *Lord* and *Christ*, even as *The Lord Jesus Christ*, but never as *God* or *Yahweh*. Any consideration of anything or anyone else as God would most likely have been unthinkable for Paul. Later thinking that the titles *Christ, Messiah, Son of God, Son of Man, Lord, Master, Rabbi* or *Teacher* mean *God* is a result of indoctrination by subsequent Church teachings and not a result of careful study of the content of the New Testament writings.

It might then be asked: are there any instances in the New Testament writings that suggest that Jesus was ever thought of or

addressed as being *God*? Yes, there are two instances, and one of those is oblique.

The first occurs in John 20:28. According to the Johannine account, after his resurrection Jesus met with his gathered disciples behind closed doors a second time, this time including Thomas. After Thomas saw the nail prints in Jesus' hands and put his hand in Jesus' side, he proclaimed, "My Lord and my *God*." It is interesting that Thomas addressed Jesus both as *Lord* and as *God*. The first asserts Jesus' acknowledged status among his disciples as *lord* (*master*), as discussed above. The second asserts an extension – that Jesus is also *God*. This is the only time in the four gospels that Jesus is ever addressed as or is implicated as being *God*.

The second reference in Hebrews 1:8 is considerably more oblique. It cites Psalms 45:6: "But of the Son he says, 'Your throne, O God, is forever and ever...'" The writer of Hebrews was contending that Jesus' status as *The Christ* elevated him to a status above even the angels. Placing Jesus' status higher than the angels put Jesus at the level of being at or near that of *God*.

Thus, close examination of the New Testament writings reveals that, rather than being replete with references to Jesus' being *God*, there are only two scattered references that make any claims that Jesus is considered to be *God*. How then did early Christianity come to regard Jesus as being *God*, equal with *God the Father*? That development will be explored in the next chapter.

Three particular aspects of the narrative of Jesus' life and ministry that have proven most problematic for many modern Christians will now be examined more closely: Jesus' virgin birth, Jesus' resurrection, and the interpretation of Jesus' death as a sacrifice for humans' sins.

To the modern hearer who is informed about human reproductive biology, the story of the virgin birth of Jesus is incredible – illogical. From a modern biological perspective, there is simply no possibility for that event to have occurred. If it is to be accepted as a basis for religious belief in the modern world, there must be at least a reasonable basis for concluding that it really occurred in the ancient world. Events and understandings of New Testament times will now be examined for evidence of how the account of Jesus' virgin birth could have originated.

First, among nonbiblical writings of New Testament times, almost nothing is said about Jesus' life, let alone his birth or a virgin birth. Among the few writers who do mention him, Jesus was reported to be a worker of miracles and other wonders; he was not unique in that respect, however, because there were numerous accounts of many miracle and wonder workers in the world of that time.

Most Roman and Jewish writings of the time that mention Jesus at all allude to his death by crucifixion under Pontius Pilate and the claim by his followers that he appeared to them alive after his death. Some references relate that, because they thought him to be the Christ, Jesus' followers started a religion in his name, the members of which were called *Christians*. However positive his reputation was among his followers, not surprisingly, the Roman and Jewish references to Jesus generally discount the claims of his followers and/or are critical of his role in Roman and Jewish society. This latter assessment is consistent with scriptural accounts that he was rejected by Jews and their leaders and ultimately put to death by the Roman authorities. Thus, although his followers were convinced about his messiahship, other Jews and Roman subjects were not.

Because nonbiblical historical references to a virgin birth for Jesus are nonexistent, other possible origins of a virgin birth for Jesus can be explored.

It is noteworthy that only two gospels include anything about Jesus' birth: Matthew and Luke. As indicated earlier, they were written between 75 and 85, at least 80 years after Jesus' birth in about 4 BCE. A probable 40-50 year life expectancy of the time would mean that any adult writer of the gospel would have been at least two generations removed from the time of Jesus' birth. Clearly, the accounts of Jesus' birth did not originate from eye witnesses who were writers of the gospels.

The gospel of Matthew cites Jesus' birth to the Virgin Mary as the fulfillment of the Isaiah 7:14 passage: "Look, the virgin (Hebrew *almah*) shall conceive and bear a son, and they shall name him Emmanuel" (NRSV). While that was a correct citation of the Greek translation of the Old Testament (Septuagint) that the writer of Matthew used, it has long been known that a more appropriate translation of *almah* in the original Hebrew Isaiah passage was "a young woman of marriageable age," although "virgin" was also a proper but less common translation. Beyond that, Old Testament scholars long ago concluded that the Isaiah passage was referring to some near-future event within perhaps twenty years of the time of its being spoken, not to an event 700 years in the future.

An even more significant consideration concerns the concept of human reproduction in biblical times. Today it is understood that a zygote (new embryo) begins when an egg is fertilized by a sperm; except for certain factors in the egg cytoplasm, the male sperm and female egg make equal genetic contributions (23 chromosomes each) to the zygote. This pattern of equal male and female contributions is and has always been true for human reproduction.

In biblical times (and continuing until the Middle Ages and beyond) it was thought that the male was hereditarily totally responsible for the new baby. Using an analogy, when a radish seed is planted in the garden soil, it grows into a radish plant. Although the garden soil provides nurture and nutrition to the growing plant, the soil provides no hereditary contribution to the plant; if no seed is planted, no radish plant will grow in the garden. In the male-dominated society of biblical times, it was thought that the male planted the human "seed" into the woman's womb. The womb was thought to provide only nurture and nutrition, like the soil in a garden. The male contribution was thought to determine everything about the nature of the baby who developed.

This notion of human reproduction coupled with the earlier discussed ideas of emperors and kings as gods and sons of gods combined to produce an account of Jesus' birth that seems preposterous today. The idea that the young Mary should be impregnated by God (*the power of the Holy Spirit*) and give birth to the Son of the Most High (Luke 1:32; NRSV) is analogous to what was considered to be happening in human reproduction in society at that time. As noted earlier, a reigning emperor was considered a "son of god," because his deceased father, the previous emperor, had been declared a god. The emperor would be considered fully a "son of god," because his father had made the sole hereditary contribution to his origin. Similarly, Jesus would have been fully the Son of the Most High, because God ("the power of the Holy Spirit") was the sole hereditary contributor to his origin. Mary's being a virgin ("having not known a man") was necessary in the account to ensure that Jesus was the Son of God and not the seed of a human father; her virgin womb was the pure garden soil in which the seed from the Most High was sown.

The introduction to Table 8.2 lists common parallels between the stories of heroes and gods in different ancient cultures and periods, in particular illustrating the similarities between Jesus of Nazareth and Dionysus of Thebes. In order for pagan religious heroes of the time to have popular appeal, it was expected that their origin be associated with an extraordinary birth. Consequently, it was commonplace among pagan religions that religious heroes were the children of a god-father and a virgin human-mother. As indicated in the table, the pagan hero/god Dionysius of Thebes was considered to be the son of Zeus, king of the Greek gods, and Semele, the virgin princess of Thebes. The gospels of Matthew and Luke accomplished this extraordinary birth for Jesus using the vehicle of a virgin having been impregnated by "the power of the Holy Spirit."

Wondrous celestial events were often also associated with the births of ancient pagan religious heroes. Matthew accomplished this by having Jesus' extraordinary birth celestially proclaimed by the star that led the Magi to his birthplace. Luke's parallel celestial event was the angel's announcement to the shepherds and the subsequent song of the heavenly hosts.

If a new religion was to gain adherents and to become established among the various already-existing religions of New Testament times, it was necessary that it contain elements found in other popular religions with which it was competing.

Table 8.2 lists a number of parallels between the received life stories of Dionysus of Thebes and Jesus of Nazareth. Jesus' virgin birth, together with its associated celestial phenomena, was one detail that served that purpose well. While the account of Jesus' virgin birth appears so supernatural to modern readers that it seemingly could not have been included in the Jesus narrative unless it actually happened, it would hardly have raised eyebrows among the religious stories and writings of its time; it would simply have allowed Jesus' birth in the Christian story to fit in with the births of other gods/heroes of the day.

Thus, I conclude that there is no evidence that Jesus' virgin birth was a historical occurrence; rather, it was a theological construction drawn from contemporary pagan religions that served well to enable the early Christian narrative to fit in with and to compete for adherents of other religions in the Roman Empire.

A second detail of the Jesus narrative that modern educated people find perhaps

Table 8.2. Comparisons of Dionysus of Thebes and Jesus of Nazareth.

Scholars of world religion and mythology detect numerous parallels between the stories of heroes and gods from widely different cultures and periods. Tales of mortal heroes who ultimately become gods characterize the ancient traditions of Egypt, Mesopotamia, India, Greece and Rome, as well as the native cultures of Mesoamerica and North America. In comparing the common elements found in the world's heroic myths, scholars discern a number of repeated motifs that form a distinctive pattern. Although Jesus is a historical figure and Dionysus a mythic being, their received life stories reveal components of an archetypal pattern, including the hero's birth to a divine parent; his narrow escape from attempts to kill him as an infant; his "missing" formative years; his sudden appearance as a young adult manifesting miraculous gifts; his struggle with evil forces; his return to his place of origin, commonly resulting in rejection; his betrayal, suffering, death, and his resurrection to divine status, followed by the establishment of a new cult honoring his name.

Dionysus of Thebes	Jesus of Nazareth
Is son Zeus, king of the Greek gods	Is Son of God (Mark 15:39)
Is son of Semele, a virgin princess of Thebes	Is son of Mary, a virgin of Nazareth (Luke 2)
Survives an attempt by Hera to kill him as an infant	Survives an attempt by King Herod to kill him as an infant (Matt. 2)
Performs miracles to inspire faith in his divinity	Performs healings and other miracles (Mark 1-2)
Battles supernatural evil in the form of Titans	Resists Satan; exorcizes demons (Mark 1-3; Matt. 4; Luke 4)
Returns to his birthplace, where he is denied and rejected by family and former neighbors	Returns to his hometown, where he is rejected and threatened with death (Mark 6; Luke 4)
Invents wine; promotes his gift to humanity throughout the world	Transforms water into wine (John 2); makes wine the sacred beverage in communion (Mark 14)
Suffers wounding and death at the hands of the Titans	Suffers wounding and crucifixion at the hands of the Romans (Mark 15; John 19)
Descends to the underworld	Descends into the Underworld (1 Pet. 3:19; 4:6)
Rises to divine immortality, joining his father, Zeus, on Olympus	Resurrected to glory; reigns in heaven at God's right hand (Phil. 2; Acts 7:55-57)
Evangelizes the world, establishing his universal cult	Directs followers to evangelize the world (Matt. 28:19-20)
Punishes opponents who denied his divinity	Will return to pass judgment on nonbelievers (Matt. 24-25; Rev. 19-20)

Source: Harris, Stephen L., *The New Testament. A Student's Introduction*, 2002 McGraw-Hill. Reproduced with permission of the McGraw-Hill Companies.

even more incredible is his resurrection from death. Again from a modern biological perspective it is inconceivable that a person who had been dead for several days could, let alone would, come back to life again. So much decay of cells, tissues and organs would have occurred that resuscitation to life and normal function would have been impossible. Thus, if it is to be concluded that Jesus' bodily resurrection actually happened, there must be incontrovertible and convincing evidence that it occurred historically.

Close examination of the gospel narratives and of the writings of Paul show that the gospel resurrection and postresurrection vignettes are fraught with inconsistencies and questionable details (indicated below in italics), none of which are independently verifiable. The details surrounding Jesus' resurrection and its discovery by visitors to the tomb lead to divergent conclusions. The oldest manuscript of the gospel of Mark ends after Mark 16:8; after being told by *a young man dressed in white* that Jesus had been raised from death, the terrified *Mary Magdalene, Mary the mother of James, and Salome* leave the empty tomb, and the gospel ends. In the Matthew resurrection story, Jesus' resurrection is accompanied by an earthquake that is theologically suggestive of an apocalyptic, cataclysmic event, similar to events that had purportedly occurred at Jesus' death: an earthquake, the splitting of the temple curtain and the opening of tombs.

In Matthew's narrative, *an angel of the Lord* was the original reporter of Jesus' resurrection to *Mary Magdalene and the other Mary*. Further expanding the diversity of details, the gospel of Luke reports that *two men in dazzling clothes* informed *Mary Magdalene, Joanna, Mary the mother of James and the other women with them* that Jesus had risen. Finally, the gospel of John reports that *Mary Magdalene came to the tomb by herself*, found that the stone had been removed and did not enter but ran back and told Peter. Thus, the gospel accounts differ as to how many women went to the tomb and who they were; they differ on who and/or how many *angels* or *men* dressed in *white* or *dazzling* clothes related the message of Jesus' resurrection. Common to all the accounts is that an empty tomb was found, but an observed resurrection was not part of any of the resurrection stories. The gospel of Matthew (28:13) suggests that, already early on, the resurrection was discredited by doubters, who attributed the empty tomb to Jesus' followers' having removed his body from the tomb where it was originally buried.

The postresurrection appearances of Jesus as related in various New Testament writings present their own inconsistencies and challenges of credibility. Chronologically, the first written references to postresurrection appearances were those of Paul in 1 Corinthians 15 (written 54-55). He wrote to the Corinthians about "what he in turn had received," which included Jesus' appearances to Cephas (Peter), then to the twelve, then to more than five hundred brothers and sisters at one time, to James, to all the apostles, and finally to Paul himself. Concerning the latter, Paul says very little in his own writings. If 2 Corinthians 12:1-5 is a reference to his conversion experience, Paul describes it much more as a vision or mystical revelation than as a physical appearance of Jesus. The details of that reference sound nothing at all like the episode described in Acts 9 as Saul's conversion on the road to Damascus. Nevertheless, Paul's mention of the postresurrection appearances in 2 Corinthians, a writing dated 55-56, indicates that these accounts were widely circulated already at that time.

Examination of the accounts of postresurrection appearances in the gospels reveals that there are significant discrepancies between them. Significantly, *there are no postresurrection appearances of Jesus in the oldest manuscript of Mark*, the first gospel to be written (ca. 70). In Matthew (written ca. 80-85), Jesus appears only twice – to the women returning from the tomb and later to the disciples on the mountaintop in Galilee when he gave them the great commission. According to the gospel of Luke (written ca. 75-85), Jesus also appeared only twice – to the two disciples on the road to Emmaus and to his gathered disciples in Jerusalem the evening of the same day, where he ate a piece of broiled fish in order to convince them that he was not a ghost. The gospel of John (written ca. 90-100) narrates appearances to Mary Magdalene, to his disciples without Thomas, to his disciples with Thomas a week later, and later to his disciples at the Sea of Tiberias (Galilee). As with the visits to the tomb on resurrection morning, there is some overlap in the accounts between postresurrection appearances, but there are more differences than there are identical details between them. It is also worth noting that in Jesus' postresurrection appearances he is not described as being normally human. In the gospel of John, he does not enter through a door to join them in a room; he simply "appears among them," as though he materialized from thin air. These details raise further questions about whether the accounts are dealing with actual happenings. All in all, considering the impossibility of biological resuscitation of a several-day-old dead body and the absence of convincing evidence from the biblical narrative or other independent sources that Jesus' resurrection was an actual happening, it is most reasonable to conclude that Jesus' resurrection from death was not a historical event.

How, then, could something so preposterous as resurrection from death have been so readily included in the New Testament narrative? Considered from a modern perspective, the claim that Jesus had risen is so out of the ordinary that it seems that it would not, indeed could not, have been included in the Jesus story unless his resurrection had actually occurred. Possible insights as to why it came to be included in the Jesus narrative can be found again by considering other (particularly mystery) religions and religious writings of the time. Pagan religious heroes who were killed were commonly resurrected to life. As shown in Table 8.2, Dionysius of Thebes, whose virgin birth was mentioned earlier, suffered wounding and death at the hands of the Titans but was raised to divine immortality, joining his father Zeus on Mount Olympus. Among other religions (Mithraism, Isis) that historically preceded Christianity, resurrections from death of some sort were quite commonplace. The story of Jesus' resurrection from death might have had different details as it was adapted and incorporated into the Jesus narrative, but it was not at all unusual among contemporary pagan religions. Moreover, many of the Gentile converts to Christianity had previously been members of pagan religions that may have included resurrections. In becoming Christians they may simply have replaced the resurrection of their former deity with the resurrection of Jesus. Even if their pagan religion did not include resurrection of a hero, the concept was not alien to them.

Consideration of the remainder of Table 8.2 shows that virgin birth and resurrection are but two of a number of details of Jesus' life and ministry that are eerily similar to the Dionysius of Thebes narrative. That many of them seem unnatural and incredible to modern people may indicate that they were not historical details of either Dionysus of Thebes' or of Jesus' life. Their being included in the narrative of Jesus' life and the rise of Christianity are, however, quite understandable and to be expected. After his death in about 30, the story of Jesus' life and ministry accrued details from the larger society, including its pagan religions, and metamorphosed into what is recognized today as the Christian narrative. Had many of these features not been included, it is unlikely that Christianity would have made successful inroads in societies where older, well-established religions already included them.

The third element of the Christian narrative that will be examined more closely concerns Jesus' death by crucifixion as a sacrifice for human sins. More succinctly and explicitly stated, a central tenet of Christianity is that Jesus' shed blood on Calvary was a once-for-all-time atonement for human sins, analogous to the way that the recurring sacrifice of animals' blood atoned for the sins of the Hebrews of the Old Testament. Consideration of that Old Testament practice in the previous chapter led to the conclusion that, while the sacrifice of "life in the blood" carried great symbolic significance, nothing physical or biological was occurring to effect forgiveness of sin or sins, whatever that might mean.

To consider this notion properly, it must be reviewed and assessed in its historical context. Perhaps the pivotal historical event in the New Testament era was the destruction of Jerusalem, including the temple, in 70. With that event everything that had occurred at the temple ceased – prayer, worship *and sacrifice*. This was true for all Jews – the small minority who believed that Jesus was the Christ as well as the great majority who did not accept Jesus as the Messiah promised of old. With the destruction of the temple and the end of animal sacrifice, a serious question arose: if forgiveness of sin was received through animal sacrifice, how could people receive forgiveness when animal sacrifice was no longer possible? It was a question that *both non-Christian Jews and Christian Jews* had to answer.

The *non-Christian* Jewish understanding of sacrifice (which remains the resolution for many Jews of today) was the following: sin against people is atoned for by spiritual honesty and cleansing of the self and by commitment to do good deeds to and for people. If sin involves hurting and harming humans, then atonement for sin entails a repentance or turning away from sin and a commitment to works of righteousness that help, heal and nurture the lives of humans – if possible, those who were originally wronged, but if not them, then other humans.

A surprising discovery is that apparently many in the emerging *Christian Jewish* community also accepted that resolution – or something like it. It was noted earlier that all four gospels were written at about the time of (Mark, about 70) or a number of years after the fall of Jerusalem (Matthew, 80-85; Luke, 75-85; John, 90-100).

All of the gospels agree that Jesus' death occurred by crucifixion at the hands of the Roman authorities. Yet, when read carefully, *none* of the gospels explicitly interprets Jesus' death as a sacrifice for the sins of humans. There are a few scattered references to Jesus' giving his life as a "ransom for many" (Mark 10:45; NRSV) and Jesus' being the "Lamb of God" (John 1:29, 35; NRSV). However, even in those cases, there is no explanation or elaboration suggesting that Jesus' death was understood by the writers as a sacrifice for human sin. Rather, the gospels are replete with examples of Jesus' calling people to repentance and of his miracles, including healing, feeding, exorcisms, and the like. All of the gospels suggest that Jesus' righteous ministry was doing good deeds for others – not ones against whom he had sinned, but simply for those who needed help that he could offer.

Perhaps the writer of the gospel of Luke most explicitly paints that portrait of Jesus. Led by the Spirit of God, Jesus forges ahead in ministry, doing what he understands to be the will of God. He is undeterred by Satan or demons, by his hometown people, by his disciples, by the Jewish religious leaders and by the Roman rulers. When the Spirit of God finally leads Jesus to run afoul of the Roman authorities to the point of being executed by them, the centurion at the foot of the cross exclaims as Jesus dies, "Certainly, this man was innocent" (Luke 23:47; NRSV). The writer of Luke pictures Jesus as a person led by the Spirit of God to live a life of obedience to God and of service to humans – to death, if necessary. According to that gospel, such was the life of Jesus, and such should be the lives of Jesus' faithful followers. Similar themes can be found in the other three gospels.

Why then does the Christian Church of today for the most part continue to teach and to profess that Jesus' death was a sacrifice for sin when the gospels do not interpret it that way? There may be additional reasons, but perhaps it is mostly due to the sequence of the books in the New Testament. As noted in Table 8.1, the four gospels (and Acts, a continuation of Luke) were positioned as the first four books, probably because they introduce and narrate Jesus' life and ministry. That the Pauline writings immediately follow the gospels (and Acts) makes it "appear" that Paul is interpreting the gospels – that Paul is explaining what the gospels mean.

In fact, that perspective is not historically correct. Chronologically, the first writings of the New Testament were those of the apostle Paul, whose writings appeared between 50 and his death in about 65. When one looks at his writings, it is abundantly clear that Paul considered the blood of Jesus' crucifixion to be a sacrifice for human sin. He wrote in Romans 3:24-25: "they are now justified by his grace as a gift, through the redemption that is in Christ Jesus, whom God put forward as a *sacrifice of atonement by his blood*, effective through faith" (NRSV). While Paul's emphasis was often on humans' access to this redemption through faith, his underlying presupposition was that Jesus' death was the human sacrifice of

Jesus for the sins of all other humans. He was interpreting Jesus' death within the framework of his Jewish faith. In Paul's world, the continuing sacrifice of animals by Christian and non-Christian Jews at the temple in Jerusalem was necessary and still ongoing; Paul considered Jesus' sacrificial death to have superseded the sacrifice of animals.

But there is a serious problem with letting Paul have the final interpretive word for all of early Christianity. *All of the writings by Paul were completed before his death in 65 – which was also before the destruction of Jerusalem and the temple in 70.* Paul never knew the Jewish religious world without the temple and without sacrifice; Paul never had to deal with how the rest of his own people might receive forgiveness of sin without animal sacrifice. Although Paul was no longer alive to deal with that question, *the writers of the gospels did have to deal with it, because they all wrote after the destruction of the temple.* They apparently did not continue to regard Jesus' death as a sacrifice for sins – as is indicated by their failure to include any such explicit interpretation in their writings.

Thus, the gospel writers present the thoughts and interpretations of chronologically later Christian writers than Paul about the meaning of the life and ministry of Jesus. The consensus of those writings does not interpret Jesus' death as a sacrifice for human sins. Yet, for the most part, Christian churches of today regard the writings and interpretations of Paul as the final word on those matters. One can understand and appreciate how this view unfolded histori-cally because of the sequence of New Testament books that was chosen, but there seems to be compelling evidence to change that view. Yet, this appears to be another case in which Christian churches prefer to stick to traditional ways of interpreting and teaching doctrines rather than *committing themselves absolutely to the truth*, wherever that might lead!

Drawing on evidence provided by historical-critical studies of the New Testament documents, I found no evidence to conclude that there were events or circumstances that imbued them with inherent authority at the outset. Certainly, the writings that later became the New Testament were revered and respected by leaders of the early Christian Church as providing valuable witness to Jesus' life and ministry and counsel on how Christians should live together in community. I found *no evidences of special inspiration* in their composition that rendered them of special authority from their composition. Rather, they were quite typical religious writings of the time, utilizing literary techniques and writing styles also found in writings of pagan religions. I found no evidence that, when they were written, the writings were associated with anything that would cause them to be regarded as the "inerrant and inspired Word of God," as they are regarded by many today. Finally, I found no evidence that the writers anticipated or considered that what they were writing was to be considered authoritative for all time. I now turn to a consideration of how that exalted status evolved.

Chapter 9

From Human Writings to *sola Scriptura* Authority

In the previous two chapters I reached two primary conclusions. First, historical-critical studies have produced no evidence that the writers of those documents that came to be included in either the Old or the New Testaments were influenced by factors other than the worldview in which they lived and the use of literary styles, techniques and practices that were common to many religious writings of their respective times. Second, the inclusion in those writings of phenomena (gods speaking to humans, virgin births, resurrections, miracles, etc.) that are not part of our experience of life today can be attributed to their being common literary techniques in religious narratives and writings of the time, even though they were not actual happenings or experiences. Thus, although they are part of the biblical narrative, there is no basis for expecting that these phenomena can occur today, no matter how much faith one brings to bear or how much one might hope that they would occur.

Yet, because they are included in the biblical narrative, many today regard them as actual historical happenings in the past and, therefore, realistic possibilities and expectations for the present. Some posit a simple rule of acceptance: "If the Bible says it, that's enough; I believe it." How, it might be asked, has the Bible come to have such absolute, and seemingly unwarranted, authority in people's lives today? Why do people not apply a healthy and proper skepticism to details of the biblical narrative in the same way that they apply a healthy and proper skepticism in other domains of their lives?

Before proceeding with the formation of the New Testament canon, that process must be placed in its larger ecclesiastical and historical contexts. As noted earlier, in church parlance a *canon* refers to a standard for determining whether a teaching or practice is consistent with the accepted doctrines of a religious group. In a specific sense, that term has been applied to the official list of writings that are considered to contain the teachings of the Church. For much of Christianity, the Bible consists of the Hebrew Bible (arranged as 39 books in The Old Testament) plus a collection of 27 Christian documents (The New Testament) that were appended to it. In an earlier chapter it was noted that the final content and arrangement of the Hebrew Bible probably reached its present form near the end of the first century CE. As Christianity developed, it accepted and adopted the canon of the Hebrew Bible as it had been constituted by the leaders of Judaism. This chapter documents the process whereby early Christian writings were gathered together to form the New Testament. As will be noted toward the end of this chapter, there is still today not complete consensus within Christianity concerning which writings should be included in the Christian Bible.

As mentioned previously, when Alexander the Great had established the Greek Empire around 330 BCE, he ordered that Greek become the *lingua franca*, the official international language. When the Roman Empire supplanted the Greek Empire in the first century BCE, the Romans retained Greek as the *lingua franca*. Thus, the original documents of what became the New Testament were written in Greek. As time passed and Christianity spread throughout the Roman Empire, some or all of these documents were translated into other languages so that they could be better understood in the various local settings.

As indicated in chapter eight, all the documents in the present day New Testament were written in Greek between about 50 (1 Thessalonians) and 150 (2 Peter). No original manuscripts of any of the writings exist; the oldest available manuscripts are probably copies of the original writing, and some (probably most) may already be copies of copies of the originals. The earliest known document of any New Testament book, dating to about 125, is a small papyrus fragment of the 18th chapter of the gospel of John that was discovered in Egypt. Although originally written in Greek, it had already been translated into Coptic, the local language in that region of Egypt.

Because their respective writings occurred at scattered places around the Roman Empire, each document was likely for a time restricted to the Christian community to or for whom it was written. Probably among the first to be collected near the end of the first century were the Apostle Paul's actual writings together with the pseudonymous writings of his students to various congregations in Asia Minor. The congregations that he founded were in communication with each other; as they became aware of letters written to other congregations, they perceived that the issues dealt with in a letter to one congregation might be of interest and importance to other congregations. One book, Ephesians, may have originally been written by a student of Paul as a circular letter to a number of congregations in Asia Minor, because the earliest available copies do not included the phrase "in Ephesus," suggesting that it was not written to any particular congregation.

How was it determined which writings should be included in the New Testament canon – that list of writings to be regarded as faithful and appropriate witnesses to the early Christian faith? In the previous chapter it was noted that the present-day New Testament includes 27 documents or books. However, it was not pointed out that those 27 books were selected by early church leaders from perhaps fifty or more documents written by many early Christians in many places around the Roman Empire. As with the canonical books, in some cases the authors of these noncanonical documents are known; most noncanonical documents are anonymous – the author is unknown. Today partial or complete copies of many of the noncanonical writings are known. They had names not very different from those writings that were ultimately included in the New Testament, such as: *The Gospel of Peter*, *The Epistle of Barnabas*, *The Acts of Paul*, *The Infancy Gospel of Thomas*, *The Shepherd of Hermas*, and *The Apocalypse of Peter*.

Although the titles of many of these noncanonical writings, like the canonical books, seemed to have connections to leaders of the early Christian Church, the contents of some of them were ludicrous. For instance, *The Infancy Gospel of Thomas* purports to relate stories of how Jesus as a boy was learning to properly use his unusual powers as he was growing up. In one story, when a young playmate of Jesus disrupted pools that Jesus had made in a stream, Jesus furiously cursed the playmate, who then withered into a prematurely aged person. In a second story, when another child running through the village accidentally bumped into Jesus, Jesus struck him dead. In a third story, when one of Jesus' teachers corrected him, Jesus sent him crashing to the ground with a stroke. In a final example, the boy Jesus had profaned the Sabbath restriction against doing any work by molding a number of clay birds from wet clay. When his father confronted Jesus about his error, Jesus clapped his hands and the clay birds came to life and flew away, thereby eliminating the evidence of his misdeed. Writings containing such fanciful and incredible stories were not considered appropriate by early church leaders to be included in the canon as witnesses to a proper understanding of the faith; yet writings containing accounts of equally fanciful (from today's perspective) but more respectful acts (miracles, virgin birth and resurrection in the gospels) were included in the canon, because such extraordinary phenomena were typical components of other religious writings of the time.

On the other hand, many of those writings that early church leaders decided not to include in the New Testament contained sayings of and stories about Jesus that are also found in those writings that were included in the canon. A consideration of the totality of these writings reveals that there was a wide diversity of teachings and writings about Jesus in the different and far-flung communities of the early Christian Church. As noted in chapter eight, even among the writings that were included in the canon, the four gospels paint markedly different portraits of Jesus' life and ministry. Perhaps this was to be expected, because the spread of the Jesus narrative in the early church to the distant parts of the Roman Empire occurred by *oral transmission* – preaching, teaching and the telling of stories about Jesus. There were few checks on how the Jesus stories mutated and metamorphosed as they passed from apostles to hearers, from one hearer to another, from community to community, and from generation to generation. In order to set some boundaries on what were considered orthodox teachings and doctrines, local and regional church leaders considered it important to draw up what they considered official lists – canons – of authoritative writings.

Between about 150 and 300, various canons appeared. Many of them contained the majority but not all of the writings included in the present-day New Testament; most of them also included several to a half-dozen or more books that are not included in the present-day New Testament canon, and in different communities those *other* writings were different combinations of writings. It was not until 367, more than 330 years after Jesus' lifetime, that Bishop Athanasius of Alexandria, in a circular Easter letter to the congregations in his see, presented a list of authoritative writings that is identical to the present-day New Testament canon. However, even at that time and until well after 400, there still existed other canons that differed from the canonical list presented by Athanasius. Gradually over the next hundred years or so a consensus emerged for the adoption by the Church of the Athanasian canon.

Thus, 250-300 years passed between the writing of the last book that would be included in the New Testament (2 Peter about 150) and the emergence of any sort of consensus about which writings should be included in a Christian canon. The canonization process was a long and arduous one; it was made by popes, bishops and other regional church leaders, who used their best individual and collective judgments to determine which of the many early Christian writings merited inclusion in a canon – a list of writings that faithfully witnessed to the life and ministry of Jesus the Christ. Those writings that were included in the different canons indicated that there was a wide diversity – not unanimity or even uniformity – of understandings about Jesus. Furthermore, there is no evidence of divine intervening events that indicated which writings should be included and which should not. The canonizing decisions were rather the actions and decisions of church leaders, acting within their own communities and larger ecclesiastical jurisdictions. They used their own worldviews and best understandings of the Christian message to judge which writings to include and which ones to omit. Those leaders would have regarded their selection processes as reflecting the spirit of their communal understanding of Christianity. They surely would have considered that they were making decisions of importance about church and spiritual matters for their local and regional Christian communities, but their decision-making processes were nevertheless fully human and natural.

Concurrently with the discussions and decisions concerning the development of a New Testament canon, debate was occurring in the Church concerning the relationship between God (the Father), Jesus the Christ, and the Holy Spirit – the *Trinity*. It should be noted that the word *Trinity* is found nowhere in the Bible; rather, the content and use of the word arose in the context of this debate. Were Jesus Christ and the Holy Spirit equal with God the Father (Yahweh) and therefore to be regarded as God? Or was God (the Father) alone to be worshiped and adored as God, as Christianity's Jewish roots so strongly held, with Christ Jesus and the Holy Spirit being regarded as emanations or agents of God? This Church debate reached such a highly divisive tone within the Roman Empire that Emperor Constantine (ruled 288-337) convened a council of the whole Church at Nicea in 325 to resolve the issue for the Church.

The general movement and development of the concept of the Trinity can be discerned by a comparison of the *Apostles' Creed* (also called *Old Roman*) and the *Nicene Creed*. The *Apostles' Creed* probably originated in the second century and was apparently the first, if not the only, statement of faith used in the Christian Church before 300. The *Nicene Creed*, formulated at the Council of Nicea in 325, significantly altered and expanded what the Church claimed to be its beliefs about Jesus Christ and the Holy Spirit. An article-by-article comparison of those two creeds illustrates how the doctrines were changing.

The First Articles of the two creeds, dealing with God the Father, are essentially equivalent:

"I believe in God, the Father almighty, maker of heaven and earth." (*Apostles' Creed*)

"I believe in one God, the Father almighty, maker of heaven and earth and of all things visible and invisible." (*Nicene Creed*)

In both creeds this article appears to retain the images attributed to the monotheistic deity (Yahweh) of Judaism.

The Second Article of both creeds deals with the Lord Jesus Christ. The *Apostles' Creed* states:

"And in Jesus Christ, his only Son, our Lord:
who was conceived by the Holy Spirit, born of the virgin Mary, suffered under Pontius Pilate, was crucified, died, and was buried:
he descended into hell, the third day he rose from the dead, he ascended into heaven, and is seated on the right hand of God, the Father almighty, whence he shall come to judge the living and the dead."

By comparison and contrast, the *Nicene Creed* confesses the following about Jesus, with enhancements and additions indicated in italics:

"And in one Lord Jesus Christ, the only-begotten Son of God,
begotten of the Father before all ages,
God of God, Light of Light, very God of very God, begotten not made,
being of one substance with the Father,
through whom all things were made:
who for us men and for our salvation came down from heaven,
was incarnate by the Holy Spirit of the virgin Mary, and was made man:
who for us, too, was crucified under Pontius Pilate, suffered, and was buried:
the third day he rose according to the Scriptures, ascended into heaven, and is seated on the right hand of the Father:
he shall come again with glory to judge the living and the dead, and *his kingdom shall have no end.*"

The *Nicene Creed* thus makes more exalted and elevated claims for Jesus than the simple "who was conceived by the Holy Spirit, born of the Virgin Mary" that is found in the

Apostles' Creed and also restated in somewhat different form in the *Nicene Creed*.

In chapter eight it was concluded that Jesus' titles (Lord, Christ, Son of God) in the New Testament writings granted him elevated status as a "human" but did not equate him with God. Rather, in the totality of canonical New Testament writings, only once in the gospel of John and once in the book of Hebrews was Jesus in any sense ever considered to be God. Thus, the above findings lead to the conclusion that, at the time of the writing of the documents that became the New Testament canon and of the adoption of the *Apostles' Creed*, Jesus' status was that of a highly revered, honored and respected human. Then, for whatever reasons, between the time of the writing of those earlier documents (and the *Apostles' Creed*) and the time of the Council of Nicea, Jesus' status was elevated from Lord, Christ and Son of God (all a revered human) to Lord, Christ, Son of God *and* God (divine LORD). Perhaps this elevation of Jesus from revered humanity to worshiped divinity was possible because by 325 Christianity had been separated from Judaism long enough (since about 90) that Christianity was no longer so strongly anchored in the strict monotheism of Judaism, although many of Christianity's early writings attempted to claim that it still was.

The Third Article of both creeds considers the statuses of Holy Spirit and of the church. The *Apostle's Creed* states:

"I believe in the Holy Spirit,
the holy Christian church, the communion of saints,
the forgiveness of sins,
the resurrection of the body, and the life everlasting. Amen.

In the *Apostles' Creed*, the Holy Spirit is merely named as an object of faith, without specifying what that could mean. No special attributes or functions are enumerated.

The *Nicene Creed*, however, makes additional claims (*italicized*) not found in the *Apostles' Creed*:

And in the Holy Spirit, *the lord and giver of life,*
who proceeds from the Father and the Son:
who together with the Father and the Son is worshiped and glorified:
who spoke by the prophets.
And I believe one holy, Christian, and apostolic church.
I acknowledge one Baptism for the remission of sins,
and I look for the resurrection of the dead and the life of the age to come. Amen.

In addition to the role of speaking through prophets in both Old and New Testaments, the *Nicene Creed* then also declared the Holy Spirit to be lord (perhaps connoting LORD) and giver of life (perhaps meaning Yahweh, the Creator). The Holy Spirit then also proceeded from the Father (God) and the Son, who in the Second Article above was declared to be God. Having also been declared God, the Holy Spirit was now also to be worshiped and glorified.

The biblical case for a Triune God (Trinity) is by no means pervasive in the New Testament, and its persuasiveness rests principally on two passages. In Matthew 28:19, Jesus commanded his disciples to baptize "in the name of the Father, and of the Son and of the Holy Spirit" (NRSV). While it is true that the three titles are linked together by coordinate conjunctions in that text, there is no explicit indication that all three are God or should in any way be regarded as equal and as God. An interpretation that Father, Son and Holy Spirit are equal and that each is God can perhaps be extracted from the text, but does not necessarily follow from it.

The second passage is from 2 Corinthians 13:13: "The grace of the Lord Jesus Christ, the love of God, and the communion of the Holy Spirit be with all of you" (NRSV). As noted previously, a careful study of Paul's writings indicates that he referred to Jesus as Christ, Lord, Son of God, Son of David and other titles of honor and reverence *as a human being*. However, because of his strong traditional monotheistic, Jewish background, Paul *never* referred to the Lord Jesus Christ (or the Holy Spirit) as God. While he considered himself a servant/slave of his Lord Jesus Christ, he also considered Jesus to have been a human sent by God in order to be a sacrifice to redeem humankind. But he always made a clear distinction between Jesus Christ and God, because it would surely have been unthinkable for him, a strict monotheistic Jew, to regard anything or anyone (even his Lord Jesus Christ) as God (Yahweh)!

It is worth noting that, while the debate regarding the *Trinity* (ca. 325) was ongoing, the New Testament canon as it is constituted today did not yet exist until after 367. Rather, there were various canons circulating in different parts of the Roman Empire, many of which contained most of the documents found in the present-day New Testament. As noted above, within and among those documents that finally comprised the modern New Testament canon, the doctrine of the *Trinity* is certainly neither pervasive nor persuasive and is perhaps even tenuous. However, on the basis of extended arguments almost 300 years following the lifetime of Jesus and 150-200 years removed from the writing of the books that were included in the New Testament canon, the *Nicene Creed* was formulated by a church council and given momentous authority. Thereby, the concept of the Hebrew/Jewish strict monotheistic God was transformed into the Christian Triune God. Buttressed by the weakly Trinitarian *Apostles' Creed* and extrapolated more completely in the later strongly Trinitarian *Athanasian Creed* (not examined here, probably written in the late fifth century), the doctrine of the *Trinity* became firmly established in Christendom.

During and following the Constantine era, events unfolded that would have important consequences for later Church and scriptural authority. From its beginnings in the late first century, Christianity was a religion that was invading the pantheon of religions in the Roman Empire. Under Roman emperors prior to Constantine, Christianity had experienced various fates. Some emperors had tolerated Christianity as a benign cousin religion of Judaism, which had earlier received privileged tolerance as a non-Roman religion in the empire. Other emperors sought to rid the empire of Christianity, sometimes resorting to severe persecution in efforts to eradicate it. By the time of Constantine (ruled 288-337), the Roman Empire seemed to be starting to come apart at the seams politically, with some of the forces tearing it apart being attributable to the disparate factions of Christianity across the empire.

In his dealings with the Christianity problem, Constantine set a course that changed the fate both of the Roman Empire and of Christianity. As he was attempting to consolidate his power and become the sole emperor in 312, a fearful Constantine was entering a crucial battle against Maxentius to capture Rome. He reportedly had a vision that indicated that his armies would prevail if he placed his faith in the cross; he invoked its power and was subsequently victorious in that battle. Following that, he issued the Edict of Milan in 313, which stated that all religions would be tolerated throughout the empire, with Christianity having a favored status. Thus, Christianity went from being a suspicious and sometimes persecuted religion to one that was promoted within the empire. Over the next ten years Constantine's military endeavors continued to be successful, so that by 325 he was the sole emperor of the Roman Empire, which then included most of Europe and Asia Minor. He then moved the empire's capital from Rome to Byzantium, which he renamed Constantinople ("Constantine's city" – modern Istanbul, Turkey). In addition to taking other actions that favored the Church, Constantine in 325 convened the earlier-mentioned Council of Nicea – ostensibly to unite the disparate, contending factions of Christianity, but he probably also had the equally pragmatic goal of fostering political unity within his newly consolidated empire.

In the half century following Constantine, the fortunes of Christianity waxed and waned within the Roman Empire. Finally, in 381 Emperor Theodosius I decreed that Christianity should henceforth be the official religion of the Roman Empire. Through this action the religious influence of the Christian Church became yoked to the authority of the dominant political government. The Church thereby began its accrual of authority over the lives of people in much of Europe and Asia Minor. Linked with the governments of various rulers through the centuries, that authority would increase and hold sway for more than a thousand years, lasting many centuries after the Roman Empire had collapsed.

It is important to note that *the newly-acquired authority within Christianity lay with the Church and not with the Hebrew Bible and the collections of writings that were maturing into the New Testament canon.* The first appearance of the present-day New Testament listing (the Athanasian canon) appeared in 367 in Alexandria, Egypt, only 14 years before Christianity was declared the official religion of the Roman Empire by Theodosius I in 381. By the time that the Athanasian canon was generally accepted, many decades had passed, and the Church was exerting its religious and political authority, whether or not that authority emanated from Christianity's Scriptures.

In the late fourth century, the Roman Empire was centered in Greek-speaking Constantinople. The Christian Scriptures at that time consisted of the Septuagint (Hebrew Bible translated into Greek) and the emerging New Testament canon, the books of which had also been written in Greek. However, in the western part of the Roman Empire, Greek was rapidly being supplanted by Latin as the dominant language, including within the Western Church headquartered in Rome. In order to have the Scriptures more accessible, various attempts had been made to translate the Septuagint and the books of the emerging Christian canon into Latin, but the results were of very mixed quality and generally unsatisfactory. Finally, one year after Christianity had been declared the official religion of the Roman Empire, Pope Damasus in 382 commissioned Jerome to begin a systematic translation of the Bible into Latin. Although beginning his efforts in Rome, he was forced to leave that city and ended up settling in Bethlehem in Palestine, where he completed his work in 405. After becoming frustrated while first attempting to work from the Septuagint and earlier Latin translations from it, he then turned to using the best Hebrew manuscripts of the Hebrew Bible to produce the Old Testament in Latin. In translating the documents of the emerging New Testament canon, he also used the best available Greek manuscripts. His completed translation became known as the *Vulgate*, because the Scriptures had been translated into the *vulgar* (common) Latin of the Western Roman Empire.

Jerome began his efforts to translate the Hebrew Bible using the Septuagint, which, as noted in chapter seven, contained the non-canonical (Deuterocanonical) books. He translated those books as well and termed them *apocrypha*, noting in the prefaces to his translations that they were not included in the Hebrew canon. Over time his preface notes were omitted or ignored, and the Deuterocanonical books became included with the canonical books of the Old Testament. More than one thousand years later, in 1546 the Council of Trent declared Jerome's translation of the Bible, including the Apocrypha, to be the official Roman Catholic version of the Bible. With few modifications from Jerome's original work, it remains the version of the Bible used in Roman Catholicism today

After Jerome completed his translation, the *Vulgate* became the version of the Bible used in the Western (Latin) Church. During the course of the development of the Scriptures and doctrines of Christendom, a key principle had become established: the Church, acting through its leaders, had the authority to establish both what were to be regarded as authoritative writings (Scriptures) and how those Scriptures were to be interpreted. The Scriptures were informing the Church's decisions in determining Church doctrines and practices but were not the sole and perhaps often not even the principal determinants of them. The ultimate authority in all these matters lay with the Church, not with Scriptures. That almost no one except Church leaders both were able to read and had access to the Bible meant that the Scriptures had as much or as little authority and influence as Church leaders wanted them to have and found useful in their governing roles.

After Constantine moved the capital of the Roman Empire to Constantinople in 325, the relationship between Christendom in the East (Greek) and in the West (Latin) through the centuries was often contentious. Perennial disagreements and disputes caused the two branches to drift apart, and they often functioned nearly independently of each other. Finally, in 1054 the *Great Schism* occurred, which resulted in the western (Roman Catholic) and eastern (Orthodox) branches of Christianity permanently separating and going their independent ways. Because the events that are most relevant to scriptural authority occurred in Western Europe, where Roman Catholicism predominated, developments there will be followed more closely, beginning back at an earlier time.

By the end of the fifth century, the Roman Empire in the West had declined and was no longer strong either politically or militarily. While the decline of the Roman Empire in the West allowed greater independence and autonomy for the Roman Church, it also meant that the Church's headquarters in Rome were perennially vulnerable to invasion and destruction. Germanic barbarian tribes from the north moved freely into and around in Italy, sometimes capturing and holding Rome for periods of time. From that time on the Western (Roman) Church was concerned and often preoccupied with survival and with coexistence with the leaders of these barbarian tribes.

Over time, some of the barbarian leaders and their followers converted to Christianity, and Christianity became the established religion in their territories. The struggle then centered over who had authority over the Christianity in those domains outside of Rome and its surroundings – the Pope and the Church in Rome or the leaders of the barbarian tribes and the ones whom they appointed to lead the Christian churches in their respective domains. This sparring continued until the year 800, when on Christmas Day Pope Leo III crowned Charlemagne (Charles the Great, Karl der Große) emperor of the Holy Roman Empire. This event signified that the Pope and the Church in Rome possessed the religious validating authority for the secular rulers of the emerging Holy Roman Empire.

Prior to 800, territories in northeast and central Italy had been recaptured by Pepin, King of the Franks, and given to the pope; these territories became the Papal States. By administering the Papal States and his exercising authority to crown its emperors, the pope acquired both political and religious power and authority *vis-à-vis* the Holy Roman Empire. One likely consequence of this was that papal rule of the Roman Church came to utilize management methodologies that often reflected the pragmatism and sometimes ruthlessness of a political ruler more than the scripturally-influenced sensibilities and sensitivities of a benevolent church leader.

Although his authority was sometimes supported and buttressed by the decisions of Church councils, most often the pope claimed and exercised the Church's authority by issuing edicts and decrees that established the doctrines, practices and traditions of the Church. While this nearly absolute Church authority might seem from a modern perspective to have been unwise and unwarranted, it was in at least one sense somewhat salutary, because over time it served to contemporize Church teachings and practices. By this process the principles and wisdom of the Scriptures (as interpreted by the pope and Church leaders) and the accumulated Church traditions were continually being contemporized to the worldview of the time that each edict and decree was being formulated and pronounced. Through the centuries, the cumulative body of church doctrines, teachings and practices aggregated to become the Church's traditions. Their volume and momentum came to influence contemporary decision-making to a much greater extent than biblical teachings and principles. Also, because popes often resorted to the pragmatisms of governing the Church as a political state, many of the Church's traditions and practices came to reflect what seemed beneficial for the Church as state rather than for the Church as Church. Consequently, questionable practices became increasingly common within the Church, including some that seemed directly contrary to the Scriptures.

Probably one of the most blatant of these was the sale of indulgences – the Church's requirement of payment of money for the remission of temporal punishment for sin. By claiming and exercising the authority to determine both how much punishment for sin a person in purgatory was due to experience and how much money that person's living relatives had to pay for the remission of that punishment, the Church had access to a huge and continuing source of money. Critics of the Church perceived this practice as a crass means of raising money to support the Church's vast building projects and what they regarded as the lavish and lascivious lifestyles of its increasingly corruptible and corrupt leaders. From the perspective of the critics, it was a "sin tax" in a twofold sense. Moneys that were exacted from living persons to atone for the sins of their dead relatives and get them out of purgatory were,

in turn, used to finance the sins of the pope and other leaders of the Church.

Dissident voices were raised, criticizing these practices of the Church and its leaders. The Church's response was to expel and/or to destroy the messengers rather than to reform the Church's corrupt system and practices. Calls for reform by people such as Jan Hus (1374-1415) and Girolamo Savanarola (1452-1498) led to their being burned at the stake or executed. Isolated and localized at first, the calls for reform soon came from more people in more places. The would-be reformers also received an unexpected boon from newly developing technology, when the invention of the moveable, metal-type printing press in the middle fifteenth century gave wings to the words and voices of dissent and reform.

The most well-known of the sixteenth century voices of reform were Martin Luther (1485-1546), Ulrich Zwingli (1484-1531) and John Calvin (1509-1564). They contended that the corrupt practices that they perceived in the Roman Church (indulgences, etc.) were the consequences of the traditions component of the Church's claimed dual authority of *Church traditions and Scriptures*. They reasoned that, if traditions derived from corrupted human thinking of the pope and other Church leaders produced corrupt practices, then removing Church human-leader-derived traditions and basing Church doctrines and practices on *Scriptures alone* should result in correct Church doctrine and practices. Therefore, they proposed a *sola Scriptura* basis for Church authority in all matters of faith and life. The important consequence of that notion for all descendant denominations of the Protestant Reformation was that authority in the church had shifted from *tradition and Scriptures* to *Scriptures alone*. That decision for their respective church bodies meant that scriptural authority had been transformed from one (and likely the weaker) of two legs on which the Roman Church had stood to the only leg on which the teachings and practices of Protestant Churches were based. Thus began in Protestantism an elevation of the authority of Scriptures to a level previously unknown in Christendom.

While these reformers idealized that Scriptures alone should produce a sound and reliably authoritative basis for Church doctrine and practice, they seemed not to recognize the potential outcome of their proposal. In implementing this principle, they, human reformers of diverse backgrounds and mindsets, would have to read and to interpret the Scriptures. What each reformer apparently meant in his respective critiques of the Roman Church was that Scriptures "as interpreted by him and his followers" were the true and correct understanding of Scriptures and therefore the basis for correct church doctrines and practices. The consequences were that each of the Reformers became the *de facto* official interpreter of Scripture for his own denomination. Although each claimed to root his denomination's religious authority in Scriptures alone, not everyone who looked at the same scriptural texts reached the same conclusions concerning their interpretation and meaning.

An additional contention of the reformers was that not only Church leaders but lay members as well have the privilege and the responsibility of interpreting Scriptures. While that notion contributed to a greater sense of egalitarianism between Church leaders and lay members in Protestantism, it also created its own set of problems. Because of the ecclesiastical principle that anyone in the Church can interpret Scriptures for her- or himself, Protestantism has been characterized from the outset by perennial division and schism. This tendency has been hyperbolically characterized as follows: whenever two or three members of a Protestant denomination are gathered together to study and to interpret Scriptures, therein lies the potential formation of two or three new denominations. By contrast, Roman Catholicism remains essentially monolithic to the present day.

The official biblical canon chosen by Protestantism differed from that of Roman Catholicism. As noted earlier, by a decision of the Council of Trent in 1546, the Apocrypha (Deuterocanonical writings) were officially included in the canon of the Roman Catholic Bible. When Luther completed his translation of the Bible into German in 1534 in order that lay members as well as clergy would have access to the Scriptures in their own language, he also included the Apocrypha. However, like Jerome more than a millennium earlier, he noted that, although the apocryphal books were useful and edifying documents, they were not part of the authoritative biblical canon. From that precedent forward, official Protestant Bibles have excluded the books of the Apocrypha from their official canon (although some still contain the apocryphal writings between the Old and New Testaments). Ironically, although they are not regarded as authoritative Scriptures, two apocryphal books (Tobit and II Maccabees) were each cited on several occasions to support theological positions and/or teachings in *The Book of Concord* – the formal confessions of Lutheranism.

Another consequence of the *sola Scriptura* approach to Church authority in Protestantism was that it put a tremendous burden on Scriptures to be able to address "all issues in all matters" of faith and life. If Scriptures were "the authority" on all matters of faith and life, then they were expected to address "all issues of all times," irrespective of whether or not a current issue or question was part of human experience and of the worldview when the biblical books were written. Because of that, people searched Scriptures in order to find passages that they claimed were addressing contemporary issues. However, this often led to the citing of "proof texts" that were only tenuously, if at all, related to the contemporary issue. Yet for a while this approach seemed workable – as long as the worldview of the biblical narrative was more or less congruent with the contemporary worldview.

Over time, however, the Renaissance gave way to the Enlightenment, the commonly accepted worldview changed dramatically, and it became apparent that this simplistic approach was unworkable.

Intimations of this unworkability appeared quite early. Even as Luther and his followers continued to claim *sola Scriptura* as their guiding principle, they were busily engaged in writing documents that complemented and supplemented Scriptures – or, as they phrased it, *that were true and faithful interpretations and expositions of the Bible*. From 1529-1537 Luther and his close reformer associate, Philip Melanchthon, wrote *The Augsburg Confession*, *The Apology of the Augsburg Confession*, *The Smalcald Articles*, *Treatise on the Power and Primacy of the Pope*, *The Small Catechism* and *The Large Catechism* in order to present and to defend their theological positions. Already it was becoming apparent that *sola Scriptura* needed some help in becoming evident as truth and an authority on all matters for all times.

After Luther's and Melanchthon's deaths in 1546 and 1560, respectively, disagreement and discord continued to abound among the followers of the Lutheran reformers. There was danger of serious and irreversible division within Lutheranism. Finally, in 1577 rapprochement-minded Lutherans gathered and wrote the *Formula of Concord* (*statement of agreement*). This document together with the Apostles', Nicene and Athanasian Creeds were added to the aforementioned writings of Luther and Melanchthon and compiled in 1580 as *The Book of Concord*; formally that book is often referred to as *The Lutheran Confessions*. To the present day, Scriptures and *The Lutheran Confessions* – claimed as true and faithful expositions of the Scriptures – remain the foundational documents of traditional Lutheranism.

But even the combination of Scriptures and *The Lutheran Confessions* has not succeeded in keeping Lutheranism united. Today there are at least dozens of Lutheran denominations around the world. Each claims its own understanding of Scriptures and *The Lutheran Confessions* to be the true and correct one. The juggernaut of *sola Scriptura* continues to bedevil even the followers of the great reformer Luther!

In the foregoing I have addressed the trajectory of *sola Scriptura* in Lutheranism; it is the one with which I am most familiar because it was the denomination that spiritually formed me. Similar divisions and discords have occurred in most other daughter denominations of the Protestant Reformation. Many have their own writings analogous to *The Lutheran Confessions*. Different understandings and interpretations of Scriptures and of these definitive writings occur in these denominations as well. Over time they resolve either in schisms to form new denominations or in retention of a single denomination coupled with valiant attempts to hold the diversity together.

Amid all the tension and turmoil of the Reformation, the reformers did not, and perhaps could not have been expected to, envision the juggernaut that they were creating with their *sola Scriptura* mantra. The Roman Catholic Church approach used Scriptures to inform (even if only weakly, sometimes) Church edicts and decrees that were drawn up in a worldview contemporary to the time at which they were issued. The *sola Scriptura* approach within Protestantism implied that a correct understanding of Scripture in its original contextual setting also provided the correct understanding for the time of the later interpreter, because scriptural authority was considered timeless. To derive meaning and application for today, an interpreter must retro-view the present issue and situation through the worldview and understandings of the times when the Scriptures were written and then try to assess Scripture's relevance for the present question or issue. Through this process, the biblical worldview and the contemporary worldview of the interpreter tend to be conflated into one and the same; to do otherwise is to diminish the Scriptures' ultimate authority for all time, including life today.

This legacy of the Reformation in time resulted in the elevation of the status of the Bible to absolute authority – "the" source and norm on all matters of faith and life for the Protestant churches and their members. If the Bible is "the" authoritative source of counsel and direction for a church and its members, then much is at stake in arriving at "the" correct interpretation of what the Bible has to say. Arriving at an erroneous interpretation and understanding of Scriptures could have drastic, negative consequences for a church and its members; eternal life may hang in the balance. The expectation for biblical authority alone to provide the absolute truth had become complete – and ultimately unsustainable.

At this point I can summarize the nature and basis of religious authority in Christendom. When the dust had settled from the Reformation, the ultimate authority in Roman Catholicism still lay with the Church through its papal edicts and decrees, often supported by church councils. As these edicts and decrees were being drawn up, they were informed by the Church's previous traditions and the Scriptures – whose sole official interpreters were the Church leaders, but their authority derived primarily from their having been issued by the Church leaders and secondarily from their having been informed by or based on Scriptures.

In Protestantism, on the other hand, Scriptures alone were claimed to be the authority on all matters of faith and life. Despite the fact that church leaders and lay members (who could also interpret Scriptures in Protestantism) in different denominations interpreted Scriptures to mean different things, it was believed that relying on Scriptures alone would avoid the errors that had crept into Roman Catholicism because of the tradition component of its dual authority of tradition and Scriptures. Despite their *sola Scriptura* claims, most Protestant denominations also drew up additional documents that they claimed to be true and faithful expositions of the Bible and therefore valid documents to buttress scriptural and Church authority.

As for the biblical content, its narrative contained material that was regarded as *the word of God* for reasons discussed in the previous chapters. Because of the high esteem and increasing authority of Scriptures, biblical content was accepted at face value. Eventually, the whole of Scriptures came to be regarded as the authoritative word of God. Without detailed knowledge of the nature of religious writings and of the worldview contemporary to the time of writing of the biblical documents, there was little reason to think otherwise.

A consequence of *sola Scriptura* was the vulnerability for church doctrine and practice that it introduced. As long as Scriptures were viewed as a fixed and unchanging bedrock that could be straightforwardly interpreted, there was at least an idealized hope that authoritative truth could be found. However, if that bedrock somehow were to become unstable or even shifting sand, then many truths might be found – a very disturbing possibility for those who contended that *sola Scriptura* authority could provide "the" absolute truth about everything for all time.

As will be shown in the next chapter, the religious authority of both Roman Catholicism and Protestantism would soon be challenged by emerging movements in the wider society.

Chapter 10

Challenges to and Decline of Church and Scriptural Authority

I turn now to a consideration of those wider societal movements that began to challenge religious authority in Christendom, by first describing the settings in which they occurred and then looking at specific instances of how those struggles played out.

In Europe during the Late Middle Ages (1100-1300) human knowledge was more or less holistic and unitary. It was collectively referred to as *science* (knowledge) and was interpreted and understood, for the most part, from a humanistic perspective: humans were deemed the center of God's creation, and perfect worship consisted of living faithfully in that context. To the extent that different thought disciplines were developed, theology was considered central – "the queen of the sciences," and all other areas were in service to it. Scientific thinking and the natural sciences had not yet arisen as a differentiated domain of knowledge; many understandings of the origins and functions of the natural world were derived from the biblical narrative as it had been conditioned by centuries of Church teachings and traditions. The holistic understanding of the Judeo-Christian narrative was deemed to contain the deep religious truths of the human situation.

Within the biblical narrative, the distinction between story and history was not yet well-developed. Little thought or concern was given to whether the biblical narrative details were chronologically ordered historical persons and events or nonhistorical illustrative details of God's perceived activity in the world. Because that aggregate biblical narrative was regarded as the story of God's actions in the lives of God's people throughout history, it was considered the appropriate framework for self-understand-ing for the Christian Church – God's people of that time. Moreover, because the prevailing worldview stemmed from the Church's interpretation of Scriptures and was taught with the authority of the Church, it was generally unquestioned and accepted. The Church deemed itself the custodian of people's lives, and its members had little need, desire or ability to question the Church's authority. Using Martin Luther's earlier-mentioned characterization of a peasant's or a coal miner's faith, most church members held a simple faith perspective: "I believe whatever the Church believes."

In that societal setting two developments occurred that would impact authority in Christendom. First, a rediscovery of Aristotelian logic facilitated the blossoming of the Renaissance. Observation, critical thinking and logical analysis over time came to be regarded as the appropriate way to acquire the best possible knowledge and understanding of life and of the natural world, rather than relying on long-held societal understandings and traditions based on the authority of the Church or of highly revered individuals. While the principles of critical thinking and logical analysis of the early Greek thinkers were utilized, many of their conclusions were discarded, because they were inconsistent with the emerging contemporary worldview. New understandings were increasingly secular rather than being based on traditional Judeo-Christian teachings. It was even deemed appropriate to apply these critical and inquiring analytic techniques to religious writings and truth claims: if these were indeed valid and true, it was thought, they should stand the tests of logical, critical analyses. The further trajectory of this kind of critical thinking was leading to the development of the scientific method. In its earlier stages, however, it was more often applied to the critique of contemporary traditional teachings and understandings.

The second development was the rise of the university. These academic institutions were learning centers in which students of the natural world, in particular, used the above analytic techniques to acquire knowledge and understanding about the world around them. Although many of them were Christian or had been influenced by Christianity, their goals were to find truth and understanding – however and wherever they could find it. Because they were for the most part not under the rigid and close control of the Church, they had considerable freedom to arrive at understandings that were at variance with official Church teachings and traditions, sometimes even being completely secular. At first, this secularization occurred primarily in the natural sciences; with the later rise of modernity it permeated most other disciplines as well.

Perhaps the highest profile early conflict that arose because of the clash between understandings derived from application of the above methodology and the teachings of the Church concerned the structure and function of the solar system. From antiquity, the Church, supported by its official biblical interpretations, had held and taught that the earth was the center of the solar system – the so-called "geocentric" or Ptolemaic system. On the other hand, although over many centuries numerous people had presented evidence and then claimed that the sun was the center of the universe, it was the Polish astronomer Nicolaus Copernicus (1473-1543) who applied observations, critical analyses and mathematical understandings to formulate what came to be called the "heliocentric" or Copernican system of the universe. Many, including some within the Church, were convinced of the correctness of the Copernican understanding. Although Copernicus was a Church official and his heliocentric model contradicted the Church's

official teachings of a geocentric solar system, his post at Warmia, Poland was geographically a long way from Rome; therefore, his work was not highly scrutinized or strongly opposed by the Church. Moreover, at that time the Roman Catholic Church was preoccupied with theological matters stemming from the Protestant Reformation (1517), which was challenging its authority as the official interpreter of Scriptures and as the leader of Western Christianity.

Through his university education, Galileo Galilei (1564-1642) became aware of and concurred with the Copernican heliocentric theory of the solar system. When he later made his own observations of the orbiting of the moons around the planet Jupiter, he became convinced of its correctness and wished to publish his results supporting a heliocentric solar system. However, as a devout Roman Catholic in Padua, Italy (much closer to Rome than Poland was), he was forbidden by the Church from doing so. While historians have suggested many subplots in the interaction between Galileo and the Church, the overriding factor does appear to have been the question of the Church's authority to suppress the dissemination by its members of ideas and understandings that contradicted official teachings of the Church, based on its sole authority to interpret Scriptures and establish doctrines.

Galileo made efforts to find accommodation with the Church. Convinced that the Church's official teaching of a geocentric solar system was incorrect, he proposed that the Church's authority was appropriate in spiritual and theological matters but that it should concede authority and accede to the methods of the emerging field of science in matters relating to the understanding of nature. He is reported to have said something to this effect: "The Bible tells us how to go to heaven; science tells us how the heavens go." However, stung by setbacks to its authority in the Reformation, the Roman Catholic Church refused to yield, and Galileo was forbidden to publish his findings and interpretations of them.

Despite the Church's suppression of Galileo's efforts, the heliocentric solar system model was becoming more generally accepted in the larger society: the sun rather than the earth was recognized as the center of our solar system. To many people, it was becoming apparent that the official interpretations of the Bible as dictated by the Church did not always agree with the emerging understandings of nature. The official position of the Church could be in error on some matters.

The Galileo matter of the early seventeenth century was a geographically proximal problem for the Roman Catholic Church, because Galileo was one of its members and lived in Italy. However, it appears not to have created that much stir in Protestantism, although many in that movement were aware of it. Galileo's proposal of a heliocentric solar system clearly appeared to be in conflict with the view of the solar system presented in the Bible – Protestantism's absolute authority on all matters. However, most Protestant denominations were still relatively young and were deeply embroiled in debates and conflicts over theological issues more central to Christianity. But they would not be spared from involvement in it and related scientific conflicts for long.

Among those who studied natural phenomena, there was an emerging school of thought that the orderly operation of the physical and biological worlds, rather than being under the direct control of divine, mystical or even magical forces, was governed by laws inherent in nature. More and more inconsistencies were appearing between understandings derived from the religious narrative and scientific understandings based on direct observations of the surrounding world and their interpretations. Still many, perhaps even most, people who held these new scientific understandings attempted to integrate them into their religious framework, although that frame-

work was becoming more often not Trinitarian Christian but rather what later came to be known as Deism – the notion that God had instilled into the universe forces and laws at creation and then left nature to operate on its own according to those mechanical principles. That theological adaptation would later have its own problems, but early on it seemed an appropriate accommodation of the understandings of science with traditional notions of God.

The shift from acceptance of the geocentric to the heliocentric structure and function of the universe also had important theological consequences that have not often been noted and addressed. The traditional geocentric model of the time still contained many elements of the three-tiered model of the universe that had been accepted with some variations by all civilizations of the Ancient Near East. As noted previously, that model posited the bottom tier as the realm of the dead somewhere below the surface of the earth; the middle tier was the earth's surface, which was inhabited by living humans and other organisms; and the upper tier was the realm above the dome of the sky – the abode of the gods who controlled all the events that went on below the dome of the sky. The biblical concept of the Judeo-Christian God and the narrative of God's people in the world developed in that conceptual framework – God is in the heavens and rules and directs the operations and events in the world below. With acceptance of the heliocentric solar system, that traditional notion of the relationship between God and the world no longer had the same meaning. Although the understanding of the earth's place in the solar system changed, the traditional understanding of God did not. God was still conceived as being "in the heavens" and directing activities in the broader universe and on earth. In one sense, the transition from geocentric to heliocentric models of the universe resulted in the Judeo-Christian God's being left "hanging in space." That conception of "where God is" is still prevalent in many parts of Christianity and even the wider world today. A mocking caricature of that notion was expressed in 1961 by the first Russian cosmonaut, Yuri Gagarin, when he stated from space, "I don't see any god up here."

As scientific studies provided more and more instances that accorded with people's experience of living in their natural environment, the principle was accepted that a proper understanding of the physical and biological world could better be obtained through direct observation and analysis of nature rather than from interpreted views and perceptions of ancient writers with ancient worldviews. For its part, the Church steadfastly resisted these new views and understandings until forced to accept them reluctantly because of overwhelming scientific evidence and acceptance by society. Overall, such occurrences tended to erode the authority and credibility of both the Church and of the Scriptures. Moreover, it raised even larger questions: if the Church and the Scriptures could be so stubbornly in error about these matters of nature, what about its authority in pronouncing other "absolute truths" about spiritual and theological matters as well?

The critical analytic techniques that were spawned during the Renaissance were even more extensively utilized in the Enlightenment – and not only pertaining to the natural world. Traditional views in all disciplines of human learning and understanding became subject to critical study and scrutiny, including those of history and religion. Beginning already in the seventeenth and continuing through the twentieth century, biblical scholars and archeologists began to examine critically the details of the biblical narrative, using historical-critical methods of analyses. In the earlier chapters on the origins and history of the Old and New Testament writings, much information has already been presented that was derived from those methods of analyses.

Archeological and other studies were carried out to find evidence independent of the biblical narrative to substantiate the historical existence of persons, events and places mentioned in the Bible. Some were authenticated; many were not. Comparisons of biblical writings to contemporary pagan religious writings showed that they contained many elements in common: gods speaking through and directly to people, miracle workers and miracles, virgin births, resurrections, etc. Biblical scholars questioned whether and how these could have actually happened in ancient times but no longer occur today. How could these happenings be claimed to have been real, actual events in the Judeo-Christian Scriptures but only fictional events when included in pagan narratives? Biblical scholars concluded that the biblical narrative was an interwoven admixture of actual persons, events and places in history with other details that were not historical. Nonhistorical components of the biblical writings included stories, poems, songs, legends, myths and folktales that circulated within the religious communities and in the larger societies and world settings where the religious communities existed. Those nonhistorical elements were incorporated into the biblical narrative because they were part of the worldview contemporary to their writing and were accepted inclusions in all religious writings of the times.

This questioning of the historicity of the biblical writings accompanied another important change in the sociological landscape – the emerging distinction between story and history. Today, when something is labeled as history, modern readers have certain expectations. Although the writing of history always involves interpretations by its writer, today it is expected that the events, people and places in a history were actual realities; it is taken for granted that the sequence of events in the history occurred in the chronological order in which they are presented, unless the writer indicates otherwise. There are certain "rules" for writing modern history. When history is read, events that happened at an earlier time can be chronologically reconstructed.

Such was not the case when ancient stories and narratives including the biblical documents were written. In ancient times there was no strong expectation that actually occurring events necessarily be told in the order that they happened. Two examples from New Testament biblical writings illustrate this. The first is the story of Jesus' cleansing the temple. In the gospels of Matthew, Mark and Luke, this event is related as occurring within the last week or so of Jesus' life, just before his crucifixion. In the gospel of John this event is related as occurring at the beginning of Jesus' ministry, perhaps some three years before his crucifixion. Similarly, a careful study of the four gospels indicates that Jesus' last meal with his disciples (The Last Supper) occurred on the evening *of* Passover in the gospels of Matthew, Mark and Luke, but happened on the evening *before* Passover in the gospel of John. In these two examples, the gospel writers presumably are referring to the same events in the life of Jesus but relate them differently in their respective stories because of how they interpreted the theological significance of those events in their respective narratives of the Jesus story.

Thus, biblical scholars recognized that ancient religious writings (Hebrew and Christian as well as pagan) were written using practices that allowed the incorporation of actual as well as fictitious persons, actions and places; the actual events might be included in the order that they actually happened, but they could also be presented in some other order, if doing so served the purpose of the writer. What this meant, of course, was that one neither could nor should attempt to interpret these ancient writings using modern historical interpretive presuppositions and assumptions. To attempt to do so is the equivalent of trying to pull a rabbit out of a hat when no rabbit has previously been put into the hat. Even magicians cannot do that!

With these new understandings of the Bible, how was the Bible to be regarded? As to authorship, biblical scholars concluded that the biblical writings, rather than being special revelations from God, were documents that were fully human writings. To be sure, these writers were revered religious leaders who were addressing religious, societal and cultural issues with their understandings of what God's perspective and judgment were in the worldview of their respective times. Nevertheless, the writings were fully the product of human authors. The authority of the biblical writings was established when religious leaders of Judaism and Christianity made the decisions regarding which writings should be included in or excluded from the scriptural canons of both the Old and New Testaments, respectively.

As to content, how was the biblical narrative to be regarded? It was certainly not history, as history is understood today; yet it contained some historical persons and events. Using historical-critical methods of analyses, biblical scholars concluded that the biblical narrative was a mixture of historical people and events interwoven with non-historical, contemporary religious stories and ideas. As earlier noted, they designated this genre of writing as myth described as: "a traditional story whose author is unknown. It has its roots in the primitive folk-beliefs of cultures and uses the supernatural to interpret natural events and to explain a culture's view of the universe and the nature of humanity." The composite biblical narrative presents a mythical story that contains the traditional self-understandings of the Hebrew and Christian peoples. The writers of the biblical narrative express their interpretations of God's actions in the lives of these two peoples. The biblical writings present these understandings in different literary genres contemporary to the times of their writings: saga, narrative, legend, poetry, song, history, etc. They are framed in the worldviews contemporary to their times of writing. Included, of course, are the stories of actual historical Hebrews and Christians. However, the nonhistorical components in the narrative are so tightly interwoven together with the historical components that it is often impossible to distinguish the latter from the former. The contents and styles of writing reflect what were considered effective and persuasive religious writing of the time. While these forms of writing might seem arcane and perhaps even deceitful to modern readers, they were the commonly-accepted forms of religious compositions at the times of their writing.

The conclusions of historical-critical studies that the Bible is not the literal word of God, does not contain quotes of God, and is the product of human composition and writing rather than of some direct God-inspired revelation further eroded scriptural authority. This was less of a problem for Roman Catholicism, where ultimate authority lay with the Church through the edicts and pronouncements of its popes and other leaders. For Catholicism, Scriptures had always been used to inform but rarely if ever as absolute determinants of its doctrines and traditions. The changed view of Scriptures meant that the Bible's role as an informer of church traditions changed, but it did not detract greatly from the Church's authority unless it stubbornly held on to erroneous biblically-based views as it had in the earlier noted geocentric-heliocentric solar system controversy.

On the other hand, the conclusions of the historical-critical studies were devastating in Protestantism, where the Bible was considered "the sole and absolute authority (*sola Scriptura*) on all matters of faith and life." If the conclusions of historical-critical studies were correct, that which had been regarded as the rock-solid foundation for authority in Protestantism since the Reformation now appeared to be a foundation of shifting sand, perhaps even quicksand. The claims that God could do in their lives what the biblical narrative said that God had done for God's

people in ancient times were no longer a basis for credibility, trust and hope. If the accounts of miracles, virgin births and resurrections in the biblical narrative could no longer be regarded as actual historical events but were rather included as fictional components of religious stories from biblical times, then what was there left in Scriptures to depend on? If these historical-critical findings were indeed correct, it was impossible to find out or to know the truth. Biblical authority had collapsed like a "house of cards."

Through use of historical-critical methods of analysis, many (perhaps most) Protestant biblical scholars, who studied at universities and other academic institutions, came to regard the biblical narrative as mythological rather than as any sort of historical account of the origins of the Hebrew and Christian religions. By the late nineteenth and early twentieth centuries, theologians, notable among them Rudolf Bultmann in Germany, were insisting that, in order to continue to be meaningful, the Scriptures had to be *demythologized* – properly understood in the context of the worldview of their times of writing and reinterpreted for possible meaning in the context of the modern worldview.

However, for Protestant church leaders and parish pastors, the conclusions of the historical-critical studies were more than an inconvenient truth. This stemmed from the fact that, although university professors and seminary academicians were insulated and often isolated from the laity in Protestantism, church leaders and pastors were not. By the 1800s the authority of *sola Scriptura* was well established and accepted as the preeminent guiding principle in Protestantism. Moreover, since the Reformation, more and more church members were literate, and the Bible was becoming available in lay people's various languages. The "priesthood of all believers" principle of the Reformation meant that all members of the Church could and should have access to the Bible, because the biblical content was considered transparent and therefore could be read and understood in a straightforward manner not only by Church leaders and clergy but also by lay members. Lay people were encouraged and conditioned to read the Bible in much the same way that they read history in their schools – that is, to interpret and to understand its content quite literally and at face value; it meant what the common use of its words appeared to say. If Genesis said that God created the earth and all creatures in seven days, that is what it meant. If the Bible said that God spoke to Abraham, that is what it meant. If something in the text was identified as God's word, that is what it meant.

For Protestant church leaders and pastors at that time to embrace or to even allow questions about the veracity of the Bible would have been extremely problematic. While some disputed the findings of the historical-critical studies, many recognized their validity. Yet they took little or no action to modify church worship practices and church teachings accordingly, even to the present day. Several examples can be cited. When the lectionary readings are read during Lutheran worship, the Bible is referred to as "God's word" or "the word of the Lord." When the biblical narrative is referenced, it is referred to as "the *history* of God's actions with God's people." When the *Apostles'* and *Nicene Creeds* are confessed, their tenets are recited as recounting historical actions of the Trinity, including the virgin birth, the descent into hell, the resurrection of Jesus and his ascension into heaven. The implication of these worship practices is that a straight-forward correspondence of the meanings and beliefs of the early Christian Church and of the Church today is entirely appropriate and proper, in spite of the known marked differences in meaning and context between the biblical and present-day worldviews.

In congregational Bible studies also, there is little effort to *demythologize* the biblical narrative. Few pastors have the courage to present the results of the historical-critical methods of study that would enable laypersons to acquire more informed and enlightened views of the biblical writings. This is so in spite of the fact that, during their seminary training, most pastors-in-training have studied and have become familiar with these findings. Rarely, if ever, are laypersons encouraged to critically examine and to carefully scrutinize the biblical narrative or the Church's teachings regarding that narrative, in order to determine whether its contents measure up to the standards of modern history. Rather today, because of nearly five centuries of accrual of biblical authority following the adoption of the *sola Scriptura* mantra, many laypeople consider it tantamount to blasphemy for anyone, including their pastors, to suggest anything other than a straight-forward, *literal* interpretation of the Bible. In effect, Biblical authority has become an almost insurmountable obstacle to seeking and to acquiring truth. Few pastors and church leaders are willing to risk the alienation from and rejection by their congregational members that are likely to result from pursuing such studies.

If the changes in church liturgy and teaching necessitated by the results of the historical-critical biblical studies were troublesome for clergy in the nineteenth and early twentieth centuries, they are even more problematic today, the beginning of the twenty-first century. As a result, there is today an uneasy, sometimes nearly hostile, relationship between university and seminary biblical scholars and parish clergy. Biblical scholars recognize the need and importance of presenting the results of historical-critical studies in order for Christians today to have more open and enlightened views of their religious roots, and they consider it the responsibility of pastors as congregational leaders to implement these educational reforms. Pastors, on the other hand, recognizing the risks of such activities, are likely to regard college and seminary biblical scholars and professors as "not understanding life in the parish." The result is that in congregational life most of the findings of historical-critical studies that are at all threatening to traditional teachings and liturgies continue to be inconvenient truths and are, therefore, ignored or even denied.

Not unrelated to the way that the church has dealt with troublesome discoveries about biblical writings is the way that it deals with many new discoveries in the scientific world. If new findings are at variance with views based on traditional biblical understandings, the church is likely to seek how the new scientific understanding can be molded to be consistent with traditional church views. These efforts are the modern form of the branch of theology known as apologetics – the defense or proof of traditional Christian teachings. The presupposition of these efforts is that the church's traditional teachings are correct and that any new piece of information or new understanding can be accepted only if it can be harmonized and accommodated with the traditional, authoritative Christian teaching. Members are admonished that the Church has to exist "in" the world but that it should not be "of" the world, meaning that members should not allow themselves to be influenced or persuaded by any modern knowledge that conflicts with official Church teachings and doctrines. Unfortunately, apologetics has more often been concerned with a defense of traditional church practices and teachings rather than with discovering truth about the modern world, especially if that means changing traditional Christianity's practices or teachings. When viewed retrospectively from some time in the future, these efforts will prove to have been impediments to the relevance of the Church's teachings and practices in the modern world.

The foregoing discussion has shown how knowledge acquired from historical-critical studies of the Bible weakened the authority of both Scriptures and the Church; but more challenges were to come. Drawing on an analogy from boxing, if the results of biblical analyses were body blows to scriptural authority, another event occurred that many deemed a knockout punch to scriptural authority – the publication of *The Origin of Species* by Charles Darwin in 1859.

By the nineteenth century science had accumulated a comprehensive body of knowledge that transformed the understanding of the natural world. The orderly operation of nature, rather than being the direct actions of God, was understood to be attributable to laws inherent in nature. Paleontological and geological studies provided physical evidence that the earth was much older than the 6,000+ years posited by the biblically-derived Ussher chronology. Fossils from different rock strata demonstrated that living forms had changed over hundreds of millions of years and that species were not fixed "kinds," as had been supposed from the Genesis creation account.

Drawing on the above knowledge and informed by his own learning as a naturalist on round-the-world travels of the *HMS Beagle*, Darwin proposed his theory that all species of plants and animals had arisen through a natural evolutionary process. Natural selection, acting on subtle differences between individuals in populations, was responsible for adapting populations of species to their specific environments. Small adaptive changes accrued during the course of millions of years of earth's history, and the accumulation of these adaptive differences resulted in the emergence of all living species.

Not only did this theory not conform to the biblical creation story or to the age of the earth that had been deduced from the Genesis narrative, it seemed to include no role for God at all. And if that was not bad enough, in 1871 Darwin published *The Descent of Man*, in which he contended that humans had arisen from prehuman animals through that same evolutionary process. The crown of creation that the biblical narrative described as being created "in the image of God" had been demoted to a mere animal – and perhaps a rather brutish one at that.

Because of the impact of Darwin's work and of the historical-critical conclusions, by the 1880s the authority of the Bible for many educated people seemed on the verge of being totally discredited. For Christians, especially Protestants who depended on the absolute authority of the Bible in all matters of faith and life, that outcome was untenable and completely intolerable. Over the next thirty years, various reactionary developments occurred among those who felt it necessary to assert and to uphold the authority of the Bible; if the Bible were the sole source and norm for Christian faith and life, the authority and veracity of its contents needed to be unequivocally established, whatever it might take to do that. Some decided to assert that the results of historical-critical methods of study were invalid; others asserted that the then-well-established *sola Scriptura* authority superseded and trumped any other authority – especially scientific authority. These groups simply ignored most results of the historical-critical methods of study.

A culminating resolution of those wishing to maintain absolute authority for the Bible occurred around 1910. A group of North American Protestants agreed that certain absolute and uncompromisable "fundamentals" of Christianity would and should be maintained: 1) the total inerrancy of the Bible, 2) Christ's virgin birth, 3) Christ's substitutionary atonement, 4) Christ's bodily resurrection, and 5) Christ's second coming. The first fundamental asserted that everything that a literal reading of the Scriptures said was to be regarded as absolute and irrefutable truth. The second and fourth asserted that the Jesus' virgin birth and resurrection were historical events. The third asserted that Jesus' death was a sacrifice for human sins but superior to Old Testament sacrifice because Jesus as God was a divine lamb. Finally, the fifth fundamental asserted that, as described in the gospels, Christ will return to judge all humans and to consign them to heaven or to eternal punishment.

While it had had an approximately thirty-year gestational period, the formal birth of American Protestant fundamentalism was set in concrete with this event. For that group of Christians, human fiat had elevated those early human writings to the absolutely authoritative Word of God that was to be interpreted literally. What had started at the Protestant Reformation as a trend toward greater biblical authority – relying on *sola Scriptura* – had now come full circle: Scriptures now had been vested with complete and absolute "literal" authority. Even today, these "fundamentals" remain central to many Christian denominational understandings.

The significance of declaring the total inerrancy of the Bible can hardly be overstated. In effect, it attempted to "historicize" the entire contents of the Scriptures – declared everything to be historical occurrences whether or not they actually occurred. While it appeared to establish those things that its declarers most desired, it also historicized elements that are patently absurd, such as talking snakes (Genesis 3:1, 4) and talking donkeys (Numbers 22:28). The present-day fundamentalistic approach to interpreting the Bible has been caricatured facetiously as follows: "for fundamentalists, the Bible has the authority to tell God what he has or has not done and what he can and cannot do."

While fundamentalism is fully subscribed to by many conservative and evangelical denominations, many of its tenets appear in so-called mainline denominations as well. My own formative heritage – Lutheranism – subscribes to Christ's virgin birth, substitutionary atonement, Christ's bodily resurrection and Christ's second coming. In discussing these topics, pastors and church leaders "dance around" literal interpretations, but few are willing to acknowledge outright that these and other elements of the New Testament narrative (Jesus' miracles, angels, Jesus' ascension, heaven, hell) were symbolic or metaphoric, or were simply characteristic inclusions in religious writings of the times. While some in Lutheranism disavow total inerrancy of the Bible, others fully subscribe to it.

When a person is ordained as a pastor in the Evangelical Lutheran Church in America (ELCA), he or she pledges to faithfully preach the gospel of the Church that "confesses that the Holy Scriptures are the Word of God and are the norm of its faith and life." The pledge continues: "We accept, teach, and confess *the Apostles', the Nicene,* and *the Athanasian Creeds.* We also acknowledge the *Lutheran Confessions* as true witnesses and faithful expositions of the Holy Scriptures." Thus, the authority of the Lutheran Church derives from its faithful preaching of the gospel – the Word of God, Holy Scriptures, the Bible – which is regarded as God's self-revelation to humans. Because the Holy Scriptures are "the Word of God," they have the implicit and inherent authority to direct the faith and life of the Lutheran Church and its members. The three Ecumenical Creeds and the Lutheran Confessions are deemed true witnesses and faithful expositions of the Bible; as such, they present and support additional doctrines and teachings of the Christian faith as understood and practiced by Lutherans.

Some Lutheran and other Protestant pastors have serious doubts about the historicity of some tenets of Christianity and may personally find the conclusions of the historical-critical approach to biblical study much more convincing. However, they are not usually free to express openly their acceptance of those findings and conclusions, because doing so would be professional suicide. The juggernaut of *sola Scriptura* in its mutated form, the inerrancy of Scripture, has so permeated much of even mainline Christianity that it wields a lethal club over the head of anyone who dares to challenge it.

I testify to that from personal experience. As a pastor of a congregation in the ELCA, I attempted to invite a more open consideration of the Scriptures. In studies of the biblical writings, I presented the traditional Lutheran understandings; however, I intentionally also raised possible questions and criticisms to those traditional understandings and introduced findings of the historical-critical studies that related to the biblical writings being studied. Some members of the congregation who had already on their own questioned the appropriateness of literal interpretations of the biblical writings welcomed those considerations as a "breath of fresh air"; others found those considerations troublesome; still others found anything other than a literal interpretation of the biblical writings to be heretical and even blasphemous. Increasingly in Lutheranism today, and perhaps in other Protestant denominations as well, there appears to be a presupposition that being based on *sola Scriptura* means being based on the literal interpretation of inerrant Scriptures. If one interprets Scriptures literally, one is considered orthodox; if not, one is presumed to be heretical.

From my perspective, that approach bodes catastrophe for Lutheran churches and other denominations that embrace that approach. Even if one embraces a general biblical authority, there are problems from the outset. From what might be considered a "technical" perspective, inerrancy of Scriptures is untenable, because even today older and better manuscripts of the biblical writings are being discovered; so even the biblical texts themselves continue to change. Moreover, when the worldview of biblical times is presupposed to be appropriate for today, serious misinterpretations of those texts result. If biblical writers presupposed a three-story universe in writing about Jesus' ascension to heaven or descent to hell, there is great difficulty in making any sense out of that depiction with the present-day view of the earth as part of our solar system. If biblical writers presupposed that males made the total hereditary contribution to a new embryo, it made sense in their worldview; but it makes absolutely no sense in the modern context of human reproduction. Informed people "know" the world in which they live, and it is not the biblical world-view.

As time passes, the biblical worldview, including the ideas of its Christian and pagan religions, becomes more quaint and irrelevant to people with the modern worldview. Already that disconnect has caused many to dismiss Christianity's relevance to the present world setting. Those who continue to embrace Christianity are forced to distort and to contort either the biblical worldview or the present worldview, or both, in attempting to find some congruence between them. The lack of congruence between the biblical and present worldviews coupled with insistence on the absolute authority of inerrant Scripture causes people to think that having faith is a "blind acceptance" of the biblical narrative and its claims, because there seems no logical or rational connection between the two. With the passage of more time, the situation will only become worse.

For whatever reasons, there seems to be a perverse relationship between a religion's having sacred writings and its inability to adapt to the changing times and worldviews of its adherents. This appears to be true not only for Christianity but also for the other great world religions that have sacred writings. At its beginning "oral" stage, a religion is pliant, flexible and adaptable. It is free to change with the passage of time in order to meet people's needs in their ever-changing life settings, including even incremental changes in worldviews. However, once the content of the religion is committed to writing, it becomes frozen or set to a fixed pattern, and the plasticity is lost. The religion loses its ability to evolve, particularly once a canon of writings is adopted that sets the boundaries and designates those writings that are "the" faithful witnesses to that religion. From that point forward in time, practice of the faith becomes a matter of interpreting the increasingly aging and ultimately ancient writings. The greater the amount of time between the writing of the documents and the time in which they are interpreted for contemporary relevance, the greater the challenge of making a connection in meaning between the two times, particularly if the passage of time is also accompanied by paradigm shifts in worldviews. This is complicated even further when a literal interpretation of the Scriptures is used in attempting to find meaning in the context of a much-changed worldview. When adherents insist on literal interpretations, fundamentalistic forms of the religion result, which can be catastrophic for society. This is especially observable in modern forms of Christian and Islamic fundamentalisms.

What is it about the adoption of a set of religious writings as an authoritative canon that causes a religion to become resistant to changing worldviews? It cannot be known for sure, of course, but one possibility seems intriguing – that it is related to the nature of written language itself. Writing involves the use of sets of symbols organized as words and sentences to conceptually represent thoughts, actions and ideas that are transcendent to the words and sentences themselves. Written language is a relatively recent addition to the set of uniquely human capacities, arising within the last ten thousand years and becoming well-developed only within the last five thousand years or so. Moreover, for most of that time only relatively few people in society – religious and governmental leaders – were literate; the vast majority of the populace could view the symbols (letters, words and sentences) and were told that those symbols meant something specific and transcendent – in some sense like their notions and ideas about their invisible and transcendent gods. This transcendent property gave written language a mysterious and mystical aura and authority that spoken language (which everyone including the least educated could do) did not possess. Remnants of that notion still persist even today, in that, rightly or wrongly, people tend to ascribe greater truth and authority to something that they have learned through reading a book than they would to the same information that they heard through oral conversation. When someone says, "But I read that …," the clear implication is that whatever was read has greater validity and authority than something that was merely heard through oral communication.

How can these sorts of fundamentalistic developments be avoided? What can be done to move away from those fundamentalisms that exist? Within Christianity, disavowing and overthrowing the *sola Scriptura* tyrant would eliminate much of the grist from the mill that produces Christian fundamentalisms. The Reformers had no way of knowing that a seemingly good short-term solution to the problems of their times would eventually mature into an excruciating curse for Christianity. Perhaps another Reformation is needed to move Protestant Christianity from its present state of being enslaved, perhaps even tortured, by the tyrant of *sola Scriptura* to a time of freedom in which it is recognized that Scriptures can be inspirational and benevolent advisors but are unbearable taskmasters.

Perhaps it is worth noting that Christian fundamentalism is a much more prevalent phenomenon in Protestantism than in Roman Catholicism. Earlier it was noted that in Roman Catholicism Scriptures inform but do not dictate Church doctrine and practice. Thus, the Scriptures are advisory but always contemporized by the pope and councils that issue the decrees and edicts of the Church. To be sure, the Roman Catholic Church on the basis of Scriptures has often resisted, sometimes vigorously, such modern notions as the heliocentric universe and biological evolution, but these and other verified modern understandings ultimately have been accommodated into Roman Catholic doctrines and teachings. In Protestantism where *sola Scriptura* prevails, accommodation of such understandings into a presumed authoritative ancient worldview occurs with much greater difficulty. One may question the desirability of the Roman Catholic hierarchy's having that magnitude of authority,

but it does appear that Roman Catholicism is much less affected by the fundamentalisms that plague Protestantism.

In the last three chapters I have looked at what historical-critical studies have concluded about how the writings of the Hebrew Bible (Christian Old Testament) and the New Testament were created. Each of the biblical documents came into existence when a human religious writer or writers addressed specific situations in their own faith communities and settings. When they wrote, they used accepted religious writing practices of their respective times and expressed their messages in the contexts of their contemporary worldviews. There is neither need nor evidence for invoking any type of supernatural intervention or infusion of divine inspiration. Because those writing styles and worldviews contained many elements (miracles, virgin births, resurrections) that are not part of people's experience today, I concluded that there is insufficient evidence that they actually occurred then. Rather, they were considered to be appropriate inclusions in religious narratives, even though they were not actual historical events. Because there is insufficient evidence that they occurred then, there is certainly no basis for me to expect those sorts of events to happen in my life today. Moreover, attempts to historicize such events become patently absurd. Prayers for things that did not and cannot happen will not make them happen – no matter how much faith and hope I might have.

I have looked at how Hebrew and Christian religious leaders selected from a wide array of religious writings those documents that they considered to witness reliably and validly to their respective faiths. These selected writings became the canons of the Hebrew Bible and the Old and New Testaments of the Christian Bible, respectively. It was the selective processes by religious leaders that gave these canons authority – not some supposed supernatural designation or infusion of divine inspiration into the writing of the documents.

The absolute authority given to Scriptures in some Christian denominations today came about through much later processes. The *sola Scriptura* principle of the sixteenth century Reformation set in motion a trajectory, particularly in Protestant denominations. The Renaissance and Enlightenment encouraged critiques of all traditional knowledge and understandings, including those of religion, history and science. The threats that the results of these types of studies posed for the authority of Scriptures led some conservative Protestants in the early twentieth century to declare certain Christian "fundamentals" to be absolutely true – including the total inerrancy of Scriptures. Thus, these fundamentalists by fiat gave Scriptures absolute, unchallengeable authority that it had not had even with *sola Scriptura*. To a greater or lesser extent, this view of the authority of Scriptures has permeated even so-called mainline Protestant denominations today. To the extent that it has permeated Christianity, it has become tyrannical and a barrier to open inquiry and consideration of Scriptures.

I began this journey of inquiry into the origins of Christianity because of my sense that my traditional Lutheran faith did not sustain me through the intense crises of my life. Already prior to these crises, I had dismissed the notion that Scriptures as interpreted in my traditional Lutheran faith were an authority on matters of science and the secular world. However, I had tried to hold on to those matters pertaining to my spirituality – faith, God, sin, salvation, prayer, heaven, hell, etc. My explorations of the histories of these matters led me to conclude that they, too, were in most instances products of the particular religious settings and worldviews of ancient times. Unlike

earlier and present Church leaders and members, I cannot ignore those many evidences derived from historical-critical studies that called into question the historicity and actuality of many elements of the biblical narrative. For me, a rather clear conclusion has emerged: those events in the biblical narrative that seem incredible because they do not happen today did not in reality happen in antiquity. Thus, to a greater or lesser extent, the "truth" of Scriptures on the "spiritual" aspects of Christianity had no more valid and reliable bases than its statements on nonspiritual matters. Above all, *there was certainly no evidence that the Holy Scriptures are the Word of God* that warranted their being an authority as "the norm of faith and life." No amount of Church assertion or insistence on the authority of Scriptures gives them a free pass from critical examination and analysis. To be considered as a valid and reliable basis for faith, tenets of belief must be congruent with and relevant to the world in which I live today.

As indicated in the foreword of this book, that Scriptures do not warrant having authority as the sole source and norm of my faith and life does not mean that they are useless for my life. Rather, it means that they do not merit the elevated status that has been given them by *sola Scriptura* and fundamentalism. As I move ahead, I shall draw on Scriptures in those cases where they have captured truths that still inform my present-day life.

In the next chapter, I want to look at how the continued trajectory of the Renaissance and Enlightenment inquiries gave rise to specific aspects of the modern worldview that further challenged the authority of Scriptures and of the Church – the origin and nature of humans and the origins and functions of religions.

Chapter 11

The Challenges of Modernity to Traditional Christianity

In looking back at and closely examining the origins of Scriptures and their accrual of authority, I have presupposed that it was valid and appropriate to do that. "Why," it might be asked, "do I not simply accept the authority of the Scriptures and the authority of the churches that claim to derive their authority from the Scriptures?" The simple answer is that our worldview continues to change. A seismic shift in worldview began with the Renaissance, reached full bloom with the Enlightenment and continues with Modernity. I will now look at some of the positive contributions that those movements have made to Western society and culture and at the impacts that those changes necessitate for Christian understandings. The paradigm shifts that affect my present interests and concerns were two-fold. The first involved a change in perception of the nature and place of humans in their larger natural setting. The second involved a change in perception of the origins and purposes of religion. The interactions between these two paradigm shifts necessitated my complete rethinking of Christianity, a process that continues today. Finally, while the fruits of the Renaissance, the Enlightenment and Modernity have greatly enriched modern living, they have in some cases overshot the mark, causing many moderns not to accept some of their positive contributions.

Through the late Middle Ages in Europe, the Roman Church (sometimes because of its associations with civil governments) had comprehensive authority over people's lives; the Church's traditions, often buttressed to a greater or lesser extent by Scriptures, determined the worldview of its members. Church authority enforced and reinforced the notion that the Church and its teachings were unchallengeable. As long as there was reasonable congruity between the Church's teachings and the world as people experienced it, there was little need to challenge the authority of the Church. However, beginning in the Renaissance and to an even greater extent in the Enlightenment and in Modernity, people began to ask whether the Church's teachings reflected and presented the true state of affairs. As noted in the previous chapter, perhaps the best-known example was Galileo's arguments with Church officials over the geocentric or heliocentric understandings of the universe. Galileo and others by careful observations had demonstrated that moons revolve around planets and that planets revolve around the sun. The eventual conclusion that the heliocentric model was correct, in contradiction to the scripturally-rooted geocentric notion, proved that both the Church and the Scriptures could not be trusted to provide accurate understandings in all matters. To an ever greater extent, people were concluding that the proper way to derive an understanding of how something functioned was to observe it carefully and to analyze the way it worked, rather than to simply take the Church's or the Bible's authority on how the world operated.

The extension of these analytical principles gave birth to modern science and the scientific method. This method of analysis arrives at the best approximation of a true understanding of physical reality by repeated testing and analyses. If an explanation repeatedly conforms to observations and survives multiple attempts of many persons in many places at many times to disprove its reliability and validity, it is considered to be a scientific principle or law – the best available truth about that phenomenon. Once a scientific principle has been established, unless and until there is ample reason to disregard it, the principle is considered to be operative now and to have been operative in the past. For example, our current understanding of our heliocentric solar system leads us to conclude that it has been organized and has functioned that way since it came into existence as a solar system; it was not a three-tiered geocentric universe at one time and then switched to a heliocentric universe, irrespective of how the ancients understood it to function. By this methodology people can construct the best possible physical worldview for orienting themselves in their world. Although people are not always conscious of the ways in which scientific information contributes to their lives, they nevertheless think and act in the context of a worldview that is informed by the truths provided by science.

Many of the first applications of the formal scientific method were used to analyze and to study physical phenomena that can be subjected to controlled conditions, and it continues to be used that way today. However, not all aspects of the natural world can be studied this way, and other approaches have been devised for the scientific study of these. One such method is historical reconstruction used in such fields as paleontology to gather information about biological evolution. In these cases the objects of study cannot be directly observed as living organisms because they have long been extinct. Rather, fossilized bones and other parts of organisms are collected, analyzed and classified according to structure. Organisms are deemed to be related if they have similar morphological features, that is, if their body structures closely resemble each other. For example, because present-day horses, donkeys and zebras are all "horse-like" animals, paleontologists

conclude that they are evolutionarily related to each other; they had a common horse-like ancestor some 50 million years ago. Additionally, if two organisms have similar morphologies but lived in very different geological times, the younger is concluded to have descended either from the earlier form or from a relative of that earlier form. Drawing again on an example from the horse family, the so-called "dawn horse," *Hyracotherium*, lived some 50 million years ago. Among its descendants are modern horses; fossils of many different transitional "horses" have been found that document the descent of the latter from the former over the intervening 50 million years.

On an even broader scale, animal body parts are said to be "homologous" (or to have "homology") if they can be shown to be evolutionarily related to each other. Thus, the front appendages of amphibians, reptiles, birds and mammals are "homologous" to each other, because they all contain the same underlying pattern of bone structure. However, the various bones in these appendages have been extensively modified through the course of evolution to become the wings of birds, the forelegs of land animals (amphibians, reptiles and mammals) and the front flippers of aquatic mammals.

In the latter half of the twentieth century, the early understandings of the evolutionary process provided by population genetics and morphological homology have been confirmed and greatly extended by information from another source – the DNA paradigm. DNA (deoxyribonucleic acid) is the genetic material that stores the information which programs the development of cells and organisms. DNA is a linear, double-stranded chemical molecule composed of an alphabet of four bases: A (adenine), G (guanine), C (cytosine) and T (thymine); this four-letter alphabet is organized into 64 three-letter words (codons), which in turn are organized into sentences; these sentences (termed genes) of varying lengths specify the manufacture and structure of all the proteins involved in all cell structures and functions. Studies of living organisms from the simplest bacteria to very complex organisms, such as oak trees and humans, have shown that virtually all biological entities utilize that same four-letter alphabet and 64-word dictionary; the few primitive entities (viruses, etc.) that do not share this system *per se* utilize a genetic system derived from it. That all living organisms utilize the same DNA paradigm for genetic information storage and function is *prima facie* evidence that they are derived from a single ancestral source. Once the DNA paradigm had arisen in ancient life, nature retained it as the "gold standard" for all subsequent living organisms

The use of the information stored in the DNA allows evolutionary biologists to trace the course of the evolution of life. Mutations are changes in the DNA in which bases (A, C, G or T) are substituted, added, deleted, or otherwise rearranged to change the sequence of bases in a gene. Using a hypothetical example from the above-mentioned horse family, a base substitution from AA*A* to AA*T* in the DNA would result in replacement of the amino acid phenylalanine by the amino acid leucine in a particular protein. If in that protein the amino acid phenylalanine was found in all horses and all donkeys but leucine was found in all zebras, evolutionary biologists would conclude that horses and donkeys are more closely related to each other than they are to zebras. Thus, each mutational difference between the DNAs of two different species represents a specific "footprint" in the evolutionary pathway of a species that can be observed and analyzed by appropriate techniques. Comparison of protein (and ultimately, gene) footprints in different species allows a determination of how similar or different the species are, of how closely they are evolutionarily related to each other. In a very real sense, these "footprints" allow scientists to trace steps back through the ancestry of organisms.

In some cases, the analyzed DNA is recovered from fossils. More commonly, DNA is recovered from present-day living species that are descendants of or relatives of fossils. The degree of similarity of two species is measured and expressed in terms of the percentage of their DNA that has remained the same over evolutionary time, with a measure of 100% meaning that their DNAs are identical. The difference between 100% and their degree of similarity represents the degree to which their DNAs have diverged over the course of evolutionary time due to accumulations of mutations. DNA sequences, including footprints of mutational changes in evolutionary pathways, are very similar, sometimes even identical, in morphologically similar plants and animals. Greater dissimilarity in morphology between two species is likely to be accompanied by greater dissimilarity in their DNAs. Overall, using this method of analysis to reconstruct evolutionary pathways is much like assembling a huge jigsaw puzzle; once a sufficient number of pieces have been assembled, a larger pattern emerges. Finally, when enough pieces are in place, the intricate details of the whole picture become evident.

Such a puzzle has now been largely assembled for the evolution of life on earth. While there are still missing pieces in the puzzle, the overall picture is clear. As indicated by the use of a common genetic (DNA) code, all life on earth is related. The evolutionary framework suggested by Darwin has now been verified; evolutionary biologists and population geneticists since Darwin have discovered the details of the mechanisms and processes by which evolution has occurred and continues to occur. Among scientists who study evolution there is no longer any doubt that this evolutionary process has given rise to all life forms – including human – that exist today. Evolution continues today, enabling present-day organisms to continue to adapt to their ever-changing environments and with the passage of time to produce new species.

Based on results gathered from the aforementioned kinds of scientific analyses, there is today no longer any doubt that humans arose from nonhuman ancestors through the evolutionary process. Evidence could be drawn from many sources, but here I cite one source that effectively summarizes the data.

In his book *The Third Chimpanzee*, Jared Diamond presents a summary of human biological and cultural evolution. Selected results from that book are presented here to illustrate the current consensus understanding of human evolution. Comparison of human DNA to that of our monkey and ape relatives, together with the estimates of the times when these various evolutionary lines diverged from each other, can be used to assess our relationship to other apes and monkeys. Human DNA is 98.4% identical to DNA of chimpanzees and pigmy chimpanzees (bonobos), from which we humans diverged about 6-8 million years ago (abbreviated mya). Human DNA and gorilla DNA are 97.7% identical, reflective of these ancestral lines' having diverged about 9 mya. Human DNA is 96.4% and 95% identical to orangutan and gibbon DNA, respectively; humans diverged about 12-16 and 25-30 mya, respectively, from these evolutionary relatives.

When proteins – the functional products specified by the genes – are compared, corresponding similarities are found. All 287 amino acids of α and β hemoglobin protein molecules are identical in chimps and humans. Comparison of nine other protein molecules containing a total of 1271 amino acids revealed only 5 amino acid differences between the corresponding human and chimp proteins, a difference of only 0.4 per cent. These examples provide incontrovertible evidence of our common evolutionary origin and on a larger scale are illustrative of how the evolutionary process has given rise to all past and present forms of life.

Although humans share decreasing DNA identity with morphologically less similar animals, even then, some human genes are very similar or nearly identical to genes in such simple organisms as yeasts. Usually,

these types of genes direct basic cellular functions common to all types of cells. These observations are consistent with the notion that early life was simple and that complex forms of life came into existence by continuous accrual of greater genetic complexity upon that early simple genetic framework.

While there are still pieces missing in the complex puzzle of determining just how human evolution happened over the past several million years, the major framework of that puzzle is well-documented. As they evolved, prehumans acquired genetically controlled and transmitted traits that enabled them to develop capacities for more complex mental processes; other genetic changes laid the morphological groundwork for sophisticated speech communication. As these morphological and physiological foundations emerged, humans utilized them in the development of complex behaviors and practices, including the development of language and writing that came to be called "society" and "culture." The ability of humans to transmit to their offspring adaptively important information – both genetically and culturally – facilitated the further coevolution of human biology and culture. That coevolution continues today, perhaps even at a more accelerated pace.

This scenario is very different from the biblical narrative of humans' having been separately created by God and then *placed into nature* to "subdue" and to "have dominion over" (Genesis 1:28, NRSV) the rest of creation. Rather, humans have *emerged within nature*. Humans are not of qualitatively different origin or substance from other living organisms in creation; at most, they are quantitatively different. Through the evolutionary process, humans have accumulated a greater complexity and sophistication of such traits as intelligence and communication, but such traits are not unique to humans. As Diamond documents and illustrates in his book, nearly all capacities and qualities that are considered hallmarks of humanity have rudiments and precursors in other animals.

Our having accrued more highly complex traits and capacities (especially our intellect) than the rest of nature does not give us warrant to "use" nature for our benefit by abusing it; rather, our ability to act to modify nature and to assess the consequences of our actions implies our responsibility to interact in ways that are beneficial to the rest of nature as well as to us humans. To interact abusively with nature is to jeopardize the evolutionary future of all nature, including our own human future – apart from any moral or ethical considerations.

Naysayers of evolution often cite the status of evolution as being unproven because it is "only a theory." After all, they say, even scientists talk about the "theory of evolution." This assessment stems from the fact that the term *theory* connotes a very different meaning in a scientific context than it does in everyday, street usage (similar to the difficulties caused by the differences between the literary and vernacular usages of the term *myth* discussed in earlier chapters). Scientifically, a theory is a group of general propositions used as principles of explanation for a phenomenon. The scientific method begins with the observation of a natural phenomenon. A *hypothesis* – a plausible or probable explanation – is then proposed to explain and to account for the phenomenon. That proposal is considered a "working" hypothesis as it is then subjected to multiple experimental tests to ascertain its validity and consistency with the characteristics and properties of the phenomenon. Specific experiments are designed and conducted to try to disprove the hypothesis. When multiple experiments have established facts and principles relating to the phenomenon and efforts to disprove it have failed, a working hypothesis becomes a "theory" of understanding.

On the other hand, street usage of the term *theory* more commonly connotes a proposed explanation that is conjectural, often supported by a hunch or even a guess. Street theories often stem from feelings or suspicions about an idea or a phenomenon. If a street theory were placed in the context of the scientific method, it would perhaps be equivalent to a hypothesis – a plausible explanation, but nevertheless one that has undergone no testing to establish its validity and reliability.

Thus, serious misunderstandings arise when people equate the two usages of the term *theory*. Those who summarily dismiss biological evolution because it is "only a theory" do so because of a lack of knowledge and understanding about the amount and the rigor of the scientific research that has been conducted to establish the theory of evolution. Moreover, in their everyday lives they depend on other "theories" for their understanding of the world and for their own personal well-being, as illustrated by the following two examples.

First, today biologists know that all living organisms are composed of cells. Living organisms may be composed of single cells, such as prokaryotic bacteria or eukaryotic amoebas; or they may be composed of many eukaryotic cells, such as pine trees or humans. Biologists know that all living organisms are composed of one or another type of cell. People do not doubt that organisms are composed of cells simply because biologists refer to that scientific principle as the "cell theory" of living organisms. That understanding is regarded as so true today that it is a first order assumption that is made about living organisms – they are composed of some type of cells.

Second, if moderately educated persons are asked why they or their children get a cold or throat infection, they are likely to respond that somehow, somewhere they became infected with the cold virus or a bacterium. The scientific understanding that a cold virus causes a cold or that a *Streptococcus* bacterium causes a throat infection is still referred to as the "germ theory" of disease. People do not ignore or discount its validity because it is called the "germ theory" of disease; they seek medical treatment and take necessary sanitation precautions, in some cases staking their own or their children's very lives on the truth of this "theory."

That the foregoing two well-established biological principles are still referred to as *theories* does not discount their validity or universality. They are as true and foundational as any other principles of biology. The same is true of the "theory of evolution."

But not only has our understanding of the origin of the human species changed. Current investigations are causing us to rethink what comprises individual human being. I begin this consideration by examining the modern understanding of human ontogeny – how an individual human being comes into existence

A recognized principle of modern biology is that living cells arise from living cells. Living cells do not arise from inanimate material or from dead cells. Although inanimate materials (water, minerals) and components of dead cells (sugars, fats, amino acids, vitamins) can be utilized by living cells to grow and/or to reproduce, new living cells arise only from previously existing living cells. In today's world spontaneous generation of living cells is not known to occur, and dead cells do not become living cells. A dead cell or a collection of chemicals cannot be activated by some vital force to become a living cell. Given this understanding of the nature of living cells today, how is the origin of an individual human understood today?

Normal human sexual reproduction involves two sexually mature humans – a man and a woman. Like other sexually reproducing animals, human reproduction alternates between haploid (containing 23 chromosomes) and diploid (containing 46 chromosomes) phases. In females, *living* diploid cells through the process of cell division known as meiosis and oocyte maturation produce *living* haploid cells called eggs that will contribute 23 chromosomes and virtually all the cytoplasm to the zygotes. In males, *living* diploid cells through meiosis and sperm maturation produce *living* haploid sperms that will also contribute 23 chromosomes when they fertilize eggs. When a *living* sperm fertilizes a *living* egg, it forms a *living* zygote that is diploid – it contains 46 chromosomes. The 46 chromosomes of the zygote contain the genetic informational blueprint that will direct the development of the emerging organism. The zygote divides by the process of cell division known as mitosis to produce an embryo consisting of many genetically identical cells. Yet, because of programmed differential gene expression in different groups of cells, these genetically identical cells gradually become differentiated or specialized into the many diverse tissues and organs of the developing organism. The first visually recognizable structures are groups of cells that will become the heart, the vertebral column and the eyes. After some weeks, functional muscles gradually develop that are able to move the developing legs, arms and trunk under the control of the brain and central nervous system, which have been developing concurrently. This accrual of structures and functions that will ultimately produce the fully developed baby in about 40 weeks has been termed an epigenetic process, meaning that each developmental stage is genetically programmed and builds on top of previous stages that were also genetically determined. Although the developmental stages termed embryo (fertilization to 8 weeks) and fetus (8 weeks to birth) suggest discrete steps of development similar to a stairway, human ontogeny is rather a continuous process, much more like an inclined plane.

Yet most ordinary religious thinking and speaking about human ontogeny continues to reflect a traditional Christian understanding of an individual human being. While that Christian understanding included elements from Ancient Near East and Greek thinking, it derived primarily from the description of the creation of the first human by God in Genesis 2:7:

> "Then the LORD God formed man from the dust of the ground, and breathed into his nostrils the breath of life; and the man became a living being" (NRSV).

In describing and talking about an individual human being, such terms as *body*, *soul*, and *spirit* are used. The term body usually implies the physical matter – the inanimate, albeit organized, chemical composition – that comprises the morphological makeup of a person. In a sense the body is what remains when a person dies; the idea that this is inanimate and inert is consistent with the ultimate decay of a body to "dust and ashes." According to the Genesis account, this mass of dirt formed by God became a living being (Hebrew *nepeš hayyâ*) when God breathed into its nostrils the "breath of life" – the "breath or wind of God" [(Hebrew *rûah*); Greek pneuma ($\pi\nu\varepsilon\upsilon\mu\alpha$)]. Indeed, according to the Genesis creation story, the first man, *adam* (Adam), was derived from *adamah* – the Hebrew word for ground or soil. This "breathed-into" living form has been variously translated as a *being* (NRSV) or a *soul* (King James Version).

While the term *soul* in Scripture often refers to a living being – the composite of the body and the breath of God, in ecclesiastical usage it is sometimes used in reference to that which leaves the body when a person dies. It is said that the *soul* leaves the body at death to be reunited with the body in the resurrection on the last day.

This understanding of living human being derived from the Genesis 2 creation narrative implies that something nonliving becomes living – that some kind of life force is added to physical material to bring it to life. Moreover, according to the Genesis narrative, God's creation of humans was unique: only in the creation of humans (Adam) did God specifically breathe in the breath of life. For all other living organisms God summarily spoke a creative word and they came into existence. That distinction has given rise to the notion that humans, as a separate and special creation, are somehow qualitatively different from other living species. According to this understanding, at the beginning of a human being, this life force enters inanimate material to create life that becomes a person; at death this life force leaves the human person, and the dead body is again inanimate material.

While the Genesis characterization of the origin of humans provides an idyllic picture for the biblical narrative and was an appropriate understanding for the time when it was written, it causes problems when applied to the present-day understanding of the ontogeny of human beings. When sufficient human knowledge was acquired to know that human life begins as a single cell which develops during the course of gestation into a newborn baby, the question arose: when does that developing entity become a living human being? Some argue that human life begins at fertilization – the single-celled zygote formed by the union of an egg and a sperm. Others argue that it begins at "quickening," that time at about the fourth month of gestation when the mother first senses movement of the fetus. Still others argue that it begins at about twenty-six weeks of gestation – the time at which, if it is prematurely born, the fetus can be cared for and nurtured to survive. Yet others insist that human life begins at birth or some days after birth when a baby can survive by receiving normal maternal care without technological and medical assistance.

With the Genesis human creation picture as a backdrop, the implication of these understandings of the origin of human being is that at some claimed point in development, the "spirit" or "breath" of God enters the developing cell/embryo/fetus/baby, and it becomes a human being. A person's selection of one of these points in development as the beginning of human life provides a basis for specific moral and ethical views in the present-day contraception, abortion and human cloning debates.

If one acknowledges that the above biblical understandings of the origin of humanity and of individual human being originated in worldviews that are no longer regarded as valid, can a new framework of understanding of the origin of an individual human being perhaps be derived to eliminate the above dilemmas?

Clearly, as described earlier, human development always involves *living* human cells, whether a haploid egg or a haploid sperm before fertilization, the diploid zygote, or any postzygotic diploid cell. *Living* human cells always derive from preexisting *living* human cells. No external spirit or life force is internally or externally added during ontogeny that causes something that was inanimate, prehuman or nonhuman to become human. The undifferentiated cells of early development are fully as human as the cells of the newborn baby or of the mature adult. Taking an even longer view, every human cell of every human today exists in a living continuity with the cells of all of our evolutionary ancestors.

Thinking of the origin of human being within the framework of the modern understandings of human ontogeny does not remove moral and ethical dilemmas in the contraception, abortion and cloning debates. However, looking at these issues in the light of modern understandings can eliminate constraints imposed by outmoded aspects of ancient Judeo-Christian worldviews.

A second dimension of human culture that has undergone extensive critique and revision since the Enlightenment is the modern understanding of the origins and natures of religions. The meaning of *religion* is rather clear today, but its etymology is considerably more enigmatic. The Latin *religio* included such concepts as "what attaches or retains, moral bond, anxiety of self-consciousness, scruple." Cicero said that the word religion came from *relegere* – to

read again, to reexamine carefully, to gather – and held that it meant "to carefully consider the things related to the worship of gods." Later, Lucretius, Lactancius and Tertullianus held that its root was *religare* – the bond of piety that binds to God. In its initial use for Christianity, the term *religion* extended to all forms of social demonstration in connection with the sacred. Although these are diverse strands of meaning, it is apparent that religion has something to do with tying together and giving meaning to the various facets of human experience in relationship to *Unseen Ultimate Reality* (*UUR*).

When considered from the perspective of the development of what is today called "religion," it would seem that the *religare* notion would necessarily have preceded the *relegere* understanding. The latter presumes that there are sacred writings to be read, considered and investigated for insight and guidance concerning life. Chronologically and historically, however, the composition of sacred writings for any religion that has Scriptures does not usually occur until years, perhaps even centuries, after the origin of the religion itself. In earlier chapters it was documented how this occurred for both Judaism and Christianity. As further detailed below, a religion originates when a group of people begins to formulate ideas and understandings about invisible, incomprehensible and transcendent forces and powers beyond their control (*UUR*). In many religions, rituals and practices are developed that enable their adherents to relate to this *UUR*. After that system of thoughts and practices becomes rather well-developed and the community develops or acquires a written language, sacred writings are produced by the leaders of many religions for the ritual rehearsal in worship of the principal tenets and understandings of those religions. After numerous sacred writings are produced, religious leaders collect and select from among them those that they deem appropriate witnesses to the faith and designate them as the official Scriptures of that religious group. These Scriptures perpetuate the transmission of these ideas and understandings to succeeding generations, who read, reread, examine and reexamine them in order to better understand the faith. Seen from this perspective, the *relegere* notion of religion could only have appeared some period of time after the development of the *religare* notion of religion. Thus, while both notions of religion might accurately reflect practices and understandings of a religion at any time after its development and the appearance of its Scriptures, the historical unfolding of a religion would seem to have occurred from *religare* to *relegere*.

Anthropological investigations have provided much information to expand the above implications of religion's etymology. Early human forms differed from their nonhuman ancestors in several important ways. One was their consciousness and self-consciousness – their awareness of themselves and their mortality. They came to understand that they came into existence – birth – and they ceased to exist – death. The idea and awareness of dying, of passing into nonexistence, brought anxiety and fear, so they created rituals and burial practices to enable them to deal with those negative emotions associated with the human condition.

These early humans also recognized their being situated in a mostly uncontrollable and largely incomprehensible natural setting. They deduced that beyond their bodies' abilities to sense physically, there must be much larger and much more powerful transcendent forces than they possessed. There seemed to be transcendent powers or spirits controlling the regularity of seasons and the movements of the sun, moon and stars. They reasoned that ultimate forces or spirits must exist that were somehow controlling these phenomena. It seemed reasonable that the same transcendent spirits that were controlling external nature around them were also controlling the births and deaths of humans. Those ideas and practices which arose among early humans were consolidated into

religion – understandings and rituals that tied together the disparate strands of life and the self-consciousness of the human situation with it.

As human sociological and cultural organization continued to develop greater complexity from roving nomadic bands and tribes to villages and cities, more individual self-control and social order were necessary to maintain stable community living. Laws and rules were devised; to exhort and to enforce obedience of these community expectations, consequences of obedience and disobedience were linked to the blessings and punishments by these transcendent spirits. Religion had now yoked thought patterns and rituals with ethical behavior and morality.

Early humans were simultaneously evolving in many places on earth. Because the natural setting in China was very different from those in the Congo, Peru, Borneo, Europe, Palestine or Mesopotamia, the sets of beliefs and practices that constituted the religions of these areas emerged in different forms. In each of these settings a different perception of transcendent, ultimate spirits or forces (*UUR*) developed, conditioned by the natural setting in which it arose. Buddhism developed as a very different religious system than that developed by the Incas or the Hebrews. Yet, each of these religions was functioning to enable its adherents to deal in some way with what are today termed the existential questions of human existence: Who am I? Where did I come from? Why am I here? What happens to me when I die? What are my responsibilities to other humans and to the rest of nature? Each religion fulfilled for its adherents those functions that religion as a human phenomenon evolved to fulfill; each religion was valid in the context of the worldview of its adherents.

Thus, the modern understanding is that religions arose and evolved as functional cultural and societal phenomena concomitant with the emergence of modern humans from prehuman ancestors. This notion starkly contrasts with the traditional Judeo-Christian understanding derived from the biblical narrative – namely, that Yahweh through self-revelation externally introduced first to the Hebrews and subsequently to Christians "the" true form of religion, ideally to become the religion of all humans.

I now examine the implications of combining the modern views of the origins of humans and of religions. While doing that, I will compare and contrast specific tenets of traditional Judeo-Christian understandings with their modern counterparts.

As noted earlier, the biblical narrative relates that humans were especially (and in Genesis 2, separately) created by God and placed "into" the natural setting of the Garden of Eden. According to the modern understanding, humans arose and emerged "within" nature through an evolutionary process. Until this point I have not yet considered the ultimate causes in the evolutionary process, but I shall do that later. At present I simply affirm that humans are a product of biological evolution and are inextricably integrated "within" nature, as opposed to the biblical special, separate creation and being placed "into" nature.

According to the biblical narrative, humans were created in a state of perfection, deemed to exist as such because God was incapable of creating anything with imperfection. According to the modern understanding, over long periods of evolutionary time prehumans gradually accrued the genetic modifications that facilitated the emergence of those traits and characteristics that are found in modern humans. Humans have never existed in a state of moral or physical perfection. Their ancestors had aggressive and selfish behaviors that had survival value in their prehuman condition; where necessary, through adoption of culture and religion, those behavioral patterns that were disruptive and harmful to the community were curbed, controlled and forbidden by human societal decisions.

The biblical narrative relates that humans lost their condition of perfection through disobedience of God's order not to eat of the fruit of the forbidden tree of knowledge of good and evil. This act of human disobedience has been called *The Fall*, although that term is not used in Genesis. According to the modern understanding, there was no Fall, because humans have never existed in a state of moral sinlessness and physical perfection. Rather, they continue to be influenced by residual expressions of animalistic behaviors that were adaptively functional in their prehuman state, but many of which are disruptive and destructive of communal human society.

According to the Christian rendition of the biblical narrative, the consequence of The Fall was alienation from God; that alienation could only be reversed through reconciliation accomplished by a savior – Jesus the Christ. Considered from the modern perspective, there was neither physical and moral perfection nor Fall, so there was, of course, no need of a savior – at least not as a redeemer from any sort of "fall" from perfection.

To be sure, humans do commit harmful and malicious acts against other humans and against nonhuman nature – what might traditionally be called "sins." But these wrongs are not the consequence of being descendants of fallen, originally perfect parents; rather, they are consequences of being descendants of prehuman ancestors that expressed those behaviors. In *The Third Chimpanzee*, Diamond cites two examples of genocide in gorillas and chimpanzees, both of which, like humans, exhibit *xenophobia* – a recognition/fear of and a different treatment of members of other groups of their own species. Chimpanzees have been observed to carry out planned killings, extermination of neighboring bands, wars of territorial conquest and abduction of nubile females from neighboring bands. Gorillas of one troupe have attacked a neighboring troupe, killing the adult males but sparing the adult females and adding them to their harems. That genocide and xenophobia in humans are vestigial behaviors of prehuman ancestors does not make them any less atrocious from a human moral and ethical perspective. However, understanding their origins in evolutionary biological roots rather than as a Fall from original innocence and perfection may provide some insights in helping humans deal more effectively with those problems today.

Traditional Christian views contend that the physical death of living organisms, especially humans, was a consequential punishment of all of nature by God for the human Fall. Modern understandings contend that, ever since living organisms arose, they have always come into existence and died. Death has always existed as a natural and normal component of the life cycle of biological organisms, including humans.

Consequently, I am left with key elements of traditional Judeo-Christianity — separate creation of humans by God, human moral and physical perfection, the Fall and subsequent need for a savior, Christianity as the desirable or even mandatory religion for all humans, and the origin of human death — having no validity in the context of the modern understanding of the origins of humanity and of religions. Moreover, the foregoing are only a few examples of Judeo-Christian tenets that could be examined and critiqued. Continuing to maintain traditional Christianity in the context of the modern worldview ensures a lack of meaningful connection and relevance. One simply can neither find nor create congruity between the two views. Given more time, it would seem that traditional Christianity will continue to atrophy because of its increasing irrelevance to the modern understanding of the universe and of human life within it.

In my earlier consideration of the origins of religions, I described how each religion developed in and emerged out of the context of a local geographical setting and worldview. Each society existed in a specific local setting; therefore, an emerging religion would only have functioned for the members of that community if it contained elements that enabled people to orient themselves existentially in that setting. Because the far-flung societies and cultures of the ancient world were vastly different from each other, it should not be surprising that religions also differed greatly.

Despite the diversity of religions that arose, most contained some concept of *Unseen Ultimate Reality* (*UUR*) – the notion that transcendent powers, forces, and/or spirits were in control of the natural world and of people's lives. In many, but not all, religions, *UUR* was conceptualized as a god or gods. Although most religions were polytheistic, I will address the issue in the singular. Each god was "real" in the sense that the perceived results and consequences of the activity of the god could be observed in the surrounding world, but the god itself was invisible and could not be objectively described. Because the god appeared to have power and control over everything, it became important for humans to establish an amiable and amicable relationship with the god.

For humans to think and to communicate meaningfully about something that is sensorially inaccessible, they developed the linguistic tool called a *metaphor*. Although in the present context metaphors are used in talking about gods (*UUR*s), their application is also useful in thinking about concepts in the physical world, such as subatomic forces and particles and string theory. Through a metaphor, attributes and properties are symbolically ascribed to this inaccessible entity, drawing on sensory perceptions of the physical world and/or human emotional and intellectual experiences. In using a metaphor, it is acknowledged *a priori* that the sensorially inaccessible entity cannot be comprehensively or completely described or understood and that the metaphor cannot be checked for accuracy in describing the entity to which it is applied. It is possible, perhaps even likely, that some aspects of the metaphor may even be misleading and erroneous.

To minimize the false implications of a metaphor, it can be analyzed and checked for its logical and internal consistency and for its coherence. Thus, at best, through the use of a metaphor the transcendent entity is being thought about symbolically. Nevertheless, in spite of these limitations, metaphors remain useful, because they are the best that humans can do with respect to those things that cannot be directly sensed and experienced.

Gods, being transcendent and sensorially inaccessible, can only be thought of and spoken of by using metaphors and symbols that draw on "human" perceptions and "human" experiences. Because in any specific worldview the most readily accessible agents of activity and partners in relationships were people, it is not surprising that gods were envisioned as quasi-humans with exceptional and specialized human powers and human responsibilities.

Most religions of the Ancient Near East were polytheistic, as were those of the Greek and Roman Empires that followed. Hebrew monotheism arose in that context, for reasons that are not altogether clear. However, as noted in chapter seven, even though the Hebrew religion was monotheistic, it was not statically monotheistic. A careful study of the Old Testament narrative reveals that the notion of Yahweh as the sole deity was not fully developed from the beginning. Rather, the concept of Yahweh developed slowly over the course of many centuries. Included were notions that Yahweh was the one and only God, the chief God among many gods, a warrior God who fought for his people's freedom and led them out of Egyptian bondage to the Promised Land, a jealous God who expected sole allegiance to and full obedience of his laws, the God of the mountains, and others. On the one hand, Yahweh was so holy – transcendent and completely separate – that his name could not be spoken and no images could be made to represent him. On the other hand, he was immanent, frequently communicating tenderly with and to his chosen people. Thus, the concept of Yahweh was characterized in many ways in the Hebrew Bible narrative.

Still, it must be recognized that *Yahweh* was the Hebrews' metaphor for *UUR* in their particular setting. It was an acknowledged truth among the Hebrews that no one had seen Yahweh. Therefore, all the attributes and characteristics that were attributed to Yahweh were not based on direct observation or experience of Yahweh, but rather were abstract and absolute extensions of attributes and characteristics that the Hebrews observed in humans. The Hebrews, like all other people, could only conceptualize *UUR* in terms of their worldview and their life experiences. The Hebrew God, Yahweh, like the gods of other religions and nations, was one particular human conceptualization of *UUR*. As such, it had and has no greater validity than the metaphors for *UUR*s of any other religions of the world, despite its foundational primacy for Judaism, Christianity, and Islam.

Considering the foregoing, from the modern perspective there is an ironic twist relating to the "image of God." The writer of Genesis 1:27 states, "God created humankind in his image, in the image of God he created them; male and female he created them" (NRSV). Through the ages Judeo-Christian theology has insisted that humans are special and different from the rest of creation, because they were "created in the image of God." The irony is that the notion of *UUR* derived by the Hebrews was God (Yahweh) conceptualized in the image of humans; that humans were said to be created "in the image of God" was but a secondary reflection of their efforts to conceptualize *UUR*.

My consideration of the biblical narrative's perspectives of the origin and nature of humans has been largely critical. The Genesis myths of origin sustained and supported the Hebrews and later the Christians because they were expressed in terms of the Ancient Near East worldview. The lack of congruence between that worldview and the modern one results in little relevance of the Genesis account for understanding the modern situation. Yet, from time to time I have noted that the biblical account does provide important insights for understanding human life; I now consider one such example from the Genesis narrative.

The two specially noted trees that God had planted in the Garden of Eden were the *tree of life* and the *tree of the knowledge of good and evil*. Humans were not to eat of the tree of the knowledge of good and evil (Genesis 2:17). Although they may have been permitted to eat of the tree of life before The Fall (Genesis 2:17), they were prevented from eating of that tree after The Fall (Genesis 3:22-24).

The desire to eat of these two "trees" appears to identify two deep human yearnings: the desire to live a meaningful life that lasts forever and the desire to know and to understand all things. People's desire to live forever arose from and is thwarted by their self-consciousness that they will someday die and cease to live on this earth. Most religions have developed elaborate burial rituals and myths of afterlife to help people cope with the deep fear of becoming non-existent at death. The afterlife of most religions is a way to live forever – to eat of the tree of life and be like the gods.

Humans (*Homo sapiens*, "wise man") also have an insatiable appetite for knowledge, not only of good and evil but of all things. Through knowledge comes power – control over nature, over fellow humans, and perhaps even ways to influence and to control *UUR*. If humans could only eat of the tree of knowledge, they "will be like God" (Genesis 3:5) – not only knowing good and evil but all things. Then they would know everything and be able to control everything, like their anthropomorphic conception of an omniscient and omnipotent God.

Thus, the idealized situation would exist for humans, if only they could live forever – eat of the tree of life – and have all knowledge in order to control all things – eat of the

tree of the knowledge of good and evil. Then, except for their lack of transcendence, they would indeed be "like God." It seems that these two trees in the mythical Garden of Eden just as accurately capture and reflect truths about modern humans.

Thus far, I have treated the developments of the Renaissance, Enlightenment and Modernity as being positive contributions to human society and culture. Understanding nature in terms of inherent principles and laws provides a much more stable worldview in which humans can orient themselves than dealing with decisions by the fickle and capricious spirits of earlier worldviews. Virtually all of the improvements in modern medicine and nearly all forms of modern technology were made possible by contributions that science of one form or another has provided. To be sure, questionable uses of science and technology have engendered problems such as environmental pollution and destruction and global warming. Yet, if given the choice, almost everyone in modern developed countries would prefer to live in their present settings rather than in the harsh settings of their ancestors of the Middle Ages or even of two generations ago. Most people in Second and Third World settings aspire to the greater possible quality of life in First World settings. Moreover, the negative consequences of science and technology are amenable to correction. The problem-solving capacity of humans enables us to reverse and to correct the negative impacts of humans that have accrued with the arrival of modernity, if we are persuaded or forced to do so.

Yet, one aspect of modern scientific understanding has proven very dissatisfying to many people, particularly Christians. The discovery of more and more scientific principles and laws enabled much of the Industrial Revolution to occur. Early on, many scientists attempted to incorporate their scientific understandings into their religious framework. The laws of nature became the principles incorporated into creation by God. Analogous to humanly-created machines, physical and biological nature and the solar system came to be viewed much as machines created by God. For Deists, God became the Great Watch-maker, who at creation had made his instrument, wound it up, and started it to run in perpetual motion. Although the absence of any role for Jesus the Christ in Deism was very troublesome to traditional Christians, God still had had a necessary role in the world's existence and function even for many scientists.

Increasingly, however, more and more of the natural world came to be understood as a large complex phenomenon controlled by forces described by the principles and laws of nature. The universe and living organisms could be understood in terms of energy and forces inherent in nature. There seemed to be a decreasing need for God. God became a "God of the gaps"; those gaps in human understanding of nature that had not been analyzed as scientific laws or principles were attributed to God's activity. However, as scientific momentum accelerated, more and more laws and principles were discovered and described. The gaps disappeared and so did the need or even any role for God. For many people, especially scientists, the oper-ation of the physical universe and biological nature could be entirely accounted for and explained mechanistically, because the properties of the physical materials were considered sufficient to define, to describe, to account for and to understand everything in nature. This approach to understanding reality has been termed *scientific reduc-tionism*. People who held or who hold this understanding of reality are referred to by several names: *mechanists*, *physicalists*, *materialists* and *naturalists*. Common to all of them is the notion that reality can be entirely accounted for by the physical properties of materials as they interact in predictable, mechanical ways: understanding reality can be "reduced" to the laws of nature discernible by science.

Respectable, established science became atheistic. The notion that nature was opera-ting mechanistically meant that it was "going" but not necessarily "going some-where." If nature was not going towards some specific end or goal, it must be mean-ingless and going nowhere. Philosophically and religiously, participating in a life that is going nowhere was not an acceptable alternative. Such a conclusion seemed to mean that life was ultimately purposeless and meaningless. The answers to the existen-tial questions "Who am I?", "Why am I here?" and "What is the meaning of life?" cannot be satisfactorily answered by: "I am the product of a biological machine, and my life is ultimately meaningless and pur-poseless."

Scientific understanding seems like a fabric that is logically, tightly woven togeth-er; if one accepts the fabric, one must seem-ingly accept the fibers from which the fabric has been woven. Or are there other possible alternatives in dealing with this dilemma?

Some people sense that science has provided a reliable and valid description of reality but do not accept the notion that the universe and life are going nowhere. Many Christians are eclectic, choosing elements of traditional Judeo-Christianity that include a role for God in the functioning world as described by science. That role may range from God the puppeteer to God the fine tuner who for God's purposes tweaks the laws of nature. Their lives thereby become purposeful narratives, enabling them to find meaning and fulfillment in life.

Some people who see no role for religion or any concept of *UUR* simply dismiss any religious interpretation of life as a useless vestige of the primitive human condition. They accept the premise that life is not moving toward some goal or purpose but is simply a mechanistic process. These people have meaningful and purposeful lives with-out adopting a particular religion, perhaps even having a wholly secular perspective of life. These people have arrived at a philosophy of life that fully meets those existential needs that are filled by religion in the lives of religious persons.

Other attempted resolutions of the conflict between science and religion could be described. But rather than seeking additional resolutions to the conflict, I might simply ask: Is that conflict necessary? Has it always existed? If not, can I determine how it arose and perhaps find helpful hints to resolve the conflict, at least for my own life? In the next chapter I consider those questions.

Chapter 12

Discovering My Own Worldview and Recognizing Its Importance

We are not victims of the world we see.
We are victims of the way we see the world.

Shirley MacLaine

Early in my life, the traditional Lutheran faith into which I was indoctrinated by my parents and my local congregation served me well. It enabled me to orient myself in my world and to develop into a responsible human being. Enclosed in this family-Church cocoon, I was unaware that any elements of that religious perspective might be in conflict with other understandings of life and of the world outside that context. However, particularly when I entered high school and became aware of modern scientific knowledge, it became apparent to me that there were major inconsistencies between those scientific understandings and the views that my Church still insisted were correct. I came to question the Church doctrines and teachings which had formed and informed my traditional Lutheran faith. Increasingly, I saw the Church as being resistant to necessary changes in its doctrines and teachings. For example, I learned that, historically, the Church had reluctantly accepted the notion of a heliocentric universe when it was forced to do so, long after the larger culture and society had accepted it and moved on. Similarly, the Genesis account of the creation of the universe and life within it continues to be held as valid by many in the Church, although modern science has provided convincing evidence that the universe and life within it are the result of an evolutionary process that began billions of years ago and continues today. Moreover, modern understandings of the origin of the world and of

life are accepted by many Christians only if they can somehow be made compatible with the biblical narrative. Still other traditional biblical concepts, such as Jesus' virgin birth, physical bodily resurrection and ascension into heaven, continue to be held as credible Church teachings based on historical events, although historical-critical investigations have provided ample evidence that these were not historical events but were rather mythological notions that were incorporated into Christianity because they were also commonplace components of contemporary pagan religions of the time.

This erosion of my confidence in the authority of the Church and of its doctrines and teachings occurred gradually and piecemeal over the last fifty years of my life. As I learned and reflected on what the Church presented as truths about life, I sensed that many of these "truths" did not resonate with my experiences and understanding of the world. While I recognized that I was gradually discounting the reliability and validity of most of what my Church continued to teach as "the Truth," I was not aware of all of the factors and influences that caused me to question my traditional Christianity more and more. I certainly knew that what I was learning from my education in the natural sciences and later in my career as a research geneticist seemed to resonate much more with my experiences of life than the assertions of Church teachings and doctrines about "the true nature of life." Through much reading and many conversations over the years, I have come to have a better understanding of what has been occurring over the course of my life and continues today: *my worldview has been changing constantly.* I did not understand fully all that was and is involved, but I know that what has been and is occurring there is fundamental to my life.

What is meant by a worldview? Linguistically, the word is a transliteration and translation of the German *Weltanschaung* – "worldview" or "world outlook." A search of English dictionaries and internet sources yields a variety of definitions, some having specific and others having more general applications. From them I have synthesized an operational definition that I will use as the framework to delineate my own personal worldview: *my worldview is that set of presuppositions with which I experience and interpret my life. It includes my beliefs about fundamental aspects of reality that ground and influence all my perceiving, thinking, knowing, and doing. It is the sounding board that I use to interpret and to make sense of my life experiences.*

Seven dimensions or elements are commonly listed as comprising a worldview: *cosmology, anthropology, metaphysics, theology, epistemology, teleology* and *axiology.* They could be listed and discussed in any order, because details of each element are often interdependent and interrelated with details of other elements. In the following I present the specifics of my own presuppositions regarding each of those elements, utilizing the above arbitrary sequence. In many cases I draw on data and conclusions from earlier chapters. In some cases I cite sources that have influenced me towards my present thinking in that area and give my reasons for moving away from the traditional, Christian position about that element.

Before proceeding further, I wish to place into perspective much of what I have related in previous chapters and what I will say in this and the remaining chapters. Having lived and worked in research and academic circles for most of my life, I am aware of the formal expectations and requirements to document the development of intellectual ideas and frameworks by attributing them to their respective sources. To do so in the present context would be extremely difficult, because the ideas and conclusions presented here are an eclectic collection of materials and reflections from more than fifty years of my personal, adult-life experiences. To document each source would be nearly impossible. Documentation beyond what I have provided in the References and Citations may be obtained by interested persons by consulting books and extensive internet sources. Moreover, the search for ideas and the intellectual and emotional processing and interpretation of them were occurring and continue to occur in the context of the specifics of my personal life. Undoubtedly, my search, my recall, and especially my interpretations have been and are strongly colored by the particulars of my life experiences, especially the adversities. Therefore, to all – scholars, academics and others – who are offended by my approach of not tracing and attributing each idea to its original source, I apologize.

Elements or Components of My Worldview

1. *Cosmology.* The cosmological component of my worldview deals with my beliefs about the origin and nature of the universe and of life, especially humans. It seems to me that our best modern scientific analyses and understandings indicate that the universe has come into existence through an evolutionary process that began with *the big bang* nearly 15 billion years ago and continues to unfold in the present. After the cosmogony of our solar system had given rise to our earth with an appropriate environment about 4.5 billion years ago, primitive precursors and then early forms of life arose because of spontaneous capacities within that natural system. Molded by the action of natural selection on naturally occurring mutations, from that original simple form of

life the evolutionary process has given rise to evermore complex organisms over the last 4-4.5 billion years. About 6-8 million years ago, the prehuman ancestral line diverged from the common ancestor that we share with common and pygmy chimpanzees. During the past million years the prehuman ancestral line has continued to evolve by developing skillful bipedal locomotion that freed the forelimbs for tool and other uses, and the brain has become larger and acquired the capacity for complex mental activities, for innovation and for spoken and written language.

Although this understanding accounts for the "what" and the "how" of the origin of the universe and of life on earth, it does not address the causative agents or forces that were responsible for originating and sustaining this evolutionary process. Those issues will be addressed later in the metaphysics section.

2. *Anthropology*. The anthropological component of my worldview pertains to my beliefs about the nature and purpose of humans. As mentioned above, the human species has arisen through the same evolutionary process that has given rise to all other forms of life: humans have been birthed and created within nature by natural processes. The hallmark human capacities, such as complex logical reasoning, innovation, and oral and written languages, have emerged through natural selection's acting on naturally-occurring mutations in genes that affected the morphology and function of the brain, just as is true for all adaptive physical features of humans. The emergence of the complex brain enabled the development of consciousness and self-consciousness, of awareness of self and other, and of complex reasoning and mental processes. The human capacity for awareness of the environment and recognition of invisible forces acting to bring about seasons and other natural cycles stimulated early humans to posit spirits and transcendent, supernatural forces as the agents of control over these natural phenomena, including over their own lives. Their desire to please, to appease and to curry the favor of these superhuman, invisible forces and spirits led to their creating religious rites, rituals and myths. Their emerging recognition of the significance of death as the end of human existence led to their conceiving of continued existence in some form of afterlife in order to avoid the emotionally-unacceptable notion of their passing into nonexistence at death.

Our knowledge about the origin of our own species, *Homo sapiens*, provides much important information about the nature of humans, or as we are wont to call it – human nature. All of our biological functions and sensory capacities occur in other animals and are sometimes developed and refined to a much greater degree in other species. The roots and rudiments of virtually all human behaviors, both altruistic and destructive, are present in other animal species – with many particularly being found in our closest ape relatives. Most of these behaviors in non-humans are controlled or at least strongly influenced by the genetic program that directs the ontological development and characteristic patterns of behavior within those species. In humans what has been termed *free will* has emerged; to a much greater degree than is known in any other animals, this capacity allows humans through mental processes to undertake courses of action that override the influences of the underlying genetic program on our behavior.

This knowledge of our evolutionary origin is cause for concern and yet provides hope for humankind. Because we arose from animal species in which behavior was overwhelmingly controlled by their genetic programs, we humans retain genes whose actions provided adaptive advantages in our prehuman and early human ancestors. For example, aggressive behaviors that pertained to obtaining food, to finding and retaining sexual partners, and to acquiring and protecting territory were essential to our very survival. The benefits of these behaviors far outweighed the costs when our early human ancestors were small roving troupes or bands of related families; however, these same behaviors became problematical when our ancestors began living in villages, towns and cities where unrelated families lived in close proximity. Those behaviors that had earlier contributed to survival were now disruptive to the community. In order to curb those destructive behaviors, communities devised, adopted and enforced mores and laws to maintain order in their respective societies. These humanly-devised ways of ordering and maintaining community remain foundational to society and culture today.

That the roots of some of our aggressive and destructive behaviors are grounded in the genetic program that we inherited from our evolutionary ancestors might at first seem grounds for permanent pessimism. However, there is an important upside possibility to our human destiny. Because of our human capacities to assess and to evaluate the consequences of our behavior and because of our free will to determine and to control our behavior, we are neither fully controlled nor limited by the influences of our genetic program on our behavior. Rather, by reasoning and innovation we are able to conceive possibilities and to adopt behaviors that transcend and override the effects of underlying negative genetic influences on human well-being. Moreover, as noted in an earlier chapter, our human capacities to control and to alter our own biological circumstances have important consequences for our evolutionary destiny. In those genes that influenced the aggressive behaviors that were positively adaptive in our evolutionary history, naturally occurring mutations that result in less aggressive behaviors are likely to occur. Selection by modern human societies for less aggressive communal behaviors by rewarding positive behaviors and by discouraging and punishing negative behaviors will tend to replace alleles (mutations)

that influence us towards aggressive, disruptive behaviors with ones that are less aggressive and beneficial to society. Undoubtedly, that process has already been occurring for hundreds of generations; however, evolution is a slow process, and many more generations will be required to reduce and, hopefully, ultimately to eliminate those genetic factors that influence us towards aggressive, antisocial behaviors. As a global community, it is important that humans continue to adopt societal standards that reduce the opportunity or perceived need to express those once-beneficial but now disruptive behaviors, in order that the selective, evolutionary process can continue to rid us of those aggressive factors that influence us towards negative social behaviors. In addition, we humans have the intellectual and innovative capacities to conceive of and to implement social practices and policies that can influence our free will to choose behaviors that are socially beneficial rather than destructive. In that way, we can override those genetically influenced negative behaviors that are still part of our evolutionary genetic heritage.

One aspect often included in the anthropological component of worldview is the purpose and meaning of human existence. From a strictly biological perspective, *Homo sapiens*, like all other species, has evolved and continues to evolve in order to fill a particular niche in nature. The niche of the human species is its particular relationship to other species and to the nonliving components of its ecosystem. Through natural selection's action in the evolutionary process, a particular species evolves to more effectively utilize resources and space in the environment than other cohabiting and perhaps competing species. Humans have evolved to occupy a previously unoccupied niche; at present it appears that the niche occupied by humans in the modern world is not seriously challenged or threatened by any other species. But humans' greatest threat to our continued existence is *we ourselves*, a concept to be addressed later.

But accounting for our biological emergence does not, *per se*, identify purpose and meaning for existence of the human species. Later, under the metaphysical and teleological components of worldview, I shall address these issues more fully.

3. *Metaphysics*. In the cosmological and anthropological components, I have presented the best modern, scientific understanding of "how" the physical universe and living organisms, including the human species, have arisen. Those understandings are derived from the material aspect of reality that I can experience with my senses and interpret with my intellectual capacity. However, there is a dimension of reality that was already intimated in arriving at those understandings: What is the nature of the forces/factors/entities that lie behind the principles, laws and theories of nature that human knowledge and understanding have discovered and formulated? These considerations concern the component of my worldview termed *metaphysics*. It deals with questions and issues that are *meta* – quite literally "beyond" or "behind" – the physical realm that I can sense, experience and comprehend. Metaphysics deals with such questions as the following: What was the origin and source of the physical material that has evolved into our universe and, ultimately, living organisms including humans? What are the ultimate causes operating in the creative evolutionary process? Why does something exist rather than nothing? What is the ultimate nature of existence, reality and experience? What are the basic categories of reality? How does the world that I know and understand relate to entities, factors and forces that I do not (and perhaps cannot) know about and understand?

Previously, I have adopted the term *Unseen Ultimate Reality* (*UUR*) to address the issues related to this worldview component. The capitalization of this term is reflective of its centrality as a worldview element: it refers to what in the Judeo-Christian traditions is symbolized as Yahweh or God. Thus, metaphysics is closely related to the worldview element theology – reflecting on and thinking about God, which will be addressed after metaphysics.

Not surprisingly, dealing with this element has been most challenging and provocative for me, because, when I question myself about these issues, I am inquiring about the core sources and causes of existence – my own and the universe that birthed me and the rest of the human species. Consequently, dealing with the metaphysics of my worldview requires a more elaborate explanation.

I started this inquiry from a dual and conflicted perspective. Having had a faith formed in a conservative Lutheran Christian tradition, I had pursued a career as a research geneticist – a scientist who studied how genes function in directing the development of individual organisms as well as how genes have changed in various species through countless generations of evolutionary history. My formative faith claimed that authoritative truth about life is derived from scriptural and Church sources, irrespective of whether the tenets from those sources were consistent with reason and my lived experience; this religious truth was claimed by the Church to be fixed and valid for all time. My scientific training claimed that authoritative truth about life is derived from empirical evidence obtained through careful observation, analysis and interpretation of my experiences of life in our world – that is, from sources that my senses can detect and from evidence that my mind can interpret. Such scientific truth is thus always and only the best available knowledge and understanding of a phenomenon available at a given time; it is always subject to modification and even rejection, if better and more complete data and information are discovered. My caring and well-intentioned parents, religious mentors and cohorts had warned me to be suspicious of truths derived from science, because they would tempt me to fall away from the "Truths" of my faith – at the risk of my eternal perdition. Such an ingrained fear was not easily dismissed even in adult life. Nevertheless, as the answers of traditional Christianity became less and less satisfactory in addressing my questions stemming particularly from the tragedies in my life, I was driven to seek answers other than the traditional ones that my Church provided. Finally, I concluded that the pain of living with the Church's answers was more unbearable than the fear of "losing my faith" but perhaps finding more satisfactory answers elsewhere.

I surmised that I might not be alone in struggling with these issues, so I sought counsel by reading the works of other Christians who seemed also to be dealing with the questions that I was having – in what I had by then learned was termed the science-religion conflict or debate. For a long time I was frustrated, because it seemed to me that Christian writers who claimed to be searching for truth were, in reality, apologists for and defenders of the traditional Christian perspective. Creationists of various stripes for the most part proceeded from their fundamentalistic presupposition that the Bible is the inspired word of God and that the Genesis narrative is at least a quasi-historical account of creation. Proponents of Intelligent Design, most of whom are Christian, seemed to be "soft" creationists; they proposed that an Intelligent Designer (although many would deny that this is equivalent to God) has been and continues to be involved in the creation of the universe and of life (many would say through the evolutionary process) by tweaking the laws of nature to achieve the Intelligent Designer's creative purposes. Close scrutiny reveals that the foregoing are seeking resolutions that presuppose and defend the validity and reliability of traditional Christian teachings, in spite of whatever clear and transparent evidence to the contrary might exist. While they might make some allowances for different worldviews, they insist that any resulting resolution has to be compatible with traditional Judeo-Christian notions of God and to retain the authority of scriptures and of the Church and its teachings, while accommodating in some way the findings of modern science. Following my scientific inclinations, this approach has not been satisfactory at all to me, because it seems not to be seeking truth – the most valid and reliable understanding of a phenomenon – but rather to be protecting scriptural and Church authority.

While there are also other aspects to metaphysics, I now want to focus on the nature and origin of complexity in the natural world. In short, it is finding a satisfactory answer to the following question: how can I best account for the source and origin of complexity – the intricate order, organization and function that I observe in the natural world? How best to account for the complexity and order in the universe has captured people's interest for thousands of years. As noted in an earlier chapter, this question and people's answers to it very likely contributed to the origins of most religions.

While searching for my own answers to these questions, some years ago I read two books by Gordon Kaufman that reflected the course of his struggles with the same issues with which I was dealing. In the first book, *God the Problem*, Kaufman documents how the traditional Judeo-Christian concept of God presents many problems in attempting to characterize *UUR* in our modern world understanding. After considerably more thinking and struggling with this and other issues, he wrote *In Face of Mystery* (*IFOM*). In that book, he presents his rethinking of traditional Christian theology so that it *incorporates, rather than just accommodates*, both the most valid and reliable current scientific understandings of nature and life and of the best historical understanding of the origin and development of religion. Because his ideas have been seminal to my own thinking, I elaborate here on the relevant contents of *IFOM*.

Kaufman proposes that all theological

150

thinking must be *critical, contextual* and *constructive*. Briefly, this means that understandings and traditions that are received from our religious forebears must be *critically* scrutinized in order to determine whether they are still valid and reliable, that is, asking whether they are still true in the modern *contextual* setting. To the extent that they are no longer valid and reliable, they must be newly *constructed* or *reconstructed* to make them "ring true" in the modern setting.

Kaufman generally embraces the modern understanding of how religions originated as human inventions and constructions, much as presented in earlier chapters of this book. Each religion arose as humans in a specific geographic environment grappled to comprehend *UUR* in their particular setting. Because each group was drawing on the different specifics of its particular human setting, the conceptions of *UUR* of different religions reflected these social, cultural and natural environmental differences. Kaufman terms these symbolic representations of *UUR imaginative constructions*. Yet each and every attempt to name, describe or talk about *UUR* is metaphoric, meaning that it utilizes images and concepts available from human experiences to think and to talk about an entity that is inaccessible to sensory perception or to any form of human experience and therefore not ultimately verifiable. Each imaginative construction symbolizes *UUR* to those who conceive it and constitutes a useful and practical conceptual framework with which to think about *UUR* within the context in which it was conceived. Yet, it can in no way be considered an objectively accurate description or characterization of *UUR*; it is something that can be conceived by the human mind but not perceived sensorially nor verified by human experience.

Perhaps the most-cited argument for the existence of God is the intricate order and operation of the physical and biological realms of nature; in the Christian tradition this type of knowledge has been termed *natural knowledge of God*. When accounting for the order and intricacy in nature, the early Hebrews imaginatively constructed *UUR*, using the best experiential image available to them in their particular historical setting: noetic human agency – that is, a rational, reasoning entity. Yet, to be "ultimate," this noetic agent had to be free of the limitations of human agency. Thus, it was necessary that this transcendent, supernatural agent be eternal, omnipotent, omniscient and to possess all the other attributes that they ascribed to Yahweh-God. It is that symbol of *UUR* bequeathed to us by our Judeo-Christian tradition that we attempt to continue to use with our modern understanding of reality. That symbol ceased to function appropriately for Kaufman, is no longer functional for me, and apparently is no longer satisfactory for increasing numbers of other people as well. Can a more productive framework or paradigm be found?

The recognition that any and all designations of *UUR* are metaphors that each arose and had meaning in a particular context means that metaphors that arose in one context may no longer be appropriately meaningful in another context. Utilizing his criteria that all theological thinking must be critical, contextual and constructive, Kaufman examined the traditional Judeo-Christian concept of God. Biblical names and designations of God include the unspeakable Yahweh, Creator, Lord of Armies (Sabaoth, Hosts), King and Father. Each of these symbols carried meaningful implications within the particular biblical context where they were conceived and used. Yet, some (Yahweh, Lord of Armies, King) have little or no meaning for most persons today. Even the designation Father presupposes a protecting, caring and providing image, a situation too often not present in modern father-child relationships.

While the metaphor Creator still conveys the idea of God as the source and origin of all that is, the Genesis narrative depiction of

God as Creator is still problematic when considered alongside our present understanding of the origin of our universe and of life. Thus, drawing on our present knowledge that our universe and life have arisen through an evolutionary process in which simpler forms have given rise to increasingly complex forms, after much discussion Kaufman selects *serendipitous creativity* as his imaginative construction that best symbolizes the modern understanding of how *UUR* is present and acts in the world today. Serendipitous creativity is the creative force or capacity that has been and is working in the evolutionary process to create evermore complex and intricate forms of life. *UUR* is no longer effectively symbolized by the noetic agent God that the early Hebrews created in their own human image and which was later adopted and modified by Christianity and Islam. Because of the foregoing and many other traditional connotations that have accrued to the symbol/designation God, Kaufman considered whether to retain the symbol God for this serendipitous creativity. In the end, he retained it, because he concluded that the symbol God has important positive implications for the larger Christian tradition that he is trying to reconstruct as a viable religion for the modern world. For Kaufman, to abandon altogether the symbol God would perhaps reconstruct Christianity so thoroughly that it would no longer be a recognizable extension of the traditional religion.

Kaufman's resolution of the "God problem" in relationship to the modern understanding of the structure and operation of the universe, of the origin and nature of living organisms, and of reality in general stimulated me to explore beyond the range of his considerations. His positing that all theological (metaphysical) thinking should be *critical, contextual* and *constructive* seemed so obviously correct to me that I found it difficult to believe that I (or anyone else) would have ever thought otherwise. Using that approach, I considered the following question. *If my purpose is not to reconstruct tradi-tional Christianity for the modern world but rather to create an imaginative construction of UUR reflective of modern understanding (but without respect to earlier Judeo-Christian notions), what might that imaginative construction of UUR be?*

Asking the question in this way widens the perspective from a religious/theological search to a metaphysical inquiry, yet one in which Kaufman's *serendipitous creativity* seems a productive starting point. Putting aside its association with the symbol God, the creativity in nature that has given rise to the entire physical and biological world could be considered *UUR*. I now want to explore some ramifications of that proposal.

Briefly and broadly stated, the proposal is the following: starting with *the big bang* and proceeding to the present, creative forces inherent within nature have operated to form the physical universe containing our solar system. Within that solar system, the earth has evolved, ultimately giving rise to an environment in which life could emerge. Simple life then arose under specific conditions that existed at that time but no longer exist today, thus explaining why life no longer spontaneously arises today. Having once arisen, simple life has evolved to its present array of variety and complexity, including humanity with all its biological, social and cultural dimensions. Creative forces inherent and immanent in nature account for all that has occurred in creating the reality that exists today. No noetic agent, acting either externally or internally, needs to be metaphorically invoked in order to account for what exists today.

Although the evidence that physical and biological reality has arisen and continues to arise because of capacities in nature seems convincing, the conclusion that these capacities in nature are "all there is" is dissatisfying to many people. Is this lack of emotional satisfaction because of weaknesses in the substance of the case or because of some other factors? In the following, I present a case for its being the latter.

Complexity in a modern scientific sense

has elaborate connotations. It can be thought of as intricate levels of order and organization compounded upon previously existing levels of intricate order and organization. Two terms are often used to characterize complexity: *organicism* and *emergence*. *Organicism* holds that the organization of the whole organism, rather than the structures and functions of its component organs or systems, is the determinant of life processes. Using nonbiological terminology, *the whole is more than the simple sum of its parts*. The term *holism* is often used to connote very much the same meaning as organicism.

If organicism is seeing the whole organism as more than the sum of its component parts, *emergence* considers the perspective from an organism's component parts to the whole. *Emergence* refers to the appearance of novel properties and characteristics of a composite that cannot be predicted from the properties and characteristics of its lower-order components. It refers to the new levels of organization and intricacy that appear when one level of order is compounded upon an existing level of order. A chemistry example is that the physical-chemical properties and characteristics of sodium chloride, salt, cannot be predicted from knowledge about the physical-chemical properties of sodium and chlorine. In biology, the behavior of flocks of birds cannot be predicted by understanding the behaviors of individuals within that flock. Emergence gives rise to the complex novelty that has repeatedly appeared during the evolution of the universe and of life within it. Through emergent processes the raw materials of *the big bang* gave rise to the complex universe of today. Through emergent processes the simple life that emerged 4-4.5 billion years ago has through the process of evolution given rise to all the complex forms of life that now exist in the biological world.

Science attempts to discover, to describe and to understand the complexities of nature through the use of analytic methods. The strengths of scientific methods of inquiry are that they rigorously establish organized bodies of data, facts and interpretations. Scientific methods of inquiry are capable only of analyzing phenomena which are tractable to perception and measurement by our physical senses (although now often assisted by technological tools). Using techniques of observation and measurement, data are acquired which can be analyzed and interpreted by the rational human brain (assisted by technology such as computers) to provide some understanding of how that phenomenon exists and operates in the real world. A phenomenon is considered to be well understood scientifically when its characteristics and behavior can be shown to follow precise mathematical formulae. When precise and detailed mathematical description is achieved for a natural phenomenon, its degree of understanding is referred to as a well-established theory, principle or law of nature.

However, here a confounding problem is encountered. Nature is exceedingly complex. An organism is comprised of compounded emergent components and complexities; yet scientific inquiry attempts to understand the organism in terms of its component parts. In order to deal with the acknowledged complexity, a scientific experiment is designed to keep constant all possible known variables in the system except one, in order that some valid conclusions about the system can be drawn when different values for that one variable are introduced into the study. When an experimental system is thus simplified, a linear mathematical equation can often be used to model the system; even then, there is often a disconcerting amount of "noise" (unexplainable variation) in the system. Although the results of such an experiment provide significant insights into the natural system being studied under the specific conditions of that experiment, they are acknowledged not to reflect the full complexity of nature, because in the natural system all values that were held constant in the experiment are actually variables that can take on many values.

Particularly in biology, the evolutionary process has accrued layers upon layers of emergence and complexity. Even if each layer of emergence could be mathematically modeled with a linear equation (an unlikely achievement), attempts to model the compounded layers of emergence would still involve higher order equations in order to account for the extensive complexity.

A rather unexpected finding occurred when it was discovered that this extensive complexity in both physical and biological systems can be modeled by equations from the mathematical field called *chaos theory*. The general concept of chaos has been known for several thousands of years, and the term was often applied where much disorder and disorganization appeared to exist. However, during the last half of the twentieth century the mathematical field of chaos theory has received significant attention. Briefly defined for this context, *chaos is order and organization that is so intricate and complex that it appears to be disorder, disorganization or randomness.* Chaotic systems exhibit mathematically deterministic functions but are nearly impossible to predict, because chaotic systems are extremely sensitive to slight differences in the initial conditions. The mathematical complexity of chaotic systems prevented their detailed analyses until the development of powerful computers with their extensive iterative capacities. Visualization of at least some of the complexity of chaotic systems can be facilitated by the use of fractal geometry.

Even after they were understood mathematically, for a time it was thought that chaotic systems might be mathematical peculiarities unrelated to the natural world. However, chaotic systems were soon found to exist in physics and chemistry, where they pertain to such phenomena as turbulence, fluid behaviors, electrical circuits, lasers, clashing gears, pendulum systems and chemical reactions. In biological systems some phenomena that were long considered too complex to analyze appear to exhibit the behavior of chaotic systems: disease outbreaks, heart rhythms, electrical brain activity, arterial and venous blood systems, circadian rhythms and animal population size fluctuations. Other additional interesting features of many chaotic systems are that they appear to have self-organizing and inherent equilibrating capacities. That is, they create stable new levels of order and organization. Moreover, when these new systems are externally perturbed from their equilibrium states, they have the inherent capacity to restore the system to equilibrium. These are precisely the properties that appear to be involved in nature's accrual of emergent complexity in the evolutionary processes. Thus, mathematically-modeled chaotic systems may reflect nature's capacity to generate the extensive complexity that is seen in nature in the phenomena of emergence and organicism. How commonplace or prevalent chaotic systems are remains to be determined.

Other recent concepts and discoveries in the physical sciences, such as string theory, M-theory, dark matter and dark energy, may also further impact our understanding of cosmological and biological evolutionary processes, although at the present there is no way of knowing how or to what extent. The point of mentioning them is to indicate that, while at present scientists have important and oftentimes substantial insights into the origin, structure and function of the natural world, there is still much more to learn about the complexity of nature – probably much more than what is already known.

Thus, the metaphysical question regarding the *UUR* that is responsible for the evolutionary development of nature can be answered as follows: the best current understanding, arrived at through scientific investigation, indicates that the evolution of nature can be accounted for by forces and capacities that are immanent and inherent in nature itself. I choose the term *Nature's Creativity* to denote this comprehensive capacity for nature to give rise to emergent novelty and complexity. From that perspective, the use of a term rooted in the word *nature* is particularly meaningful. The English word nature is derived from the Latin *nasci* – "to be born" and *natus* – "born." While birth is usually thought of as the process by which we humans enter the world after a forty-week gestational period, in another literal sense nature has birthed us humans. Through the evolutionary process over millions of years, nature has created and continues to create us *Homo sapiens* and all other species.

Yet, it must be noted that there is not anything like a comprehensive and complete understanding of everything that is going on in nature's evolutionary birthing processes. Indeed, the philosophical presupposition of scientific inquiry is that no phenomenon of nature is ever completely understood. As newer tools for more precise measurements and newer technologies, such as computers with greater power for analysis and interpretation become available, the body of science in a particular area continues to be elaborated, refined and corrected. Thus, the body of scientific understanding regarding any natural phenomenon is always proximate. Although the goal of science is to inquire for penultimate and ultimate understandings, the presupposition of scientific inquiry is that ultimacy will always be beyond human attainment. Ironically, if ultimacy were achievable and finally achieved, the purpose and need for scientific inquiry would cease.

Then, even if we acknowledge that the best scientific understanding is never complete and ultimate, it is still the most valid, reliable and complete understanding that is available, but it is not "all there is" to know and to understand. Use of the term *Nature's Creativity* invokes only capacities and powers that are inherent and immanent in nature. There is neither any evidence to support nor any need to invoke the notion that other forces or capacities, supernatural or otherwise, are involved in the creative processes of nature.

It seems to me that, in stating what science has learned, scientists have often reported scientific information and understanding with an attitude that "our scientific methods have discovered natural laws that fully account for all that is observed in nature; what remains to be discovered are details that may or may not be significant or important." Such an attitude belies the sea of incompletely understood and not yet even anticipated phenomena that from time to time cause paradigm shifts in our understanding of nature. For example, it is estimated that our universe consists of four percent matter, 22 percent dark matter and 74 percent dark energy. While there is solid evidence that dark matter and dark energy actually exist, almost nothing is known about them except that they exist. So far as we know, all knowledge of astronomy, physics, chemistry and biology pertains to the four percent of the universe that is matter, and there remains much to be discovered about matter. Thus, any claim that a complete understanding of the universe is available overstates the case to a large but unknown degree. Indeed, there is still much in nature for which the term *mystery* is an apt characterization.

In the foregoing I have answered only the metaphysical question of "how" the matter resulting from *the big bang* gave rise to the existing natural world. How do I answer the question of "why" there is something rather than nothing – of what was the cause and the origin of *the big bang*? Ever since Einstein presented the theory of general relativity, physicists and cosmologists have been seeking to discover what has been termed "the theory of everything" – an understanding of "why" the universe and the laws of nature came into existence. There were insights and intimations from what is known, but no one had synthesized a satisfactory comprehensive model.

That was the status of things as I worked through the foregoing rationale that led me to select *Nature's Creativity* as my imaginative conception for *UUR*. Then in 2010 Stephen Hawking and Leonard Mlodinow published *The Grand Design*, in which they seek answers to the following questions: *"Why is there something rather than nothing? Why do we exist? Why this particular set of laws and not some other?"* Noting answers that people have given to these questions over the past several thousand years, they focus on clues provided by scientific studies in the fields of physics and cosmology that began with Newton's laws in the late seventeenth and early eighteenth centuries and continue today. Specific insights occurred with Einstein's presentation of the theory of general relativity and with the later development of quantum theory. Since the early formulation of the two foregoing theories physicists have been searching for a theory of everything – a single unified theory that would comprehensively account for the origin and existence of the universe. Concerning the results of that search, they state the following.

> Dualities like this – situations in which two very different theories accurately describe the same phenomenon – are consistent with model-dependent realism. Each theory can describe and explain certain properties, and neither theory can be said to be better or more real than the other. Regarding the laws that govern the universe, what we can say is this: There seems to be no single mathematical model or theory that can describe every aspect of the universe. Instead, as mentioned in the opening chapter, there seems to be the network of theories called M-theory. Each theory in the M-theory network is good at describing phenomena within a certain range. Wherever their ranges overlap, the various theories in the network agree, so they can all be said to be parts of the same theory. But no single theory within the network can describe every aspect of the universe – all the forces of nature, the particles that feel those forces, and the framework of space and time in which it all plays out. Though this situation does not fulfill the traditional physicists' dream of a single unified theory, it is acceptable within the framework of model-dependent realism. (Hawking and Mlodinow, p. 58)

In a later chapter the authors conclude that at present M-theory is the "only" candidate for a complete theory of the universe, although details remain to be proven in order to conclude that this is a model of a universe that creates itself.

Hawking and Mlodinow point out that, at the molecular and subatomic levels where both the theory of relativity and quantum theory are applicable, time and space behave in ways that are very different from and often counterintuitive to our experiences in everyday life. For example, the early understandings of *the big bang* theory supposed that our universe had a beginning point someplace in the continuum of time. However, when the effects of quantum theory are integrated with the theory of relativity, space-time warpage occurred to the extent that time existed only as a fourth dimension of space. That is, under the conditions that existed at the very early stages of *the big bang*, time as we know it did not exist. Rather, time arose from the fourth dimension of space during the early inflation stages of the universe's creation. Thus, the realization that time arose from a fourth dimension of space solves the puzzle pertaining to the time of the universe's beginning: time arose and began as one product of the universe-creating process. Moreover, the foregoing considerations mean that the beginning of the universe unfolded according to the laws of science rather than requiring action by some entity such as a god.

Although there is not yet a complete quantum theory of gravity, the authors describe the importance of gravitational force in the creation and continuing operation of the universe. They answer their earlier posed questions as follows:

Because gravity shapes space and time, it allows space-time to be locally stable but globally unstable. On the scale of the entire universe, the positive energy of the matter can be balanced by the negative gravitational energy, and so there is no restriction on the creation of whole universes. *Because there is a law like gravity, the universe can and will create itself from nothing* in the manner described in Chapter 6. *Spontaneous creation is the reason there is something rather than nothing, why the universe exists, why we exist.* It is not necessary to invoke God to light the blue touch paper and set the universe going. (Hawking and Mlodinow, p. 180; *italics* mine)

The conclusion of Hawking and Mlodinow that spontaneous creation gave rise to the universe is fully consistent with my proposal that within *Nature's Creativity* lie all the capacities necessary for the emergence of our universe, of our earth, and of all the life forms that have arisen on it. While their proposal emanates from the best scientific understandings of physics/quantum theory and cosmology, my conclusions derive from several considerations. First, the biological evidence arises from scientific studies that consistently and repeatedly demonstrate that forces and actions inherent in nature are responsible for creating living organisms and adapting them to their environments. Second, considerations of supernatural and other nonscientific explanations purported to account for the origin and operation of the universe have shown that they arose in and reflect elements of ancient worldviews that are no longer considered valid for our modern world. For example, the Hebraic-Christian notion of God as creator arose several thousand years ago as a human imaginative construction that seemed to issue logically from worldview presuppositions of the time regarding the origin of the universe and life. However, those presup-positions share almost no common elements with presuppositions of the modern world-view that led to the conclusions of Hawking and Mlodinow and to my own conclusions.

The human scientific endeavor has made much progress in our understanding of the origin of our universe. With determination we will continue to use our human curiosity, investigative skills and technologies, and reasoning capacities to inquire further into the deep questions of nature. As was noted earlier, at the deep levels of nature at which exploration is now being carried out (theory of relativity and quantum theory), many findings and conclusions run counter to our intuitions, which are based on what we can sense and experience in everyday life. This requires that we create imaginary constructs and models pertaining to things that we cannot directly sense and experience but for which we can use symbols and metaphors to aid our understanding. This process is not unlike what we use in our conceptualization of *UUR*, as described earlier. I do not know how deep we humans can go or what we might find at the deepest depths that we are able to probe. Because of our tenuous access to the deep secrets of nature, it seems to me important that we approach these deep mysteries with awe and wonder as well as with modesty and humility.

At the beginning of this section the question concerning the basic categories of reality was posed. My answer to that question is that reality has only one category – *nature* or *the natural*. Everything that exists is attributable to capacities and forces in nature. Humans' capacities for experiencing this unitary reality can be thought of as a continuum. At the one end of that spectrum are those natural capacities and forces that are directly accessible to our senses, from which we receive stimuli and input that we can interpret and understand as the theories, principles and laws of nature, which we can then utilize to orient ourselves in life. At the other end of that spectrum are capacities and forces that are not directly accessible to our senses and experience; our understanding of those aspects of reality can be apprehended only through the use of symbols and metaphors supported by mathematical equations and characterizations. The acquisition of valid and verifiable human knowledge and understanding of the natural world through human history has been an incremental movement from interpreting sensory observations towards understanding symbols and metaphors. Although we have acquired much knowledge and understanding about the world in which we live, those forces and capacities in the latter mode of understanding may remain accessible to us only through great effort; some may even remain inaccessible to us. There undoubtedly remain unknown forces and capacities that we cannot even address symbolically and metaphorically. They are now, and perhaps will always remain, mystery. Even so, these are forces and capacities that innately inhere in nature – the single, unitary category of reality.

Thus, I can summarize my metaphysical presuppositions as follows. All of present reality exists because of *Nature's Creativity* – forces and capacities immanent and inherent in nature that through evolutionary processes have created and continue to create the emergent complexity in the physical and biological world from the primordial materials produced by the originating event that we term *the big bang*. I believe that humans have discovered information that allows us to have valid, but still very incomplete, insights into how that has occurred and continues to occur. Although current scientific studies are discovering details and formulating models that allow us to reach reasonable but still tentative conclusions about why *the big bang* occurred, many aspects of *UUR* activity in that process remain for me ultimate mystery – something that I do not know whether we humans will know or even can ever know.

4. *Theology*. The theological element of worldview, as its etymology indicates, is concerned with thinking and beliefs about God or gods. Because I have conceptualized *UUR* as *Nature's Creativity*, there is, literally speaking, no god – no *theos* – in this element of my worldview. Historically, the term *natural theology* has been applied to a theology that holds that knowledge of God can be acquired by human reason without the aid of divine revelation. Because use of human reason has been primary and central to my thinking about *UUR*, that aspect of natural theology might appropriately apply to this element of my worldview. However, my conceptualizing of *UUR* as *Nature's Creativity* rather than as any sort of noetic agent (God or gods) portends a very different trajectory than traditional natural theology. Much of my thinking about *Nature's Creativity* has already been presented in the earlier discussion under the metaphysical component of my worldview and will not be repeated here.

In the following I recount how the use of reason informed by the historically and scientifically established presuppositions that undergird the modern worldview have at first led and finally driven me from traditional Christian theology to the aforementioned qualified natural theology.

While exploring the dimensions of this element of my worldview, I came to realize why I have had such problems and conflicts in dealing with these complex issues. Formally, my theology and theological thinking deal with "what" and "how" I think about *UUR*. However, in traditional Lutheran Christianity I began my theological journey *wondering whether such thinking was even appropriate for me and, if so, what freedom to think I had in pursuing that journey*. The traditional faith that formed me inculcated in me the notion that the authority of the Scriptures had delegated to the Church the authority to proscribe the limits of how and what I could think about *UUR* (God) and that use of my reasoning capacity to reach beyond those limits was wrong and not to be pursued. Drawing on that scriptural authority, the Church of my formative faith claimed the power to ensure that its interpretations of Scriptures were faithfully accepted and practiced by all its members including me. Thus, the first step of my theological journey was to determine the validity of both the Church's and the Scriptures' claimed authority to proscribe what I should and should not think and believe about *UUR*.

After being convinced of the truth of Kaufman's premise that all received religious traditions should be critically, contextually and constructively analyzed, I concluded that all aspects of my traditional faith should be subjected to these criteria. In the following I draw summarily on church history, on the results of historical-critical studies of the Scriptures, and on the modern understandings of the origins of religions in order to reach conclusions about whether the Church and the Scriptures have the authority to influence and to control my theological thinking in the way that my traditional faith claimed.

Although understood somewhat differently by Roman Catholics and Protestants, the authority of the Church is claimed to derive from the Church's having been "instituted by Christ" (understood to be God) in the scriptural narrative (Matthew 16:13-20), after Peter's statement that Jesus was "the Christ, the Son of the Living God." A study of the history of that time reveals that, if there were any actual events in Jesus' life that lay behind this segment of the biblical narrative, they must have happened during the adult life of Jesus (around 30). Yet, both secular history and the biblical narrative agree that Jesus was an observant Jew during his entire lifetime. Thus, there simply is no historical evidence to suggest that Jesus had anything to do with the founding of the Christian Church; on the contrary, after his lifetime, it was his disciples and other followers who undertook the establishment of the religious group that came to be called Christians, and it was not until some thirty to sixty years *after* Jesus' lifetime that Christianity separated from Judaism and became an autonomous entity. Moreover, Christianity remained powerless, even to the point of frequently being persecuted in the Roman Empire, until Constantine in his Edict of Milan in 313 included it in the panoply of accepted religions in the Roman Empire. My earlier examination of the history of the Roman Empire indicated that the Church derived its authority in society from Christianity's being designated the empire's official religion in the late fourth century (381) by a political edict of Emperor Theodosius I. Over the course of time as the Roman Empire waned, the Church continued to accrue additional power unto itself until it became by the Late Middle Ages the preeminent authority in Western Europe, both politically and religiously. In addition, because of its claim to be the sole authoritative interpreter of the Scriptures, the authority of the Scriptures in the early Roman Church and in later Roman Catholicism has through the years tended to be as much or as little as was needed by the Church in order to maintain its ecclesiastical and political authority.

On the other hand, the Churches of Protestantism, which included traditional Lutheranism that formed my faith, claimed to derive their authority directly from their correct understanding and faithful adherence to the Scriptures and the implied authority that they possessed. Yet, historical-critical studies cast considerable doubt on those claims of authority for several reasons. First, content-wise, the biblical writings include some unusual events and phenomena. The biblical narrative takes for granted that God communicates with people by directly speaking to them and by visions, dreams or signs; it also relates a virgin birth, resurrections from death and ascensions to heaven – phenomena that seem so esoteric and out of the ordinary that, in order to have been included in the biblical narrative, modern readers conclude that they must have been actual events. Yet, these same phenomena and literary devices were also commonplace inclusions in the theologies and written narratives of pagan religions contemporary to the times of composition of the biblical writings. How could these seemingly "supernatural" phenomena have been part of Jewish, Christian and pagan religions and their respective writings in those times but seem incredible and preposterous today? It was because those phenomena were consistent with the metaphysical presuppositions of the worldviews of those times; people unquestioningly accepted such supernatural phenomena as part of their mythical narrative. My critical consideration of and skepticism about those claims which seem incredible and impossible today parallel my consideration of and rejection of the biblical notion of the three-tiered universe discussed earlier, even though it was the commonly accepted cosmological presupposition of the worldview of the time. Thus, the results of historical-critical studies lead me to conclude that biblical phenomena that seem impossible today also did not occur as actual events then either; they are included in the biblical narrative because they reflect different presuppositions of the worldviews of the times rather than because they were actual historical events and occurrences. Given that conclusion, I certainly cannot conclude that the Scriptures inherently possess the authority to proscribe the limits and content of my thinking about *UUR* and related issues in my life in the setting of our modern worldview.

Secondly, the Scriptures are said to have authority because God inspired the writers of its component documents and guided the selection of those books that became the Hebrew Bible and the New Testaments. However, the results of historical-critical studies have shown that the documents that came to be included in the Bible were written by religious leaders who were expressing for their respective communities their understandings of what their God (imaginatively conceived *UUR*) willed and demanded of their collective religious com-

munities and individual members. As indicated above, they expressed those understandings utilizing commonly-accepted literary devices used in religious writings of their times and placed their narratives in the context of their contemporary worldview presuppositions. From a large number of such writings, contemporary and later religious leaders selected and gave authority to those that they considered faithful witnesses to their understandings of their God and of their faith and aggregated them into what became the Hebrew Bible and the New Testament canon. These selected writings accrued further authority over time as they were repeatedly read before the religious communities gathered in worship and became the authoritative expressions of their faith. The elevated statuses of both the Old and New Testaments are thus entirely attributable, respectively, to the actions of Hebrew and Christian religious leaders. Therefore, the Old and New Testaments are considered as "the word of God" not because God specifically inspired and chose them as supernatural communications with or revelations to God's people but rather because they were written when the metaphysical element of the worldview deemed such communications between gods and humans commonplace. In reality, *human* church leaders chose from a large array of *human* religious writings that reflected *human* understandings of their God and of the divine will for their communities.

The Bible's further accrual of its extremely authoritative status in Protestantism can be largely attributed to two additional factors. The first occurred at the time of the Reformation, when primary ecclesiastical authority shifted from the Church to the Bible through the Protestant reformers' adoption of the *sola Scriptura* mantra. They did this as an antidote to their conclusion that corrupt (Roman) Church traditions arose because they originated from sinful and corruptible human Church leaders, whereas they thought that the churches of Protestantism would remain free of those errors because their church doctrines and practices were guided by Scriptures alone, which they deemed to have emanated directly from a holy, just and sinless God, for reasons cited above. The subsequent, repeated splintering of Protestant churches has proved this ideal to be an illusion, because the Bible still needs to be read and interpreted by *humans*, who often reach quite different conclusions as to the correct and proper meaning of the biblical content. Thus, claims of dependence on *sola Scriptura* also have not resulted in any unified consensus of scriptural authority.

The second major contributing factor to the accrual of biblical authority, particularly in American Protestantism, was the development of Christian fundamentalism. When the conclusions of modern scientific and historical research conflicted with long-held Christian traditional understandings for most of Protestantism, the notion of the Bible as "the" authority for all matters of faith and life was seriously called into question. To stem and hopefully to reverse this erosion of biblical authority, a group of American conservative Christian theologians adopted a set of five fiats or fundamentals, the most important of which for this consideration was the assertion that the Bible is the inerrant word of God that is to be literally interpreted. In addition to giving the Bible absolute authority, the notion of the biblical writings as "the literal word of God" made them incontestable and incontrovertible. Adoption of this tenet asserted that persons and actions in the biblical narrative were historical facts and that a straight-forward, literal reading of the Bible would provide persons with the necessary guidance for eternal salvation and for Christian living, without regard to any differences in the elements of the worldview of the times when the biblical documents were written and the worldview of today. Moreover, the notion that the biblical writings were incontestable and incontrovertible rendered them off-limits and immune to judgments involving human logic and reason. Many denominations of

American Protestantism today adhere more or less strictly to the fundamental of literalism; others find it necessary to relax that principle to a greater or lesser degree, because they recognize that its strict application leads to preposterous theological thinking and conclusions.

Thus, the foregoing considerations of the origins of the authority of the Church and of Scriptures has led me to the conclusion that neither any longer holds a valid claim or right to control whether I think or what I should think about *UUR*.

Having dismissed the unwarranted authority of the Church and of the Scriptures, I was left with the possibility that *UUR* itself might have a rightful claim to authority over my theological thinking. However, in light of current understandings of the origins of religions, symbols of *UUR* in all religions are human imaginative constructions that help people find meaning and purpose in the narrative of their lives. Thus, the Judeo-Christian symbol God is but one of many such imaginative constructions derived by humans in the course of history; as such, while it was and remains important to Judaism and Christianity (and as Allah in Islam), that symbol has no priority or preeminence over any other imaginative construction of *UUR*, and neither is it exempt from critical assessment for validity in the perspective of modern understandings of the world. Because of this awareness that all symbols of *UUR* are imaginative constructions of human minds, I concluded that I must find an imaginative construct that gives meaning and purpose to my life within the perspective of the other elements of my modern worldview. For me, *Nature's Creativity* is the appropriate symbol and metaphor for *UUR*. From this point forward, my theological thinking must be directed towards understanding how orienting my thinking and my life's activities vis-à-vis *Nature's Creativity* can bring greater meaning and fulfillment to my life and can contribute to the betterment of nature, including humankind. As an imaginative construction of my own mind (informed by other forebears who have thought similarly), *Nature's Creativity* as my metaphor and symbol for *UUR* deserves my utmost reverence and respect for what it has created and continues to create and to sustain; however, it has only as much or as little authority over my theological thinking as I give it.

Although many Christians and non-Christians accept many of the same elements of the modern worldview that I accept, especially pertaining to cosmology and anthropology, they continue to accept ancient and often arcane notions and characterizations of *UUR* depicted as God in the biblical narrative. Why is that so?

There are likely multiple reasons. First, there are some notions, images and characterizations of the biblical God that people are still able to incorporate and to fit into their worldviews. For instance, they can imagine an invisible God both as an all-powerful force in cosmogony and as a fine-tuning force in the process of biological evolution, including the origin of humans.

But there are other notions, some of which have already been mentioned and others of which will be mentioned later, where primary tenets of Christianity simply cannot be reconciled with aspects of the modern worldview, and yet people continue to believe them. Perhaps a way to think about why people continue to believe these is by using an analogy with the earth and the moon which orbits around it. The moon continues to orbit around the earth because of a balance of outward forces (centrifugal) and inward (centripetal = mostly gravitational) forces between the two bodies. In the present analogy, the Church corresponds to the earth and an individual member corresponds to the moon. The positive centripetal forces that keep the individual member in close orbit around the Church include its tenets that claim authority as the access to the word and will of God, as the

gateway to eternal life through faith, as the provider of guidance for godly living, and as the setting for membership in a community of like-minded believers. Threats of the loss of any of the foregoing provisions of the Church, which could ultimately consign a person to eternity in hell, dauntingly inhibit a member's inclinations to weaken the influences that keep her/him in that orbit.

On the other hand, centripetal forces tend to be weakened and offset by centrifugal forces. The latter largely consist of rational and reasoning activities by the individual member that question and challenge the validity, veracity and authority of the above-mentioned centripetal forces. As individual Church tenets, one by one, are found not to be true in the modern worldview, the centripetal forces diminish and the centrifugal forces amplify to the point that the individual enters a more and more distant orbit from the Church and finally escapes the orbit of parochial thinking that previously kept her/him associated with the Church.

My spiritual journey has been a *prima facie* example of the above process. Having given myself more and more permission to think critically and rationally about the Bible and about the Church and its teachings, I finally escaped the orbit of the Church and have moved into a new orbit with its gravitational forces around *Nature's Creativity*. With that new center of gravity, I have found it necessary to reconsider a number of primary tenets of Christianity. In the following I document those that inhibit rather than provide meaningful orientation for me in the modern worldview and that I have therefore had to reinterpret or to abandon.

Conflicts between biblical teachings and modern understandings of anthropology are numerous and extensive. I list here those that were discussed in the previous chapter and determined to be no longer credible for orienting and ordering my life: humans as specially created, sinless creatures who were placed into nature by God; the Fall; the Fall as the origin of human death; traditional

162

redemption theology of Jesus' death as a sacrifice to God for human sin; and salvation and eternal life after death that is accessed through faith in Jesus' meritorious sacrifice.

Rather than the biblical tenets, I have accepted our modern anthropological understandings as valid presuppositions for my life. The human species is but one product of the evolutionary process that from materials produced by *the big bang* has birthed our universe and the diverse forms of life within it. As descendants of nonhuman animal forms, we still carry within our genetic heritage the roots of aggressive behaviors that were adaptive to our evolutionary prehuman and early human forebears. Rather than needing salvation from a fall into sin, we humans have developed sociological and cultural constraints to help control and "to save ourselves from" those primitive behavioral tendencies that are destructive of our modern communal life. When we die, our lives end, our bodies decay, and their elemental components reenter the physical universe to become resources used by other living organisms.

As I indicated previously, early in my life I began to question biblical teachings about matters of nature and science as taught by my church. Thinking that perhaps the church had just "gotten it wrong" about those matters, I was still accepting of its doctrines regarding what I considered spiritual matters. Later, during the illnesses of my children and wife, I turned to those aspects of my Christian tradition, believing that God could and would come to the rescue of my family members and heal them as the biblical narrative indicated that God had done for others. Surely, if God was anything like the Bible and my Church's teachings depicted God to be, it was reasonable for me to hope and even to expect God to hear my prayers – my begging – and to provide healing. Moreover, not only was *I* asking God to hear my prayers and to send healing; also vast numbers of members of the congre-

gations of which I was a member as well as of family members, friends and acquaintances in other Christian congregations and denominations were also pleading with God to send healing. However, the outcome was the same in all three cases; my family members died. I then seriously began to question whether I was not practicing my faith faithfully and responsibly; perhaps God had not answered my prayers because the practice of my faith was somehow faulty. But, if that were true, then the practices of all of my fellow Christians also must have been defective, because their prayers for my family members' healings also were not answered. I thought that somehow, some way, there must be something wrong in that big picture. A wit has said that insanity is continuing to utilize the same practice an eleventh time, expecting a different result, in spite of its not having worked for you the first ten times. Drawing on the wisdom of that witticism, I felt a deep and painful need to search for a saner, and hopefully more workable, understanding for my life,

Only later would I learn that I was dealing with an intractable problem that God-fearing people have faced since the early days of the Hebrew religion, which held that God blesses those who faithfully obey the divine statutes and punishes or at least withholds blessings from those who disobey God's commands. Theologians have termed this problem *theodicy*, often stated as a question. If God is totally good and all-powerful, how can God either cause or permit bad, destructive and evil things to happen to faithful and God-fearing people? Affirming one attribute of God demands the denial of another. If God causes evil things to happen, then God can be all-powerful but is no longer totally good. If evil things happen in spite of God's intent, then God can be totally good, but God is no longer all-powerful. The issue is perhaps the primary question addressed in the biblical book of Job, which ultimately provides no satisfying answer.

It is worthwhile to note that, among the world's great religions, this issue is especially problematic for the Abrahamic religions. When I examine the issue of theodicy in light of my earlier conclusion that all symbols of *UUR* (including God) are human imaginative constructions, I recognize that the theodicy questions arise because the symbol God has been conceived of as a spiritual entity having human agency. As a noetic agent, God makes decisions that are either good or evil, as judged by human moral and ethical standards. Because God is posited to be totally good, it is thought to be impossible for God to make evil decisions or decisions that result in evil things happening to humans. Concerning power, God is conceived of as having causative power as humans do but to an unlimited extent. Therefore, if something evil happens in spite of God's willing it not to happen, then God is not all-powerful. This dilemma will persist so long as *UUR* is conceived of as God, the supernatural human-like noetic agent. Traditionally, Christians have been counseled to resolve this dilemma by the assertion that the ways of God are beyond human understanding and therefore to be uncritically accepted; good Christians do not attempt to fathom these matters.

If, on the other hand, *UUR* is imaginatively conceived of and constructed as something other than human agency, the theodicy problem may not even arise. Such is the case when I imaginatively conceive *UUR* as *Nature's Creativity*. The events that happen are then not a result of a decision by some noetic entity but rather consequences of capacities and forces that are components of nature's operational processes. The following example can illustrate my point. Genetic mutations are changes that occur naturally in the DNA of all species. Most mutations probably result in detrimental changes – some so deleterious that organisms that carry them die. Other mutations result in changes that better adapt the species to its present environment or perhaps even allow it to occupy new environments.

Personalizing nature's creative processes, some mutations produced the more beautiful rose that grows in my yard. Other mutations caused the deaths of my daughter Tammy from Werdnig-Hoffman disease, of my daughter Bethany from acute lymphocytic leukemia and of my wife Darlene from acute myelocytic leukemia. The underlying mutational process in nature is the same; the outcome for the organisms in which mutations occur is very different.

When understood thus, bad things happen to both good and bad people, simply because we humans are embedded in nature's processes. Our being morally or ethically good or evil persons has no bearing on whether good or evil things happen to us. Of course, that is not to say that we do not experience good or bad consequences. If we make bad decisions, we are likely to suffer harmful consequences to ourselves or others. Making good decisions enhances the chances that the interplay of our decisions and nature's processes will result in favorable outcomes for us and/or others, although, of course, it does not ensure a favorable outcome. Broadly speaking, "mutations" of sorts can happen in many, perhaps all, natural processes. When they occur, what we consider good people (or animals or plants) may suffer harm. These calamities are simply part of the fabric of nature and have no relationship to human moral, ethical or even aesthetic assessment of whoever or whatever is experiencing them.

Recognizing that the problem of theodicy disappears when *UUR* is imaginatively conceived as *Nature's Creativity* provided me with one of the most convincing evidences that the symbol God in the Abrahamic religious traditions no longer functions to help orient me in the modern world. I also know that such a conclusion may not be so evident and persuasive to others. I think that the conclusion that I have reached is more likely to resonate with others who have experienced tragedies similar to mine. I am reminded of statements and belief stances of Jewish survivors of the

Holocaust, many of whom could no longer embrace the traditional Hebrew symbol of God.

Through the experiences of the losses of my family members I also came to question the efficacy of prayers to God – in particular, supplications for help. One of the conclusions that I reached during the course of my struggles was that perhaps God was for unknown reasons not listening to or hearing my prayers or those of other persons on behalf of my family members. When *UUR* is symbolized by a noetic agent (God), prayer and the expectation that prayers will be answered make sense. When *UUR* is imaginatively conceived as *Nature's Creativity*, there is simply no one or no thing to respond to prayer requests and therefore no rationale for expecting such supplicatory prayers for external intervention to be performative. To those who contend that their prayers have been answered, I note that careful studies conducted to determine whether prayed-for persons or outcomes fare better than nonprayed-for persons or outcomes generally have provided no convincing evidence for the effects of prayer. In addition, at least for individuals with respect to their own well-being, a "placebo effect" is a well-known phenomenon. Persons who are not receiving but who think that they are receiving assistance from some source, medical or otherwise, often fare better than those who do not know whether they are receiving something that might be curative. The reasons for a placebo effect are not well understood but may at least in some cases involve psychological phenomena that are mediated through endorphins, the *feel good*-inducing molecules in our bodies.

Some persons contend that "miraculous" healings that occurred in response to prayer are evidence for the power of supplicatory prayers to God – even for the existence of God. This is particularly true when a person is healed of some condition after all medical resources have been exhausted and even doctors have despaired of a cure. It is argued that such healings can only be interpreted as God's intervention in that situation to effect a healing.

When I examine the occurrence of such hoped-for, wonderful outcomes in light of *UUR*'s being *Nature's Creativity*, I can interpret it in a quite different way. First, during the evolutionary history of life, *Nature's Creativity* has not only accrued novel complexities one upon another. *It has also developed systems and processes that support and maintain the already existing complexity in life*. I think particularly of the immune systems found in many animals. Immune systems evolved to protect animals from foreign and destructive agents – bacteria, viruses, cancer cells, harmful substances from other organisms – that pose a threat to the well-being and even the life of an organism. It is prudent and pertinent to note that modern drugs and medicines do not replace the functions of the immune system. Rather, they act in conjunction with and as adjuvants to the functions of the immune system, sometimes perhaps setting the stage for it to overcome threats to the organism that it could not have accomplished without drug or medical intervention. While our understanding of immune systems is sufficient to devise and to produce drugs and medicines that work in the context of the immune system to effect cures of many diseases, such knowledge is by no means complete. Many complexities of the immune system remain to be discovered. If we extrapolate from the immune system to the entire body, the capacities of these still unknown healing processes may well account for the "miraculous" healings that happen from time to time; we are all thankful for them and marvel when they do occur.

5. *Epistemology*. The epistemological element of my worldview has to do with human knowledge. What is human knowledge? What do we know and how do we know it? What are the possible sources of

human knowledge?

What is human knowledge? There are numerous contextual definitions of knowledge. The following definition (Wikipedia) provides an appropriate starting point: "Knowledge is the awareness and understanding of facts, truths or information gained in the form of experience or learning (*a posteriori*), or through introspection (*a priori*). Knowledge is an appreciation of the possession of interconnected details which, in isolation, are of lesser value."

Not surprisingly, my epistemological views derive closely from my anthropological presuppositions. To put that in perspective, I begin by answering the question: How do we know? The simplistic answer is by using our brains. But that response would mask much background information and a number of presuppositions about our functioning brain. Because we humans are a product of the evolutionary process in the animal kingdom, our nature is rooted in precursors found in other animals. All animals have some combination of touch, taste, smell, hearing and sight through which they sense the natural world. While many other animals have one or more of these sensory systems much more highly developed than we humans have, the package that we humans have has allowed us to survive – yes, even to thrive – evolutionarily.

However, physical sensing of the environment is but one rudiment of what ultimately gives rise to our capacity to know. Many lower animals process the input of their sensory organs instinctively – almost mechanically. The relative simplicity of their brains cannot integrate their sensory input into complex mental capacities such as awareness, feelings, or relationships to other organisms. During the course of evolution, as the animal brain accrued increasing complexity – particularly in the cerebrum, the capacities for feelings, for awareness and for spatial relationships developed. For example, we and our mammalian cousins have a much higher development of the foregoing capacities than our more distant cousins – birds, reptiles, amphibians and fishes. And among mammals, our human brains have accrued far more complex functions than our closest cousins, the chimpanzees. It is important to note, however, that the rudiments of all of the capacities of our human brain are found in prehuman animal forms; that is, we humans differ quantitatively, not qualitatively, from our animal cousins in our capacities to know. All of these human capacities have arisen as adaptive functions selected for and molded by the evolutionary process. They arose as *Nature's Creativity* accrued one new complexity upon another in order to better adapt our prehuman ancestors and then us to live in our respective niches in the world environment.

Given the foregoing understanding of how through the evolutionary process *Nature's Creativity* has bequeathed us with complex mental functions, we humans create and develop knowledge to a much greater degree than any of our animal cousins; we can lay a rightful claim to our scientific name *Homo sapiens* – " the wise man." While we like other animals incorporate sensory inputs into our mental processing, they are only one component of that processing. Those inputs can be stored as memories and can be integrated with memories of previous experiences. Collections of experiences can be further processed by the brain's recall and reasoning abilities to create more complex and integrated concepts. The highly evolved capacities of the human brain for consciousness, self-consciousness, and time awareness allow us to integrate our life experiences into a personal narrative picture of ourselves and of our place in the world – our life history. If the foregoing processes occur successfully, they orient us in our world for meaningful and productive living.

In the foregoing I have enumerated capacities of the human brain that contribute to our ability to know. However, at present we have only very fragmentary knowledge about how the cells of the brain function biologically in the processes of learning and knowing. Although much current research effort is being directed towards understanding those processes, much of what we know still consists of phenomenology. It is likely that the twenty-first century will see a blossoming of our understanding of how the human brain functions in learning and memory, much as the twentieth century saw an elucidation of our understanding of DNA structure and function and what that knowledge has contributed to cell biology, genetics and evolution.

Having some appreciation of the phenomena involved in "how" we know provides a background for understanding "what" we know. What we know is knowledge – defined above as "the awareness and understanding of facts, truths or information gained in the form of experience or learning (a posteriori)." That includes not only data input from our senses, but also integration of sensory input with previously processed and organized concepts from our earlier individual life experiences. Beyond that, we can increase our individual knowledge by learning information and concepts that other people have created and transmitted to us; we do not have to experience and to process everything ourselves.

Also possessed by the human mind is the capacity for innovation – the ability to imagine possibilities beyond those which exist and occur in our natural world. Today we see the products of innovation in technology – the application of our knowledge of nature to harness or to modify natural processes towards human goals. For many years technological innovations seemingly benefited humans without apparent significant harm to the rest of nature. Unfortunately, however, since the Industrial Revolution human technological advancements have produced cumulatively detrimental effects on the rest of nature. Today some of the major problems that we face – global climate change, environmental destruction and mass species extinction – are results of the technological applications of knowledge that humans have

acquired through use of the human brain with its marvelous capacities. If there is a lesson for us in what has happened and continues to happen, it is that we as a species must exhibit much less hubris and exercise more prudence, modesty and humility as we interact in our natural world – lest we destroy that world and ourselves with it. That will involve using our intellectual capacities to inquire about the possible detrimental effects of potential technological innovations "before" we deploy them. We must live up to our name – "wise man."

Finally, as a capstone function, the human brain also possesses highly developed capacities for *abstract reasoning*, using logical powers to create new information and ideas. Often that involves the mental processing of ideas and concepts that have no physical existence and, therefore, are not even accessible to our senses; they exist only as constructs of our thinking and figments of our imagination. Nevertheless, we often utilize abstract reasoning to create new, valid and useful ideas, understandings and conclusions for orienting ourselves in life and making our lives more meaningful. Much art, music and fictional and science fictional writing utilizes this human capacity not only to entertain us but also to stimulate us to conceive or to recognize new possibilities for the real world.

For everything that has been said about "how" we know and "what" we know, the presupposition has been that the capacities to know and the content of what we know derive exclusively from natural phenomena. That is, they exist because of the capacities of the human brain as it has emerged from *Nature's Creativity* through the evolutionary process in order to adapt us to our niche in nature. There is neither evidence for nor need to invoke anything extranatural or supernatural acting either in the origins of our capacities to know or of the content of what we know. The notion that an external spiritual, noetic force influences or directs the functioning human mind or infuses specific content into human knowledge and memory gains no traction or support in the framework presupposed here.

In the previous paragraphs, I have described the possibilities that abstract reasoning and innovative thinking can contribute to the enhancement and enrichment of human life. We should not need to be reminded, but *it is important that we always keep our life's expectations grounded in the real possibilities of our natural world* as we best understand its functions today. That is, if we imagine with our mental capacities some idea or concept, we can only expect it to be a realistic possibility if its creation or existence is consistent with our best modern understandings of the natural laws of physics, chemistry and biology. As a simple illustration, alchemy does not become chemistry simply because we can imagine that it could or because we want it to.

When, for whatever reasons, we consider a fictional idea, concept or scenario as knowledge about the real world, we are likely to create expectations for ourselves that cannot possibly be met. From my own experience, I now look back and see how that happened in my life at the times of the illnesses and deaths of my family members. Many teachings of my church derive from an ancient worldview, a number of whose elements are now known not to have been correct understandings of reality, as earlier discussed. Results of historical-critical studies have shown how and why many of those elements became part of the Christian tradition. As long as I considered those impossibilities as "knowledge" on which to base my expectations in real life, I now see that it was inevitable that I would experience disappointment, disillusionment and pain. It was only when I began to critically examine those once-credible (in ancient worldviews) but now incredible beliefs that I began to set my life on a course in which my expectations of life are anchored in the realities and realistic possibilities of the ways that nature operates.

Before leaving epistemology, I want to mention the contributions of two scientists who have presented views on the nature of knowledge, especially as it relates to science and religion. The first was the late Stephen J. Gould, an evolutionary biologist who labeled himself a Jewish agnostic. He proposed the following relationship regarding knowledge in the areas of science and religion.

We may, I think, adopt this word [magisterium] and concept to express the central point of this essay and the principled resolution of supposed "conflict" or "warfare" between science and religion. No such conflict should exist, because each subject has a legitimate magisterium, or domain of teaching authority – and these magisteria do not overlap (the principle that I would like to designate as NOMA, or "nonoverlapping magisteria").

According to Gould, the magisteria or domains of science and religion are each legitimate areas of human study and realms of truth. The domain of science is the empirical universe, concerned with the physical and biological realms and with fact and theory. The domain of religion concerns questions of spirituality and of moral meaning and value. No attempt should be made to find overlap, compatibility or connection between these magisteria, because an *a priori* assumption is that none exists. Conflicts arise when people attempt to make connections where none exist. Nevertheless, inquirers in the two fields might find it mutually informative and enlightening to discuss the knowledge in their respective realms with each other.

The second scientist is also an evolutionary biologist, E. O. Wilson, who in his book *Consilience: The Unity of Knowledge* contemporizes the meaning of that ancient term. He defines consilience as "literally a jumping together of knowledge by the linking of facts and fact-based theory across disciplines to create a common groundwork for explanation." The implied assumption is that there is an underlying unitary understanding to be discovered, not only between the sciences but ultimately also with the humanities, including religion. Wilson posits that if inquirers in each discipline utilize valid and reliable investigative techniques, they will find the deepest truths of their respective disciplines. When such truths are arrived at for all disciplines, these truths will "jump together" to yield a comprehensive, unitary understanding of reality – there will be *consilience*.

It seems to me that Wilson's proposition, rather than Gould's, is a valid expectation of my own worldview. If *UUR* is *Nature's Creativity*, then all of present reality is emergent complexity produced by that creativity since the origin of matter at *the big bang*. It is to be expected that there would be an internal consistency in the creative processes. Underlying all creativity there should exist some unifying and unitary understanding – the consilient principle(s). How long it will take and how close we shall get to that foundational consilience remains to be seen. Nevertheless, seeking that consilience seems an appropriate epistemological goal as we humans continue to deepen our understanding of nature, of ourselves, and of our place in nature.

6. *Teleology*. The teleological element of my worldview concerns what I believe about purpose in the universe – for the universe as a whole, for humans in general, and for myself in particular. This aspect of worldview is very important from a humanistic perspective because it is closely tied to humans' finding meaning and purpose in life. While many people today are convinced of and emotionally comfortable with the notion that humans are the product of the evolutionary process, they find it difficult – even impossible – to accept the conclusion that this process was and is the product of random events and accidents, which reductionistic materialism seems to imply.

For many people, living in such a universe is akin to riding on a large modern jet passenger plane and hearing the pilot address the passengers on the intercom. "Good morning, passengers. I have some good news and some bad news. The good news is that the engines are working well, our fuel tanks are full, and we are making excellent time. The bad news is that our directional instruments are completely nonfunctional, and we have absolutely no idea where we are going." Living in a universe that is functioning well but going nowhere or to an unknown destination seems pointless to humans, who, to live meaningfully, must feel a part of something that is going somewhere – part of a purposeful larger picture.

On an individual level, people also need to feel that their lives are going somewhere. Many people are willing to walk or to run for hours on a treadmill, expending huge amounts of energy and perhaps ending up quite exhausted. Yet, when they step off of the treadmill, they are still at the same place as when they stepped onto the treadmill; they have gone nowhere. People on a treadmill have at least gotten some beneficial exercise that contributes towards healthy living; most people would not commit themselves to such a strenuous effort without some sense of deriving benefit. However, as a metaphor for the whole of their lives, the exercise of living intensely and having accomplished no purpose does not provide a satisfactory outcome to make life worth living. We humans need more than that.

I am typically human in that respect. I need purpose and meaning in my life. The question thus becomes for me: can I find purpose and meaning in my life, knowing that the human species and I, in particular, are the product of *Nature's Creativity*?

Before I move to directly answer that question, I want to examine the purpose and goal of life and of the universe as viewed from the traditional Christian teleological perspective. Briefly summarized, the biblical narrative relates that God created the universe and all life, including humans. Although not explicitly stated, God's apparent purpose for creating the universe was to provide a setting for God's plan for humans to unfold. The divine purpose for humans was to glorify God by living according to God's commands to them, which included being a blessing to the nations of the earth and taking care of God's creation. When God's plan was foiled by the human's use of their free will to disobey God's command and to sin, God's reconciliation plan was to redeem humans by sending Jesus the Christ, who suffered a sacrificial death by crucifixion. Humans' faith in Jesus' sacrifice restores them to a redeemed and saved relationship with God. After their mortal deaths, the redeemed exist eternally in the presence of God in heaven. The purpose of human life in this scenario is to live life according to God's will and plan, with the ultimate goal of living eternally with God in heaven.

I want to examine that overarching narrative in some detail. First, based on what is known today about the origins of religions, the Hebrew-Christian symbol God is but one of many possible imaginative constructions of UUR. Therefore, irrespective of how well it and its attendant narrative served to provide teleological meaning and purpose for the early Hebrews and later Christians, the Judeo-Christian narrative was (and is) but one narrative that was imaginatively conceived by ancient peoples. Other imaginative conceptions of UUR and their attendant narratives seem to have worked equally well for adherents of other religions. Thus, the Judeo-Christian symbol God and the attendant biblical narrative cannot be regarded as having exclusive validity or even a preferred status in filling humans' teleological needs.

That I am today critical of the Judeo-Christian symbol for God and its attendant narrative does not in any way belittle the intelligence or malign the motivations of the ancient religious leaders who imaginatively conceived them. They were most likely fully as intelligent as modern *Homo sapiens*. Their efforts to discover meaning and purpose for their communal and individual lives drew on the knowledge, wisdom and understandings of their times – all of which factored into the worldview presuppositions of their times. In their considerations of those worldview presuppositions, they discovered and conceptualized their symbol of UUR and the attendant narrative (including its teleology) that seemed to emerge and to issue from those presuppositions. If modern people (*without* modern worldview presuppositions) had been transported back to those times and been presented with the circumstances and world presuppositions of those times, they likely would have reached the same conclusions! Thus, it was not the intelligence or motivations of those who discovered and imaginatively conceived the symbols for UUR and their attendant narratives, but rather the worldview presuppositions that proscribed and influenced the content of what those symbols and narratives could be. This conclusion should emphasize to us modern humans the importance of discovering and imaginatively conceiving UUR and an attendant narrative (including teleology) that is informed by the presuppositions of our modern worldview.

Once the biblical teleology became incorporated in the Judeo-Christian narrative, it assumed the authority of the Scriptures in which that narrative was embedded. Although scriptural authority was secondary to Church authority in the pre-Reformation Western Church and later Roman Catholicism, the Church's dogmas and worship practices reinforced and perpetuated the biblical teleology. In Protestantism the same end was accomplished by adoption of the *sola Scriptura* mantra, which granted absolute authority to Scriptures. Because this biblical teleology has become so entrenched and integrated into the foundational authorities of traditional Christianity, any attempts to modify or to replace biblical presuppositions with modern presuppositions threaten the entire biblical worldview and are therefore strongly resisted and condemned by both Roman Catholicism and Protestantism.

Previously, I have inquired into the validity of the authority claimed for the Scriptures and for the Church. Based on the studies of many biblical scholars using historical-critical methods of study cited in earlier chapters, my conclusions were that the Bible consists entirely of writings of *human* religious leaders who were expressing their understandings of God's purpose and will for their respective religious communities. The writings included in the Bible were the results of decisions by *human* religious leaders, acting on the authority of the Church. That authority emanated from early Christianity's being selected by a *human* Roman Emperor as the official religion of the Roman Empire; the authority of the Church in Western European society waxed through the centuries of the Middle Ages as the authority of the Roman Empire itself waned. Finally, the preeminent biblical authority in Protestantism today reflects a trajectory that began with the selection of the *sola Scriptura* mantra by *human* leaders of the Reformation and culminated with the birth of biblical fundamentalism by *human* church leaders in the early twentieth century in North America.

Considering this big picture, then, I am left with the conclusion that the purpose and goal found in Christianity is not a teleology that came into Hebraism and Christianity from some external, supernatural or divine source, but rather it was a *humanly*-discovered and *humanly*-conceived teleology (purpose and goal) that functioned to give purpose and meaning to its adherents with the worldview presuppositions of those times. Because of that, it was woven into the Hebraic-Christian narrative through the centuries as the literary compositions that would become the Bible were being written. Thus, I conclude that, while it has served as

an inspiring teleology for several thousands of years, *it is, in fact, a teleology that was discovered and conceived by humans to give purpose and meaning to the universe and to their lives.*

While that teleology was appropriate for the times when the presuppositions of the other elements of the ancient worldviews were considered valid, in my view it is no longer appropriate in today's worldview. I need an appropriate teleology for the modern world in which I live. If ancient humans had the freedom to discover and to imaginatively conceive a functional teleology for their lives in their times, do we not also have the freedom to do so today? Perhaps we can even say that we have the responsibility and the duty to discover, to imagine and to construct a teleology that enables us to successfully orient ourselves in the modern world and to live purposefully and productively therein.

What teleology might be discovered and conceived for the modern worldview? When I consider a purpose and goal for the universe, again I come up against the same hurdle that I encountered when I tried to answer the questions: "Why is there something rather than nothing? Why does the universe exist? What was the cause of *the big bang*?" At present we do not have enough knowledge of everything that occurred in *the big bang* to discern an endpoint towards which our universe is going, if indeed there is an endpoint. While through the acquisition of human knowledge I (we) can have an informed understanding of how the universe and life have evolved to their present state, I cannot know where it is going or if there is reason or purpose for its continuing to go wherever it is going. Nevertheless, informed by our knowledge of what has gone on in the past, I can surmise that *Nature's Creativity* will continue to operate in the future as it has in the past and does in the present; but that, too, is only an informed guess.

On the other hand, it seems to me that we

can discover and imaginatively conceive purpose, meaning and a goal for our *human* existence today, just as our religious forebears did. *Nature's Creativity* has endowed the human species with its hallmark characteristics: consciousness, self-consciousness, awareness of other, concrete and abstract reasoning abilities, innovation, oral and written language communication, etc. Because of these capacities, we humans are able to comprehend our relationship to each other and to the rest of nature – how we can live compatibly and harmoniously within nature. We can understand the workings of nature sufficiently that we can to some extent control and alter its activities and processes – albeit for both the benefit and the destruction of the rest of nature and of ourselves. Utilizing our rational intelligence and innovative capacities, we can discover how the myriad of living organisms produced by *Nature's Creativity* can continue to survive and to thrive on planet earth and then commit ourselves towards allowing and, where possible, facilitating that end. Such a purpose seems all the more worthwhile and appropriate at this time, as we humans are facing the challenges of global climate change, environmental destruction, mass species extinctions and human overpopulation. Committing ourselves to achieve that goal helps to ensure that both physical and biological materials continue to exist so that *Nature's Creativity* can continue to operate. Success in achieving that goal will result in more abundant living for us humans as well as for the rest of nature. Ironically, if we choose this as the meaningful purpose and goal of our human existence, we come up with a teleology, one aspect of which is not very different from that of our Hebraic-Christian forebears – to be wise caretakers of creation.

Beyond discovering and defining teleology for the whole of humanity, I can also consider it from an individual and personal perspective. As discussed previously, we humans can think and talk about realities and notions that are not sensorially accessible to us only through the use of symbols and metaphors that draw on our experiences of the natural world and of our mental imagery. Thus, I have talked about God and gods as being imaginative constructions of *UUR*. Similarly, the notions of heaven, hell, Hades and Sheol are imaginative constructions of what some have imagined human afterlife to be like, although there is, of course, no objective description of any of them. In particular, the notion of heaven has provided an individual teleological goal of great spiritual incentive and emotional support to Christians as a place where they live on eternally in the presence of God as a reward for lives of faithfulness and obedience to God's commands and laws. In the conceptual framework that I have proposed, *UUR* is imaginatively conceived as *Nature's Creativity*, and human life, like that of all living organisms, is considered to end with the physical death of the individual. Within this paradigm, are there any considerations that can provide emotional and spiritual support and inspiration analogous to the notion of heaven as an afterlife?

In an earlier chapter I described human conception, in which a mother's egg is fertilized by a father's sperm forming a zygote, which through a continuous, epi-genetic, developmental process grows to form first an embryo, then a fetus and finally at birth, a baby. This entire process involves the continual transformation of less specialized living cells into more specialized types of cells, tissues, organs, systems and finally an organism – the baby. There is no point at which something nonliving becomes something living, no point at which a soul or spirit *per se* enters the developing body making it alive. From a first-person perspective, the continuity of living cells in my body ends when I die. From that point on, I as organism cease to exist. However, when my body decays, its component chemical elements and compounds are released into the biosphere and become available to provide sustenance to other living organisms. In that sense, the components of my body continue to live on, one might even say eternally, through the succession of living organisms that utilize those components after they were part of my body. In order that the components of my body become available to other organisms more quickly after my death, my desire is for my body to be cremated. In that way the gaseous products of cremation are immediately released into the biosphere for use by other organisms; the ashes that remain can be spread, perhaps in a garden or other symbolically suitable location where they, too, can contribute to the support of other living organisms. From my perspective, this manner of dealing with my body is much preferable to being buried in a sealed casket encased in a concrete vault, both of which would for a long time inhibit the return of the components of my body into the biosphere. Although not consistent with many aspects of the Christian tradition, this manner of dealing with a human body resonates with the "ashes to ashes and dust to dust" wording (extrapolated from the English burial service and from Genesis 3:19) often spoken during funerals and at gravesites.

From another perspective, I can also live on, although not eternally. If during my life I contribute to the betterment of the lives of other people and of the rest of nature, those thoughts and actions may "live on" as a legacy long after my death. Although most people do not consciously live towards the end of being remembered, it is nevertheless true that through our religious and holiday observances we remember and celebrate persons who lived their lives for ministry to and for the betterment of others: Buddha, Confucius, Jesus, Mahatma Gandhi, George Washington, Abraham Lincoln, Martin Luther King and others. They live on in us through the good that they have done. This notion is also acknowledged by the Christian tradition in Revelation 14:13, where it is said of those in eternal rest that "their good deeds follow them."

7. *Axiology*. The axiological element of my worldview concerns my beliefs about human values. What is good and bad? What is right and wrong? What are the origins of these value assessments?

My beliefs about axiological issues also derive rather straightforwardly from my anthropological, metaphysical and theological presuppositions. As far as we know, our prehuman ancestors had no complex, conceptual value systems anything like those present in human societies today. Therefore, I must conclude that in the course of evolving towards modern humanity, we humans have somehow discovered and developed our systems of values, morals and ethics in response to perceived needs for the orderly establishment and maintenance of family and of larger societal structures. Precisely how those developments occurred among early humans is refractory to anthropological investigation, because they left no traces in fossils or other artifactual evidence. Nevertheless, if we extrapolate from what is known about our closest ape ancestors to what is known about modern human society, a rather accurate scenario of the origin and development of values, morals and ethics can probably be constructed.

According to evidence presented in *The Third Chimpanzee* by Jared Diamond, many aspects of human behavior and culture have rudimentary corresponding parallels in gorilla and chimpanzee social organization. These closest modern relatives of us humans live in groups of biologically-related individuals called troupes, which are probably similar in social structure and organization to that of their and our common evolutionary ancestor. Gorillas and chimps have developed interactions that enable relatively stable social structure and order between biologically-related individuals within the same troupe. Yet, they, like humans, have an inherent xenophobia – suspicion and fear of members of other troupes of their own species that they do not recognize as being biologically-related to themselves. As noted in an earlier chapter, because of that xenophobia, both gorillas and chimps also exhibit genocide, the killing of members of other biologically-unrelated troupes or bands of their own species. Regrettably, genocide issuing from xenophobia is still too frequently also observed among humans today, quite probably as a carryover from our evolutionary past.

Early humans existed as small migrating bands of biologically-related individuals that only infrequently encountered other bands that were biologically-unrelated to them. Then they required a morality and ethics that governed primarily thoughts and behaviors between biologically-related individuals. At that stage of societal and communal development, xenophobic behaviors were perhaps at least in some ways still adaptive. However, as human populations increased in size and more densely populated the earth, bands encountered other unrelated bands more frequently. Conflicts occurred that stimulated humans to develop and to use military tools and tactics both to attack and to defend themselves from their enemies. Eventually, as humans transitioned from roving hunter-gatherers to more stationary agricultural societies and city-dwelling cultures, xenophobic and genocidal behaviors became destructtive to communal living and to societal structure. Cooperation with, rather than fear and destruction of, other biologically-unrelated humans became positive adaptive behaviors. Humans then needed to develop a *universal code* that stipulated that individuals and groups treat biologically-unrelated individuals and groups according to the same moral and ethical standards that they treated their own relatives. The adoption of a universal code enabled biologically-unrelated people to live together peacefully in villages and later cities.

Concomitant with these changes in behavior between bands of unrelated persons, there were also changes within the bands of related persons. Chimps and gorillas still have a polygamous troupe structure in which a dominant male monopo-

lizes and exclusively mates with all the adult females in the troupe, presumably like our prehuman ancestors. The emergence of the human species was accompanied by a transition from a polygamous to a monogamous relationship between adult males and females that became the precursor of the modern family. Most societies of early humans discovered and codified the notion that monogamy enhanced the successful rearing of their progeny and the stability of their communities.

These transitions in within-band and between-band relationships required altered behaviors in order for families and communities to develop as stable units of social structure. Their increasing intelligence allowed early humans to recognize the need for rules that prescribed acceptable and proscribed unacceptable behaviors between family members and between biologically-unrelated members of a community. Our knowledge that the domestication of plant and animal species associated with agriculture and the founding of the earliest towns and villages began around 10,000 BCE suggests that the development of these behavioral codes must have been ongoing at that time. Early written records, such as the Sumerian Family Laws and the Code of Hammurabi from Mesopotamia, indicate that laws and rules for family and societal behavior were well-developed and had already been codified by around 2,000 BCE (4,000 years ago). These existing written records allude to antecedents that probably originated and existed long before written languages were developed to record them.

As noted in earlier chapters, while these social and cultural changes were occurring, religions were also emerging and evolving. Different societies imaginatively conceived different symbols for *UUR*. In many tribes and chiefdoms ruled by warlords and chiefs, the power and authority of the ruler were so intermingled with that of the deity that they were considered one and the same. As tribes and chiefdoms aggregated to states and nations, this development grew even more pronounced. I earlier noted that even in Israel and Judah, which claimed steadfast allegiance to Yahweh, most of the king's names contained some root of the name Yahweh or Elohim. This close association between the human ruler and deity provided a vehicle for authority to enforce the rules that had been deemed necessary by that society (perhaps they were just edicts of the god-king) for its orderly existence. Laws that were considered the most essential to an orderly society (*i.e.* The Ten Commandments) were identified as commands of the deity, obedience of which brought blessings and disobedience of which brought punishments. Through this process, rules and laws governing society became associated with the deity's will and purpose for the followers of the deity. The societal benefit of this development was that, although kings and dynasties came and went, the religion's deity persisted and evolved to become the continual authority for society's rules and laws.

Much of the foregoing synthesized scenario is backed by established historical evidence; in places I have tried to "connect the dots" in order to give a general overarching picture of what I believe to have been the origins of human value, morality and ethics. The details of that picture show that all assessments of good and bad and of right and wrong are products of human endeavor facilitated by the evolution of the increasingly complex human brain with its greater capacities for reasoning, discovery and innovation. Humans perceived needs and discovered and devised societal values, rules and laws to meet those needs. It is likely that most early rules and laws pertained to collective rather than to individual well-being. That is, the rules and laws functioned to create and to mold individuals who were compliant members of society and contributed to its communal welfare. Most notions of individual rights and privileges are rather modern developments. In general, regarding values,

something was assessed as "good" if it enhanced the well-being of society; it was considered "bad" if it was deemed harmful to society. Categorizing a thought or an action as "right" or "righteous" implied obedience of a rule or law that was considered so important to societal welfare that it carried the status of a command or order of the deity; conversely, something considered "wrong" or "sinful" involved disobedience of such a divine rule or law. The punishments for wrong or sinful actions were generally severe, frequently being death. On the other hand, punishments for breaches of society's lower ranking rules more often involved fines and forms of restitution to the victims or to the deity. Refinement of this system of justice led to the modern principle of justice that the "punishment should fit the crime."

I can assess the origin of the Hebrew religion and the Hebraic-Christian axiological tradition in light of the foregoing scenario. For purposes of this discussion, I will assume that the patriarchs and Moses were historical persons. The earliest possible roots of the Hebrew people and religion occurred around 1800-2000 BCE, the probable time of Abraham and the other patriarchs. If Abraham originated in Ur of Chaldea, as the Genesis narrative suggests, he was very likely aware of much of the contents of the Code of Hammurabi and/or the Sumerian Family Laws. This time frame also indicates that when Yahweh was imaginatively conceived as the Hebrew symbol for *UUR* sometime after 2000 BCE, the Sumerian Family Laws and the Code of Hammurabi had already been operational for hundreds of years. Although the best estimates place the time of Moses around 1300 BCE, the oldest known documents written in the Hebrew language date to about 1100-1000 BCE. The period of the united and divided kingdoms extended from about 1000-590 BCE, during which time many of the documents were being written that would later be included in the Hebrew Bible.

Although components of the moral and religious laws undoubtedly arose during the time of the Southern Kingdom (Judah), the best biblical scholarship suggests that the law-containing books of Exodus, Leviticus and Deuteronomy probably were not compiled and edited to their final forms until the time of the Exile (ca. 590-540 BCE), some 1500 years later than the earlier Sumerian and Babylonian codes. Although the biblical narrative relates the Ten Commandments and other moral and ceremonial laws as issuing directly from Yahweh, the historical reality is that these laws and rules were conceptualized and codified by *human* leaders of the Hebrew people and acquired the authority of Yahweh in the same way that laws acquired the authority of the gods in the surrounding nations. Additionally, the best information about their time of origin suggests that the Hebrews probably drew on the societal wisdom of the surrounding nations to fashion their own axiology.

I conclude by summarizing my axiological beliefs. Human value systems arose in the context of humans' biological and cultural evolution towards their modern condition. Assessments of thoughts and behaviors were deemed "good" or "bad" and "right" or "wrong" depending on whether they contributed positively towards societal well-being or whether they were detrimental to society. Because of the greater intellectual and reasoning capacities enabled by their increasingly complex brain, humans were able to discover, to perceive and to devise the rules and laws that were required in order for families and societies to exist stably and to function in an orderly manner. The coevolution of these moral and ethical rules and laws with the religion of the community provided an association between the purposes of the rules and laws and the will of the deity for the people and their society. This association provided the necessary authority to enforce the rules and laws within that society over time. According to this view, no laws or rules were (or are) received from external authoritative sources that authorize their validity for all times or for all places. Rather, as with all other elements of my worldview, they must continually be critically examined and evaluated in the context of their use and reconstructed, if that is required for the betterment of society and/or of individuals.

Now that I have gone through the process of identifying my beliefs and presuppositions concerning each of the elements of my worldview, I recognize that I am what today is called a *philosophical naturalist*. Identifying *UUR* as *Nature's Creativity*, I attribute the emergent complexity that is present reality to nature's creative capacities that have been acting on the original materials produced by *the big bang*. All physical matter and all living organisms, including all dimensions of human being, society and culture, have arisen through natural evolutionary processes. There is neither evidence for nor need to invoke the activity or participation of any transcendent noetic agent or supernatural force(s) external to or in addition to nature. So far as I can discern, the processes of nature are "all that there is."

Yet, having concluded that nature is "all there is," I must add some qualifications that distinguish my worldview from what has been termed *scientific reductionism*, which holds that the analytic results of our scientific methodologies are sufficient to account for everything that is observed in the natural world. As noted earlier, these methodological approaches often require holding constant what are known to be variables in nature, thereby enabling valid conclusions to be reached about the single variable in the complex natural system being analyzed. While the conclusions drawn are valid for the specifics of the experiments being conducted, they do not accurately reflect the true complexity of nature, in which each of the variables in the system can take on many values. Thus, such scientific methodologies give important insights into – but not complete, comprehensive understandings of – the full complexity of nature. Moreover, scientists are beginning to learn some things about how *Nature's Creativity* includes self-organizing capacities that give rise to emergent complex novelties. Natural systems contain such emergent complexities compounded one upon another during the course of evolution. Scientists and mathematicians are discovering that at least some of this compounded complexity can be modeled by chaos theory and other complex mathematical formulae. At present, it is not known what additional creative capacities remain to be discovered. Thus, it is simply not honest to state or to imply that results of current scientific analyses permit an accounting for *all* that has arisen in nature. *While it is true that everything that is observed appears to be due to capacities and forces within nature, it is not true that present knowledge and understanding comprehensively account for all that is observed.* There is still much to be learned, for which, at least for the present, there is perhaps no better description than "mystery."

I have also dealt with the criticism that metaphysical views that identify *UUR* with *Nature's Creativity* provide no purpose and meaning for the universe or for human life within it. I noted that current understandings of the origins and development of religions indicate that whatever purpose and meaning for the universe and for human life there might be in the various religious narratives have been incorporated into those religious narratives by the human writers of the foundational scriptures of the various religions. That is, the purpose and meaning of the universe and of human life found in religious narratives occur as imaginative constructs of the human writers of those scriptures, drawing on their symbol of *UUR*, rather than as purpose and meaning introduced from external supernatural or other transcendent sources. Given that fact, we modern humans have the opportunity and responsibility to imaginatively create purpose and meaning for our lives based on our understanding of

Nature's Creativity as *UUR*. I suggest that a meaningful purpose and goal for humans today is to be caretakers for the marvelous natural world gifted and bequeathed to us by *Nature's Creativity*. This would involve addressing and correcting the problems that we humans have inflicted on nature – global climate change, environmental destruction, mass species extinction and human overpopulation. Such purposes and goals would benefit the rest of nature as well as us humans; indeed, it is not too strong an assertion to say that human and all other life *depends* on our dealing successfully with these challenges. Considered from an individual teleology, we can understand the physical elements and compounds of our bodies to be in a continuous interchange with the rest of nature; while we are alive, our bodies are comprised of components that were part of life that has gone before us, and the components of our bodies become accessible to other living organisms when our bodies decay after our deaths. We also live on after death through the ideas and services that we contribute towards making our societies and our larger world a better place for our human posterity and for the rest of nature.

Why was/is it important for me to identify my beliefs and presuppositions that comprise the various elements of my worldview? First, I have come to believe that, without doing that, it becomes nearly impossible for me to have a holistic, internally consistent and integrated understanding of reality. If I have presuppositions in one element of my worldview that conflict with those of another element, I cannot integrate them; I can continue to hold both views only by compartmentalizing them, so that they do not have to be reconciled with each other. Such was the case for me earlier in life when I tried to have one concept of the God of nature and another concept of the God of my spiritual world. I now recognize that I was trying to simultaneously hold two conflicting views of *UUR*. I somehow needed to resolve that inconsistency.

While I was gathering materials and organizing my thoughts before writing this chapter, I came across the Shirley MacLaine statement under the heading of this chapter: "We are not victims of the world we see. We are victims of the way we see the world." I was intrigued by it and thought it spoke to the content of this chapter. A victim is someone "who suffers from a destructive or injurious action or agency" (Random House College Dictionary). In the present case, the injurious actions and agency are the Church's claims that it and the Bible intrinsically have complete and unquestionable authority over all matters in its members' lives. Whenever I allow any authority, religious or secular, to impose on me tenets to be accepted without critical examination, I can become not only a "victim" of but also a "captive" of the worldview created for me by those tenets, although those tenets impede my attainment of a constructive orientation in the world. Concerning the first sentence of the MacLaine statement, when I experienced the deaths of my family members in the context of my belief in the traditional Judeo-Christian symbol of *UUR*, I did see myself and the surviving members of my family as victims of God's injustice and unfairness. After all, why should none of the three good, just and worthy members of my family receive God's healing blessing when the tradition assured me that such healings could and did happen? Later, as I was struggling along my journey of faith, I discovered and integrated into my worldview a number of the elements that are included in this chapter. It was then that I began to realize and to understand that I had been a "victim" of the way that I saw the world in which I lived; I had been a "captive" of a worldview, at least some elements of which were not congruent with the reality of the world in which I was living.

Thus, a second reason to explicitly identify my worldview presuppositions is so that I can have expectations of life that are realistic possibilities. As long as I viewed *UUR* as a God who could and would intervene and tweak the happenings of nature to effect some particular outcome – in my case, healing the diseases of my family members, I was "set up" to experience disappointment and pain and then to face the theodicy problem of why God seemed to be capricious, ignoring the pleadings of faithful Christians. Understanding *UUR* as *Nature's Creativity*, I recognize that through its long evolutionary history nature has accrued inherent capacities that enable individual bodies to heal themselves in order for a species to survive. However, sometimes it is nature's inherent healing capacities in conjunction with human medical intervention that cooperate to achieve the hoped-for healing of illnesses and diseases and restoration of the body's functioning capacities. And regrettably, sometimes even that combination is unable to effect a cure. Whatever the outcome, it was neither contingent on nor affected by my or others' supplications to an imaginatively-conceived symbol of *UUR*. Nor was the outcome dependent on how righteous or sinful were the supplicants or those needing healing. The outcome was determined by whether the self-regulating and self-healing capacities that have emerged within the human species together with the medical intervention based on modern human scientifically-derived understandings would be able to correct the malady in the human body. To be sure, my earlier fervent belief that an omnipotent God could and would intervene to effect my desired outcome was the basis for hope for a miraculous healing. Unfortunately for my family members and me, it was not based on reality but on false expectations that were derived from unrealistic presuppositions of my worldview. For my religious beliefs to help orient and sustain me in life, they must be based on expectations consistent with my best understanding of reality – and of *UUR*.

Finally, a third reason that it is important for me to know and to understand the contents of the individual elements of my worldview is in order to keep the contents of each of them up-to-date. By keeping each of them informed by the best available knowledge and understanding, I guard against their becoming outdated, as happened with my traditional Judeo-Christian worldview.

Thus, when my experiences of life are interpreted against the soundboard of world-view presuppositions informed by the best available human knowledge and understanding of reality, I am best able to orient my life for dealing with all the vicissitudes of life. I now turn to what that has come to mean for me personally.

Chapter 13

The Collapse of My Traditional Faith and the Emergence of My Authentic Faith

"My own education operated by a succession of eye-openers, each involving the repudiation of some preciously held belief."

George Bernard Shaw

The above statement by George Bernard Shaw captures the essence of my spiritual journey. Little by little each eye-opening experience eroded my confidence and faith in the system of beliefs that had been instilled in me early in my life. This chapter brings together the disparate strands of that erosive process. Although there were intimations of doubt in my early life, my efforts to process my thoughts and feelings following the deaths of my two daughters and my wife brought that process to a crescendo. Because the final collapse of my traditional faith was the culmination of a process, this chapter includes some reviews and restatements of ideas and conclusions discussed earlier.

Shortly after my birth, my parents and my Church began to indoctrinate me in the traditional, Lutheran Christianity that had been the support and mainstay of many generations of my forebears. Although the content of that indoctrination was surely considered important, equally or more important was the projected attitude with which this indoctrination was to be received: good and faithful Lutherans uncritically and unquestioningly accept the authority of *sola Scriptura* as interpreted by the Lutheran Church. Now as I look back and assess the nature of that religion, it could perhaps be best described as Lutheran fundamentalism. The faith which that form of religion engendered in me seemed adequate as long as I was safely "cocooned" within the parochial bounds of that traditional Luther-

anism. However, when in high school biology the findings of modern science broke into that sheltered sphere, I was confronted with views and understandings different from the biblical worldview presumed by that form of Lutheranism. I began to have serious doubts that its *sola Scriptura* tenets provided a true, accurate and relevant basis to orient me for a meaningful and fulfilling life in the modern world. As years passed, I eventually concluded that, with respect to modern science, the Bible was much more a hindrance than a help in my efforts to orient myself in the world.

While rejecting claims for the Bible's authority in matters of science and nature, I nevertheless persisted in believing that its claims in "spiritual" matters were valid and important for my life. Then over the course of twenty years in my adult life my daughters Tammy and Bethany and my wife Darlene died of diseases. Throughout the courses of their illnesses, my Lutheran communities and I diligently and fervently drew on all the spiritual resources of that traditional Lutheran faith – prayer, worship, prayer, healing services, prayer, pleading with God and more prayer – in the firm hope and trust that the healing and wholeness that were part of the biblical narrative would be visited by God in the lives of my beloved family members. I reasoned that, if the biblical narratives of healing were genuine and authentic, God could also heal the important people in my life. Three times

God had an opportunity to heal a member of my family; three times my family member died. After three strikes, my faith in the seemingly capricious God of my traditional Lutheran faith had struck out.

I then needed to go on a spiritual journey – to explore not only my own Lutheran Christian tradition but also the larger role of religion in people's lives. What I learned was both disturbing and revealing. It was disturbing because I learned that most elements of my traditional faith were carry-overs from religious understandings and practices from ancient worldviews, where miraculous healings, virgin births and resurrections were commonplace elements of many religions besides Christianity. Although they were parts of those ancient mythical religious narratives, I concluded that they did not actually occur then anymore than they happen now. The healings that I had asked God to provide for my loved ones were unrealistic expectations; the notion that they could occur derived from ancient religious mythologies rather than from real and actual occurrences in people's lives. I then also concluded that, for me, not only was the Bible not an authority on matters of science and nature, it was also not a valid authority for modern expectations on "spiritual matters." Although the Bible may contain truth and understandings about human beings that are instructive for living today, much more of it is chaff that must be intentionally winnowed away to get at those kernels of truth.

The collapse of the faith of my upbringing was traumatic. I felt like a traveler who had begun a journey on an interstate highway. As I started on my journey, I was advised that, if I watched and followed the informational signs, I would get to my destination safely. However, as each successive informational sign was reached, I became aware that the previous signs had contained misleading and erroneous information. With each successive sign, I had more and more doubts about my even being on the right road. Finally, I realized that the road signs were a carry-over from the precursor road that had been built centuries earlier; they gave directions and information about towns, villages and landmarks that no longer existed. I needed to have access to currently relevant sources of information in order to make this trip meaningful and productive. I needed and continue to need signs that contain valid and reliable information for orientation and meaning for my life in today's context – not the context when the original road was built centuries ago. I needed to find *authentic* faith for my life today.

A first task in seeking authentic faith was to assess what had gone wrong in my traditional faith. Two possibilities occurred to me. First, it was possible that I had not properly *believed and practiced* my traditional faith. Was it possible that God did not respond to my pleas for healing my family members because my faith was somehow shallow, corrupt or even a sham? I went through the personal self-examination of the biblical Job. I thought that, if I searched hard enough – as Job's "advisors" suggested that he should do, I might find that fatal flaw in the exercise and the practice of my faith, correct it, and all could and would be well. This process of self-examination started after Tammy's death, continued after Bethany's death, and reached its culmination after Darlene's death. I found no such flaw; rather, I concluded that no fatal flaw existed. Not that my practice of the Lutheran faith was perfect or even exemplary. No, it was not just my faith that was called into question by the outcomes of the crises in my life. It was not only my prayers to God for healing my family members that went unanswered; the hundreds and thousands of prayers of other "good" Lutherans and other Christians for the healings of my family members also were not answered. Were their faiths, too, somehow fatally flawed? Not likely! It seemed apparent that the problem did not lie in the practice of Lutheran (and/or wider Christian) faith – theirs or mine.

The second possibility was that the flaw existed not in the *practice of* but instead in the *content and substance of* my Lutheran faith. As I was growing up and trying to understand my faith, I remember thinking that many of its elements were strange and surreal. Some seemed believable, but many certainly defied credibility when viewed from the perspective of today's worldview. How could a virgin birth or a resurrection really happen? What about ascension to heaven or descent to hell? If such things can or did happen, just where is heaven and where is hell? Was it really possible to heal someone just by touching them and saying some words? Could five thousand people really be fed with five loaves of bread and two fishes, or could someone really be "raised" from death? Was it possible that these "events" were not really actual occurrences from the past but rather *fictional events* that had for some reason been incorporated into the biblical narrative? Even more basically, what and where is God? Why is God depicted as a male superhuman adult rather than as someone or something else? How could I be sure that Christians had arrived at the correct religion by adding the New Testament, whereas Judaism was in error by accepting just the Hebrew Bible (Old Testament) and not accepting Jesus as the Messiah? From a still wider perspective, I wondered: how could I be sure that my Bible-based faith and religion was correct, but that Buddhism, Hinduism and all other religions had gotten it so completely wrong?

In my formative years there was a standard answer to these questions: "If it's found in the Bible, it is true and you have to believe it, even though it does not seem reasonable. There are some things you just have to accept on faith." Looking back on those years, I now realize that I was coercively indoctrinated to adopt the authority of *sola Scriptura* and to historicize the Bible – to make details of the biblical narrative into historical events simply because they were included in the Bible.

Moreover, if the Lutheran Church interpreted the Bible in a certain way, its way was the presumed correct interpretation and understanding. What I learned much later through seminary studies and other personal reading helped to liberate me from those shackles and to free me to seek faith relevant to my life.

To assist me in finding authentic faith, I began to look into the larger question of the role of religion in the lives of humans. That part of my spiritual journey was both revealing and enlightening. I learned that religion as a human endeavor occurs in nearly all cultures and societies. In no case was it externally imposed on or introduced into societies by transcendent divinities of any sort; rather, it evolved in different forms in different cultures to assist individuals and communities in dealing with the human sense of an *UUR*, in answering the existential questions of human existence, and in authorizing moral and ethical codes of conduct to maintain order and stability in communities. To the extent that the religion of a given culture met those needs for a cultural community, it served the purpose of religion validly for that community at that time. This recognition helped me recognize that the claim of any one religion – *my own included* – that it is necessary and valid for all people in all places is both arrogant and insensitive to the meaningfulness that exists in other religions and cultures. Different religions have evolved and have been modified by people to the form that they are needed, where and when they are needed. That this evolution of religions has occurred throughout the history of humanity was instructive and supportive to me: if humans had the necessity, opportunity and freedom to modify religions to their contemporary needs in the past, do not I (we) today also have that freedom – indeed, even the responsibility and the necessity of doing the same?

I also learned that the role and function of religion is not only culturally conditioned; within each culture it is also temporally

182

conditioned. Just as cultures evolve over time, so the specific religious needs and perspectives of people will also evolve over time, sometimes in response to changes in worldview. Although these changes usually occur rather slowly over long periods of time, from time to time there are seismic changes, sometimes referred to as paradigm shifts. An example was the shift from a geocentric to a heliocentric understanding of the universe. When religions accommodate these worldview changes, they can continue to fulfill the functions for which that religion was created by humans in that culture. When religions resist such changes, they are at first merely obstacles to humans' orienting themselves successfully in life. With continued resistance to the changing worldview, religions become marginalized, because the worldview that they continue to espouse is no longer the worldview of the society in which they are supposed to function. Continued refusal to accommodate a modern worldview can only further lead to irrelevance and then to the death of a religion. It appears to me that most forms of traditional Christianity today are content to let that course of events ensue.

There are undoubtedly various reasons why religions tend to be resistant to change. They are stabilizing forces in communities. They are believed to provide *divinely* sanctioned sets of moral values and ethical behaviors that give order and security to communities; these are important and cherished qualities and contributions. The reasonable human tendency to follow the adage "If it ain't broke, don't fix it" causes people not to want to change things when they seem to be functioning properly. When moral values and ethical behaviors are buttressed either by the Church or by Scriptures that are claimed to be absolutely authoritative because they issue from "the word of God," they become even more resistant to change – even when change is much needed.

The collective set of church beliefs and

practices is called church tradition. For me it was the Lutheran tradition. One definition of tradition is "the handing down of statements, beliefs, legends, customs, etc., from generation to generation, especially by word of mouth or by practice." Traditions are usually thought of as being good, useful, important and even necessary to maintaining a stable society. And they are – usually.

The story is told of an old small country church to which a mother had taken her five-year-old son for worship, as was their Sunday morning custom. As they were walking through the narrow hallway to enter the sanctuary, the mother turned to the white plastered wall on her right, bowed and made the sign of the cross on her forehead and chest. Her son asked her, "Mommy, why do you always do that?" Her mother thought for a moment and then responded, "Because my mother taught me to do that. Let's ask her why she taught me to do that." Later that day when they gathered at grandma's house for dinner, the mother asked her mother, "Why do we bow and make the sign of the cross when we pass that white plastered wall in the hallway into the sanctuary?" Her mother replied, "Because it's a tradition that my mother taught me, but she never told me why." They could not ask great-grandma, because she had been dead for many years.

Sometime later, the congregation undertook a building renovation project that included remodeling the hallway. As the workmen stripped away the old plaster in the hallway, they uncovered a painting of Jesus hanging on the cross – at just the place where the mother always stopped, bowed and made the sign of the cross. Generations before, when the painting was visible, people had begun the reverential tradition of bowing and crossing themselves before that picture: it was then a meaningful practice. At first when the picture had been plastered over, people remembered the picture behind the plaster and continued the practice. They taught their children to do the same; but the children had no knowledge of the picture behind the plaster. The tradition was continued, but it no longer had the same meaning for those doing it.

In light of the above anecdote, it is interesting to look further at the etymology and meaning of the word *tradition*. It comes from the Latin *traditio*, which means "a handing over or down, transfer, surrender, or betrayal." Yes, *betrayal*. Traditions that continue to be practiced after they have lost their meaning can betray the persons who perform them. The persons believe that they are doing sacred and reverential actions, when in reality they are going through the motions of something traditional that no longer has meaning. The "doing" has substituted for the "reason for doing": a tradition has become a betrayal.

Has much of traditional Christianity become a betrayal? Are Christians today being betrayed by continuing to believe religious tenets and to perform religious rites and rituals that had meaning in the context of ancient worldviews but have little or no meaning today? Each person must answer those questions for her/himself. My own experience in facing the challenges and losses in my life and the struggles that followed convinced me that the Lutheran tradition had betrayed me; as I was indoctrinated to practice Lutheranism, it pretended to offer me something that it did not – and could not provide. It claimed that the earnest and faithful practice of rites and rituals, including prayers to God, were effective in bringing healing and health to my family members and to me. Until that point in my life, as in the above anecdote, I had been continuing to cross myself and bow before the white plastered wall, because I had been indoctrinated to believe that that traditional practice was a meaningful part of a proper life of Christian faith. In my case, when the plaster was peeled away, the image that was present was no longer a valid object of my faith.

It is perhaps worthwhile to note that traditional Christianity is not the only religion that seems destined for oblivion if it

continues on its present course. The same fate would appear to await all religions in which authority for modern living is derived from narrow interpretations of ancient writings (Scriptures) that are given strong or absolute authority. It cannot be overemphasized that the reason that those writings were foundational, formative and relevant for their respective religions was because they were written in and spoke to the worldviews of their respective times of writing. The context of their composition was the same context as their interpretation and use; they were relevant because they were understood in their contemporary setting – a worldview based on the best knowledge and understanding available at the time. But, while times and worldviews changed, the writings remained static; they were in a sense "set in stone." Although the modern practice of a religion of ancient origin can be loosely tethered to and informed by ancient writings, it cannot be fully determined and authorized by them without becoming first passé and finally irrelevant.

In order to live meaningfully and productively, I need to have faith. But my life experiences, particularly the deaths of my family members, had taught me that it could not be just any faith. Although it was highly revered and esteemed by my ancestors, the traditional Lutheran faith that had nurtured and sustained them for many centuries was not performative for me; it could not deliver what it claimed it could. How or where, then, might I turn to find an authentic faith for me – one that would nurture and sustain me, that would help me orient myself productively in life?

In previous chapters, I have often used the terms *faith* and *religion*, sometimes almost interchangeably. It is now important that I clearly distinguish between them, because each has come to have a particular meaning for my life.

First, what do I mean by *faith*? Formal definitions of *faith* include terms and phrases such as "confidence or trust in a person or thing; belief that is not based on proof." My faith or belief is my confidence and trust that a person or thing (object of faith) is reliable in producing that good, meaningful or worthwhile outcome which I expect of the object of my faith. My confidence and trust in the object of my faith may be fostered and supported by my knowledge that it has previously provided the desired outcome. Nevertheless, I believe in and trust the object of my faith without proof or certainty that the desired outcome will happen.

That faith is not based on proof, however, does not mean that faith is based on an inability to understand. The religious tradition that formed my early faith emphasized the nonunderstandability of matters relating to faith, but I have learned that that notion is quite often not true and may, in fact, be detrimental to developing a viable and mature faith. I may have faith in something that I fully or partly understand or completely fail to understand. Because something is partially or fully understood does not disqualify it as the object of my faith. In some cases my understanding of an object of faith or evidence of previous effectualness may foster and bolster my confidence that it is reliable and worthy to be an object of my faith. For example, I go to my doctor and utilize modern medicines because I have faith and trust that they can cure and heal me. These medicines are used because those who devised or created them know how they work in cooperation with the body's natural processes to heal and to cure my body of diseases and illnesses. If I have sufficient knowledge, I too can understand how and why they work. My knowledge of the accumulated understanding of the modern medical profession can provide evidence that causes me to put my trust in it – to have a reasonable expectation that modern medicine will work towards my benefit – rather than my doing nothing or resorting to witchcraft or magic. That my doctor and the medicine that he prescribed have previously cured me

of my ailment is evidence for me to have faith that I can be cured again. Yet, I know that some who use these medicines are not healed or cured; my use of these medicines and techniques is not proof or a guarantee that I will be cured or healed.

From my perspective, faith is confidence that life is sufficiently organized and dependable that I can live meaningfully and productively; faith is trust that life is predictably worth living – that is, dependable and grounded in something reliable. I can expect life to unfold in a positive and predictable way, and I can expect to find meaning, fulfillment and happiness in life. I can expect that, having been born, I have a life expectancy of 70-80 years and that I will someday die. The unfolding of human life is sufficiently regular that I can have confidence and trust that I might also experience that.

Of course, I have no proof or assurance that that will happen. Although I know that bad things can happen, they are uncommon. Some are attributable to factors over which I have some control; I have within my power the ability to maximize the possibilities of my living a long life. I can eat healthy foods, exercise properly, get proper rest, and get appropriate medical checkups and treatment; I can avoid putting myself in situations where accidents might harm or kill me or where I might be exposed to diseases that could kill me. Yet, my life is also contingent on things outside of and beyond my control. Even doing everything within my power to maximize my life expectancy, I know that illness, disease or accident could cut my life short. Yet my faith in the predictability of life is sufficient that I have the confidence to participate in its unfolding. Thus, I will use the term *faith* to refer to this confidence and trust to participate in and to find meaning in life.

What do I mean by *authentic* faith? The Random House definition of *authentic* includes such words and phrases as "reliable, trustworthy, genuine, real, and entitled to acceptance or belief because of agreement with known facts or experience." Although not etymologically related, authenticity depends on the authority of the reasons for having faith. If something is deemed *authentic*, it is "entitled to acceptance and belief because of agreement with known facts or experience." For me, then, a faith is *authentic* when it is credible, because it is based on the authority of the known facts and experiences of my life. My faith is *authentic* when it is grounded in the authority of the presuppositions of my worldview that I presented in the previous chapter.

My faith is *authentic* only when it is an informed faith. It was not until I was able to describe in detail the cosmological, anthropological, metaphysical, theological, epistemological, teleological and axiological components of my worldview that I recognized what an authentic faith is for me. My faith is authentic when it is fully consistent and congruent with and informed by what I believe to be the authoritative truths about reality. Such a faith effectively supports, sustains and orients me to the greatest extent possible, because it is informed by and based on the authority of the best human knowledge and understanding of the natural world and of my place in it. It can reliably sustain and nurture me because my expectations of life arise out of real possibilities in the world. An authentic faith gives me no guarantees about life, but, because it is based on the authority of the best understanding of nature and of human life within nature, it gives me sufficient trust, confidence and hope to fully commit myself to living in the world in spite of the vicissitudes of life.

Taking into account the foregoing discussion of an authentic faith for me, I conclude that *Nature's Creativity* – my imaginative conception of *UUR* – is the worthy and appropriate object of my faith. From *Nature's Creativity* have emerged and arisen all the capacities and all the conditions that made my life possible and that support it in the present; its provisions make possible

my having a life with meaning and purpose. It is the groundwork for all the real possibilities in and for my life.

There is ample evidence that *Nature's Creativity* is a worthy object of my authentic faith. That it has been acting for more than 10 billion years to give rise to the marvelously complex universe, including the solar system and all the complex forms of life within it, indicates to me that it is reliable and worthy of my trust in it. It has first created an earthly environment in which life could originate and then through the biological evolutionary process populated it with the marvelous array of living organisms that are observed today. With such a track record, I can confidently place my faith in its being capable of continuing to provide for me and other humans, as well as all other living organisms.

To live with authentic faith means that I cannot function well in any setting that asks or requires me to ignore, to distort or to deny any of my authoritative worldview presuppositions. For example, I cannot imaginatively conceive *UUR* both as the Hebraic-Christian symbol Yahweh-God and as the symbol *Nature's Creativity*. I cannot simultaneously hold as valid understandings of the origin of the natural world both the Genesis narrative in which God's spoken words externally imposed order on the natural world and the evolutionary process in which immanent and inherent creativity is the source of natural reality. These are mutually exclusive alternatives. If I attempt to simultaneously hold both views, I end up with a conflicted worldview. My life experiences inform and convince me of the problems in trying to do that.

If my authentic faith is trust and confidence to live in the world with *Nature's Creativity* as the object of my faith, how is my *religion* related to my faith? As discussed earlier, there have been two historical understandings of the etymology and definition of religion. That practiced today in most Protestant denominations today derives from the *relegere* (literally, "rereading") root. According to its presuppositions, denominations, congregations and individuals strive for a true understanding and practice of Christianity by reading, rereading and interpreting the Bible; Scriptures are searched and studied in detail, because they are presumed to hold the answers for all matters of faith and life for all time. The second, and presumably earlier, understanding of religion derived from the word *religare*. Its root *"lig"* connotes a binding together, and the prefix *"re"* indicates a recurring happening. Its meaning connoted the bond of piety that binds to God or the gods. The *religare* domain would seem to be wider in scope than the *relegere* understanding, because the former would seem to access a broader range of resources in order to achieve its goal than the latter, which relies primarily or exclusively on Scriptures. *Religare* seems to have been involved in the original formation of a religion, while *relegere* became the understanding when a religion was sufficiently developed to have written and adopted its sacred Scriptures.

In arriving at an operational definition of religion for myself, I began with the *religare* concept and expanded it even further to the following. *My religion is that set of practices that I use to maintain, to correct and to construct my worldview so that it continues to serve as the best possible paradigm for orienting my life.* Using Kaufman's earlier-mentioned theological principles, this would mean that I continue to *critically* examine each presupposition of my worldview to determine whether it still represents the best understanding arrived at by human study and analyses in the *context* of wider human knowledge. If it continues to pass muster, it is retained. If not, that presupposition must be *reconstructed* and corrected.

This definition of religion accommodates, and perhaps even presupposes, the earlier-mentioned notion of consilience – the expectation that, if valid and reliable investigative methodologies are used in probing for the truths of the various fields of human inquiry, the results will "jump together" to yield a unifying consensual truth regarding an understanding of reality. Because everything involved in humans' capacity to reason, to analyze and to know are the products of *Nature's Creativity*, the practice of this definition of religion ought always to provide the best possible worldview to support my faith.

What are the consequences and implications for me of "practicing" this notion of religion? First, my religion is moved from a stance of being in opposition to much of modern knowledge to one of being in the midst of the human search for truth about the world and humans' place in it. Thus, as I continue to inform and to update my worldview presuppositions, I am free to draw on all valid sources of human knowledge and understanding – including those aspects of my traditional religion that remain valid in the context of the modern worldview. Although I have been highly critical of many elements of my traditional Lutheran faith, it would be neither prudent nor wise for me to "throw out the baby with the bath water." I will now sort through the components of that traditional faith to winnow out those that no longer have meaning and relevance for me.

To be sure, there are paradigm-shifting changes. Imaginatively conceiving *UUR* as *Nature's Creativity* brings with it certain global changes. The mysterious Hebraic-Christian symbol of Yahweh-God as a transcendent, superhuman, noetic agent is replaced by immanent creative forces in nature that evoke the same sense of awe and mystery. The teleological plan of Yahweh-God in the biblical narrative is replaced with the trajectory produced by nature's emergent creativity. While the writers of the biblical narrative claimed to know the teleological endpoint of God's plan for creation (a rather grand assumption!), I must humbly acknowledge that I do not know the final purpose and goal of nature's emergent creativity, if indeed there is an ultimate goal and purpose. Perhaps *Nature's Creativity* will just continue on and on without end to produce more marvelous creatures as it has since *the big bang*.

Other significant changes in understanding pertain to the origin and nature of humans. Our best current knowledge of our human origins indicates that we have evolutionarily descended from prehuman animal forms whose sometimes very aggressive behaviors were mostly instincts determined by their genetic programs. Because we have inherited residues of those determinants in our genetic program, we are still influenced towards aggressive behaviors that were positively adaptive during our evolutionary past but that are disruptive and destructive to modern human society and culture. That, together with our sometimes irrational use of our free will, accounts for our "sinfulness." Thus, the biblical notions of a human "fall" from perfection and sinlessness to sinfulness are no longer valid understandings of the human situation. Consequently, all tenets of so-called classical redemption theology lose meaning and purpose and become nonoperative. There is no need for a savior to offer a sacrifice to pay the price for sin to a just and holy deity in order to restore the original perfect relationship between humans and their God. Any "salvation" for humans in the new paradigm involves the human institution of societal rules, laws and practices that curb our residual, innate aggressive tendencies and protect us from the harm produced by those destructive behaviors.

Several other traditional beliefs are no longer tenable. According to traditional Christian theology, the aforementioned redemption took place in order that humans might spend their postearthly lives eternally with God. However, historical analyses reveal that the notions of heaven and hell evolved in pre-Christian and early Christian times from ancient ideas about the abodes or realms of the dead, examples being Sheol and Gehenna for the Hebrews and Hades for the Greeks. From those, the concept of heaven evolved to designate the place where those who lived God-pleasing lives, especially in the face of persecution for their faith, were rewarded with eternal life in the presence of God. On the other hand, the concept of hell evolved to indicate the place where the enemies of God were consigned to live eternally tormented and separated from God. There is and never has been any objective evidence for the existence of either heaven or hell. Claims of knowledge about postdeath experiences in nonearthly places almost surely derive from artifactual effects on the mind and consciousness when the brain is deprived of sufficient oxygen and nutrition. On the edge of cell function and on the verge of cell death, nerve cells are likely to create bizarre images and unnatural "experiences." According to the new paradigm, I know that, when I die, my existence as a person will end. What, if any, kind of existence I will have after death is unknown and unknowable. However, most likely my body will experience what happens to the bodies of my animal cousins; they die and decompose into the chemical elements and compounds from which they were constituted during growth and development; those chemical components then become nutritionally available to the array of living organisms that is the continuity of life.

Also rendered purposeless is the practice of supplicatory prayers to God. Such have meaning only if *UUR* is imaginatively conceived in the image of a transcendent, noetic, personal agent, who can hear and respond to such requests. When *UUR* is imaginatively conceived as impersonal *Nature's Creativity*, there is simply no receiver or responder to such requests. To the extent that it is a meditative process in which people get in touch with their deep inner selves, prayer may serve a salutary effect. To the extent that it unites groups of people together in common endeavors and towards common goals, prayer can foster communal benefits. However, these benefits are attributable to not-yet-understood intrapersonal and interpersonal psychological effects rather than to activities and forces infused into life's happenings from transcendent external sources. Whatever are the observed effects of prayer, they derive from capacities that have emerged within human individuals or groups during their evolutionary journey to present-day humanity.

To have jettisoned so much of traditional Christianity might seem to many people indeed to have "thrown out the baby with the bathwater." Some might argue that all that remains is a few soap bubbles or the ring around the tub. I would now like to turn to those aspects of Christian tradition that I think continue to contribute positively to help people orient themselves for productive living in the modern world. If the premise that we humans continue to deal with sub-human attitudes and behaviors that are rooted in our genetic heritage from our prehuman ancestors is acknowledged and accepted, then I think that traditional Christianity gives us much to hang on to and to work with. Indeed, some of it can be instructive and constructive in leading us to a better world.

In considering wisdom from the Hebraic-Christian tradition that offers insights into modern life, I cite references from the Scriptures. In doing so, I must remind myself of all the qualifications and limitations relating to the origin and nature of the Bible's contents that were noted earlier. I am referencing literature that witnesses to the Hebraic and/or Christian faiths; I am not citing history, although those writings contain some actual historical events. However, even if none of the "events" and "persons" of the narrative are historical, it is still possible to discern attitudes and behaviors of the Hebrew/Christian people towards other people in the narrative and towards nature. I will now attempt to show that it is precisely in those areas that we can draw important insights for today.

The overarching question to be answered is the following: how did humans evolve from prehuman animals that expressed much aggressive behavior towards each other to modern humans who are usually able to live peaceably together and even to love one another? Under that umbrella question, I want to look for evidence of how the early Hebrews and later the Christians regarded and related to persons who were not members of their own ethnic and religious communities.

It was previously noted that, like our anthropoid relatives, we humans exhibit xenophobic hostility – aggressive and often harmful attitudes and behaviors towards other biologically-unrelated members of our own species. This inclination seems to be rooted in our evolutionary genetic heritage; that is, it tends to come "naturally" to us because it is conditioned to a greater or lesser extent by our genes. This xenophobic proclivity most often results in our treating our biological relatives more favorably than we treat biologically-unrelated persons. All too frequently, however, this tendency negatively escalates to genocide – killing members of other human groups that are somehow different from us. I do not need to document the cases of genocide that have occurred during the twentieth century and those that are happening even today. It was earlier noted that one of the important advancements in social interactions that occurred as human culture evolved from isolated roving bands of relatives to aggregations of unrelated persons in towns and cities was the recognition of the need for a so-called "universal code." This code specified that humans should attitudinally and behaviorally treat biologically-unrelated persons in the same positive ways that they treat their biological relatives. Although this behavior was and is contrary to our natural instincts, it was and remains absolutely essential to establishing viable and orderly human communities that include unrelated persons.

The struggles that were involved in the

development of the universal code can be followed in the biblical narrative. From the earliest point in the narrative that the Hebrews considered themselves Yahweh's chosen people, there are references to their desired impact on larger humanity. In "conversations" with Abram/Abraham (Gen. 12:3; 22:18), Isaac (Gen. 26:4) and Jacob (Gen. 28:14), God tells each of the patriarchs that through their offspring "all the nations of the earth will gain blessings for themselves," although the nature of those blessings is not specified. The writers of Exodus and Leviticus narrate God's giving of the laws that include how they should live with other people. The writers of Deuteronomy (*the second law*) relate many of the same things, but in their narrative Moses relates all the laws that Yahweh had earlier given to him to give to the Israelites in order for them to obey Yahweh faithfully. The prescribed punishment for disobedience of many of the laws involving behaviors towards Yahweh or other Israelites was death by stoning. Other lesser offenses involved the *lex talionis*, or law of retaliation. According to this law, "the injury inflicted is the injury to be suffered"; from this came the "fracture for fracture, eye for eye, tooth for tooth" rule (Exodus 21:23; Leviticus 24:19-20). By today's standards, all the foregoing would be regarded as brutal standards of punishment that might be reflective of a quite harsh and perhaps closed society. Yet there were specific laws that prevented oppression of non-Hebrew resident aliens (Exodus 22:21; 23:9; Leviticus 19:33-34); the reason stated for this law was Israel's having lived as aliens in the land of Egypt. With regard to legal treatment, "You shall have *one law* for the alien and for the citizen" (Leviticus 24:22; cf. Deuteronomy 1:16), meaning that Israelites and resident aliens were to be treated equally before the law. Another law specified that Israelites had to return an *enemy's* ox or donkey that was going astray (Exodus 23:24). It is no surprise that the Israelites were told not to "hate in your heart anyone of your kin," but they are

also told to "love your neighbor as yourself" (Leviticus 19:17). Thus, it can be seen that the universal code for treating unrelated persons in the same benevolent way that one treated one's family or fellow Israelites was well-developed in Israelite law – at least if that alien or stranger was living, presumably peaceably, in their land.

Yet Israel appears to have been schizophrenic with respect to its behavior towards other unrelated groups. According to the narrative, an important part of Yahweh's promise to Abraham and to his descendants was that the land of Canaan would someday be theirs. Following that promise, much of the narrative is concerned with Abraham's descendants' becoming a "great nation" and their moving in to occupy that land. Thus, as the Exodus journey was ending, Moses tells the Israelites:

> When the LORD your God brings you into the land that you are about to enter and occupy, and he clears away many nations before you – the Hittites, the Girgashites, the Amorites, the Canaanites, the Perrizites, the Hivites, and the Jebusites, seven nations that are more numerous than you – and when the LORD your God gives them over to you and you defeat them, then you must utterly destroy them. Make no covenant with them and show them no mercy. (Deuteronomy 7:1-2; NRSV)

> You shall devour all the peoples that the LORD your God is giving over to you, showing them no pity; you shall not serve their gods, for that would be a snare to you. (Deuteronomy 7:16; NRSV)

In these passages, Moses is telling the Israelites that Yahweh has commanded them to commit what today is called *genocide*. The justification is that doing so is fulfilling Yahweh's promise to provide land for his people. The seven nations ("seven" symbolizing totality) were to be conquered by Yahweh so that Israel could occupy their land. They were to be annihilated by the Israelites so that there would be none left to practice religions that might ensnare the Israelites away from the worship of Yahweh.

When the foregoing passages are analyzed in the context of our modern understandings of the nature of humanity and of the development of religion, the details of the narrative can be understood. The xenophobic proclivity present in people became a vehicle for justifiable genocide when it was authorized by religious conviction: the commands of Yahweh to occupy the land and to utterly destroy all its inhabitants not only authorized but demanded the extermination of peoples of different ethnic origin and of different religions in order that Israel might take over their lands and remove all possible threats to its religion. The continuation of the biblical narrative in the books of Joshua, Judges and 1 & 2 Samuel relates how that unfolded until the time when King David captured Jerusalem and established the Israelite monarchy. Because this narrative was composed by Hebrew religious leaders who were often authorized by and/or beholden to the kings, it is not at all surprising that the ethical assessment was favorable to the perpetrators rather than to the victims of these atrocities.

Over the years, people, including many from the Hebraic-Christian tradition, have been very troubled by this segment of the biblical narrative, because they are able to see clearly the moral and ethical wrongness of those atrocities. Other Jews and Christians, on the other hand, often justify it as being ethically acceptable, because it was part of Yahweh's plan for his people. It was necessary for Yahweh's chosen people to have land in order for his plan for them to unfold, and the Promised Land was the place and the way in which Yahweh chose to do it. Because Yahweh was deemed both omnipotent and sinless, therefore what happened was morally correct and ethically proper.

There is, however, extreme danger in that rationale. By this "reasoning," any time that anyone of any religion proceeds to carry out an activity – no matter how reprehensible, if it is carried out in the name of religion – especially if authorized and commanded by the deity, it is not only a permissible but a mandatory action. By that "reasoning," the Oklahoma City and World Trade Center atrocities were completely justifiable to those who committed them. The perpetrators of those atrocities were acting in the firm belief that their deity was calling and authorizing them to carry out their respective actions. Utilizing this rationale, any tenet of any religion can be distorted and fanaticized.

It is not easy to see how such perversions by extremists of any religion can be prevented, as long as *UUR* is conceived of as a superhuman agent with the authority to command humans to behave in ways that rational and reasoning minds conclude is madness. When *UUR* is conceived of as *Nature's Creativity*, it is not an entity from which emanates authority for any moral standard or ethical behavior. In the latter case, all moral and ethical authority derives from use of humans' evolutionarily-derived discovering and reasoning capacities. To be sure, such capacities can be used to atrocious ends. However, when groups of humans utilize their collective reasoning capacities to arrive at acceptable moral and ethical standards for the benefit of their larger communities, there is a larger touchstone of propriety at work that warrants the adoption of genuinely good community standards. In our evermore global world of today, such collective adoption of standards becomes even more important.

While I have singled out Israel's conquest of the land of Canaan as an atrocious misuse of religion, I must acknowledge that my own Christian tradition has more than its share of atrocities to account for. They are well-documented historically, and I do not have to enumerate them. Rather, I now want to recount how later Jewish tradition went on to develop moral and ethical standards that provide a positive model for humans to live together in our global community.

As discussed in an earlier chapter, the early Hebraic concept of forgiveness of sin was related to animal sacrifice. If a person sinned against Yahweh or other humans, forgiveness of that sin (redemption) was obtained by offering the blood ("life") of an animal as a sacrifice to Yahweh. This notion persisted in Judaism, and its efficacy was not challenged until the Temple, including its sacrificial altars, was destroyed in 70 CE. Following that, there was a need for Jewish religious leaders to rethink how forgiveness might be obtained without sacrifice. Their resolution can be generally stated as the following: if sin is committing a wrong against Yahweh or another human, then forgiveness involves some restitution for the wrong committed. Forgiveness for a wrong involves somehow trying to right that wrong. If Yahweh or the person wronged cannot be helped directly, committing acts of kindness and benevolence to other people indicates an attitude of self-examination and repentance – a "turning around" of one's life from evil towards good. That new foundational understanding of Judaism provided a wellspring for the many humanitarian contributions of Judaism in the following two millennia. This Jewish understanding of righting wrongs would seem to be a very deeply meaningful and appropriate perspective for all people to emulate.

I earlier documented that, even as most of Judaism was arriving at the aforementioned understanding of repentance and forgiveness in the late first century CE, a small sect of Judaism called Christians claimed that the Messiah of the Hebrew Bible had finally come in the person of Jesus of Nazareth. The earliest preserved writings of that group, attributable to the apostle Paul, clearly interpreted Jesus' crucifixion and death as a sacrifice for human sin. The gospels, on the other hand, depict Jesus the Christ (Yahweh's anointed) as a human *par excellence* – not God, but the supreme example of human existence. They depict Jesus' life as redeeming by being a moral model for humans. His life of teaching, ministry and healing serves as a model for his followers to emulate. When necessary, that model also included his challenging of religious traditions, which ultimately led to his demise, as religious leaders conspired to have the Roman authorities execute him by crucifixion. Thus, his death was not deemed a sacrifice for sins in any sense; rather, it was the possible and even likely outcome of a life of faithfulness to God. According to this understanding, Jesus is the *savior* of humans by teaching them what it means to live a moral and ethical life; what it means to minister to others by providing healing, food and spiritual nurture; and what it means to live a life of faithfulness, even if that commitment results in forfeiting one's life. This understanding of Jesus' life and ministry is fully consistent with the above notions of repentance and forgiveness arrived at by the early Jewish community.

Why then did the Pauline view of Jesus' death as a sacrifice for sins persist and become the predominant understanding in traditional Christianity? It seems to me that this occurred for at least two primary reasons. First, it was an artifact of the process whereby the writings that became the New Testament were collected and organized – namely, the fortuitous sequential listing of the Pauline writings closely after the gospels. This gives the impression that the Pauline writings, which include almost nothing about the life of Jesus, are interpreting the meaning of Jesus' life as narrated in the gospels. However, this conclusion belies historical evidence (See Table 8.1). Paul's life and writings, which explicitly and unquestionably describe Jesus' death as the sacrifice of God's anointed human (Messiah/Christ) for the sins of humanity, *preceded* the destruction of the temple and the end of animal sacrifice in Jerusalem in 70. Because animal sacrifice was ongoing during the whole of Paul's life, it was theologically consistent for Paul to interpret Jesus' death by crucifixion as a once-for-all-time sacrifice for sin that super-seded Jewish animal sacrifice. Thus, *the Pauline writings express a pre-gospel rather than a post-gospel understanding of the meaning of Jesus' life and ministry*. On the other hand, the gospels were written *after* Paul's death and *after* 70. That the gospels do not explicitly interpret Jesus' death as a sacrifice for human sins strongly suggests that the consensus (four out of four gospels) of emerging post-Pauline Christian thought viewed Jesus' life more as a moral model rather than his death as a sacrifice for human sins. Thus, it appears that the Jewish follow-ers of Jesus (at least the writers of the gospels), later to become the Christian Church, had accepted the same resolution regarding repentance and forgiveness reached by their fellow Jews who were not followers of Jesus. That is not surprising, because, although there were strong tensions and disagreements between the Jewish followers of Jesus and Jewish nonfollowers of Jesus, they were still part of the same larger Jewish community that had reached the aforementioned understanding of the meaning of and ways to obtain forgiveness. The formal separation of Christianity from Judaism most likely occurred around 90, about the time that the gospel of John was written and sometime after the other three gospels had been written.

Second, by the time of Augustine of Hippo in the fourth and fifth centuries, the above-mentioned sequence of the New Tes-tament canon was already well-established, giving rise to the previously mentioned impression that the Pauline writings were interpreting the gospels. Early redemption theology in the Western (Latin, later Roman Catholic) Church drew heavily on the writ-ings and understandings of St. Augustine, who championed Pauline theology. A mil-lennium later, when Luther and other reformers also picked up on Augustinian theology, the Pauline understanding also became firmly entrenched in Protestant theology.

Thus, my own conclusion concerning Jesus is that his early followers perceived him to be God's "anointed one," that is, a fully human person who exemplified their notions of what their God intended that an ideal moral and ethical human should be and do. Hence, I conclude that understanding Jesus as a "savior" entails his being a moral model and ethical example for me. If I emulate his life of care and service towards other people, I am "saved" from those primal behavioral tendencies that are still con-ditioned by genes in my evolutionary genetic heritage that predispose me to antisocial, immoral and unethical ("sinful") behaviors. Moreover, I do not need to believe that he was God in order for him to serve as a preeminent moral model for me.

Jesus' being a moral and ethical model included not only practicing the religious traditions and understandings of his time but also challenging them when he considered it necessary. Later, I will document several instances of that.

Whatever one might conclude about Jesus' deity or nondeity or about the mean-ing of his life and death by crucifixion, the early Christian narrative can be examined to see if there are principles and guidelines appropriate for modern life. I now turn to some of the pronouncements and teachings of Jesus that address larger questions of how humans should live together, particularly in relationship to biologically-unrelated hu-mans.

Here again in the gospels, not knowing what are actually historical events and what are nonhistorical inclusions in the gospel narratives complicates straightforward anal-yses. Nevertheless, because the contents of the gospels are attributable to the followers of Jesus, I will assume that they correctly reflect Jesus' attitudes and teachings.

First, I address Jesus' comments regard-ing *neighbors*, who, I will assume, refer to or at least include nonfamily (biologically-unrelated) persons encountered by those being addressed by Jesus. His teaching concerning neighbors was drawn from the second great commandment of the Hebrew Bible: "You shall love your neighbor as yourself" (Matthew 19:16; 22:39: quoting Leviticus 18:5). He also stated the same teaching even more inclusively: "In everything do to others as you would have them do to you; for this is the law and the prophets" (Matthew 7:12). Jesus again drew on the content of the Hebrew Bible (*the law and the prophets*) to indicate that people should treat everyone, not just neighbors, as they themselves would wish to be treated. In this directive Jesus is telling his followers to live according to what has been termed the *universal code*: treat people who are not your biological relatives as you would like to be treated, which is presumably also the way that you treat members of your family.

And then come Jesus' teachings which are likely to push people considerably beyond their comfort zone and natural tendencies:

"You have heard that it was said, 'You shall love your neighbor and hate your enemy.' But I say to you, Love your enemies and pray for those who persecute you, so that you may be children of your Father in heaven; for he makes his sun rise on the evil and on the good, and sends rain on the righteous and on the unrighteous. For if you love those who love you, what reward do you have?" (Matthew 5:43-46, NRSV)

"But I say to you that listen, Love your enemies, do good to those who hate you, bless those who curse you, pray for those who abuse you. If anyone strikes you on the cheek, offer the other also; and from anyone who takes away your coat do not withhold your shirt. Give to everyone who begs from you; and if anyone takes away your goods, do not ask for them again. Do to others as you would have them do to you." (Luke 6:27-31, NRSV)

In these passages Jesus commands his hearers to engage in behaviors that were well beyond common expectations of society of his day and of ours as well.

Perhaps a few words of clarification about "turning the other cheek" are in order. Striking the cheek of a person was a way of insulting or socially demeaning the person being struck; it was not an attack that was intended to kill or even physically harm the other person but rather to humiliate the other person. To "turn the other cheek" could have two beneficial results. First, it indicated that the one who was struck was choosing not to respond in a retaliatory way that might well escalate to further and greater violence. Second, it indicated to the one who did the striking that the recipient was not accepting the humiliation. In effect, "turning the other cheek" was an action that said, "You may be able to strike me, but you cannot take away my dignity – even if you strike me again (on the other cheek)." "Turning the other cheek" was a way to demand respect in a non-violent manner.

In his command to "love one's enemies," Jesus was "pushing the envelope" in today's phraseology. "You have heard it said 'You shall …. hate your enemy.'" may be another way of saying that people's natural instinct for fairness tells them that the proper attitude is to hate their enemies – those who are intent on harming or perhaps even killing them. That would, after all, be consistent with "an eye for eye, tooth for tooth" – hate for hate retribution. But here Jesus commands commitment to behaviors that make one vulnerable. To "love one's enemy" with *agape* love is to deal with him or her from a selfless perspective. It means that one acts to benefit the enemy, quite possibly at some personal cost or risk. From a natural selection perspective, such behavior would appear to have an adaptive advantage of zero. But here humans' capabilities of informed reasoning and innovation enable them to move beyond a natural, instinctive response to a behavior that promotes reconciliation and peace. Selflessly ("agapeically") "loving one's enemy" may be an occasion to remove or to disarm the reason for the relationship of enmity. Beyond acting to minimize violence and discord, loving includes forgiving the person who did the wrong, which psychologically frees the wrong-doer as well as the person wronged, because she/he no longer has to expend physical and emotional energy to maintain the grudge or hatred. Whatever its outcome, loving one's enemy is much more likely to achieve a peaceable relationship between the two parties than could be accomplished by aggressive retaliation.

While some have concluded that the intent of these commands to love one's neighbor and to turn the other cheek mean that one should not protect oneself if attacked in a potentially injurious or life-threatening manner, such is not the case. Jesus nowhere says that one should allow oneself to be harmed or killed by anyone attempting to do either. Rather, the impetus of his commands is to attempt to choose behaviors that are likely to bring reconciliation rather than behaviors that would further exacerbate the estrangement between people.

Thus, I can summarize how I think the biblical narrative informs and extends positive relationships between people. Historically, interindividual relationships have moved through a continuum. From a strictly biological perspective, parental care and altruistic (benefiting another person at some "cost" to the individual doing it) behaviors towards genetically-related persons were evolutionarily adaptive because they fostered the transmission of genes to subsequent generations. These behaviors were already present among our prehuman ancestors. However, among them xenophobic behaviors towards biologically-unrelated persons were still probably the norm, because they were strongly conditioned by their genetic heritage. Later, in order to live in villages, towns and cites, early humans had to overcome their xenophobic tendencies. They

did so by discovering and imaginatively conceiving the universal code, which specified that people should treat people who were not their biological relatives with the same benevolence that they treated their relatives. This code enabled people to live together, as long as there were not serious disputes. Moreover, in addition to the universal code, humans also developed altruistic behaviors towards biologically-unrelated persons. Although also observed in other animals, the extensive altruistic and reciprocal altruistic behaviors observed in humans may have been considerably strengthened with the emergence of conscience – a sense of moral right and wrong. In the Hebraic tradition, that behavior was incorporated into the "love your neighbor as yourself" command. Still needed, however, were principles and rules for dealing with nonrelatives when conflicts arose between biologically-unrelated members within the community or between different communities – when interpersonal animosity reached the point of the two parties' considering each other as enemies. It is at that point that Jesus' command to "love your enemies and do good to those who hate you" extends human relationships beyond our natural instincts and even justice to love – acting benevolently towards someone (whether biologically-related or not) who regards you as an enemy and whom you may regard as an enemy. It should be noted that the above precepts are found in many world religions, which in many cases predate Jesus' teachings and even the Hebrew religion.

Thus, the Judeo-Christian tradition bequeaths to us a number of sound principles for human interactions. As the diverse peoples of planet earth increasingly become one global community, we need to draw on the more nuanced of these principles in order to promote peace and tranquility in our world. We may even have to further draw on our imaginative creativity and innovative capacities to envision other pathways towards world peace.

Another dimension of traditional Christianity that seems to me eminently important is the sense of community. As I noted earlier, at the times of the illnesses and deaths of my family members, the most important way that congregations helped me was through the "ministry of presence." I was supported, nurtured and embraced by the members of the congregation as I struggled to deal with my pain and grief and to move ahead. The Greek word εκκλήςία (translated "church") means "a gathering or an assembly," and it seems to me that the church is at its best when it invites and gathers people into and supports them in community. We humans are evolutionarily social creatures; we thrive best when we communicate and are in community with other members of our own species. In this modern age of urban anonymity, in which by chance or by choice we often do not get to know well even those living in close proximity to us, a congregation can be a place where people can be accepted "agapeically" more than in any other setting.

Even in the absence of personal crises in people's lives, the importance of the congregation as community was illustrated for me by events that occurred when my wife Linda and I were copastors of a congregation in which about 125 people worshiped together on an average Sunday morning. One of the reasons that we were called to the congregation was to help them introduce a contemporary worship service to supplement their traditional worship service. After about one year of getting settled into ministry, a contemporary service was begun. It started with about 30-35 people in attendance, with the remaining 90 attending the traditional service. During the course of about a year, attendance at the contemporary service grew to about 110. About 20-30 of those were new worshipers drawn in from the surrounding community; the remaining 80-90 were members who had been attending the traditional service but who had switched to the contemporary service because they had found it more meaningful

and/or convenient. Meanwhile, attendance at the traditional worship service had dwindled to 30-40. This caused great concern and consternation for those attending the traditional service, the reasons for which I could not understand at the time. It was not that the "traditionalists" did not want the contemporary worshipers to experience meaningful worship, but the traditionalists just were not happy, although they were using the same worship settings, singing the same hymns, and saying the same prayers that they always had used in worship. The resulting conflict from that "worship war" was one of the primary reasons that my pastoral ministry could no longer be effective there. As I now reflect on that situation, I think that the conflict had almost nothing to do with worship style and almost everything to do with a "loss of sense of community." When the traditionalists were worshiping with only 25-30 others, they were doing the same worship activities that they had always done, but it felt different. They no longer felt that larger sense of community that had been present when they were part of a worshiping group of 125 people. When the sense of community is lost by a group, it has lost a good part of the reason for its existence. It has lost a component of its full humanity.

The word *church* as a "gathering" or an "assembly" can refer to a local congregation, but it is also used to refer to the gathering of all people who identify themselves as Christians (often called the Church Universal). In this latter context, every Church belief and action should always facilitate its being inclusive and inviting within the larger setting of the world community. However, such is often not the case today. Many denominational teachings and doctrines claim that their specific denomination has what they regard as the correct and true understanding of Scriptures, while contending that other congregations and denominations have inferior and false interpretations of the Scriptures. Such elitist attitudes often include explicit or implied mandates for the "true believers" to separate themselves from and/or to not associate with individuals, congregations or denominations whose teachings are regarded as somehow inferior. This tendency is especially prevalent in Protestantism, where the Bible is regarded as the source and norm for all of faith and life. The application of this notion has contributed to the proliferation of the literally thousands of Christian denominations that have arisen since the Reformation. Continued adherence to this way of thinking will serve to further splinter Christianity. Beyond that, it promotes even further separations from, rather than community with, people who are members of other world religions.

In light of the modern understanding of the origin and development of religions, this is also especially unfortunate. Recognizing that each and every religion has evolved within a specific societal and cultural setting that allowed a local people to relate to *UUR* as they understood it and to derive their own answers to the existential questions of the human situation in their specific context, I conclude that there is no single true and correct religion. On the other hand, there are many valid religions, each functional in its own particular setting. Continuing to hold elitist and exclusivist attitudes regarding one's own religion is divisive and detrimental in the modern world, where people of diverse religions seek commonality and reconciliation as we are becoming one global community. What is needed are religious attitudes, teachings and practices that promote harmony and unity rather than ones that foster differences, separations and divisions. What is needed are religious tenets that promote the universal code, treating our neighbors as ourselves and loving our enemies rather than religious tenets that reinforce our xenophobic proclivities. By that measure, all religions, Christianity included, have much room for improvement.

Thus, it seems to me that the Hebraic-Christian tradition brings much of value to inform our efforts as we seek to find ways for all humans to live together in one global community. To be sure, we will need to let go of much of that tradition, which, when examined critically and contextually, no longer has credibility and relevance. Other parts still have relevance, although they, too, may have to be continually reconstructed in light of our ever-changing worldview. Such will require spiritual work, but we really have no choice if we hope to survive and to thrive as a species in our natural setting here on planet earth.

I want to now consider another pronouncement of Jesus that I think has profound implications for today – particularly for this book, although Jesus undoubtedly had his own specific understanding in mind that may have been quite different from what I will attribute to it:

> The sabbath was made for human-kind, and not humankind for the sabbath. (Mark 2:27 NRSV)

First, a consideration of the quote itself is in order. Found only in the gospel of Mark, it is given in the context of Jesus' commentary on sabbath laws. As described earlier, the most commonly accepted understanding of the origin of the gospels of Matthew and Luke is that their writers constructed their gospels primarily by drawing and elaborating on the gospel of Mark to paint their own respective pictures of Jesus' life and ministry. While Matthew and Luke both include the accompanying "the Son of Man is lord even of the sabbath" (Mark 2:28; Matt. 12:8; Luke 6:5), neither includes the above verse from Mark. Perhaps the writers of Matthew and Luke considered it too controversial or radical to include in their writings. There are numerous other examples when the gospels of Matthew and Luke include "toned down" versions of Jesus' seemingly harsh or radical words or actions as related in Mark. Also, while the gospel of Matthew does not include the above quote, it does include a number of cases in chapter 5 in which Jesus reinterprets long-held understandings of Hebrew Scriptures: "You have heard it said..., but I say...." These further illustrate that, when Jesus felt it necessary to challenge long-held views and traditions, he considered it his responsibility to act on his convictions.

What then was the meaning of Jesus' statement: "The sabbath was made for humankind, and not humankind for the sabbath"? By "the sabbath" Jesus presumably meant all the rules and regulations that Jews had to obey in order to properly "observe" the sabbath – the seventh day of the week. According to Genesis 2:3, after completing creation God rested on the seventh day; following God's example and commands, humans were also to rest on the sabbath. Certain maintenance and emergency tasks could be carried out, but there was to be a complete cessation of daily work activities. The sabbath was for rest and renewal of the human body and spirit and for proper reflection and attention to their relationship to Yahweh.

The sabbath "was made." The sabbath and the rules for observing it did not always exist. They were brought into existence "for humankind"; "for" in this case implies "for the benefit and well-being of humankind." Observation of the sabbath was for the re-creation and renewal of humans.

"And not humankind for the sabbath." The sabbath and the rules were not created first by God, and then humans "plugged in" at the appropriate places and times in order that there be someone to obey them. If humans did not exist, there would have been no need for the sabbath and the rules for its observance.

Thus, the meaning of Jesus' statement appears to be this: the sabbath does not exist for its own sake, with humans serving as accessories to accomplish the ends of the sabbath. Rather, *the rules of the sabbath were created for the benefit of humans* – to give them time to refresh, to renew, to re-create and to reflect.

Before Jesus' defining statement on the sabbath, he had mentioned the case of David's and his companions' having eaten the bread of the Presence (also called Show-bread). The bread of the Presence consisted of twelve loaves of specially baked bread that sat in the holy place to symbolize that they were in Yahweh's presence. These loaves were baked fresh each week, and the old loaves from the previous week were then eaten by the priests in the holy place – a practice specified by Levitical law. However, in this case David and his companions were famished and no other bread was available. In order that their human needs might be served, the priest set the Levitical law aside and fed David and his companions with the bread of the Presence, thereby using sacred materials for everyday human needs. The principle is clear: the sabbath and the rules for its observance are for human benefit; humans do not exist to serve the sabbath. Jesus' mentioning that incident indicated that both he and the Old Testament narrative approved of that action.

What meaning might this have for today? If *sabbath* is thought of as a metaphor for *religion*, a direct paraphrase might read: "Religion was made for humankind, and not humankind for religion." Religions in their various forms have come into existence for the purpose of serving human needs. Various societies and cultures have created and modified rites and rituals that enable them to face and to deal with the challenges of the human condition: consciousness, self-consciousness, the need to find meaning and purpose in life, human mortality, etc. Religions would not exist were it not for humans and their needs that religions serve for them.

Thus, indeed, "the sabbath was made for humankind": religions have validity and purpose only as they serve to meet the needs of their adherents. "And not humankind for the sabbath": humans were not created for the purpose of observing the sabbath – following the rules of externally imposed religions.

Not surprisingly, this pericope (a selection or extract from the Bible) is not an oft-used text for sermons in any denomination. It seriously calls into question the exhortations for "serving the Church," particularly when "serving the Church" comes at the expense of humankind – the individual members. It seriously calls into question the exhortations for remaining faithful to the Church's teachings and traditions, when those teachings and traditions have little or no reference and relevance to the worldview in which Church members live but seem more contrived to serve the stability and longevity of churches and their leaders. In short, it seems to me that this pronouncement of Jesus is particularly applicable and relevant today – for the many reasons that I have presented in this book.

In dealing with this pronouncement Jesus was doing critical, contextual and constructive theology, using the terminology of Gordon Kaufman. Jesus was interpreting the sabbath laws in the context of how those laws were beneficial to the needs of humans in specific situations. Apart from their serving human needs, the sabbath laws had no standing or authority. "Sabbath laws" of today should be held to the same high standards.

That churches and their leaders today are reticent to consider this text seriously and act on its implications should come as no surprise. Its ramifications are simply and straightforwardly too threatening to the Church establishment and its teachings – just as they were at Jesus' time. When Jesus addressed the issue, he experienced resistance, rejection and threats to his life. After Jesus' pronouncement of the above statement challenging the sabbath laws, the gospels of Matthew, Mark and Luke conclude that the religious leaders "immediately conspired…., how to destroy him" (Matthew 12:14; Mark 3:6; Luke 6:11).

Finally, I wish to cite another statement of Jesus that, I think, has widespread implications for the issues addressed in this book. It comes from one of Jesus' teaching discourses in the gospel of John:

> Then Jesus said to the Jews who had believed in him, "If you continue in my word, you are truly my disciples; and you will know the truth, and the truth will make you free." (John 8:31-32; NRSV)

Again, while Jesus intended a particular meaning in making the statement in the context of his teaching, I think that the clause "and the truth will make you free" informs the issues addressed in this book. It is, if you will, valid as a stand-alone statement: "the truth will make you free."

As I began my life's journey as an infant, I began to be indoctrinated in the "Truths" of Lutheranism, and I was assured that the Lutheran interpretations of Scriptures and of the Lutheran confessions derived from these Scriptures were the fixed and unerring "Truths" according to which I should live my life. However, as I grew older and continued my education, experienced tragedies in my life, and then began to question the veracity of these "Truths," I began to see that the authority of those "Truths" could only be maintained if the ultimate authority of the Bible and of the Church were unchallenged and postulated to be unchallengeable. However, when I delved into the history of the origins of the Bible and of the Lutheran confessions, I learned that many tenets of my traditional faith did not stand up to the validity and credibility of truth standards of today. They were not only challengeable, but they needed to be challenged, and it turned out that many needed to be discarded or replaced. Having come to regard "truth" as the most valid and reliable understanding that is based on the best knowledge and information available today, I recognized that for me many of the Lutheran "Truths" were not truths at all, but rather they were teachings that derived from mythological religious understandings from ancient and no-longer-credible worldviews. As such, they were and are no longer a credible foundation on which to build my faith and to orient my life.

Truth about reality for me now consists of the most valid and reliable knowledge and information available that is consistent with and informs human experience. Scientific methodologies can provide valid and reliable knowledge and information, but that alone as a source is not sufficient. Also needed is the reasoning capacity of the human brain to assess and to interpret this knowledge and information in the context of lived experience to make sense of what life is ultimately all about – to gain insights and to point towards *UUR*. This collective information and knowledge available to me causes me to conclude that the ultimate source of all that physically and biologically exists and of humans' capacities to understand those realities is *Nature's Creativity* – nature's immanent and inherent self-organizing capacities to compound one emergent complexity upon another in order to produce the marvelous totality that is collectively called "creation." That "truth" has freed me to live in what my life experiences tell me is the real world.

To be sure, I still live with the challenges and limitations of being human. I still have the existential questions: "Who am I?" "Why am I here?" I still know that I will someday die, and I still do not like that at all. But because my interpretations of my life's experiences are now grounded in the most reliably and validly informed worldview available to me, I am enabled to have *authentic faith* to live as freely as I can. I live with realistic expectations of life. I know that I will die because that event is part of life, just as my being born was. Every death including my own is part of the course of natural events and not a consequence or punishment for anyone's sins. The truth has made me as free as I can be, while still being subject to the limitations of being human. I still cannot possess the unlimited capacities and freedoms of the "gods" that I can imagine, but I can live with authentic faith as freely as possible within the bounds of human existence.

I began this spiritual journey with a commitment to "an absolute devotion to truth," in the words of Albert Schweitzer. Having done my best to adhere to that principle along the many roads of that journey, I now feel a sense of "being free indeed."

The notion of nature or some aspect of it as the object of faith is, of course, not new. Ever since religion arose in human culture, some facets or aspects of nature have been integral parts of many religions, including Christianity. Recently, however, an increasing number of writers are addressing the incongruity between traditional Christianity and the modern worldview. As already noted, Gordon Kaufman, who contends that all designations for *UUR* are and always have been imaginative constructions, refers to the immanent capacity of nature to create and to sustain life as *serendipitous creativity*. Because he wished to reconstruct traditional Christianity into a relevant modern form, Kaufman retained the concepts of God, the world, humanity and Christ as components of his theology; within that framework he used *serendipitous creativity* as a metaphoric understanding of God. Kaufman's expanding the concept of God beyond its traditional roots was very instrumental in stimulating my thinking about a valid object of a modern faith. Kaufman's numerous writings on rethinking Christianity are too extensive to attempt to summarize here; persons struggling with the relevance of traditional Christianity for the modern world will find his insights very helpful.

John Haught, another Christian theologian, has sought to integrate traditional Christianity with the scientifically understood modern worldview. In *God After Darwin* and *Deeper Than Darwin*, Haught acknowledges the validity of the modern, science-based worldview but rejects the conclusions of scientific reductionists who claim that the scientific understanding of today is sufficient to account for everything; he insists that there is something "deeper than Darwin." He briefly alludes to chaos theory and complexity as possibly providing important insights and inroads to that which is "deeper than Darwin." Those two books also provided provocative stimulation for my own thinking.

Donald Crosby has presented a case for nature as the object of religion in his book *A Religion of Nature*. Like me, he gravitated to that position from a conservative Protestant Christian position over the course of his lifetime. His positions and arguments overlap some of the ideas that I have presented; however, his arguments are more philosophically nuanced and academically supported than the case that I have presented here. His book effectively draws on the particulars of his life to explore implications of a religion of nature. It is a good read for persons who are open to going on that same journey.

My life with *Nature's Creativity* as the object of my faith requires that I have guidelines and rules for living, just as I did living under the traditional Christianity which has heretofore been the source of the moral and ethical codes that informed and guided my thinking and acting. As discussed in this chapter, some of those moral and ethical values remain valid, reliable and operative for me when *Nature's Creativity* is the object of my faith. I now turn to expanded moral and ethical considerations within this new paradigm.

Chapter 14

Reframing and Refocusing Morality and Ethics

Like nearly all other organisms, we humans live in communities with other members of our own species; in our evolutionary heritage, we humans received those genetic influences that are conducive to living in community with biological relatives. However, unlike other organisms whose community members are most often biologically-related, we humans also have complex communities called towns, cities and metropolises in which we live in close proximity to hundreds, thousands and even millions of other people who are not our biological relatives. To be able to live together in relative harmony with large numbers of biological nonrelatives, we humans have had to transcend the xenophobic behaviors that exist in our animal cousins, at least some of which are probably rather strongly genetically-conditioned. That such complex concentrations of human populations could develop in history occurred because humans have discovered and developed principles and rules for coexisting together in close proximity. We call these principles our moral and ethical codes. They detail how we are to think about and to act towards other people living in our communities in order to have a civilized society.

In this chapter I want to examine the origins and roots of our moral and ethical codes and then look closely to see whether these codes are still adequately meeting the needs of our complex modern society.

Traditional Christianity has attributed the origins of its moral and ethical codes to the Judeo-Christian God. According to the biblical narrative, Yahweh gave his chosen people instructions and sets of laws from time to time in order that they might live in

faithful obedience to him and in harmony with other people. Because his chosen people regarded Yahweh as having absolute authority, they were to obey his commandments. Later, in the New Testament narrative, Jesus iterated, amplified and extended Yahweh's laws to provide guidance and direction for the Christian community of the New Covenant.

Although the biblical narrative attributes the origin of the Judeo-Christian moral and ethical codes to God, a modern historical understanding of how religions arose and of how morals and ethics evolved has led me to quite different conclusions. The contents of the Judeo-Christian moral and ethical codes are, for the most part, not unique to Judaism and Christianity. Many of the elements of these moral and ethical codes are common to nearly all civilized peoples. Certainly, they were common to a number of civilizations of the Fertile Crescent that surrounded early Israel, some of which were considerably older than Israel. Thus, rather than originating in Israel, most components were adopted and adapted by Israel from already existing moral and ethical codes and incorporated into its own.

I can also view the biblical claim in the larger historical context of the development of human society and culture. Early on, as groups of biologically-unrelated humans began aggregating into villages, towns and cities, they had to discover ways to overcome the xenophobic tendencies (fear of biologically-unrelated persons) that had contributed to their well-being when they were wandering nomadic tribes and clans. In order to accomplish this, they found it necessary to institute rules and regulations that would govern their living together in community. These moral and ethical codes were the reasoned formulations of rational humans' discovering how to survive and to thrive in community. The codes of all these urban communities had to deal with the same problems: not harming or killing but rather respecting other people, maintaining stable family structure, not stealing each others' properties, not slandering or defaming one's neighbors, etc. Only when these rules for living together were enforced and obeyed could there be safety, security and harmony in the community.

Enforcement of these rules probably first began with the authority of tribal and clan leaders. Later, as towns and cities were ruled by chiefs and kings, they became the enforcers of the moral and ethical codes. Their physical presence and their power and authority exerted through their police and military forces were visible, physical reminders to their subjects to obey the community rules.

As early community structures were evolving, their religions were also changing. An important development occurred when obedience of the laws for stable communal living became the will and commandments of the deity of the community's religion. Once the moral and ethical codes had attained the status of being enforced by the authority of the "god," they were well-established in governing the life of the community. Moreover, unlike their human leaders who died, the gods of their religious narratives and their authority persisted through the generations and provided continuity in enforcing these codes, which could then expand as necessary to meet the needs of an increasingly complex community.

In my earlier considerations of the development of religions, I concluded that the gods of all human societies and cultures are imaginative constructions of the human mind that attempt to conceptualize *UUR* for that community. Because those powerful controlling forces in life (*UUR*) are not accessible to our senses, we humans can

only think and talk about them by means of symbols and metaphors that draw on our life experiences and sensorially detectable realities. Thus, *each symbol and metaphor, including the Judeo-Christian God, was an imaginative construction of UUR by a particular community* that drew on the specific social, cultural and geographical circumstances at the time when it was conceived.

For my purposes, the important conclusion from the foregoing review is that moral and ethical codes are and always have been the product of the rational human mind, as humans used their reasoning and innovative capacities together with their knowledge and experience of living in order to discover and to formulate the rules and regulations necessary for living together in community. Moreover, the authority that was drawn on to enforce and to compel obedience to these moral and ethical codes originated from gods, which were themselves imaginative constructions of human minds. Thus, neither the moral and ethical codes themselves nor the authority to evoke and to compel obedience to them came from external sources or origins, but both were rather discoveries and products of the rational human mind.

Because the use of our human reasoning capacities has served us well in giving us the moral and ethical codes that have ordered our communal lives until the present, it seems to me that we would do well to use those same reasoning processes to determine what elements to incorporate into moral and ethical codes that are appropriate for living in the modern world. In the following I will first review the content of the Judeo-Christian moral and ethical codes that have guided us heretofore. Then I will critique them from my own personal perspective for their adequacy for the present time. Finally, I will suggest how I think that they may need to be modified for the present and for the future.

As I examine the contents of the Judeo-

Christian moral and ethical codes, it is helpful to review the presuppositions on which they are based. The groundwork is already laid out early in the biblical narrative. The fundamental tenet is that humans (Adam and Eve), created by God in perfection, willfully disobeyed God's commands (sinned) and thereby became "fallen" creatures, alienated from and needing to be reconciled with God. That state of "fallenness" – including moral depravity that prevented them from doing anything God-pleasing by their own abilities – has been hereditarily transmitted to all their human descendants. In order for humans to be reconciled with God, God called a chosen people (Israel), and from time to time gave them commandments and laws that detailed how they were to live as his faithful followers. Probably most familiar are The Ten Commandments, which specify how God alone should be worshiped and obeyed and how people are to live in a God-pleasing relationship with one another. There were also other significant expansions to this basic code. For example, orphans, widows and aliens (non-Israelites who lived in their land) were especially singled out to be cared for and treated with dignity and respect. Because being an Israelite and belonging to a nuclear family with a male head of the household was so important in Israel's social life, these three classes of people were especially vulnerable to neglect or mistreatment because they often lived outside of such a nuclear family.

Later, in the New Testament, Jesus summarized the content of Jewish law quite succinctly. When asked which commandment in the law was greatest, Jesus answered, "You shall love the Lord your God with all your heart, and with all your soul, and with all your mind. This is the greatest commandment. And a second is like it: You shall love your neighbor as yourself" (Matt. 22:37-38, NRSV). These moral and ethical codes have served as the core principles for Middle Eastern and Western European civilizations that were influenced by the monotheistic religions – Judaism, Christianity and Islam.

Before moving on to critique the adequacy of the Judeo-Christian moral and ethical codes for living in the modern world, I want to examine the credibility of the presuppositions that undergird them. From the results of historical-critical studies of the biblical origin and contents, I know that the biblical narrative of "The Fall" is mythological and has no actual historical basis. It has nevertheless persisted as a principal tenet of the Judeo-Christian narrative because it appears to provide an etiological account for human sinfulness – the capacity, tendency and even proclivity for humans to think and to act wrongfully against their God, against other humans and against nature.

However, it is known from paleontological, archeological, genetic and other scientific evidence that *Nature's Creativity* has produced humans through a long evolutionary process, in which our prehuman forebears were animals with aggressive behaviors that functioned for survival and reproduction of their own species. Viewed from our humanistic perspective of today, many of those behaviors were indeed cruel and animalistic. As *Nature's Creativity* continued, intellectual capacity and innovative abilities accrued atop these survival instincts. Early humans discovered that some behaviors were necessary for ordered and organized human society and culture, while other behaviors were detrimental to humans' living together in community and needed to be suppressed. Even as humans were adopting and implementing behaviors that were supportive of organized society, they still had to deal with the vestiges of aggressive behaviors from their evolutionary past, at least some of which had and still have a hereditary basis. That tension persists in human societies today. For various and often not well-understood reasons we humans still engage in actions that are harmful to ourselves and to other people. In religious terms, we sin. Later, I shall explore possible

204

biological roots of those behaviors.

Yet, to acknowledge our biological roots is not to accept the premise that we humans are a "fallen," retrograde species. Rather, our modern understanding of human origins informs us that we are a quite highly-specialized and complex product of *Nature's Creativity* and that we appear to be becoming more so. *Nature's Creativity* has endowed us with what we are and the capacities that we have. Our status is one of elevated complexity and capacity, although we are still too frequently haunted by the baser behavioral instincts that still inhere within us from our animal roots. But our long human track record of having created increasingly organized and complex societies through discovery and through rational and innovative thinking gives us hope and confidence that this trend from baser animality to fuller humanity can and will continue. Moreover, to the extent that these baser animal instinctive behaviors are genetically conditioned, our societal actions to curb and to eliminate them should over extensive time help rid the human gene pool of those alleles (forms of genes) through the same selective processes that have molded us as a species to the present time.

Elements of the Judeo-Christian moral and ethical codes inform the morality and ethics of our country, the United States of America. Our Founding Fathers wished to establish a nation of laws and justice but without the religious domination and intolerance that had plagued the countries of their European ancestors. As a justification for seeking our independence as a nation from Great Britain, they wrote in the second paragraph of the Declaration of Independence:

We hold these truths to be self-evident, that all men are created equal, that they are endowed by their Creator with certain unalienable Rights, that among these are Life, Liberty and the pursuit of Happiness.

Interpreting "all men" to mean "all people," their statement echoes the second great commandment expressed by Jesus: "You shall love your neighbor as yourself." It should be noted, however, that the Founding Fathers' statement "universalizes" Jesus' statement. It says that *all* people have the same inalienable rights, not just the people of the new nation that they were hoping to create. If *all* people of *all* nations of the world are created equal and with the unalienable rights of life, liberty and the pursuit of happiness, then we are being unfaithful to the moral principles on which our nation was founded whenever we in any way think or act to deprive any other human of any nation of the inalienable rights that we claim for ourselves. Thus, in the United States of America we find ourselves living with moral and ethical codes that commit us to treating *all people* as having the same rights and privileges that we have, simply based on their being fellow humans.

These Judeo-Christian moral and ethical codes seem to have served Middle Eastern and Western European civilizations rather well for several thousands of years. It is probably not an overstatement to say that without them Western civilization might well not have developed at all, or at least not as we know it today. Yet when some aspects of modern life are examined, it can be seen that some serious frays and tears are appearing in the fabric of our society. I now turn to looking at them more closely, in particular to determine if they are related to inadequacies and/or misapplications of our moral and ethical codes. Because I am a member of collective American society, the following discussion and commentary is narrated in the first person plural, except for those details from my personal life experiences

The *first great commandment* cited by Jesus concerns humans' relationship with

God, the transcendent, superhuman-like noetic agent who is the Judeo-Christian imaginative conception of *UUR*. Because I have conceived *UUR* in this book as impersonal *Nature's Creativity*, many aspects of the Judeo-Christian moral and ethical codes that relate to a personal God have little or no meaning in relationship to *Nature's Creativity*. Nevertheless, I shall return to a consideration of my relationship to *Nature's Creativity* later in the chapter. However, I now consider whether "obedience" to the *second great commandment*, "Love your neighbor as yourself" – together with its American elaboration of universal human equality of persons, rights and opportunities – is functioning adequately in our modern society.

The above-cited phrase "pursuit of happiness" in the Declaration of Independence was a parallel phrase to Adam Smith's "pursuit of property." Later that phrase came to be understood as the opportunity for all persons to engage in the free enterprise economic system, which has metamorphosed into the capitalistic free enterprise system that is the primary economic basis for our society today in the United States of America.

Among the premises offered by proponents to recommend the capitalistic free enterprise system is the notion that people are most highly motivated to succeed if they are permitted to freely engage in economic activities that bring them personal benefits, rewards and wealth. It is undoubtedly true that humans are likely to engage wholeheartedly in activities that will accrue economic benefits to themselves. However, the capitalistic free enterprise system ultimately works well only if humans' economic desires and goals also factor in considerations concerning the benefit and the well-being of the larger human society rather than of just the individual.

Such wider consideration is frequently not the case today. When I assess current business practices – particularly those of large multinational corporations, it seems

that they can have devastating consequences. The purpose of corporations is to create wealth by maximizing the profits for shareholders and management. Maximizing profits involves minimizing costs, which often translates into reducing the labor force to the absolute minimum necessary to conduct business operations. Reducing the labor force means that people lose their jobs. In losing their employment, people also lose their sense of dignity, identity, fulfillment and self-worth – their sense of being fully human. They can no longer support themselves and their families. They are destroyed emotionally, psychologically and socially as surely as if they were physically maimed or killed. Yet because our economic system considers competition as the grist mill for greater profits, this cost in human capital is considered a necessary price to pay in order to maximize profits – "the cost of doing successful business." To add even further insult to the victims of this system, corporate officers who execute these moves towards greater profits with the highest efficiency (i. e., reducing the work force to the smallest possible minimum, thereby depriving people of meaningful employment) are rewarded with the most obscene salaries and benefits packages (sometimes when their management of the corporation leads to losses or even to failure of the company rather than to profits). It seems absurd that those who act most aggressively and efficiently to destroy the lives of others by eliminating jobs in order to increase corporate profits receive the greatest benefits from our economic system. Moreover, as we move towards a global economy, the notion is prevalent that, if these practices can be streamlined, exported and implemented on a world-wide basis, the epitome of economic success will have been achieved.

Traditional Judeo-Christian morals and ethics have acted more or less successfully to curb the physically-aggressive and harmful behaviors towards other humans. That is, societies have conceived and instituted morals and ethics that curb and prevent people from behaviors that "physically harm or kill" each other. On the other hand, our society has created, legitimized and even sanctified practices that *economically* and *emotionally* destroy our fellow humans. Our championing of competition and maximizing profits in the free enterprise system posits that we can rightfully destroy someone economically and emotionally by disposing of their jobs, depriving them of a livelihood or putting them out of business.

If we inquire into how and why these practices have evolved, we can identify factors that dehumanize people in our economic system. The size and power of publicly-owned corporations have increased exponentially, even as the size and influence of forces acting in the interests of individuals in the labor force have correspondingly decreased. The "public good" is seen as maximized corporate profits. It is noteworthy that our governmental economic reports have been depersonalized and sanitized of human consequences. Creation of wealth through business activity is reported as gross national product, while the cost in human suffering is measured as *job losses*, as though the people losing their jobs were some impersonal commodity. Even as this trend was happening, our society was preoccupied with maximizing ease and convenience through the use of disposable products in almost every area in our daily lives. In such a "disposable society" it should not surprise us that people became disposable chaff winnowed from the economic mill. Societal acceptance and endorsement of such economic *modi operandi* will in the long run fracture and destabilize society; perhaps we are already seeing evidences of such societal instability.

The above-described economic system has developed under the auspices and tutelage of two overlapping sets of moral and ethical principles. Proximally in time, it seems impossible to reconcile with the stated purpose of our Declaration of Independence, which asserts "that all men are created equal and that they have the inalienable right of the pursuit of happiness." More distally in time, it contradicts traditional Judeo-Christian moral and ethical principles under which humans have been exhorted "to love your neighbor as yourself." Our failure to achieve either the goals of traditional Judeo-Christian moral and ethical goals or their expanded American counterpart is a sure signal that their practice in our society needs to be seriously reassessed.

Unfortunately, the above societally legitimized economic destruction of our fellow humans is exacerbated by yet two other trends – the increasing individualism in our society and the notion that life is all about accumulating wealth and enjoying leisure. Both are, in one way or another, societal expressions of individuals' tendencies towards self-gratification and self-indulgence.

I cite several examples from my own experience to illustrate this point. In the early 1960s as I was moving through my teens and beginning to consider a career, I was counseled by my parents and mentors to find a vocation that would be of significant service and benefit to others, that would be intellectually and emotionally meaningful and fulfilling to me, and that would provide a satisfactory livelihood. Through high school and college I explored the possibilities of finding that combination, and I finally discovered that for me that vocation would involve education and teaching. I think that my experience was not unique or even atypical. While others of my contemporaries chose other vocations for their own specific reasons, the counsel and advice given to them was much the same as that given to me, and they, each in their own respective way, attempted to follow that advice.

Later, when I began my career as a research geneticist in the mid-1970s, from time to time I interviewed persons for technician positions to work in the laboratory that I managed. The sequence of questions by job applicants generally went something like the following. "What will be my duties in this job?" "What training and skills will I need for this job?" "What will be my work schedule?" "What will be my opportunities for additional training and job advancement?" "What will be my salary and fringe benefits?" "How much vacation will I have?" By the time I left that position in the early 1990s, the sequence of questions as asked by many job applicants was almost completely reversed. The primary interest in the job was the benefits that accrued to the employee; of secondary interest were the responsibilities, requirements and demands of the job, and the contributions of the job to some larger cause.

Another incident from my college teaching in about 2003 is particularly illustrative. One student, a junior, arrived for class about ten minutes early and took his seat. Attempting to engage him in conversation about his life, I asked him, "Tommy (not his real name), when you dream about your ideal life five or ten years down the road, what would it look like?" Without hesitation he answered, "I'd like to have a job where I can earn enough money so that I can sit and watch television and drink beer." And he was serious.

To be sure, this was not the career advice that Tommy was getting from his mentors at Catawba College. Service to others and contributions to larger causes in society are lifted up as important avenues to personal meaningfulness and fulfillment as students are counseled about choosing a vocation, much as I received earlier in my life. Yet for many students that advice seems a whispered voice lost against the background of society's loud din that puts the highest priority simply on finding the job that will earn an individual the most money and will provide the greatest opportunities for leisure and self-indulgence.

The youth of today learn those values by absorbing them from adults in society. The development of our free enterprise, econom-

ic system in American society has increasingly resulted in our assessing the status and importance of people by their economic success – their financial success. *When asked who we are, we often reply, not by telling the questioner who we are, but rather what we do* – where we fit into the socioeconomic fabric of our society, which often implies how much money we earn. A person who has amassed great wealth is deemed to merit social prestige, power, influence and privilege. A person is especially admired and respected if he/she has "taken some idea and run with it economically." Whereas, in the past, ideas had intrinsic value because they contributed to the betterment of human society, in the present it seems that too often ideas are considered to have no value unless they somehow allow someone to "make money," especially lots of it. This emphasis on the importance of ideas based largely on their economic potential seems to cheapen the intent of our Founding Fathers and of the wider Western heritage, who and which, respectively, have regarded the free exchange of ideas to be the fountainhead of knowledge that would enhance liberty and justice for all people – not just or even primarily to create wealth. We seem to be abandoning the use of our intellectual capacities to improve the human situation by prostituting its use for the creation of wealth and the self-indulgence that comes with it.

The combination of our growing obsessions with accumulation of wealth and with individualism has led to a narcissistic vision of the American dream. Seemingly, the ideal American life has become consumed with earning as much money as possible, as fast as possible, in order to retire as young as possible, and to spend the remainder of life enjoying as much leisure as possible for as long as possible. And all along the journey, we seem obsessed with looking and feeling as young as possible in order to withstand and to enjoy the whole adventure as much as possible. This characterization is obviously a caricature. Yet to the extent that any of it

208

"rings true," it should cause us concern that over the last half-dozen decades or so the priorities of our lives have shifted so dramatically from communal well-being to individual and oftentimes selfish considerations.

Another current fixation is that one must, while finding the job that pays the most money, become an adored and worshiped idol or hero. Often the "occupations" that pay the most money are in the sports and entertainment industries, where stars receive extravagant, even obscene, sums of money for "jobs" whose primary activities provide little or no discernible contribution to the betterment of society. Unfortunately, perhaps even tragically, most of our idols and heroes of today's society can claim no feats – no extraordinary, or even notable, achievements to benefit humankind; rather, their "jobs" pander to our desires for spectator self-indulgence. To cite further evidence, whereas formerly television programs sought to identify persons with genuine, artful talents and abilities, such programs are now searches for "American idols," who often turn out to have the "clayest" of clay feet. And all of this is happening in our nation, which claims to be guided by Judeo-Christian morals and ethics.

It is noteworthy that, although the *second great commandment* tells us to "love our neighbors as ourselves," it is remarkably silent on what is entailed in "loving ourselves." In Matthew 7:12 Jesus states, "So in everything, do to others what you would have them do to you, for this sums up the Law and the Prophets." The presumption was that one would do only things for one's self that were good and pleasing and that this principle should be a guide to one's actions towards one's neighbors. But that directive gives no specific guidelines as to what to do. Another possible reason for the silence on "loving ourselves" concerns the status of the individual in Hebrew and early Christian societies. While individuals were viewed to have intrinsic worth and value, their impor-

tance stemmed primarily from their relationships to communal groups – families, clans, tribes, Israel, the Christian community. Because their importance was viewed in the context of their belonging to and contributing to community, there was little emphasis or attention paid to what the individual did vis-à-vis herself or himself.

The Declaration of Independence states that all persons have the inalienable right of the pursuit of happiness. This ensures us of the right and privilege to seek after that which brings us happiness. The *second commandment* quoted by Jesus was "You shall love your neighbor as yourself." This presupposes that we "love ourselves" – that we think and act in ways that genuinely contribute to our personal well-being. With our present obsession with individualism and self-indulgence, we achieve neither. We can never acquire or possess enough wealth and fame to achieve happiness. Instead, we indulge ourselves with food, alcohol, tobacco, licit and illicit drugs, sex, entertainment, and the like. Through this undisciplined self-indulgence, we are destroying ourselves; following our misguided thinking, we are "loving ourselves" to death.

Our capacity to indulge and to harm ourselves has also been facilitated by yet another modern technological "advancement," the so-called "virtual world." It is a "world" that in our minds can seem to be real but is actually only imagined. Both the possibilities and the limitations in the virtual world have little or no relationship to actual possibilities and limitations in the real physical and biological world. This virtual world phenomenon has led many to conclude that, if something can be imagined, it can become real; that is, if something can be dreamed, it can be accomplished – that we can interchangeably intermingle the elements of this virtual world into our dealing with life in our real world. Although the creativity and innovative capacities of the human intellect surely can inspire us and are conducive to marvelous advancements in human accomplishments, when they delude us into thinking that we are no longer subject to fundamental physical and biological laws of nature, they become dangerous to human well-being. Because we can imagine that we humans can grow wings and fly in a virtual world does not make it a real possibility.

Living in this virtual world can also delude us into thinking that we can escape the consequences to ourselves and to others of our bad decisions and actions in our real world. I illustrate the implications of this by using my own life as a hypothetical example. In reality, before I was anything else, I was a biological organism – a baby. I needed food, shelter, care and nurture. Throughout life, I continue to be a biological organism, whose existence and well-being can be fostered and enhanced by healthy lifestyle choices in a life-supportive environment. On the other hand, my life can be endangered or ended by bad decisions and risky behaviors such as drug, alcohol, food, sex and other abuses and addictions. While I might be able to escape the consequences of self-destructive behaviors in a virtual or imaginary world, the consequences of having engaged in risky or outright self-harmful behaviors cannot be ignored or imagined away in reality. The *real life* consequences of bad decisions are that I suffer *real* harm and/or *real* death. All of modern technological, medical and other advances do not free me from personal and collective responsibility for and consequences of my actions. That is true for me as well as all other members of the human species.

Living in the unrealities of a virtual world is akin to living today in the unrealities of a religion situated in an ancient worldview – a "virtual" world of another time. Both foster illusory expectations that have no possibility of being realized. Deriving expectations in life from either is guaranteed to bring disillusionment and disappointment – and ultimately failure and destruction. In order to live a meaningful and fulfilled life, I must always make my life's decisions and base my expectations on presuppositions that are *grounded in reality* – on what the best human knowledge and my life's experiences inform me can actually occur. To do otherwise is to live unrealistically and foolishly.

Today's society has a rightful concern for discovering and developing the abilities and skills of all individuals in order that they can pursue happiness. However, it seems that, in striving to accomplish that goal, it has forgotten the notion that those skills and abilities should also contribute to the betterment of the larger society in which we live. The balance between seeking personal happiness and economic success and contributing to society has been strongly skewed towards the former at expense to the latter.

There is no doubt that modern society and technology have brought us many medical and technological advances, which enable us to live longer and healthier lives that are as meaningful and as fulfilling as has ever been possible. However, the emergence of many aspects of individualism and self-directed behaviors at the expense of the welfare of wider society and of nature is a troubling omen. History tells us that such decadence and self-indulgence within societies are symptoms and signals of empires and nations in decline rather than in ascendancy. Our nation would do well to learn from history rather than to repeat its mistakes.

Thus, I must conclude that our traditional Judeo-Christian moral and ethical codes must be substantially reassessed and revised if we are to live in such a way that we truly love ourselves and that we love our neighbors as ourselves – that is, we interact in ways which ensure that all humans have the same inalienable rights that we claim for ourselves.

While very serious in their own right, the shortcomings of our Judeo-Christian morality and ethics in self-loving and in human-to-human relationships are not their only or even their most serious deficiencies. The life-threatening issues of today deal with the human-to-environment relationships. I now turn to an examination of these concerns.

"Scientific man is already on the moon, and yet we are still living with the moral concepts of Homer," said Italian modernist film director Michelangelo Antonioni. Homer, if there was actually a Greek of that name, probably lived about the eighth century BCE. Many of the primary moral and ethical principles of the major world religions were codified and written down during the two millennia bracketing the time of Homer. Chronologically, Islam arose later, but it inherited many of its moral and ethical precepts from its older siblings, Judaism and Christianity. The foundational writings of the major world religions date to that Homeric period of time, and they are still considered the authoritative determinants of the doctrinal teachings and moral and ethical codes of their respective modern religions. Thus, Antonioni's statement is a fairly accurate reflection of what has occurred historically.

I can speculate as to why we humans have been unwilling to move beyond "the moral concepts of Homer." First, perhaps it is because most religions consider their moral and ethical codes to be the will and even the spoken commands of their respective deities and/or human founders and that they are, therefore, not to be changed. In the Hebrew Bible there are strong admonitions against changing the law: "You shall not add to the word which I command you, nor take from it, that you may keep the commandments of the Lord your God which I command you" (Deuteronomy 4:2). "Whatever I command you, be careful to observe it; you shall not add to it nor take away from it" (Deuteronomy 12:32). "Do not add to His words, lest He rebuke you, and you be found a liar" (Proverbs 30:5-6). Similar counsel was given by Jesus: "Not one letter, not one stroke of a letter, will pass from the law until all is accomplished" (Matt. 5:18; cf. Luke 16:17). Such biblical threats are surely not inviting of changing those commands. Second, perhaps there has been little felt need for change, because the received moral and ethical codes seemed, for the most part, to be working. Whatever the reasons, we still live essentially with "the moral concepts of Homer."

But it is precisely the challenges and problems that have arisen because of "scientific man" that have exposed the shortcomings of our traditional moral and ethical codes in dealing with life in our modern world, particularly our relationship to nature and to our environment. And there are recognizable reasons why we have lagged in our sensitivities to these issues. Traditional Christian morals and ethics have been predominantly both humanistic and anthropocentric. They have strongly emphasized moral and ethical considerations of how humans should relate to God and to other humans. According to the biblical narrative, Jehovah God was surely the "holy other" from whom everything originated and emanated, yet the principal plot of the story was the relationship of God to humans. In that narrative, *nature* is regarded as a creation of God into which God then introduced "specially-created" humans. The biblical notion of the three-tiered universe is strongly anthropocentric. It presupposed humans at the center of the middle tier with the surrounding animal and plant life in service to them, with the sun, moon and stars in the upper tier ministering to human needs during life, and with the lower tier Sheol attending to humans after their deaths.

Because the biblical narrative presents nature as having been created by God for human use, we have deemed ourselves to have primacy and the privilege – indeed the right – to exploit nature with hubris. Using biblical terms, humans were "to have dominion over it" and "to be fruitful and multiply, and fill the earth and subdue it" (Genesis 1:26-28). And we have exploited it – in both senses of the word. We have sometimes respectfully and prudently utilized nature's resources for our own benefit. Especially recently, however, we have exploited nature in a negative way. We have used its resources with hubris and without regard to the harmful, even catastrophic, effects that we are inflicting on nature.

Although recent environmental concerns have caused a reconsideration by Christians of all stripes of what is entailed by responsibly "having dominion over" and "subduing" the earth, it is, nevertheless, still true that the Christian focus of the human-to-nature relationship is predominantly humanistic and anthropocentric – the concerns of the *two great commandments* stated by Jesus: "to love God" and "to love one's neighbor as oneself." These concerns are elaborated explicitly in the Ten Commandments. However, it is noteworthy that neither the word *nature* nor anything relating to its care and well-being is mentioned in The Ten Commandments and the commentary on them that is presented in Luther's Small Catechism – the primary teaching tool that was used for Lutheran indoctrination during my youth and is still used today.

A brief consideration of the acute problems facing human life on planet earth today documents the inadequacy of traditional Christian (and other religious) morality and ethics in relationship to nature. The recently coined terms *biocide* and *ecocide* refer to the rampant killing of living organisms and to the destruction of their ecological environments, respectively. Global warming/climate change, attributable mostly to human use of fossil fuels, threatens to alter and to destroy environments that are today occupied by humans and other living organisms. Habitat destruction through deforestation, mining, agriculture and other human activities is causing extinction of species of plants and animals at a rate estimated to be 100-1000 times as high as at any previous time in humans' existence on the earth. Each year humans are eliminating millions of acres of forests – which utilize carbon dioxide – even as we continue to increase the amount of carbon dioxide that

we release into the atmosphere from the burning of fossil fuels. Human overpopulation is intruding into the habitats of many plant and animal species, leading either to animal-human confrontations or to the disappearance of the nonhuman species. Likewise, human overpopulation is resulting in human-to-human conflict, as overcrowding leads different families, tribes and nations to fight over limited food, water and land resources. These latter struggles will only be exacerbated as the effects of global warming create greater extremes in weather and climate patterns – causing more frequent droughts and floods.

These global environmental problems have been further exacerbated by another presupposition or our free enterprise system – that the economy can endlessly continue to expand and to create more wealth. We Americans suppose that to be a viable strategy for our own country, and we also lift it up to be emulated globally. While in the world of one hundred years ago with a much smaller human population that notion seemed a reasonable assumption, we are recognizing that presumption to be a fallacy for the present day. The earth has limited – not limitless – resources. It is finite, not infinite. That means that our use of fresh water, forests and minerals will one day exhaust earth's supplies of these and other natural resources. That means that one day, perhaps quite soon, the human population will reach the maximum carrying capacity of planet earth – that number of humans who can live optimally with each other, with other living species, and with their environment. (Many argue that the maximum carrying capacity has already been exceeded!) And as we near that limit, the human-to-human tensions and conflicts will be aggravated and exacerbated by natural disasters such as floods, droughts and other calamities brought on by global climate change. Continued pursuit of our present ever-expanding free enterprise policies that ravenously exploit all available planetary resources will lead to the situation addressed by the wisdom of a Native American adage: "Only after the last tree has died, the last river has been poisoned, and the last fish has been caught will we realize that we cannot eat money."

In his book *Collapse: How Societies Choose to Fail or Succeed*, Jared Diamond documents how such nonjudicious use of natural resources by various societies within the past several thousand years has led first to internal conflicts and finally to their ultimate collapses. While these instances for the most part occurred in isolated areas of the earth, such will not be the case in the modern world. Today there are no longer isolated areas of the earth. We all live in one global community. We are all aboard the same ship; if and when that "Titanic" goes down, we all perish together. Unless we rethink our personal, national and global economic strategies in terms of long-term, sustainable existence, our global community will experience the same fate as these earlier isolated communities. The important difference is that the next collapses will be simultaneously local and global.

Our pursuit of living in a sustainable relationship with our ecosystem has been adversely complicated by yet another factor. For much of human history, commerce and economic interchange were motivated by mutual *needs* of people for resources available from other people in their own communities or in other geographic regions. By exchanging resources, people were able to meet their needs for food, clothing and shelter. To be sure, nonneed items such as jewelry and other decorative and artful items were also traded, but they were generally "over and above"; that is, they were traded when the basic needs for survival had been met. Moreover, as a proportion of people's total economic activity, these exchanges were often quite limited, because most people had limited resources to purchase much beyond their needs.

During the twentieth century – not only in the United States, but especially here –

business entrepreneurs concluded that if business enterprises could depend only on meeting the *needs* of society, their prospects for continued expansion of their businesses and profits were rather limited. After all, people had only a limited number of needs, and those needs were being met with a decreasing proportion of their financial resources. Rather, if businesses wanted to exploit a seemingly limitless potential for profits, they had to appeal and to cater to people's *wants* rather than to their *needs*. *While people's needs were limited, people's desires and wants rarely had bounds.* To achieve that goal, businesses began sophisticated advertising strategies. If only people could be convinced that they would be happier, healthier, sexier or otherwise better people by using a particular product, then a *want* became a *need*, and seemingly limitless sales potential could follow. Idealized models of fashion or fitness became the standard against which people were encouraged to compare themselves, and of course, they always came up wanting. They then "needed" the product being sold in order to measure up to the ideal. After all, everyone owes it to her/himself to be the best person that she/he can become!

The transition from a needs-based to a wants-based economy catered to our desires for self-indulgence and escalated into our lavish, modern consumerist way of life. Advertising allured us into thinking that wants were needs. Charge and credit card purchasing meant that we did not have to wait to earn the money to purchase the desired item; we could have it immediately. And when the desired item was on sale "for a limited time only," we were lured into impulse buying – purchasing an item without due thought or consideration as to whether we could afford the item or whether it would in any way better our lives. The underlying economic assumption was that humans have limitless wants that can produce endless economic expansion, thereby creating countless new opportunities to generate more wealth for new entrepreneurs to conceive and to sell new products for self-indulgence. Little or no thought was given to whether this way of life improved the well-being of either the individual or of larger society. If anything, such considerations were discouraged, because they impeded "economic progress."

Moreover, the above economic transition occurred as Americans prospered and had more disposable income. They had money to seek and to satisfy more and more of their wants. Today it has reached the point that many Americans spend much of their time seeking new ways to spend their money in order to find and to satisfy new wants – new ways to indulge themselves. There is, of course, nothing inherently immoral or unethical about seeking and satisfying our needs and even many of our wants. The moral and ethical problems arise from two consequences of these economic practices. First, all of this has occurred without any consideration of the consequences and impacts that such behaviors have on our natural setting. Satisfying these wants most often comes at some, and often not small, expense to our environment. A sustainable relationship with our natural environment means that we cannot exploit its resources without limit. There may be no limits to our imagination of wants, but there are limits to our environment's capacity to provide resources to meet those wants. Second, the founding principle of our nation that all people have inalienable rights – the same rights that we have – means that in meeting many of our *wants* we are, in fact, depriving other humans (of our nation and of the larger world) of their rights to meet their basic *needs*. In our global economy such inequities will threaten and destabilize a harmonious global community. Stated in traditional Judeo-Christian terms, we are to live so that we "love our neighbors as ourselves." As a society, we need to balance our needs and wants both with a sustainable relationship with planet earth and with the rights and privileges of our global fellow human and nonhuman inhabitants.

In summary, traditional Christian morals and ethics have attempted to address the people-to-people conflicts – including family relationships, fratricide, homicide and respect for humans' property rights. While those concerns have to some extent been addressed and met with some success, further attention to those matters is still needed. Beyond those concerns, it is clear that traditional Christian morals and ethics have been completely inadequate in dealing with biocide and ecocide – the wanton destruction of nonhuman life and the ravenous consumption of earth's resources, both biological and physical. These call for a major rethinking and refocusing of our moral and ethical concerns towards living in a compatible and sustainable relationship with nature and *Nature's Creativity*, because the above-mentioned natural crises are already serious and are becoming even and ever more so.

How can we deal with these *problems-becoming-crises*? Sometimes we can begin to remold our thinking by looking at the etymological and historical roots of words, as we did earlier when comparing our modern definition of *religion* with its Latin root *religio*. The Random House Dictionary defines the word *economic* as "pertaining to the production, distribution, and use of income, wealth, and commodities," and that definition captures the connotations and implications of our common usage of the word today. However, the English word *economic* is etymologically derived from the Latin *oeconomic(us)* and the Greek *oikonomikōs*, which mean "relating to house-hold management." According to this understanding, we are managers or stewards of the household bounty with which we have been endowed by *Nature's Creativity*. We individuals may have wealth, deeds and other documents of *ownership* during our lifetimes. However, when we consider our threescore and ten or even five-score years of life in the time perspective of the billions of years of age of our planet and universe, our life spans are indeed short, and our *ownership* is transient, to say the least. And, as the saying goes, "we can't take it with us." When we die, that *ownership* passes to someone else. Thus, in the perspective of cosmic time, the terms *manager* and *steward* more aptly describe our relationship to earth's household resources than the word *owner*. The term *owner* tends to perpetuate the anthropocentricity discussed earlier, together with the malignant presumptions that go with it. The terms *manager* and *steward* imply our overseeing the household of nature for the benefit of the rest of nature as well as of ourselves.

Moreover, our human "household" today is global – planet earth. We live in a global community and economy. We are managers and stewards with all other humans. We must manage earth's resources so that all inhabitants of that global household can live with the "inalienable rights of life, liberty and the pursuit of happiness." Drawing on both secular (Abraham Lincoln, June 1858) and religious (Jesus, Matthew 12:25) wisdom, "A house divided against itself cannot stand." We cannot consider it fair to other humans when we claim a disproportionate share of the earth's bounty for ourselves. We are morally and ethically obligated to consider the well-being of other humans in the present and in all generations yet to be born. Just as important, we are related to all other forms of life and to their (and our) environments that also have necessary and important roles and functions in the web of life. They have no less "right" to live than we humans do. Our moral and ethical thinking must take all of the above factors into our deliberations.

How can we proceed to conceive of and to implement morals and ethics that better serve us for living in the modern world? Perhaps we can begin by better understanding ourselves as humans – both our origins and who we are.

Earlier, I compared and contrasted the nature and origin of humans as understood from the biblical narrative with that provided by modern scientific investigation. I concluded that we humans are not a "fallen" (retrograde) species as described in the biblical narrative but rather a highly specialized and complex product of *Nature's Creativity*, whose fuller humanness and humaneness promise to emerge in our future. We have the capacity to become more than what we are. Moreover, with our incrementally growing understanding of the workings of nature and of *Nature's Creativity*, we have the potential to participate wisely and constructively in the unfolding of our future. Nevertheless, despite our "risenness" from prehuman forms through the evolutionary process, we are individually and collectively subject to all of the moral and ethical shortcomings and failings that are attributed by traditional Christianity to our "fallenness." In Christian terms, we sin. Stated from a secular perspective, we fail to obey the moral and ethical codes that society has formulated for us to live by. That is, *we are who and what we are, irrespective of how we came to be that way*. We are individuals who tend to act in our own self-interest and to indulge our individual wants and desires, often in opposition to what our higher reasoning powers tell us are good and right things that we should do.

Awareness of this human proclivity is not new. It was already addressed by St. Paul in Romans:

> I do not understand my own actions. For I do not do what I want, but I do the very thing I hate. ...For I do not do the good I want, but the evil I do not want is what I do (Romans 7: 15, 19).

Rather early in traditional Christian theology, St. Augustine of Hippo referred to this human tendency with the Latin *incurvatus in se* – "turning inward or curving inward on oneself". It was also elaborated by Martin

Luther in his commentary on the epistle of Romans. Stated succinctly, this innate tendency for us humans too often to think and to do selfish and self-serving things that our higher reasoning powers tell us not to think and to do is part of being human. Unless we accept that about ourselves, we are not dealing with reality.

While the earlier characterization – that modern humans have the capacity to become more than what we are – is both affirming and optimistic, it leaves us with the challenge of how we might achieve a fuller humanness and humaneness. First, we must recognize *who* and *what* we are today. We are learning that our human "beingness" consists of a *who* situated atop a *what*. Our *who* consists of the human capacities of consciousness, self-consciousness and reasoning, which are functions of the higher part of our brain, that part of our brain that has evolved most recently. Those rational and reasoning capacities are situated atop a *what* – a pyramid of lower brain functions that we share with our less- and non-reasoning animal cousins. Those lower brain functions control autonomic functions and instinctive behaviors, many of which are apparently quite strongly genetically-influenced or even genetically-determined. Those lower brain functions act to control and to sustain the biological functions that are common to all animals. However, they also interact with our higher brain functions to give emotions and feelings to our consciousness. Those emotions can distort and color our reasoning capacities so that we are sometimes influenced to think and to act in ways that are very different from how we might think and act in the absence of or with other emotional influences.

One current example of such individual irrational behavior relates to the problem of obesity in our society. We humans can understand through our reasoning capacities that eating too much food leads to obesity and that obesity is a threat to our individual health. Why then do we continue to overeat to the extent that more than half of our society is overweight and a significant proportion is morbidly obese? In the course of their lives, our animal cousins face abundance and scarcity cycles in food availability. They eat large amounts of food when it is abundantly available in order to store up reserves to be used in times of food scarcity. This highly functional evolutionary adaptation is probably significantly genetically-conditioned and is most likely mediated through the lower, nonrational functions of the brain. In our genetic heritage from our prehuman ancestors, we received the genes that influence us towards those same behaviors – specifically, eating much food when it is abundantly available. For most of us, that means all the time. Unlike other animals, we are almost never faced with food shortages when we would use up the stored energy. Those conditions combined with our increasingly sedentary modern lifestyle result in our continuing to accumulate excessive calories. Moreover, our society constantly seduces us to experience new and different kinds of food and further entices us with the "all you can eat" for a relatively small price. Being "value-conscious consumers," we certainly want "to get our money's worth." This is a very obvious example of how our lower brain functions override what our rational brain informs us is good for us – both individually and societally.

Thus, although we humans have rational and reasoning capacities, we are not "programmed" to use them mechanically. Rather, while at times we use them to completely think out and to program our behavior, at other times their functions are strongly influenced or even overridden by the input from the nonrational parts of our brain. It is the rational and reasoning parts of our brain that enable us to conceive of and to construct moral and ethical codes for the purpose of guiding and directing us. At times, our feelings that bubble up from our lower brain functions allow and even enable us to act fully consistently with our moral and ethical codes. At other times, our thinking and behaviors are being influenced by input –

feelings – from the autonomic and instinctive parts of our brain; then our feelings influence us to think and to act in immoral and unethical ways.

How might we have evolved from an early species in which our behaviors were determined largely by our lower brain to modern rational humans? We do not yet have the answers to that question, but we can hypothesize how it might have happened. In our prehuman and early human ancestors instinctive and autonomic, physically-aggressive (selfish) behaviors helped to sustain and to support life. For those ancestors, physically aggressive behaviors that provided food for an individual and its offspring, that conquered and protected territory, and that obtained a mating partner in order to have the most possible offspring contributed a competitive, adaptive advantage to the individual exhibiting them as well as to the whole species to which it belonged. When those brutish physical behaviors were gradually supplemented with purposeful and guileful manipulation enabled by increased mental capacity, they became even more successful. Thus, among our ancestors of long ago these behaviors were necessary and adaptive for survival.

However, in most human societies today the needs of food, living space and the acquisition of a mating partner are met through more civilized behavioral patterns that require much less physical aggressiveness than was the case for our ancient ancestors. Thus, we no longer need to express such physically aggressive behaviors in order to meet our basic biological needs. Indeed, we have found that these aggressive behaviors are destructive and disruptive of our communal living, and we have discovered and formulated our moral and ethical codes to constrain us from expressing what remains of them. Consequently, when such primitive, aggressive behaviors are expressed in modern times, they are almost universally condemned and punished in nearly all societies.

Yet, we still have within us the genetically influenced, instinct-like, lower-brain-conditioned, aggressive tendencies towards selfish and self-serving behaviors. For the most part, instead of the overtly *physically* aggressive actions of our forebears, our residual innate aggressive tendencies are now likely to be expressed through societally-refined, softer aggressive behaviors that involve self-pleasure, self-indulgence and self-gratification. Our human capacity and desire to "feel good" influences us towards many "self-" inclinations and behaviors: self-admiration, self-advancement, self-absorption, self-centeredness, self-deception, self-dedication, self-delight, self-devotion, self-fulfillment, etc. Probably more often than not, these self-serving behaviors benefit us individually at the expense of other humans or other components of nature, even though they involve little or no physical aggression.

Thus, the reality of our current situation is that we humans are still too much influenced by those self-serving animalistic tendencies that, while serving well to ensure the survival of prehuman species, turn out to be disruptive and destructive to human society and to our global environment. Despite our having been endowed with elegant rational capacities by *Nature's Creativity*, we are still too often driven by selfish interests that fail to consider a balancing of the benefits to ourselves with those of other humans or with our global environment. Simply knowing the good and right things to do is not sufficient to give us the ability and the will to do them! Somehow, we have to discover and to implement a rationale that will make it feel right for us both to think and to do the right things.

Given that the above is our present human situation and promises to be for the long foreseeable future, how might we rethink and reframe our moral and ethical codes to help us live in ways that "love" ourselves and our neighbors in a sustainable relationship with our environment? Evolving prehistoric and early historic humans drew on their emerging rational and innovative abilities to discover and to discern what was necessary and then to devise moral and ethical codes in order for people to live together peacefully in towns and crowded cities. We today are using those same intellectual capacities to explore and to understand the intricacies of nature and of what we must do to live in sustainable relationship to it for both nature's and our own benefits. In order to develop moral and ethical codes for living in our world today, we should draw on our life experiences, informed by the best available modern scientific knowledge, in order to reason out what is conducive to the well-being of nature and of humans' living within nature. That corpus of scientific knowledge and understanding, constantly being updated, is the best possible authority that our life experiences and reasoning capacities can draw on to enlighten and to instruct our formulation of the most practical and relevant moral and ethical codes for living in a harmonious and sustainable relationship with nature. The compelling reasons and considerations for adopting and enforcing these morals and ethics are ones of human self-interest – survival of our own species and of our environment, planet earth.

In the following, I attempt to lift up what appear to me to be important principles of a moral and ethical code that presupposes *Nature's Creativity* as *UUR*. Although they are my personal conclusions about what is necessary and appropriate, I will speak of them collectively, because it seems to me that the whole of humanity will ultimately have to embrace a set of principles something like this. First, we should acknowledge and respect *Nature's Creativity* as the ultimate source of all reality. It has birthed all of nature, including us humans. Although we have achieved important insights into the operations of *Nature's Creativity*, there is still much that remains shrouded in mystery – that is not yet, and may never be, fully

accessible to human understanding. The understandings that we acquire cause us to respect and perhaps even to stand in awe of what *Nature's Creativity* has given rise to through the evolutionary process. While this reverential attitude is not worship in a traditional religious sense of "loving God with all one's heart, soul, mind and strength," our attitude towards *Nature's Creativity* should be one of deep reverence and respect. Maximally, that attitude should lead us to want to understand the intricacies of our relationship to nature and then to live in harmony with it. Minimally, it should evoke in us a sense of reticence and hesitancy to perturb or to disturb the complexities that *Nature's Creativity* has so intricately assembled over billions of years.

Second, we must commit ourselves to living compatibly with *Nature's Creativity*. From an individual perspective, each of us should live so as to optimize her/his own personal well-being – we must "love" ourselves. This involves adopting attitudes and behaviors that promote and encourage the health and wholesomeness of our *individual* physical, mental and emotional being. Positive actions towards these ends include proper diet, sufficient physical exercise and stimulating mental activity. It involves self-discipline and self-control in order to avoid addictive behaviors to food, drink, sex and other self-indulgent behaviors. Just as important, we should avoid exposure to harmful factors, including toxins, such as licit drugs (alcohol and tobacco), many currently available illicit drugs (marijuana, cocaine, methamphetamine, etc.), and the many other toxic chemicals that are introduced into our environment through our technological "advances." Each of us honors what *Nature's Creativity* has endowed us with – our individual selves – when we care for ourselves with the greatest possible diligence. While taking this individual responsibility for ourselves does not guarantee that we will live wholesome and fulfilled lives, it surely optimizes and maximizes the chances that we will have the opportunity to do so.

Third, we must commit ourselves to living in a sustainable relationship with our communal environment – our fellow humans and the rest of nature. Employing a term from traditional Christian terminology, our thinking and actions towards the rest of nature should reflect *agape* love – acting with care and concern for the well-being of the other. We must expand loving our "neighbors" to include not only other humans but also other living organisms and our physical environment. We humans are situated in an integrated web of life. We exist in a balance of nature that consists of a slowly changing equilibrium over evolutionary time. We humans can claim no primacy that warrants our exploitation of nature to our benefit and to the detriment of other living organisms or of our physical environment. When we make decisions and take actions to benefit the whole of nature, we also act morally and ethically to benefit ourselves. *In the end, when we love our environmental neighbors, we love ourselves.*

As to specific actions, we must immediately take steps to stop and to reverse the rampant biocide and ecocide that is currently occurring on our planet. We must replace anthropocentric thinking and behaviors with biocentric- and ecocentric-focused considerations that enable sustainability in our living patterns. We must immediately take steps to stop and to reverse global climate change by modifying or replacing our use of fossil fuels with energy sources that leave as small a carbon footprint as possible. Future technology must always be introduced and deployed only after considering its impact on the well-being of all living organisms and their environments, not just on what convenience, ease, leisure or profit it brings to humans. Many other specifics could be listed. In short, we must formulate moral and ethical codes for the world of "scientific man" to update or to replace "the moral concepts of Homer."

For an individual, compliance with and obedience to moral and ethical codes issues from our conscience – that inner sense of what is right and wrong. Each person's conscience is formed and informed by input from what she/he deems to be valid and reliable sources – appropriate authority on which to think and to act morally and ethically. In traditional Judeo-Christianity, the authority of moral and ethical codes has depended primarily on two factors. The first was the authority of the lawgiver. Because the commandments and laws are described by the biblical narrative as being oral and/or written directives from God, they are regarded as having divine authority and are to be obeyed absolutely and unquestionably. For believers in that God, there can be no greater authority mandating obedience. Second, according to the Christian tradition, during their lives and after their deaths, humans are judged by God concerning whether they have obeyed God's laws and commandments. If they are judged by God to be obedient, they are rewarded with blessings during their temporal life and with everlasting life with God in heaven after their deaths. If they are judged to have been disobedient, they are chastised and punished by God in their mortal lives and/or condemned to an eternity separated from God in hell. This combination (God's authority as lawgiver, the promise of blessings during life and of eternal life in heaven for obedience, and the threat of temporal and eternal punishment in hell for disobedience) has served and continues to serve effectively to enforce the Judeo-Christian moral and ethical codes.

With the intent of distinguishing itself from the "legalism" of God's covenant with Israel and its implied obedience because of "fear" of God, Christianity has attributed Christians' motivation to obey God's laws and commandments to "love" of God, made possible by the Holy Spirit's transformation of the sinful heart into a sanctified heart through the redemptive work of Jesus Christ. Irrespective of the specific motivations, all of the foregoing achieve compliance and obedience to the Judeo-Christian moral and ethical codes because of relationship to God, the absolute and ultimate transcendent authority in humans' lives. That is, humans obey because they are responding to an "exterior" authority – something *outside* of themselves.

Under the new paradigm presented in this book, *UUR* is symbolized by *Nature's Creativity*, an impersonal, self-organizing, creative capacity deep within nature. This metaphor involves no transcendent, super-natural, noetic entity having a personal relationship with humans. The absence of this personal godlike figure to whom humans are accountable means that humans have no external authority to enforce obedience and compliance with whatever moral and ethical codes they see fit to establish. Therefore, they must rely on other motivational factors to invite and to enforce compliance with society's moral and ethical codes.

An obvious, simple solution is for humans to use self-discipline and self-control to obey society's moral and ethical codes. However, in my earlier consideration of the problems being faced by modern society, I concluded that, if there are common underlying weaknesses of modern humans, they probably relate to our lack of self-discipline and self-control and to our proclivity towards self-indulgence – the op-posites of what are needed to comply with our moral and ethical codes. We humans are too often influenced and even controlled by the baser impulses of our lower brain func-tions to do what "feels good" and to indulge the self rather than what our reasoning capacities tell us is good and right. The question then becomes: how can human societies achieve compliance and obedience to its updated moral and ethical codes, without an exterior godlike authority to whom they are accountable and responsible?

This dilemma is not new. In *Doubt: A History: The Great Doubters and Their Legacy of Innovation from Socrates and Jesus to Thomas Jefferson and Emily Dick-inson*, Jennifer Michael Hecht cites the writings of doubters throughout history – persons who questioned or outright rejected the predominant religious views of their society and the moral and ethical consider-ations that emanated from them. These writers recognized the importance, indeed the essentialness, of the contributions of traditional religions in various cultures. Because of the authority of the god or revered human religious leader, compliance with moral and ethical codes has been elicited, and improper human behaviors that would be destructive to these societies have been curbed. At the same time, these doubters recognized that the philosophical and historical underpinnings of these ancient religious authorities did not meet the standards for validity and credibility in the context of our modern understanding of the world. In choosing between societal chaos on one hand and societal order and stability on the other, many doubters reluctantly but ultimately conclude that the order and stability that these religious influences con-tribute to society are so necessary and important that, at least for the present time and the foreseeable future, religious author-ity must be retained and tolerated in order that organized societies can persist.

However, that solution is not very satisfying. Ultimately, it seems disingenuous and lacking integrity to justify and to con-tinue doing the right things for the wrong reasons. Identifying valid philosophical and authoritative bases for compliance with our modern moral and ethical codes seems much more satisfying.

Using our discovering and reasoning capacities informed by our bodies of scien-tific information and historical understand-ings are our best resources for determining *what* we are to do morally and ethically and *how* we are to do it. Therefore, they are probably also our best resources for identi-fying authoritative reasons *why* we should think and act morally and ethically. Simply stated, the compelling reason *why* we need to obey our moral and ethical codes that pertain to living in a sustainable relationship with nature is that *we must do so in order to survive and to thrive*, both as a species and as a global ecosystem. If we deem our continuing to live as being the preeminently good, moral and ethical outcome, then it follows that we must commit ourselves to do whatever is necessary to ensure that outcome. Contrasting our present situation with the judgments of human actions by the traditional gods, which often pertained to blessings and punishments in the "afterlife," we have a more urgent challenge. If we do not learn to live by moral and ethical principles that our reasoning capacities tell us are necessary to live in a sustainable relationship with nature and *Nature's Creativity*, we may be "judged" in the "present life" by causing our own extinction and the destruction of the rest of earth's ecosystem.

So what *authority* can be invoked to make it all work? As has been noted previously, when we humans act *individually*, we are still too often negatively influenced by our lower brain functions to reliably and consistently think and act morally and ethically. Conversely, the *collective reasoning capacities* of human community informed by our best scientific information and historical understandings enable us to formulate sound moral and ethical principles for living in a sustainable relationship with nature and with *Nature's Creativity*. Reasoning collectively, we are able to compensate for and to overcome the foibles and shortcomings of individual thinking and acting. Because it has been the *community's acting collectively* that has proven to be our best compass in charting life's waters throughout human history, it is the community acting through its informed rational decision-making that should be our ultimate authority for formulating and for enforcing our moral and ethical codes. The informed, deliberative community should decide what inducements to obedience and what reprimands and punishments should be imposed on those who fail or refuse to live according to those moral and ethical codes.

Informed communal deliberation can best decide the seriousness of the infractions and the appropriate communal sanctions.

When compared with the authority for moral and ethical codes in traditional religions, some similarities can be found. It was the early *community* leaders in many places around the world who recognized the need and formulated the moral and ethical codes for living together in community. The authority for enforcement and compliance emanated from the leaders' interest in their community's well-being. It was only later that the moral and ethical codes which the leaders had formulated and imposed became integrated and conflated with the gods of the various religions that arose in different geographical areas around the world. In the traditional religions, the moral and ethical authority originated with the community leaders and was subsequently transferred to their gods. In the present scenario, the authority originates from the rational, informed deliberations of the community, and it stays with the community – where its function is needed. There is neither need nor purpose to transfer it elsewhere.

The community's having this degree of authority seems unduly authoritarian in this present era of highly prized individualism and personal freedom and liberty. Yet, a review of our history as recently as the first half of the twentieth century shows that when the citizens of a community respect and comply with the community's mores and ethics, the community enjoys a greater sense of safety, security and stability. The rise of individualism and increased self-indulgence in the second half of the twentieth century has been accompanied with centrifugal forces that are fracturing and destabilizing modern society. "Doing our own thing" is the antithesis of communal harmony and well-being. Informed reasoning should prompt us to return to those communal practices that contribute to the stability and well-being of our society.

I noted earlier the fragmenting influences

that individualism and self-indulgence are having on modern society. It is because of the *individual's* inability to live according to a community's moral and ethical codes that the highly-prized individualism of modern society is so problematic. The libertarian notion that each person is free to do what she/he wants to do as long as it does not harm someone else neglects the self-deception and self-delusional influences of a person's lower brain functions on their thinking and acting, as noted earlier. Whenever an individual thinks and acts without a sense of accountability and responsibility to the community and its well-being, she/he has a "blind spot" regarding her/his thoughts and actions. The result is that individually determined and derived moral and ethical decisions suffer from all the deficiencies of humans' acting autonomously, and they lack all the benefits of informed humans' acting in communal deliberations to formulate their moral and ethical principles with a subsequent accountability and responsibility to the community.

In his book *The Assault on Reason*, former Vicepresident and Nobel Peace Prize Laureate Al Gore explores the premise indicated by the book title. When the Founding Fathers drew up the constitution of our country, they determined that our government would be one of *laws* rather than of *people.* Their experiences unambiguously illustrated that kings or small groups of people often did not enact laws that were for the best general well-being of all the citizenry. To overcome those weaknesses, they determined that laws would be enacted after informed, reasoned public deliberation and debate in two large legislative bodies (House of Representatives and Senate), followed by a signing into law by the president. If necessary, the laws and their applications would be reviewed by the judicial branch. This method of enacting laws presupposed that public discourse considering old and new ideas relating to communal life was the best process that would lead to the

formulation of laws that served the needs and interests of all citizens.

Gore argues that for many years that process seems to have worked rather well, but that recent societal developments have caused it to work less well. With the advent of radio and television, the public discourse became a one-way conversation, with the broadcast information and perspectives presenting particular views of one or a few people that were not subject to the debate, deliberation and critique of the general public. Public discourse was stifled and soon atrophied. Persons seeking power soon realized that they could influence, form and manipulate public opinion by controlling the content of the information and views broadcast to the public. More recently, even among our elected leadership, sectarian and special interest groups have hijacked the ship of state by suppressing not only participation in but even awareness of the occurrence of and of the contents of policy deliberations by evoking fear in citizens that carrying out open and public deliberation would "jeopardize national security." Gore's conclusion is that, unless informed public deliberation and discourse is somehow restored within our nation, the principles and practices that have enabled our nation to become a thriving democracy will continue to atrophy, and we are likely to devolve into an executive oligarchy.

Gore believes that the internet, with its opportunities for input, response and reaction to online posted information and views, offers the possibility to resurrect and to revitalize the public discourse that is essential to a vibrant democracy. From my own perspective, although that potential seems to exist, participation in online interchanges is fraught with its own set of problems and shortcomings. The interchanges are in many cases not in any sense *informed* public debates at all. Rather, the contents consist of persons' posting words and ideas, whether or not they have been reasoned out. This is exacerbated by the individualistic and self-indulgent attitudes that pervade our present-day society. Too often people say something because they want to "be heard" rather than because of their having something to contribute that is "informed, reasoned and significant." Without rules of critique to referee the online inputs, it is difficult to know when anything of substance and importance has been presented. Under such circumstances, any given statement is perceived by uninformed readers as being as valid and authoritative as any other. Without implementing touchstones of validity and reliability to discriminate between informed, reasoned input and online babbling, the internet interchange is unlikely to revive the meaningful public discourse necessary to energize and to support the further development of our democracy. All in all, it seems that in our country today there is an increasing tendency to ignore and to abandon reasoning as the preferred approach to dealing with and solving issues and problems, even when there is not an outright "assault on reason."

On this journey to finding truth and authentic faith, I have from time to time found it helpful to look at the etymological roots of words. The Random House College Dictionary defines *patriotism* as "devoted love, support, and defense of one's country; national loyalty." Today, the word is most often used to describe the sacrifices of military personnel, police officers, firefighters and others who selflessly devote and risk their lives in the public and national interest. In this day and age when much of the public appears obsessed with making money and amassing wealth, these public servants accept modest salaries to promote and to defend the safety, order and freedom of our national community. Common symbolic tributes to these public servants include displays of our nation's flag or of medals and ribbons that designate specific acts of valor and heroism or other contributions to the public's welfare. It is important for our communal psyche and well-being that we acknowledge and honor these public

servants.

Patriotism is related to *patriotic*, and both of these are derivatives of the root *patriot*, derived from the Greek *patriōtēs* and *pātrio(s),* which means "of one's fathers," and from *patris*, "one's fatherland." As was noted earlier, our Founding Fathers drew up and ratified our constitution to provide a government of *laws* rather than of *people*. They specified that the laws that would govern us would be molded and honed by informed public debate and deliberation, in the belief and the trust that that process would utilize the informed reasoning of many people to craft the best possible laws. Thus, we would do well to expand our understanding of the term *patriotism* to include honoring not only military, police and fire-fighting personnel, who defend our freedoms, principles and laws, but also those who commit themselves to maintaining and recovering the *processes* by which our freedoms, principles and laws are established. In this day and age when there seem to be combinations of intentional and unintentional assaults on reason, the commitment to preserve and to recover the processes instituted by our Founding Fathers is very demanding. In that sense, public and political leaders, press and media persons, teachers and other educators who tend to the integrity of the political process are patriots in the full sense of the word: they are dedicated and committed to maintaining and recovering the intended governmental processes "of our fathers." The contributions of these kinds of patriots are equally essential, especially at this time, if our democracy is to survive and to thrive.

From the previous discussion, the importance of the community both in formulating moral and ethical codes and in enforcing them can be recognized. Reasoned public discourse informed by life experience and the best available objective understanding of reality is our best available approach to enacting good laws and to formulating good moral and ethical principles. Although we may in the future discover other better processes, for now we are well-advised to use the best resource that we have – informed reasoning. While not guaranteeing perfect laws, moral and ethical codes, it does provide for a honing process in the formulation of the principles and laws that govern our communal life.

That honing process allows the detection and removal of propositions that would not be in the public interest. First, individuals or groups who knowingly intend to think or to act immorally or unethically towards other people understandably do not want their thoughts and actions opened to public scrutiny, because their harmful and evil intents will be exposed; therefore, in order to accomplish their goals, they attempt to act in secret and without public awareness. Informed public discourse serves to expose such nefarious attempts and leads to their removal in the course of enacting public policy.

Second and more problematic for society are people who genuinely intend to think and to act in the public's well-being but whose reasoning processes are deceived and beguiled by their self-serving lower brain functions and influences. Because they honestly think that they are acting in the public's best interest, they are unaware of the lower brain functions that cause them to think and to act in their own self-interest. They are in no sense evil. Their wronging of other individuals or of society is unintentional; it occurs in spite of their good intent but because of the shortcomings that exist in all of us humans. Such self-deception and self-beguiling is most likely to occur in individuals and in small groups of people who have similar interests and goals in life. The most effective way to identify and to expose those self-serving motives is through informed public debate and deliberation involving large groups of people with varied interests and goals in life and a greater likelihood of seeking the common good.

In the foregoing paragraphs, I have contended that public debate informed by life experience and by an objective understanding of the world in which we live is the best way to derive our moral and ethical principles and to enact the laws and policies that govern our communal life. During our American history the two issues of gender and racial equality have been publicly discussed and debated at length. Conservative religious voices, often on a biblically-based rationale, have opposed equality for women and African Americans. Yet, progress has been made in that both of these constituencies now have constitutionally guaranteed voting rights. Furthermore, practices of discrimination on the basis of gender, race, religion, ethnicity and sexual orientation are being outlawed through state and federal legislation and judicial rulings. In dealing with these issues, sectarian arguments that issue from bygone worldviews have been supplanted by the egalitarian notion mentioned earlier that all persons possess the inalienable rights of life, liberty and the pursuit of happiness. While egalitarian treatment is still not always realized by everyone in the workplace and before the law, clearly much progress has been made.

Yet, as I will now document with several examples, even informed public discussion and debate do not always ensure that the laws and public polices adopted are in the best interests of either the public or of individuals. Perhaps the most glaring example is that of our public policy regarding the use of tobacco products. There is no longer any question that the use of tobacco, whether smoked or smokeless, causes cancer and cardiovascular and pulmonary diseases that result in much individual pain and suffering at a tremendous cost and burden to our health-care system. The conclusions drawn from objective scientific research and our life experiences are overwhelmingly clear: the use of tobacco products is harmful to users as well as to bystanders who inhale secondhand smoke. Its continued use has no justifying counterargument. The reasonable conclusion is, therefore, that its use should be banned. Yet, it remains a legal scourge of society, because those who stand to make huge amounts of money through its continued use have through expensive lobbying efforts influenced legislators not to act in the public interest by banning tobacco use. Particularly insidious is the fact that the tobacco product manufacturers have long known that the nicotine in their products is addictive and also quite probably that tobacco use had numerous harmful effects on users. They intentionally suppressed that information in order that huge numbers of people would become addicted to ensure their long-term profits through the sales of their products. They also advocated the libertarian argument that people ought to have the right to use a product that is harmful to them, if they choose to do so after having been informed of its known harmful effects. Additionally, very disturbing is the fact that tobacco products are being exported for use in countries where ignorance regarding its use prevails and where public policy requires no disclosure of the harmful effects of tobacco use. As a society, we are ever so slowly moving towards policies and laws that informed public debate tell us we should have implemented decades ago. Public policy in the form of smoke-free public areas and of increasing taxes to discourage the use of tobacco products are moves in the direction of individual and public welfare. This whole episode is a particularly disturbing case of businesses' deeming commercial profits more important than individual and public welfare.

A second example is the gambling and gaming industry. Its appeal is undoubtedly based on various appeals to the human psyche, among them the desire to get a big reward for an apparent small cost – crassly stated, "to get something for nothing." While that possibility may be realized for a relatively small number of participants, overall the vast majority of players are losers, because the operators of the industry,

whether private or state-sponsored, have a substantial "take," ensuring that the payout is less than the total input of the players. Moreover, there are significant negative impacts of the industry. A substantial number of people become psychologically addicted, leading to personal financial ruin and family disruption. The poor, who can least afford it, are enticed to spend significant amounts of their limited income to try to better their situation. Almost universally, whenever gambling and gaming industries have been introduced, graft, corruption and criminal involvement have permeated the system. Perhaps the most important reason in the present moral and ethical context, the potential of "getting something for nothing" flies in the face of the time-honored economic principle of earning money through useful employment. Thus, there is no moral or ethical justification for the industry.

Yet, several reasons are offered to provide justification for the industry. Perhaps the most common are that the state can use this mechanism to support and to improve education and that it provides jobs. There is almost universal agreement that support of public education is good. Using state-generated lottery proceeds to support public education links the industry with a good purpose, implying that the lottery is useful and, therefore, good. In reality, proceeds from lottery systems frequently do not "supplement" legislatively appropriated funds but rather "replace" them. What the foregoing charade masks is that public officials cowardly turn to the lottery to support public education because they are unwilling to take the unpopular stance of enacting and imposing the taxes that are necessary to support strong public education. Moreover, from a moral and ethical perspective, solid financial support of public education is much too important to our society to be left to the outcome of a "crapshoot." The second justification – that the gaming industry provides jobs – is a shallow one. If a "job" provides no useful contribution to society or even contributes to its demise, the very existence of the "job" begs the question. By that logic, we could create many "jobs" by growing poppies and producing opium!

A third example, alcohol use, is more complicated. On the one hand, scientific studies have shown that moderate use of alcohol is beneficial because it helps reduce the harmful effects of stress on the body. On the other hand, alcohol is a much-abused, addictive substance in society. Adding to the potential for alcohol abuse is the fact that significant numbers of people, usually unsuspectingly, carry particular genetic variants that increase their susceptibility to alcohol and other addictive substances. Thus, when properly used, alcohol use can be a benefit to society; but when improperly used, it is a bane not only to the user but also to other people who are impacted through family conflict, automobile accidents, and the like. Because our experience and informed societal discussions and debates have identified both positive and negative effects of alcohol use, our societal decisions have attempted to permit and to regulate its proper use and to prohibit its improper use. Overall, our success in dealing with this issue has been modest.

If one looks for a common thread relating to the use of tobacco products and alcohol and to participation in the gambling/gaming industry, it would seem to lie in our strong human desire to indulge and to pleasure ourselves. Both alcohol and nicotine in tobacco stimulate our brain's pleasure centers. Initially this feeling of pleasure occurs at lower blood concentrations, but with continued use higher levels are required to achieve the same level of pleasure, and finally addiction is reached when the user can no longer bear to go on in the absence of the addictive substance. With regard to gambling, the appeal of "getting something for little or nothing" quite likely relates to the same appeals (perhaps instincts) that underlie free enterprise capitalism: when an individual has the opportunity to become

involved in an endeavor that can benefit her/himself, she/he is likely to commit her/himself wholeheartedly to that activity. In the case of gambling/gaming, the potential reward is a jackpot that could provide money for pleasure and self-indulgence on a scale previously only imaginable to the participant. That lure is hard to resist. As in the case of chemical substance abuse, seeking to satisfy the imagined pleasure that winning the jackpot would bring can lead to addictive, self-destructive behaviors.

In summary, although we humans are best able to address societal concerns through public debate informed by experience and objective knowledge about our world, we still have difficulties reaching decisions and enforcing them when it comes to matters relating to our strong human desires for self-pleasure and self-indulgence. In spite of our best collective and communal efforts, we sometimes still fail to adopt good public policy.

Although traditional Judeo-Christian moral and ethical codes are in need of extensive modification and updating, in the foregoing I have acknowledged the contributions that they have made to the development of Western civilization. Because there is nothing to be gained by our "throwing the baby out with the bathwater" and then having "to reinvent the wheel," it seems worthwhile to retain those components that remain valid and functional principles and practices to guide communal life today. In the following I explore the proposition that the dynamics of *repentance* and *forgiveness* may have profound implications pertaining simply to our being human rather than to our being Christian or even religious.

In dealing with the failures of humans to live morally and ethically with each other, the traditional Christian paradigm has used terms such as *sin* and *transgression*, *contrition*, *repentance* and *forgiveness*. When one person "sins" against another by transgressing some element of the communally accepted moral and ethical code, the trust relationship between the two persons has been injured or fractured, and it does not heal itself spontaneously. Some contrition on the part of the wrongdoer (sinner) must happen both to signal and to effect a restoration of the broken relationship. This often takes the form of the sinner's expressing remorse for having done the wrong and asking the wronged (sinned against) person for forgiveness. The wrongdoer may offer to compensate the wronged person for the damage done. This repentance and contrition on the part of the wrongdoer evokes from the wronged person forgiveness – a commitment that the wrongful act will no longer act as a separation or barrier between them. Religiously, this reconciliation is interpreted to serve two purposes. First, the relationship between the humans is restored. The wronged person has given up any right to retribution or revenge that "an eye for an eye or a tooth for a tooth" justice might deem appropriate. The forgiven wrongdoer has been accepted back into a trusting relationship with the person whom she/he had wronged. Second, when the repentance and contrition of the wrongdoer is seen by God as an acknowledgement of her/his sin, God forgives the sinner and accepts her/him back into God's good graces. Thus, blessings of forgiveness to the repentant wrongdoer include restoration of relationships with God and with the wronged human.

Although repentance and forgiveness have specific meanings in the context of Christianity, they may point to deep, and perhaps essential, psychological interactions between humans that maintain and restore relationships, apart from any specifically religious application. Humans' possession of self-consciousness, consciousness and personal awareness of other individuals permits us to develop psychological and emotional relatedness and connectedness with other humans that are qualitatively much more intense and integrated than appears to exist in any of our animal cousins. We humans live in a trust relationship with other humans that is described and defined by our moral and ethical codes – the principles that we humans have at some point in history agreed should guide and direct our communal lives. We are betrayed and emotionally wounded when that trust relationship is transgressed. This wronging of one person by another, whether deliberate or unintentional, has the consequences of separating and alienating humans from each other. Trustful human bonds and social relationships are fractured. The restoration of a trusting interpersonal relationship requires psychological transactions that both symbolize and effect reconciliation. The first step towards the rectification of the wrong is repentance – a turning around or turning away from the behaviors that fractured the harmonious relationships with the other person. Minimally, that involves stopping the unethical behavior; ideally it involves replacing the unethical behavior with a loving behavior – one that contributes to the well-being of the person who had previously been wronged. Although the *Nature's Creativity* paradigm does not involve a noetic God whose forgiveness is needed, the blessings of forgiveness in the present context involve the wrongdoer as well as the wronged fellow human. For the wrongdoer, the psychological-emotional transaction that occurs in repentance and forgiveness seems important to our human consciousness of what is good and bad and what is fair and just in our relationship to other people. In human-to-human relationships, the blessings of forgiveness in this setting accrue to the wronged and to the wrongdoer in much the same way as in the traditional Christian paradigm.

The concepts of repentance and forgiveness might also be explored in the context of our relationship to nature and to *Nature's Creativity*. Repentance would involve a turning away from ideas and practices that knowingly or unknowingly destroy nature and replacing them with ones that uphold and support what *Nature's Creativity* has produced throughout the history of our universe. Disregard or willful disobedience of mores and laws pertaining to living in a sustainable relationship with nature also fractures human society, because if continued such behaviors will ultimately destroy both human society and our natural environment.

When humans wrong impersonal nature, there can, of course, be no *personal* forgiveness of the repentant wrongdoer by nature or *Nature's Creativity*. On the other hand, because *communal* society formulates and enforces its moral and ethical codes that pertain to living in a sustainable relationship with nature, it can offer forgiveness to the repentant wrongdoer. The wrongdoer is thereby restored to relationship with the community, which includes humans as well as their environment. The blessings of that harmonious restored relationship accrue to present and future generations of humans as well as to other living organisms and to their environment.

Adoption and application of the moral and ethical principles that permit us to live in a sustainable relationship with nature have implications for our living in the modern world. As I have documented, our nation has dealt and is dealing with many substantive moral and ethical issues and problems. It seems that there is so much to do, and we must act quickly to deal with these urgent issues. Implementing the necessary changes might seem such a daunting or even impossible task that we might ask ourselves: can we do all that is necessary? I might counter that question with another question. If not here, where could those problems better be solved? We live in the United States of America, the longest-running experiment in democracy in the history of the world. Through the free exchange of ideas we of all people should have the best opportunity and capacity for resolving the problems at hand. Informed by our scientifically established knowledge and utilizing our communal reasoning and innovative

capacities, we have the resources to determine what is good for our environment as well as for us humans. As we rationally understand the urgency of taking action to reverse our abuse of our fellow living creatures and of our environment, we will be compelled by our reasoned conclusions to make the appropriate changes in our lifestyles in order to do what is ethically necessary to live in a sustainable relationship with nature. For the most part, we already know what to do. What we most need is to choose local and national leaders who are committed to lead us in effecting those changes. In the absence of those leaders or even in addition to them, we can mobilize a groundswell of informed citizenry that demands actions of our leaders towards those goals.

I can now summarize my reframing and rethinking of society's morals and ethics. I have concluded that "the moral concepts of Homer," while having served reasonably well to tutor and to guide the development of Western civilization, are now in serious need of being updated to meet the needs of "scientific man." Throughout human history, moral and ethical codes have emanated from the discovering and reasoning capacities of humans. Through rational processes they recognized the needs for organizing complex human societies and then proceeded to develop and to implement the principles that would meet those needs within the communities' time-conditioned mythical understandings of the world. Later, for various reasons those moral and ethical codes became conflated with their religions and the authority of their gods. Those associations served to foster the growth of complex societies but have also hindered the updating of moral and ethical codes to meet the needs of the modern world. What is needed today is a return to the basics of human problem-solving. Informed by life experiences, by our best scientific knowledge and by our best historical understandings, our collective communal reasoning capacities must be used

228

to draw up and to implement moral and ethical codes in which humanistic and anthropocentric emphases are replaced by biocentric and ecocentric considerations that promote our living in a harmonious and sustainable relationship with other humans, with other living organisms and with our global environment. Informed communal deliberations can determine the appropriate incentives for obedience and the sanctions for disobedience of the modern moral and ethical codes. Because global well-being transcends sectarian interests, specific religions may contribute towards but should not have ultimate authority regarding the formulation and implementation of modern moral and ethical codes. Finally, because our human reasoning capacities are unduly influenced by our lower brain functions, we as individuals do not have the necessary self-discipline and self-control to live consistently and reliably according to the moral and ethical codes that our communities formulate as earlier described. Therefore, in order to comply with the moral and ethical codes of the community, individuals must have responsibility and accountability to the communities in which they live.

Chapter 15

Living in the Present and into the Future

"It is quite true that philosophy says that life can only be understood backwards, but it must be lived forwards."

Søren Kierkegaard

"Hindsight has 20-20 vision," states a hyperbolic adage. Usually, we quote it after we have made a significant mistake, when we later become aware of information that would have caused us to make a different earlier decision. While we never reach the stage in life when it is possible to look back and to have enough information and wisdom to have made all the right decisions, with the cumulative life experience that comes with advancing age we gain sufficient perspective to identify the significant events in our lives that have made us who we are: we to some extent "understand our life backwards."

In the previous chapters I have been engaged in efforts to understand my life backwards, particularly as it relates to my spiritual journey. I have identified the most important influences that formed my early worldview. I then documented how later tragic experiences in my life caused me to reexamine those early presuppositions and how what I learned led me to replace them with presuppositions that enable me to have authentic faith for the modern world – faith that is valid and reliable for the world that I live in today. In this chapter I summarize the major events and discoveries of that journey. Through "understanding my life backwards," I have reached several conclusions about not only the specifics of my life journey but also about the process itself. Finally, I address how what I have learned in understanding my life backwards is enabling me to live forwards.

My early faith was formed by home and Church indoctrination into conservative Lutheranism and served me rather well in that parochial setting. However, already during my education in the local public high school, I was beginning to recognize that some of my Church's teachings did not "ring true" to my life experiences and my expanding understanding of the world outside that setting, particularly as they pertained to science and nature. After completing college and getting married at age twenty-two, the next twenty-five years of my life were punctuated at approximately ten-year intervals by the deaths of my two daughters, Tammy and Bethany, and finally of my wife Darlene. Wrestling with trying to understand those tragedies led me to critically examine the practice of my faith and the content of my traditional faith, including the nature and even the existence of the Judeo-Christian God. I gradually drifted towards what might be termed "a-theism" – a belief that that *UUR* (*Unseen Ultimate Reality*) was certainly not the Judeo-Christian God described by my traditional faith. However, because of my career experiences as an evolutionary biologist/geneticist, I continued to believe in the existence of an *UUR* that is evidenced by the marvelous, novel intricacies that have been created by nature's evolutionary processes. Later, when I read Gordon Kaufman's books, *God the Problem* and *In Face of Mystery*, I became convinced of the truth of his contention that all concepts of *UUR* are time- and space-conditioned, imaginative constructions of the human mind. This notion was further confirmed for me when I then learned how the various religions of the world have developed in scattered locations around the earth and that the founders and adherents of each religion have imaginatively conceived a metaphor/symbol for *UUR* that arose out of the specifics of their respective social and geographical settings. Kaufman, proceeding from that notion and attempting to incorporate what is known about nature from modern science, coined the term *serendipitous creativity* as his metaphor/symbol for *UUR*. While that symbol/metaphor seemed to me headed in the right direction, my own career work in genetics and evolutionary biology and my awareness of the discoveries in the wider scientific world led me to conclude that the evolutionary process is "not merely serendipitous" – producing the awesome complexities of life by chance or accident. Rather, there is a self-organizing and innovative, creative capacity inherent in nature which through the evolutionary process has systematically given rise to the compounded levels of complexity and organization that exist in the physical and biological realms of reality. This creative capacity has been implicated in the concept of organicism – that which makes the whole of nature more than a sum of its analyzed parts. As a metaphor/symbol for this capacity of *UUR*, I settled on the term *Nature's Creativity*. Our analytic probing of the activities and products of *Nature's Creativity* through modeling with chaos theory and other higher order mathematical relationships is giving us insights into what is going on in *Nature's Creativity*, although why and how *Nature's Creativity* acts still remains mostly mystery. Irrespective of our ability or inability to understand what is going on, I am convinced that these creative capacities inhere deeply within nature and are ultimately responsible for all of reality that exists today.

Thus, *Nature's Creativity* is the object of what I have come to refer to as my *authentic* faith – a faith that is "entitled to acceptance or belief because of agreement with known facts or experience" (Random House College Dictionary). For me, it is *authentic faith* because it is belief, confidence and trust in a symbol/metaphor for *UUR* that is valid and reliable for my general understanding of the world that I live in today. My faith is authentic because it is a credible faith. The worldview presuppositions for this faith are derived from reasoning that is informed by the most valid and reliable scientific knowledge and experiential understanding of reality. This worldview accepts the notion that our universe – including all physical matter and all life within it, including humans with their capacities to develop complex religious, social and cultural organization – is the product of *Nature's Creativity*, acting through an evolutionary process over billions of years. This authentic faith recognizes that we humans gain knowledge through reasoning that is informed by careful observation and logical analyses of what is going on around us in the real world. My authentic faith recognizes that we do not know the endpoint to which *Nature's Creativity* is taking us through the evolutionary process but that it is likely to coincide with the end of our earth, solar system and universe in the distant future. Finally, my authentic faith recognizes that what we humans consider good and bad, moral and immoral, ethical and unethical are all parts of systems of value judgments that have been discovered, created and developed by humans to enable and to facilitate organizing and ordering human society and culture. I have faith that the continuing operation of *Nature's Creativity* sustains me in the present and that it promises to sustain me and all other life in the future, because its past creative and sustaining operations through billions of years give me confidence that it will continue to do so.

My religion, on the other hand, is reconceived as that set of beliefs and practices that I employ to continue to update and to correct the presuppositions of my worldview. Through this constant updating, I repeatedly ligate and tie together (*religio*) the best possible understandings of the workings of *Nature's Creativity*, in order that I can live in the best possible harmony with them. Using the rational intellectual capacities gifted to humans, I can learn how to live in a sustainable relationship with *Nature's Creativity* and all that it has created. This growing understanding of what is necessary to live in harmony with *Nature's Creativity* informs me about what is desirable and good both for nature and for my living within it and becomes the compelling justification and mandate for my moral and ethical considerations.

Living into the future guided by this new paradigm means that my moral and ethical compass has been changed from one that was strongly anthropocentric and humanistic to one with broader *biocentric* and *ecocentric* concerns. In all that I think and do, I must consider the well-being of the biosphere and ecosphere, not merely the comfort, convenience and even the well-being of other humans. To use a "Yogi Berra-ism," "Not everything that is doable is doable." Not everything that is technologically possible is morally and ethically permissible. As an illustration, it is no longer morally and ethically acceptable for me to use motor vehicles that contribute to my comfort and convenience, if they are not fuel-efficient and if their greenhouse gas emissions are destroying our biosphere and ecosphere. To use technology to devise next-generation vehicles that lack maximum fuel efficiency and that produce more greenhouse gases in order to appeal to my self-indulgence by "making a statement about who I am" and/or "by projecting the image of how I want others to see me" is not a morally and ethically permissible course of action under this new paradigm. Only technological advances that, insofar as we can tell, have as little negative impact as possible on the world around us should be deployed for use in society.

Some may protest that such a stringent test for introducing new technologies would revolutionize the free enterprise business system as we know and practice it today. They are indeed quite correct in that assessment. However, we have a choice. We can continue doing what we are doing; in that case, our best scientific knowledge and information indicate that we will destroy our planet and ultimately ourselves. Considering that not to be an acceptable moral or ethical alternative, we must select the other choice – to make the extensive changes necessary in order to achieve a sustainable coexistence with our biosphere and ecosphere. That is the only morally and ethically acceptable choice – the only good outcome. The bad news is that we have many extensive changes that must be made. The good news is that we already know most of what we need to do to rectify things. What is required is our resolve and commitment to make those changes.

In the previous chapter I concluded that humans' best moral and ethical principles are derived through the process of public discussion and debate informed by life experiences and by their most valid and reliable objective understanding of reality. Thousands of years ago, as our remote human ancestors were developing human culture and community, that process served them (and us) well in formulating and enforcing mores and laws that pertained to living in family and urban relationships, to not killing other people, and to not stealing other people's property. In our world today that same process can serve us in adopting mores and in formulating moral and ethical principles that pertain to living in a sustainable relationship with nature and *Nature's Creativity*.

Why then, even if in my most rational moments I fully accept and commit myself to live by the moral and ethical principles adopted by my community, am I unable to do so individually and autonomously? It is because I am fully human and therefore have all the limitations of a human's acting individually and autonomously. I simply do not possess the self-control and self-discipline to think and to do the right things all the time. I know that, like all other humans, my cerebral, rational and reasoning capacities are situated atop a pyramid of underlying noncerebral and subconscious functions that control my more instinctive behaviors and body functions. These "lower" brain functions are largely involuntary and are impacted by emotions such as fear and anxiety, as well as by other self-serving factors of which I am consciously unaware. Some of these self-serving tendencies are probably genetically-conditioned, residual behaviors that made important contributions to survival and fitness in our prehuman ancestors. These instinctive and emotionally-influenced functions of the brain often sabotage and undercut my reasoning processes and allow or even cause me to think and to do things that my higher reasoning capacities consider irrational and unreasonable. I am also subject to the nudges and pushes towards the self-indulgent desires and tendencies that I have absorbed from growing up in modern American society. I am continually enticed by Madison Avenue seductions that promise to make my life more comfortable, easier and even extrava-gantly luxurious and sumptuous. Advertising efforts attempt to deceive me into thinking that such a lifestyle is good for me and ultimately for everyone. Stated in traditional Christian terms, I am too strongly influenced by *incurvatus in se* – that innate instinct to act in my own self-interest – to be able autonomously and individually to live consistently with my community's moral and ethical principles all the time.

Therefore, because I am *individually* and *autonomously* unable always to think of and to carry out what our informed, collective society determines to be necessary to live in a sustainable relationship with nature and *Nature's Creativity*, I must look to *communal* resources and help to influence and to assist me in living according to the *community's* moral and ethical codes. I must make a contractual commitment with my community to be guided and directed by its moral and ethical principles. I must pledge that I will give my best efforts to live according to its moral and ethical principles. In order to invite and to elicit my obedience, the community can appeal to my logical and reasoning capacities that demonstrate the importance and necessity of such obedience and perhaps offer other inducements and incentives. However, when I fail to live up to my community's moral and ethical standards autonomously, I acknowledge the commu-nity's right, authority and responsibility to hold me accountable. If necessary, the community can discipline and punish me, with its sanctions being commensurate with the seriousness of my moral and ethical infractions. Thus, by combining my own self-control and self-discipline (which suffice much of the time) with communal commitment and enforce-ment (which assist me when my individual resources fail), I have the greatest potential for succeeding in living a moral and ethical life in the modern world.

In attempting to live according to my community's moral and ethical principles, I must exercise the self-discipline and self-control to do what is good and right with respect to other humans, to nature and to *Nature's Creativity*. I must be fully ac-countable to myself and to my community for my thoughts and actions. Although I must depend on the community to help me live a moral and ethical life, when I fail, I alone am responsible for the harm that ensues to myself, to other humans and to the rest of nature. I cannot blame demons or evil spirits. I cannot beg off that "the devil made me do it." Nor am I accountable to any external deity: I do not live a moral and ethical life in order to ensure an amicable relationship with any divinity in this life or in any future existence or in order to avoid divine punishment in the now or in the hereafter. Rather, I attempt to think and to act morally and ethically because to do so is good and right with respect to other humans, to nature and to *Nature's Creativity* for both now and the future.

What specific implications does this new paradigm have for my personal life? It means that in my daily living I make choices that are informed by deliberated understandings of our knowledge about living in a sustainable relationship with *Nature's Creativity* and all that it has created for us. The principles of conservation, efficient use, reuse and recycling are the commandments of daily living. Driving an energy-efficient car and making my house energy-efficient are moral mandates not options. My community responsibilities include advocating for policies that enable a sustainable relationship between humans and nature and that eliminate our desecration and wasting of earth's natural resources. Politically, I am compelled and motivated to support candidates for public office who have a primary commitment to working towards nature-wise policies and programs. The litany of necessary and desirable moral values and ethical behaviors could be extensively continued. Suffice it to say that our continuing study of nature and *Nature's Creativity* continues to *religiously* inform my morality and my ethical behavior so that they are oriented towards what is good for all of nature including humans.

From this process of understanding my life backwards, I want to relate what appear to me to be more general conclusions about understanding life backwards – discoveries that other persons may perhaps find useful in understanding their lives backwards.

First, my personal narrative has illustrated that finding truth about faith and life is a journey, not an event or a destination. The indoctrination of my formative faith purported to give me the "Truth" to live my whole life. Not only was that "Truth" incomplete, much of it proved not to be true at all. It seems to me that it takes many decades of living in order to acquire sufficient experiences and perspective to "understand life backwards." Unfortunately, as in my case, we often do not even begin to look for that backwards understanding until we are

pushed to the brink of our existence by adversity. As I write these words and paragraphs, I have traveled more than sixty-five years along my journey. By traveling this far, I have acquired a perspective that is particular to my life. There were many *events* along my journey in the form of truth discoveries and insights. Each of these served to modify the presuppositions of my worldview in order to make them more congruent with modern understandings of reality. Yet, aspects of my worldview will continue to change. I will have new and different experiences in life; some will bring me pleasure and satisfaction, and others will bring me pain and disappointment. All of my life, I am committed to continue trying to understand life backwards in order that I can faithfully live forwards into a more meaningful future. I keep trying to find more of the truth that will make me free. My "destination" truth will reflect the worldview that I have when I draw my last breath; I trust that it will continue to be dynamic until my death. Again, I quote Mohammad Ali, "The man who thinks the same at age fifty that he did at age twenty has wasted thirty years of his life." I trust that, when I draw my last breath, I can do so with the satisfaction of having "wasted" as little of my life as possible.

Second, perhaps like many other people, I was content to live according to the adage: "If it ain't broke, don't fix it." As long as my life seemed to be going well, I had little occasion or need to examine or to challenge the presuppositions of the worldview created for me by my formative faith. My traditional religion seemed to be "working" for me. However, one, two and then three tragedies struck. At first I assumed that my Lutheran faith tradition was valid and that my "practice" of that faith was somehow defective. Upon more detailed examination, I concluded that my living of that faith was sincere, honest and faithful. I then questioned whether the "content" of my faith was valid and reliable to orient and to support me in life, and finally I concluded that it was not. That it took three such tragedies to finally shove me into such a thorough examination of my traditional faith may reflect my spiritual density. Or it may reflect what I euphemistically refer to as my resoluteness and steadfastness but which my wife less generously calls my German stubbornness. Perhaps both contributed something, but I rather think that it was also due to the thoroughness of the indoctrination process in my early spiritual formation. The presumed biblical authority coupled with the authority that my church claimed to derive from correctly teaching the Scriptures for a long time combined to make it unthinkable for me to challenge either of those claims to authority. I have no doubt that all who contributed towards instilling that faith in me were honest, sincere and well-intended and thought that they were serving God and me in a most honorable way. However, while that indoctrination and training seemed to serve me well in the cocoon of strongly religious home life and church community of my early life, it did not serve me well when I left that setting to face the challenges of life outside that context. Thus, I conclude that, at all stages of one's life, one is best served by developing the practice of critically examining and, where necessary, updating the presuppositions of one's worldview. *At all stages of life, an examined faith serves one best.*

Third, as a guiding principle, I conclude that the best way to prepare for living into the future is to understand how the past has given rise to the present. I have gained some understanding of how *Nature's Creativity* has over eons of time utilized the evolutionary process to give rise to the array of emergent complexity in the physical and biological components of nature; this has informed my worldview so that I can live in harmony with nature and have realistic expectations of life. Also, having learned about the origins and development of religions over time as human culture evolved, I can understand how Hebraism, Christianity and Lutheranism fit into that larger context and the contributions that they have made to society in general and to my life in particular. I understand better how religious writings and institutions came to claim and to hold authority in the development of human societies and cultures. Such authorities functioned positively within the worldviews in which they developed. However, that same awareness freed me to abandon numerous tenets and beliefs of my traditional faith that are no longer credible for me in the modern context.

Fourth, in facing the tragedies of my life, I have found humor to be essential. Scott Peck began his book *The Road Less Traveled* thus:

> Life is difficult. This is a great truth, one of the greatest truths. It is a great truth because once we truly see this truth, we transcend it. Once we truly know that life is difficult – once we truly understand and accept it – then life is no longer difficult. Because once it is accepted, the fact that life is difficult no longer matters.

I read that book while going through the grief process after the death of my second daughter, Bethany, and I began to come to grips with the meaning of that passage for my own life. Those statements do not say or imply that, when my life is difficult, it is not painful. Rather, when I accept that life is difficult, I can learn to deal with the difficulties of life and the pains that come with them.

For most of human history people have accepted and even expected that life would be difficult. It is largely a product of twentieth century affluence and technological advances that people have come to expect that life should be comfortable, easy and full of leisure and pleasure. Yet, it is often when we experience a reality check – when we are facing the difficulties of life – that we discover our own best resources and achieve the most personal growth. But facing too much or too intense difficulty can overwhelm one's capacities to deal with adversity. Steel is produced by intensely heating iron, but too much heat can destroy the desired properties of steel.

It is especially when life is "overheating" that I have found the following statement of Salma Hayek to be true: "Life is tough, and if you have the ability to laugh at it, you have the ability to enjoy it." That is not to say that anything about the tragedies that I experienced was humorous or funny. Rather, in spite of the seriousness and pain of my tragedies, I was still able to discover opportunities to laugh at other things in life during the illnesses and especially after the deaths of my family members. For me, the ability to find humor was therapeutically essential to my survival during these times of stress and tension, although at times I found humor and laughed with a sense of inappropriateness and even guilt. I probably learned this use and appreciation of humor from my father, who, although he has taken life quite seriously, has been able to be a jokester at times – especially in kidding and teasing my mother. Without the occasional levity and release that humor and laughter brought to my life, I am not sure that I would have survived my life's tragedies.

Until this point in life and as I continue on, I have drawn on and continue to draw courage and inspiration from many people. Recently in life, they have more frequently been persons who have questioned their traditional faiths and arrived at other understandings of life. In her book *Doubt: A History*, Jennifer Michael Hecht recounts the history of doubters – whom she describes as those persons throughout recorded history who have questioned or rejected outright many of the prevailing societal and religious notions of *UUR* (usually a god or gods) in their respective societies. She recounts and examines the writings of such persons from Hinduism, Buddhism, Judaism, Christianity and Islam, which range in time from the middle first millennium BCE until the present. Among the doubters whom Hecht

mentions, I want to cite two from my faith tradition who have been and remain moral and ethical models for my life – two persons who strove to live faithfully within the contexts of their respective worldviews.

The first was Jesus of Nazareth. In following his moral compass, he found it necessary to challenge the religious and political traditions of his society, obedience to which would have compromised his integrity and caused him to be unfaithful to his sense of God's call and will for his life. Faithful adherence to that sense of call led to his being rejected by leaders and other members of his traditional Jewish religion, who collaborated with the Roman government to have him executed. Jesus' dedication to discovering and to witnessing to what he came to understand as truth, even though it resulted in his death, has served as a powerful example for me to be faithful in my search for truth and for authentic faith, even in the face of intense opposition. Although such a high price as Jesus paid is unlikely to be exacted of me, my own sense of integrity calls me to follow my own moral compass as he did. As was true for Jesus, sometimes following my own moral compass puts me on a lonely trail, because it is difficult for others to understand how and why I have been "driven into the wilderness" to reflect on and to come to grips with the struggles of my journey and to arrive at the resolutions that I have reached. But for me to live with personal integrity, I must travel on those trails, even if that means traveling them alone.

My second faithfulness model comes from a more recent time – although still nearly five hundred years ago. While I have been highly critical of Lutheranism for a number of reasons, I lift up Martin Luther, the namesake of Lutheranism, as a second model of faithfulness, courage and tenacity for my life.

Luther's personal faith struggles tormented him already during his early life. In trying to find personal peace with his understanding of God, he turned to what he thought should be the source of forgiveness, wholeness and peace – his Church, the Roman Catholic Church. Instead of finding what he sought, he found Church practices that led him to greater uncertainty about his relationship with God and to deeper despair. Instead of practices that served to nurture and to sustain himself and other members in their faith, he found corrupt practices that preyed on their fears and robbed them of their material possessions. He deemed the sale of indulgences particularly abominable, because it extorted huge amounts of money from poor peasants to finance the lavish and lascivious lifestyles of church leaders and the profligate building projects of the Church. He concluded that "the sabbath" that should have been created for humankind was not serving them at all; rather, humankind was being abused and tyrannized by the interpreter of "sabbath" laws – the Catholic Church. Summoning up the courage of his conviction that God would be with him in his efforts to call the Church to faithfulness, he became one of the pillars of the Protestant Reformation. His confrontations led to his being excommunicated from the Church and subject to death, had he been captured. Yet his efforts were not in vain; over time the Roman Catholic Church reformed itself. Although it was not his intent to found a new Church but rather to remain a member of the reformed Catholic Church, such was not to be, because of his having been excommunicated by the Roman Catholic Church. If he and his followers were to continue to practice their faith, it would have to be in the "Lutheran" Church – as he and his followers came to be called. Over time, that church too came to have its own difficulties and problems, some of which I have attempted to address in this book. But, through it all, Luther was doggedly committed to what he perceived as God's call to his living a life of faithfulness.

Since Luther's time there have emerged within Lutheranism two different understandings of what it means to be *the Church of the Reformation*. One view holds that reformation was essentially completed by 1580, when after his death Luther's followers compiled and ratified *The Book of Concord* – which together with the Bible became a sort of closed canon of Lutheran confessions and practices. After 1580, Scriptures and their claimed faithful interpreters, the Lutheran Confessions, would henceforth be "the" authoritative touchstone for all matters of faith and life. According to this view, "The Truth" had been determined; what remained was to continue to interpret and to reinterpret it and to live it out faithfully.

However, a second view also emerged within Lutheranism and persists to the present. It posits that the actions of Luther and the other reformers were merely the *beginning* of reformation that needs to continue as long as Lutheran (and other) churches exist. Because the Lutheran Church continues to minister in a world of changing worldviews over time, reformation must continue in order for the sabbath to continue to serve humankind faithfully. This view of Lutheran reformation insists that no final form of Lutheranism (or of Christianity or any other religion) can ever exist, because changing times and worldviews will always necessitate reforms in order for the sabbath to continue to serve humankind in the best possible way.

It is difficult to know which of these two understandings of reformation would have been espoused by Luther himself. Clearly, he felt that *sola Scriptura* was "the" appropriate remedy for the Roman Church of his time, which he saw as misusing and ignoring scriptural principles in pursuit of its own corrupt self-interests. To what extent he would have seen the need for additional reformation in the church founded in his name can never be known.

It will not be surprising that I have identified with the second understanding of Lutheran reformation. Lutheranism as well as all other forms of Christianity must continually reform in order that the sabbath can "be made to serve humankind." Because I am most familiar with his life and work, I cite Luther as a model of faithfulness in attempting to bring about necessary reforms. I fully recognize, however, that before Luther there were many forerunner voices calling for reform that were ignored and/or silenced. Considering their efforts *in toto*, I take heart in knowing that voices of truth and liberation cannot forever be stifled and silenced. In every age, the time comes when the human spirit no longer tolerates tyranny, be it from secular rulers or from religious Scriptures or rulers. Human reasoning informed by life experience and the most valid and reliable understanding of reality will ultimately prevail. Drawing on other well-known sayings of Jesus, the truth shall then "make us free" and "we shall be free indeed" to discover and to be sustained by authentic faith.

I also attempt to emulate both Jesus of Nazareth and Martin Luther for another reason. Strong commitments to teaching and education were important aspects of the lives and ministries of both of them. Perhaps no other aspect of the gospel narratives of Jesus' life as a moral model was more important than his teaching ministry. Many of Martin Luther's writings reflect his activities as teacher in one capacity or another. Presumably their emphases on teaching reflected their recognition of the importance of humans' capacity for informed and innovative thinking and for considering better possible alternatives in order to improve their lives compared to what they had been thinking and doing. Teaching and education could help both Jesus' and Luther's listeners work towards those possibilities.

As I worked to understand my life backwards, I came to recognize how important education and teaching also have been in my life. At age 54 when I was graduated from seminary, I calculated that I had been a full-time student for 27 years – fully one-half of my life. And since that time I have continued to sit in on college courses and to learn what I can in other settings.

Looking back on my life, I recognize that learning has always been the wellspring of discovery and insight for me and has motivated me to excel in whatever educational setting I found myself. Later, as I was choosing a vocation, teaching became the source of my greatest sense of fulfillment. I thank my parents for encouraging and supporting me in those endeavors; I think that, although each of them had completed only eight years of elementary education, they recognized the importance of education and encouraged me to succeed in every possible way – to benefit from opportunities that they never had. I was near or at the top of my classes throughout elementary school, high school and college; I was very successful in the coursework for my three graduate degrees. Learning often came easily to me, but even when it did not, I was driven to learn and to understand. My expectation was that my life could become more fulfilling through a better understanding of the world in which I live – that, in some sense, "the truth would make me free." Indeed, as I look back, I am thankful that this strong drive to learn was instilled in me at a young age. When I later experienced the tragedies in my life, it was that drive that compelled me to pursue all possible sources of knowledge and understanding in order to deal with those losses. If I had not had that compulsion, I might well not have survived those ordeals.

Because learning has been important to me, it has always seemed to me that it should also be important to others. In addition, I discovered early in life that I felt the greatest sense of fulfillment and found the deepest meaning in life when I was teaching and helping others to learn. Thus, my going to college to train to be a teacher was a natural choice. My undergraduate degree was a Bachelor of Science degree in education with a major in biology. Initially, I planned to be a high school biology teacher. However, towards the end of my undergraduate college studies, I was encouraged to pursue graduate work that would allow me to teach in college. While working on both science graduate degrees, I earned support as a teaching fellow for undergraduate courses. After completing several postdoctoral fellowships, I ended up with opportunities to direct research programs. There I could both satisfy my intellectual curiosity by conducting investigative biological research and utilize my teaching/mentoring abilities in working with and training the postdoctoral fellows, students and research assistants and associates with whom I worked. Later, when I attended seminary, I earned support for my schooling by working as a teaching assistant for the Greek class required of all pastoral students. Still later, in the parish, I was a teaching pastor, hoping and attempting to expand the spiritual horizons of the members of the congregation through teaching sermons and group studies of various kinds. Since retiring from pastoral ministry, I have been teaching undergraduate college general education courses in biology and religion, through which it is my hope and goal that the students will become educated for lives of fulfillment and productive citizenship in the modern world.

Through the years I have become more sensitized to the subtleties of the educational process. "The art of teaching is the art of assisting discovery," wrote Mark Van Doren. The notion of discovery lifts up an important nuance of effective teaching that relates to the meaning of *educate*. The root of educate is the Latin *educere*, from which comes the English word *educe*, meaning "to lead forth, to draw out." In leading students to new learning and understanding, an educator "draws out" from them the full possibilities of their intellect – their full reasoning capacities and their particular experiences of life. Stated another way, being involved in educating people is entering their world of informed reasoning. Drawing on the life experiences of students, an educator makes available the most valid and reliable objective information to inform the learners' reasoning processes in order to help them acquire and develop worldview presuppositions that will assist them in living meaningful and productive lives. Seen from that perspective, educating is entering the sacred spaces of learners' lives. Those of us who educate do well to respect and to honor that sacred space of each and every learner. As I have matured towards being a senior educator, I have sought to become more and more a facilitator of informed reasoning in my students.

But I also share another dimension of life with Luther – the deaths of family members. In 1528, his second child, daughter Elizabeth, died at the age of five months, which was one month younger than the age at which my first-born daughter Tammy died. In 1539, Luther's wife Katherine suffered a miscarriage. In 1542 his fourteen-year-old daughter Magdalena died. During the winter following Magdalena's death, Luther, already depressed because of his own health problems, fell into a deep depression. Very likely reflective of that depression, some of his writings during that time are very disturbing: his "On the Jews and Their Lies," written in 1543, is extremely vitriolic and very anti-Semitic. Although he appears to have recovered somewhat, he was still quite depressed when he died four years later in 1546. These family tragedies only exacerbated Luther's recurrent battles with depression during the last twenty years of his life.

I can readily identify with the depression experienced by Luther following the deaths of his children. I also suffered anxiety depression following the death of my first daughter, Tammy, in 1971. Not being familiar with the grief process, I attempted to bottle up my feelings and to "tough it out." That did not work, so I eventually sought psychiatric help, which benefited me greatly. About ten years later, after Bethany's death in 1980, I began to have many of the same feelings that I had experienced after Tammy's death, and I recognized them as symptoms of the grief process. I then became involved in Compassionate Friends, a grief support group for parents who have lost children to death; my participation in that group helped me work through my grief from the deaths of both of my daughters.

Although Luther's and my losses were undoubtedly similarly painful, I am privileged to have lived at a time when the grief process is better understood, and I was able to learn about things that I could do to help myself constructively work through it. At Luther's time such a loss was most often considered a test of faith that one should use as an occasion to closely examine one's faith in and relationship to God. Because of Luther's certainty concerning the veracity and authority of the Bible, he likely concluded that his losses were somehow judgments by God of his faith and/or life; not surprisingly, such conclusions drove him to greater depression and despair. As a result of my losses, my traditional faith was also tested. Rather than assuming that my traditional faith was correct and therefore concluding that the fault lay with me and my practice of that faith (as Luther probably did), I began to question the veracity and credibility of the tenets of my traditional faith. I found my traditional faith and concept of God wanting, and I was ultimately led to my faith in *Nature's Creativity* as the most valid symbol of *UUR*.

Because the deaths of my daughters and wife occurred during the months of June and July, these remain difficult months for me every year, although the last of these losses occurred more than fifteen years ago. If I fail to remember my family members' deaths, troublesome emotions bubble up from my subconscious memory on these calendar dates until I consciously acknowledge my losses; once I have "tipped my hat" to these losses, I can move on. I have come to regard the grief process as being similar to recovering from alcoholism or drug addiction: it is something that I will continue to do

for the rest of my life.

To help me work through the grief process, I have adopted the following mantra for myself: *whenever I am feeling down and depressed, I need to remember my losses.* Earlier I have recounted in some detail the deaths of Tammy (1971), Bethany (1980) and Darlene (1991), which started me on the journey of questioning my traditional faith. While very significant, these were just the first of my many losses. I have come to realize that, while *Nature's Creativity* has provided and continues to provide many blessings and opportunities for me in life, my living meaningfully, healthily and productively depends on how I deal with *all* the losses in my life – which can be losses of various kinds.

As I write these lines, I am still dealing with the death of my mother, who died on December 1, 2005 – more than two years ago. Unlike the deaths of my children and wife, her multiple myeloma-caused death at age 85 came at the end of a full life and, therefore, seemed to follow a more "natural" course of events: parents are expected to die before their children do. Yet, my loss of her was of the person who birthed and nurtured me – her first-born. Although I very much love, admire and respect my still-living father and share many interests with him, I was emotionally closer to my mother. I continue to deal with her death. Moreover, as I write these lines, my father has passed his eighty-eighth birthday – an age at which I realize that he will likely not be with me for too many more years. So the prospect of his death constitutes an anticipated loss.

But deaths have not been my only significant losses. Soon after the death of my wife Darlene in 1991, I felt a call to pastoral ministry, where I envisioned that I could minister especially to others who had experienced similar losses of loved ones. While attending seminary, I gained a fuller appreciation of the importance of questioning elements of my faith that I had hitherto accepted on claimed biblical and/or Church authority. After completing seminary and

240

being ordained, I carried with me into pastoral ministry my inquiring mind on matters of faith and religion, and I invited the members of the congregation that I served to join me in that journey of inquiry. While many members found that approach refreshing and enlightening, others did not accept that approach and were critical and unaccepting of my doing so. A consequence of that conflict was that, after only four and one-half years of pastoral ministry, at the end of 2001, I resigned from pastoral ministry. Reflecting on that overall experience, I concluded that my divergent religious understandings and beliefs made it impossible for me to continue pastoral ministry. This disappointment and sense of failure was also a deep emotional loss with which I am still dealing. It has been said that the loss of one's job is perhaps more destructive of one's sense of well-being than is the death of a family member, because in the modern world one's job is so closely associated with one's identity and sense of self-worth. I believe that conclusion may be true for me. While my previous grief experiences were with the deaths of close family members, this loss struck more deeply at the heart of my personal being.

In addition to the "job" loss that came from leaving pastoral ministry, there was also the separation from Lutheran congregational and denominational communities that accompanied it. My spiritual journey was leading me so far afield from traditional Lutheranism that I was no longer in spiritual fellowship with those of that religious tradition. I found myself on a lonely road looking for fellow travelers with whom I could relate.

Despite the foregoing disappointment, I left pastoral ministry after having confirmed for myself that teaching was something that I could do quite well and which brought me much personal satisfaction and fulfillment. Moreover, during my half-time pastoral ministry as copastor with my wife, I had concurrently been teaching part-time for four

and one-half years as an adjunct professor of biology at nearby Catawba College, a liberal arts college of 1000-1500 students with both traditional daytime and adult evening programs. Having both an M. S. and Ph. D in the biological sciences and an M. Div., I explored the possibilities of more teaching opportunities in biology and in religion. I reasoned that, if I could demonstrate high quality teaching in courses that the college needed and wanted me to teach, the college would see fit to offer me a full-time faculty position. Through the 2001-2003 academic years I was given the opportunity as an adjunct professor to teach more courses in both the daytime and evening programs, sometimes even carrying a full teaching load or more. The student evaluations of my teaching were consistently good to excellent. My interactions with the faculty and administration were extensive and positive. I felt that things were moving positively towards a possible full-time faculty position doing what is most meaningful and fulfilling in my life.

Then in the spring of 2004 it became apparent that additional teaching staff would be needed for the following fall semester in the biology department. The course that needed to be taught was a beginning biology course that I was qualified to teach. The biology department chairman and the academic dean approached me about teaching the course. Together with the other courses that I was scheduled to teach, my teaching load would be full-time. Therefore, I was offered a visiting professor position for the fall semester that included full-time benefits. Because the situation for the spring semester was still unclear, I was told that the details for it would be worked out when specific needs for it became known.

The fall semester came and I threw myself fully into the courses that I was teaching, confident that I could teach them well enough that the college would see fit to have me continue to teach the courses that I was teaching. Perhaps the college would give me the opportunity to teach other biology courses, and hopefully even want me to teach courses that drew on my rather extensive background and experience relating to the intersection of science and religion.

When the middle of the fall semester came and I had not heard any more about the spring semester, I began to be concerned. I made an appointment with the academic dean to discuss the matter and was informed that there would not be a full-time position for me in the spring semester. The only teaching opportunities would again be as an adjunct professor, which, of course, included no benefits. I tried to make the case that I was ideally qualified to offer a course or courses that would deal with the science-religion interface and contribute towards the interdisciplinary effort that the college was emphasizing at the time. When I inquired whether my teaching was satisfactory, I was assured that it was indeed good, but that good-to-excellent teaching was not sufficient grounds to reward a person with a full-time position. I remember wondering what would be sufficient, but I was too stunned to ask.

I was devastated by the results of that meeting – so much so that as I was driving home after that meeting I was involved in a fender-bender accident with a Salisbury city bus. The accident was not serious; no one was hurt. I was clearly at fault for attempting to move my car into the lane already occupied by the bus. I am sure that I was already beginning to deal with the emotional repercussions of that earlier meeting.

I am still dealing with that loss today. It was not a loss of something that I actually possessed. Rather, it was something that I had anticipated having – and had conditioned myself to believe that I would and should have gotten. While I cannot prove that anyone at the college was dishonest with me, I feel that I was not dealt with in a straight-forward, open and professional manner. Whatever the facts of that ordeal, I am dealing with the reality of not having gotten something that would have meant a great deal to me. Moreover, it involved teaching – the vocation that I find meaningful and fulfilling and for which I have been assured by many students in numerous settings that I have considerable skills and abilities. Because this perceived loss involved teaching – something so close to my identity, I have found grieving that *loss* nearly as painful as the deaths of my family members. But I must and am dealing with it, and I will move on.

Yet another loss that I am experiencing is the biological decline that accompanies advancing age. As I am now in my mid-60s, I am quite aware that I no longer have the strength and stamina that I had twenty or even five years ago. While this modest physical and perhaps mental decline does not prevent me from doing anything that I really want to do, it does constitute another loss in my life that I must accept and deal with.

Finally, the place where I have arrived in my spiritual journey has resulted in other losses of sorts. Conceiving *UUR* as *Nature's Creativity* means that many aspects of traditional Christian mythology are lost as emotional props in my life. The notion of *Nature's Creativity* is impersonal, unlike the loving, caring and providing Father God of traditional Christianity. The notion of praying to *Nature's Creativity* in the hope and expectation of answering specific requests or in thanksgiving does not make sense any longer. The prospect of resurrection to life after death and being united with one's loved ones in heaven I now regard as an understandably motivating development in the course of early Christianity but without any basis in reality or as real possibility. Whatever does happen to us after death is unknowable, but it likely has no resemblance to the afterlife conceptions of Christianity or any other religion. These are among the most notable *losses* of abandoning the tenets of traditional Christianity and adopting authentic faith and religion for the modern world.

I noted earlier that several years after Tammy's death I was diagnosed with clinical anxiety depression, which was caused by my not grieving her death in a healthy and constructive manner. After the other losses of my life, I have also experienced transient periods of depression, although most did not reach the degree of severity of that earliest bout. Recently, I have come to better understand depression and how to deal with it in my life. In his book *The Depression Cure: The 6-Step Program to Beat Depression without Drugs,* Stephen S. Ilardi presents strong evidence that much clinical depression in modern life derives from our attempts to require our bodies and minds to do things that they are not evolutionarily adapted to do. Because our genetic heritage has changed little in the last twelve thousand years, the structures and functions of our bodies and minds remain adapted to essentially the same lifestyle of our hunter-gatherer forebears. Indeed, numerous studies of present-day hunter-gatherer lifestyles have shown them to be strongly anti-depressant; clinical depression is virtually unknown in those "primitive" societies that exist today. However, beginning with the invention of agriculture some twelve thousand years ago and accelerating especially during the twentieth century, dramatic changes in six aspects of particularly western lifestyles have occurred, and the incidence of clinical depression has correspondingly soared. First, we get much less physical activity than did our forebears, who foraged and hunted for food. Second, we are sleep-deprived; we get much less sleep than our early ancestors, who slept a goodly portion of the dark hours every day. Third, we work indoors and have much less exposure to sunlight; even well-lighted indoor work places do not provide the necessary light to meet our bodies' needs and to maintain our biological sleep clocks. Fourth, omega-3 fatty acids have profound effects on brain structure and function; since the beginning of agriculture, our diet has transitioned from one that was omega-3 fatty acid-balanced to one that is extremely omega-3-deficient. Fifth, our social structure has evolved from local, extensively interacting, extended families to geographically separated, solitary individuals and nuclear families who often do not even know the people living next door; this has resulted in inadequate social support and pathological isolation. Sixth, for various reasons more modern people seem to be involved in life activities that they do not find engaging and fulfilling; this leads to obsessive brooding and rumination about one's personal problems, which can lead to a downward spiral into depression. Applying this knowledge to myself, if I sense the onset of depression, I examine these six aspects of my life to see if any are tending away from their respective healthy norms.

It is particularly in the sixth aspect – participation and engagement in fulfilling activities – that I have been most challenged. Reflection on and retrospective analysis of my life's narrative is by its nature an introspective process; it involves recalling, reviewing and reassessing the meaning and impact of the various life events that I have experienced – particularly the tragedies. If I do this reflective and retrospective analysis appropriately, I am able to discover instructive insights for meaning and better living; if I become obsessed and ruminate over the loss that I am analyzing, I can be pulled down the spiral towards depression. Thus, when I say that *"whenever I am feeling down and depressed, I need to remember my losses,"* I must remind myself to remember them and to acknowledge the effects that they have had on me but not to ruminate and to obsess over them. Ruminating and obsessing over them gives them a continuing unhealthy influence and power over me that can drag me down towards depression. The solution to this problem, as suggested in Ilardi's book, is to decide *a priori* that I will allow myself only a fixed amount of time – five or ten minutes – to meditate on the matter and then to move on to a new thought or activity. Thus far, that approach seems to be working for me.

Even so, dealing with my losses will

remain a necessary, life-long process for me. As I live in the present and into the future, I must continue to acknowledge the foregoing variety of losses that I have experienced and will continue to experience. In dealing with my losses, I am committed to continue using informed reasoning to find truth and authentic faith for my life. When I become depressed, I need to remind myself to appropriately remember my losses. I have grieved and will continue to grieve each of them. As I grieve these losses, I move forward to discover and to adopt meaningful and inspiring thoughts and actions that support and enhance my faith in *Nature's Creativity* as *UUR*.

Living involves change. Some changes are blessings and new opportunities; other changes are losses and challenges to continued meaningful existence. Living fully involves making the most of the former and dealing with the latter as best I can. Sometimes dealing with losses means minimizing their harmful effects and impacts on my life; at other times I can try and even succeed in turning them into challenges and opportunities for growth and for good.

At the beginning of this book I recounted the details surrounding my birth and noted that my father, in his haste to visit my mother and me a few hours after my birth, left a bucket of about 120 eggs on an unheated porch of their farm house. Because my birth occurred in late January in Kansas, the eggs all froze, and my father had to find as many ways to eat eggs as possible in order not to waste any of them. In relating those details, I suggested that that incident became a metaphor for my life. In dealing with my losses and disappointments I have attempted to use my own version of an oft-stated adage: when life presents you with broken eggs, pick out the eggshells and learn how to make and to enjoy scrambled eggs. Occasionally, you may even be able to make and to savor a gourmet omelet.

The losses of earnings from leaving pastoral ministry and not receiving a college faculty appointment were deep disappoint-

ments to me. As a result, my wife Linda and I had to live on the more modest income provided by her part-time pastoral ministry and by my income from part-time teaching as an adjunct professor. Those events and circumstances forced us to assess which expenditures are necessary and important in life. The result was that we were able to simplify our lives and to live with less disposable income and therefore less "stuff." We learned that we can have as much meaning and fulfillment with a lifestyle that has been termed by some as "frugalitarian." Those experiences prepared us for "living green," the code phrase for responsible, environmental living in today's world. We can still enjoy life, perhaps even more meaningfully, as we are preparing for retirement in the not-too-distant future.

Another "omelet" came in the wake of my resignation from pastoral ministry. The loss of my pastoral ministry "job" certainly was a blow to my identity and self-esteem. Yet, it was a decision that I had to make in order to maintain my own integrity. However, as I now look back to that time, I see that at least some of the reasons that caused me to make the decision to resign came out of the struggles that I was having trying to constrain my life within the bounds of traditional Lutheran Christianity. Released from the yoke of Lutheran pastoral ministry, I was freed – yes, even impelled – to engage the struggles and to follow the journey that has led me to my current faith understanding. Remaining in pastoral ministry would have inhibited and delayed my moving forward in my journey in search for truth and for authentic faith.

Through the years, as I have continued to face calamities, hardships and disappointments, two additional adages have come to make more sense to me. The first is: "Sometimes opportunity comes disguised as hardship." The second, more hyperbolic perhaps, is: "A crisis is a terrible thing to waste." Neither of these adages suggests that hardships and crises will be without the discomfort or even extreme pain that accompanied most of my life crises. Yet, both of them imply that it is how I decide to interpret and to react to the crises and hardships – how I choose to assess them in a larger context – that determines whether only bad consequences or also some good eventualities will occur in my life. To be sure, I most certainly would never have chosen to face any of the difficulties and losses that life has dealt me. Nevertheless, it seems to me that I have learned to face crises better as each occurred successively in the past because, as I was assembling a more valid and reliable worldview, I was able to assess each new crisis and hardship in a more authentic larger context. I was better able to find and to imagine new realistic possibilities than I could with my outdated worldview. I still do not go searching for crises, but now, when they come, I am inclined to look for the silver lining in the cloud sooner than I would have in the past.

In this book I have drawn heavily on knowledge and understanding that are attributable to the scientific method and the vast body of knowledge that it has generated and continues to produce. The scientific method is important because, when properly utilized, it is a dispassionate consideration of information derived from observations of natural phenomena. Its forte is that it assiduously attempts to accurately describe and to define "what is"; it is working at its best when it keeps us from infusing into our interpretation erroneous presuppositions or feelings of what we might like them to be. It seeks to provide a straight-forward understanding of truth about reality. Its consistent and iterated use leads to truths about reality that are continually being refined and corrected. Its faithful use identifies and corrects errors in the body of knowledge that it produces. At any given time, our scientific knowledge represents our best understanding of what is going on in our natural world – both what is within ourselves as well as what is outside us.

Yet knowledge provided by the scientific method alone was not sufficient for me to "understand my life backwards." Indeed, much of the truth of the Kierkegaard statement was in evidence before the dawn of the scientific age. The truth of Kierkegaard's statement coalesced through use of the rational, reasoning capacities endowed to us humans by *Nature's Creativity* through the evolutionary creative process. The logical processing that led to "understanding life backwards" was undoubtedly informed by truths provided by scientific information, but the truth of the statement itself was not a product of the scientific method. Thus, I conclude that it is the analytical reasoning capacity of us humans that is foundational to understanding life backwards. Scientific information serves to ensure that we accurately understand life backwards in the context of the real world in which we live. In our collective decision-making, we humans have more consistently acted in the best interests of ourselves and of the world around us when we have listened to our better "angels" of deliberative reasoning informed by life experiences and by sound scientific knowledge than when we have acted on our emotions or on sectarian tenets of one or another religion. The latter have often led to catastrophes of unimaginable proportions such as we see today in forms of terrorism that derive from fundamentalistic religious interpretations.

Throughout this book I have attempted to draw on my life experiences and on my reasoning capacity as a human informed by the best human understanding of reality as provided by modern science in order to understand my life backwards. The results of this deliberative process have led me to a very different paradigm of understanding than the traditional Judeo-Christian tradition that formed me and guided me for much of my life. My new understanding of faith and religion brings me a new status. I am a member of the human species – a highly evolved, biologically and socially complex group of organisms produced by billions of years of evolution by *Nature's Creativity*, which has endowed us with an extensive capacity to perceive, to discover and to understand the world around us. Our human species appears to be evolving towards ever greater humanness and humaneness. We humans live embedded in nature. We are interconnected to all life forms within and around us and to the physical environment that supports all of the web of life.

With this understanding I "live forwards." By participating in informed public deliberations, I contribute towards my community's formulation of the moral and ethical principles that will shape our life together. I must call upon all the resources that I have in order to acquire the self-discipline to do what is good and right. Recognizing my moral and ethical shortcomings when I act autonomously, I contract with the community both to assist and to support me in positive ways and to hold me accountable and to sanction me when I fail to live morally and ethically. Ultimately, however, I alone am responsible for whether my actions are moral and ethical. I alone am accountable for my thoughts and actions – for good or harm – to myself, to other humans and to the rest of nature. I have a responsibility to join other humans in discerning how we humans can live forwards collectively in a sustainable relationship with all our human coinhabitants of planet earth, as well as with other forms of life and our physical environment.

I live forward into that new future with an understanding of faith as confidence that *Nature's Creativity* is a reliable object of my faith. I can depend on it to provide nurture and new possibilities for me in the future as it has for me and all of life in the past. As its Latin etymological roots (*nasci* – "to be born" and *natus* – "born") indicate, nature has birthed life in all its variety and with all its marvels, and it continues to sustain and to produce new forms of life. We are constantly being born anew. There are not any other objects of faith of which I am aware that

have a 14-billion-year track record. In that sense, "rock of ages" may be an appropriate traditional religious metaphor to indicate the reliability and stability of *Nature's Creativity*.

Paraphrasing several lines of another well-known Christian hymn, "'Tis nature's brought us safe thus far, and it will lead us home." Yes, it is nature that has created all life – including all humans. We can understand life backwards, and we are acquiring a rather good understanding of how, through the evolutionary process over vast eons of time, nature has brought us "thus far." In "leading us home" we can have confidence that *Nature's Creativity* will continue to provide for us, as new mutations occur and as natural selection continues to adaptively hone living organisms in the future. However, the surprise that we have in store for us is that we do not know just what that "home" will be like: it remains a mystery and a surprise for us. Judging from Nature Creativity's past activities of evermore giving rise to marvelous, novel, emergent complexities in bringing us to the present, we can only imagine what a wonderful future might be in store for us. Morally and ethically, we must commit ourselves to stopping our activities that cause global climate change, environmental destruction, species extinction and human over-population so that we do not interfere with and short-circuit *Nature's Creativity*. As I write this, I sense serious, growing global commitments both among individuals and among nations to deal with these issues. It is mandatory and worthwhile for all of us to commit ourselves to help solve these problems. If we do, we can optimistically and expectantly live forwards.

I began this chapter with the quote attributed to Søren Kierkegaard: "It is quite true that philosophy says that life can only be understood backwards, but it must be lived forwards." While that statement has been attributed to Kierkegaard, he, in turn, acknowledges it to be the wisdom that "philosophy says." That "life can only be understood backwards" is a consensus conclusion of many philosophers through the ages, each drawing on the retrospective rational analysis of the experiences and resources of her/his own life. As I look at the statement now, it seems a truism – a self-evident, obvious truth that requires no limiting qualifications.

Yet when I first read it, it somehow struck me that *understanding my life backwards* was exactly what I was struggling to do. From that point on, I felt a bond with all others who through the ages have attempted or who today are attempting to do the same in their lives. Then, even as difficult and arduous as my struggle to understand my life backwards has been, I felt a sense of exhilarating peace – yes, even of joy. I too was "surprised by joy" in a way experienced and described by C. S. Lewis in his book with that title. Something significant and important had happened to, with, for and within me. My struggles had been worthwhile. I felt a sense of deep satisfaction and meaningful accomplishment because of having arrived at a significant point in my journey – not the end to be sure, but an important milestone along the way. I was heading out of the dark tunnel of confusion and into the light of understanding on the other side. I had found some truths that have made me free. I see and understand life from a new perspective.

Understanding my life backwards has been, for the most part, a cerebral undertaking that has been important and necessary for me. Yet, even with this newfound perspective and the sense of satisfaction that comes with having discovered it, living into the future has not been and is still not free and easy. In addition to having authentic faith and to finding truth, meaningful human life also involves emotional relationships with the larger community in which I live with my friends and with my family.

I will describe those struggles in the context of my whole life. At the beginning of this book, I recounted that, as a first-born child in my family of origin and the second of two grandchildren on my father's side of the family, my first social experiences consisted of having to learn to relate to adults. During those early years I learned ways of thinking and acting that won me acceptance and approval with adults. Even as an adult, having the approval of my parents and family and of other significant adults in my life has remained important to me, even if sometimes only subconsciously.

While I have been mostly successful in getting the approval of important adults in my life, there is one important relationship that has not been all that it might have been – the relationship between my father and me. I have recounted how he and my mother diligently reared me in the best possible way they knew, including indoctrinating me in the teachings and practices of the conservative Lutheran faith that served them and their ancestors well and teaching me to be a responsible and self-disciplined person who takes life seriously.

I became aware of how my relationship with my father did not become all that it could be when as a pastor I viewed the video "The Power of a Father's Blessing" by Pastor Dick Hardel. He used the biblical model of Isaac's blessing of Jacob rather than of older twin brother Esau. Isaac's blessing of Jacob enabled Jacob to thrive and to face life's challenges with courage and confidence, while Esau lived his life haunted by being something less than his brother – of not having received his father's full blessing. Dick relates in his own life how he could never live up to his father's expectations. His father modeled high standards and had high expectations for Dick as he was growing up. His father could acknowledge and praise Dick's contemporaries, including his cousin, for their accomplishments, but it was seemingly beyond his father's capacity to affirm and to praise Dick, his own son, in the same way. Therefore, Dick lived his life without his father's *blessing* – without being fully affirmed as the good and very successful person that his colleagues and contemporaries had affirmed him to be. The absence of that *blessing* haunted Dick throughout life. Shortly before his father's death, Dick gained some insights into how and why his father was the way that he was. The video illustrates a powerful message. I recommend that all fathers view it, if only to remind themselves of the importance of "blessing their children" while parenting them.

My relationship with my father paralleled Dick Hardel's relationship with his father. As mentioned above, my father reared me to be a responsible, self-reliant and self-disciplined person. He had high expectations of me and taught me to have high expectations of myself, for all of which I thank him as well as my mother. But I do not ever recall his praising or even complimenting me on a job well done or expressing a sense of pride or even satisfaction in any of my accomplishments. The message that I always heard and felt was to try harder to do even better. It seemed that, if I got 100% on a test, complete success was getting all the extra credit also.

Then, when nearing the age of fifty, I left the LCMS and became a member of the ELCA, which in my father's eyes tolerated incorrect biblical interpretations, erroneous doctrinal teachings and lax ethical practices. He asked me why I had left the church with the correct teachings to join one that contained errors. He then had further justification for not *blessing* me. Although my brothers in most respects accomplished no more than I did, in his eyes they at least remained true to "the one true faith" in which he had reared them. To my knowledge, however, they also did not receive overt, expressed approval, but their staying faithful to "the one true faith" merited at least an implicit *blessing*. As I look back on my relationship with my father, it seems to me in a twisted sort of way that loving and being loved in this manner gave a whole new

meaning to the term *tough love*.

I have chosen to interpret my father's relationship with me benevolently. I love my father dearly, and I am sure that he loves me. He reared me in the way that he had been reared by his father, receiving few compliments and little praise but being held to high standards of self-conduct and accomplishments; and most importantly, living a life of godliness meant retaining allegiance to "the one true faith." I am not aware of any mistreatment of my father by his father that factored into their relationship, as was the case with Dick Hardel. Rather, I have attributed my father's relationship with me to the stoical, nonaffectionate demeanor that is too often observed and transmitted through the generations, particularly in males of Germanic heritage. It can promote high ideals and great accomplishments, but it does not often result in children who have a positive and satisfying self-image or who are affectionate – both of which are fostered by a sense of having been *blessed*, particularly by their fathers.

As I relate this account of my faith journey, I do so with mixed emotions. While it is an account that I relate with full conviction and confidence that it describes who I am and where I need to be in life, it is also an account that will not be well-received by many people, including especially my family and friends. Many of them continue to hold forms of traditional Christian faith that are extensions of their childhood rearing, and they will conclude that I have lost my way spiritually or perhaps that I have simply gone crazy, because I no longer continue in the faith that sustains them. I want to assure them that I have not lost my way, although I almost surely would have, had I remained faithful to the faith of my youth and earlier life. Life has dealt me a difficult hand to play; I had to draw on all the resources that I could discover in order to find healing and wholeness again. To those who doubt and question where I have arrived, I paraphrase a Native American adage: "Do not be too quick to criticize someone unless you have walked in his moccasins for thirty moons." I did not choose the hand of life that was dealt me; nevertheless, I had and still have to play it the best that I can in order to live with myself with a sense of integrity. For those who have experienced what I have and retained their traditional faith, I respect their having done that. For many and various reasons, that was not possible for me. I ask that I be respected for what I have found to be an authentic faith and the truth for me. I am doing the best that I can to understand my life backwards and then to live it meaningfully forwards.

But it is also within my immediate family that the scars of my earlier losses intervene and interfere with my present relationships. In my early life while developing relationships first with my wife Darlene and then with my daughters, Tammy, Cheri, and Bethany, I formed deep emotional bonds with them that involved extensive and intensive commitments and investments of my very being. I experienced affection with them that I had not experienced in my family of origin. When Tammy, then Bethany, and then Darlene died, I was left with a torn shred where a loving emotional bond had existed. With each death I wondered how I could go on with life. Out of a survival response, I became protective of myself. I became increasingly guarded about how deeply I could become emotionally invested in my remaining family members, because I wondered how or if I could survive if they too should die. Pragmatically, this led to my keeping a "safe," self-protective emotional distance from my surviving family members. Intellectually I know that doing this is both understandable and counterproductive. Although it is understandably self-protective from a pragmatically emotional survival perspective, it is also counterproductive, because it prevents me from experiencing the fullest possible fulfillment that deep emotional relationships might bring to my life. It remains a challenge for me to be

willing to take that risk.

But to say that losing my daughters Tammy and Bethany and my wife Darlene to death made me "emotionally cautious" does not tell the whole story. While those losses indeed were emotionally devastating for me, they forced me to identify resources outside of me but most especially within me that would assist me in recovering from those losses. I learned that opportunities for growth sometimes come disguised as hardships. I found internal strength and resources that I did not know I possessed. I learned that finding meaningfulness, wholeness and integrity in my life involves reaching peace with and accepting myself. My sense of self and the strength to continue living are foundational to my existence; they are what give rise to whatever self-confidence I have. Deep and meaningful emotional relationships with other people are flowers in the garden of my life, but they are not the garden itself. Relationships with others ultimately cannot substitute for a healthy sense of myself.

Thus, when after my first wife Darlene's death I met Linda – who would become my second wife, I was both emotionally wounded and yet more mature because I had been steeled by the forge of my losses. Linda's first marriage had ended in divorce when her first husband decided that he wanted out of their marriage. Additionally, like my father, Linda's father had shown little affection to her as she was growing up and had failed to *bless* her with affirmation, although, as a first-born, she was a responsible and reliable person as well as a good student. Thus, when Linda and I met, she was emotionally dealing with male trust and abandonment issues. Her abandonment issues resulted from males who made both conscious and unconscious decisions that had hurt her. My abandonment issues resulted from important family members having been taken from my life by death. Each of us had a wariness about becoming emotionally close to another person and, thereby, vulnerable to being hurt again.

But we committed ourselves to do just that. We have now been married for more than fifteen years, during which we have experienced much happiness and fulfillment. Our love and mutual trust have grown to levels that neither of us has known previously in our lives. However, it goes without saying that we have had struggles as each of us tested the emotional waters in order to find the warmth that brings us closer together as a married couple. Through it all we have committed ourselves to work things out – "to fight" rather than "to take flight." When we have struggles that cannot be easily worked out, we commit to "fighting fairly." Words – even strong words – are fair game, but physical abuse and flight are not permitted in our rules of engagement. We continue to struggle with any problem until we find a satisfactory resolution for both of us. We have committed ourselves "to keep on keeping on."

Most of the struggles relating to my faith that I have written about in these pages have occurred during our married life. As mentioned earlier, shortly after our marriage I began attending the same seminary where Linda was a student and where she was graduated two years ahead of me. We shared a first call together in congregational ministry. When my personal struggle reached the point that I concluded that I could no longer continue in congregational ministry, Linda continued in pastoral ministry and finds parish ministry a fulfilling vocation to the present. That she has done so indicates that she remains comfortable within the context of her traditional Lutheran faith.

Although Linda has not struggled with her Lutheran faith as I have, she has often lent me a listening ear as I have shared the struggles of my faith. At first, as I was drifting away from my traditional Lutheran faith, she was disappointed because she saw us losing something in common that we had previously shared together in life. In spite of that, from my perspective she gave me the greatest *agape* love that she could have given me at the time: without judgment or criticism she gifted me with the freedom and the space to deal with my struggles as I needed to deal with them. Today, from a faith perspective we are a "mixed marriage." Yet during the time that it has taken for each of us to reach our respective places in our faith walks, we have become closer and more committed to each other. Our love and respect for each other have grown. We look forward to retirement in the not-too-distant future and to the enjoyment and fulfillment that that stage of our lives together will bring.

One of the gifts that aging brings to life is perspective. When traveling life's journey, I have experienced mountaintop experiences followed by descents into valleys of dark shadows. When I ascend again to new high points, I have vantage points from which to look back over the places that I have been and to try to make sense of those tragedies. Different recollections and experiences of my life stand out against each other. Sometimes similarities between these elements of my past stand out, while at other times differences are more poignant. Sometimes experiences in my life show up in recycled form in other members of my family. Seeing and appreciating them are part of what brings joy and fulfillment to me as I grow older; they are the precious moments of my life. Recently, I have had several "perspective treasures" that I want to recount.

One of my first boyhood recollections of nonchurch music was going to the café in my hometown of Palmer, Kansas, where there was a jukebox that played popular music of the time. It was there that I first heard the tune "I Walk the Line" sung by Johnny Cash. While the tune was catchy and the words spoke of matters beyond my life experiences, I was particularly fascinated by the sound and rhythm of the guitar accompaniment. It sparked my interest in learning to play the guitar, a desire that I expressed to my parents. At about the time I was in the fourth grade, I received a guitar for Christmas. I began to learn to play it, and guitar-playing became an important enjoyment and relaxation for me during my life.

Although she was not very musically inclined, my first wife Darlene also was learning to play a guitar at the time of her death. Later, my daughter Cheri too developed an interest in playing a guitar, and she has kept in her house the guitar that her mother was leaning to play. Although she no longer plays it very much, it remains accessible in the room in their home where my three-year-old grandson Keaton can see it. From time to time when visiting them, I have picked up the guitar, picked and strummed a few chords, and sang a few simple songs.

While visiting in our home, Keaton has learned that I also have several guitars that I keep in a back bedroom of our house. When Keaton recently came with his family to celebrate Christmas with us, as soon as he had come into our house and we had taken off his coat, he grabbed my hand and led me down the hall to the back bedroom, opened the door and pointed to one of my guitars. He wanted me to play it for him. I played a few chords for him, he seemed satisfied and we left the room.

Later that afternoon he took my hand, led me back to that room again, and again pointed to the guitar. I again picked it up and began playing and singing "Jingle Bells," a song that he has been learning at his preschool. This time after I had played a few chords, he indicated that he wanted to strum the guitar. He then motioned that he wanted to sit on my lap and strum the guitar while I fingered the chords with my left hand. He then strummed while I fingered the chords and sang "Jingle Bells." We then joined the rest of the family in our family room and repeated our audition – to the family's delight and to Keaton's great pleasure. For me, that was a special experience and recycled the above earlier experiences in my life.

The second experience occurred with my fifteen-month-old grandson, Grady. In chapter 1, I recounted that, while my parents were potty training me, they would set me on the potty-chair and tell me, "Now Bobbo, sit still." After sitting for perhaps ten to twenty seconds, I would say to myself, "Now Bobbo, dit doo" (my way of saying "sit still") and away I would run. It was a story that was often rehearsed within my family as we recounted stories of our childhoods and one that I also shared with my wife and children. At the aforementioned Christmas get-together at our house, Grady was sitting on the floor playing with toys. From time to time he would speak the sounds and words that he knows as he is learning to talk. At one point he looked up at the adults sitting around the room and said "Dit doo." My wife Linda and I looked at each other and we both began laughing. Over the next several minutes Grady repeated it several more times. Although it was a different context, there before me was an echo of what I must have sounded like more than sixty years earlier. What made it even more memorable was that Grady's physical appearance has many resemblances to the photograph of me taken when I was one year old – a blue-eyed, fair-skinned towhead sitting in a small chair. In talking about that childhood story of mine, Linda and I had often joked that Bobbo was so unique that it was necessary to throw away the mold after making him, because the world probably could not tolerate two such individuals. After hearing Grady say "dit doo," Linda said, "Oh, no! Here we go again." Grady's uttering "dit doo" is a story I will long cherish and retell.

Finally, when my grandson Keaton turned three, Linda and I attended his birthday party to celebrate with him on a chilly, breezy February Saturday morning. While his parents were inside their house decorating and preparing for his party which would run from 11 AM to 1 PM, Linda and I went outside to play with Keaton. We crossed the street to the neighborhood school yard, where Keaton rode the new bicycle that he had gotten for Christmas. We found a penny lying on the ground that Keaton proudly put into his jeans pocket. Keaton and I played a peeking game around the trunk of a large willow oak tree. After about an hour, Linda was feeling cold, so we returned to their house across the street. Although Linda went inside, Keaton and I remained outside in the yard, where we played for a while with his T-ball set. After perhaps fifteen minutes of playing, we wandered towards the back yard, where a small flock of about ten robins was feeding on the ground. They had apparently stopped there on their early spring migration northward. As we neared the birds, they flew up and perched in the trees about twenty or thirty feet beyond where they had been feeding on the ground. After they had landed in the trees, Keaton looked up and said to them, "Birds, don't fly away. This is Grandpa Bob."

At first, I did not think much about his statement. But as I reflected later, it began to dawn on me what I think he had meant. He was telling the birds that his grandpa was not a threat to them; they had nothing to fear. I was their friend just as I was his friend, and he wanted to introduce me to them. Keaton saw us all at least as one large circle of friends, perhaps even as one big family. Although Keaton could not have known it, that he saw me both as his friend and as a friend to his animal cousins in nature affirmed me as a faithful adherent of my authentic faith in *Nature's Creativity* and of the moral and ethical living that issues from that faith. There is hope for the future, and it rests with persons like Keaton, who see all of us together as partners in nature. As I reflected more about this experience, tears came to my eyes, and I could not stop them. They were the most tears of joy that had rolled down my cheeks in a long time.

Life is again good and getting even better.

Epilog

After I had nearly completed the writing of this book, I had two experiences that further illuminated the continual processing of my life's experience. Therefore I include them in this epilog.

One experience was discovering the following statement by Albert Einstein, written in a letter to a friend in 1901:

> A foolish faith in authority is the worst enemy of the truth.

As I reflected on that statement, I concluded that it very accurately and succinctly addressed what I have written about in this book. Among the array of definitions and synonyms of the word "foolish" apropos to the above usage are "lacking caution" and "unwise."

Through their authority over me as a child and because of their perceived importance of religion, my parents and later my church instilled in me a faith which emphasized that the Bible and the church had authority over me that was not to be questioned or challenged – "a foolish faith" according to Einstein. However, already when I was a teenager and became aware of the science-religion conflict, I began feeling the need to exercise caution in accepting teachings of the Bible and doctrines of the church, particularly in matters relating to science and understanding how the world functions. Yet, only after I reached adulthood and experienced the deaths of my family members did I acquire the knowledge and summon the courage to challenge the authority of the Bible and of the church in spiritual matters. I then realized that the church attempts to interpret the biblical narrative in a manner that largely ignores the differences in the worldviews of the times when the biblical books were written and the worldview of today. I then concluded that the enlightened way to utilize and to interpret the Bible is to take into account fully the many differences between the biblical and modern worldviews and then to sift out and to give authority only to those kernels of content that remain true today. That sifting process gives rise to an *examined* faith, which I termed an *authentic* faith. According to Einstein's statement, such an examined, authentic faith would qualify as a "wise faith"; it would be a "friend of the truth" and eminently useful for orienting one's life in the modern world.

The second experience occurred when I began a search to find other people who have had experiences in life that led them to reach similar conclusions about life and faith. I was hoping to find a group of people who might be interested in forming a group in which we could share ideas and communally pursue extensions of our individual thinking. Usually this search involved having lunch with another person, asking questions and discussing topics and ideas in order to learn whether we were thinking on wave-lengths that could communicate with and stimulate each other. Unfortunately, I found few such soulmates.

However, at one such sushi lunch meeting, I met an individual who had been reared in a traditional Roman Catholic home but who many years ago had found that religious approach not to be useful in orienting himself in life and had abandoned it. After a few short exchanges at that meal, I immediately recognized that he had come to many of the same conclusions about life and worldviews that I had reached. After discovering a number of our common understandings of life, he expressed astonishment and dismay that so many modern, intelligent, well-educated people could still continue to believe ancient mythologies and to practice rituals that no longer related to modern understandings of the world.

When I asked whether he could recommend writings that he found helpful in pursuing the topics of our common interest, he said that he had discovered that the *American Humanist Manifesto* stated remarkably clearly and succinctly many of the conclusions that he had reached about living in the modern world. Not having read or heard of it previously and being familiar with the term *manifesto* only from the *Communist Manifesto* by Karl Marx and Friedrich Engels, I was initially skeptical about what it might contain. When I looked it up in the dictionary, I was surprised to learn that a manifesto is simply "a public declaration of intentions, opinions, objectives or motives, as one issued by a government, sovereign, or organization." A Google internet search informed me that the *American Humanist Manifesto* was first drawn up in 1933 (I) and was updated in 1973 (II). In 2003 it (III) was updated again and condensed into six well-crafted, topical sentences, each accompanied by a few sentences of expansion and explanation. Readers who have resonated with conclusions reached in this book and who are not already familiar with the *American Humanist Manifesto III* will find it a very useful summary of the elements of a modern worldview.

My reading and reflecting on the details of *American Humanist Manifesto III* was a kind of epiphany in that it included concise statements of many of the conclusions that I had reached in my struggling to understand my life backwards. I also understood why my friend had concluded that he could not express the concepts any better or more clearly than stated in the *Manifesto*.

I also began to see why my friend, having many years ago abandoned his traditional Roman Catholic religion and accepted the ideas and positions in the *Manifesto*, would find it difficult to understand how an intelligent, well-informed modern person could still believe and be guided by ancient mythological understandings. As I reflected further, I realized that the contents of the *Manifesto* are clearly obvious and credible to someone *who has already worked through the struggles from a traditional religion towards acceptance of a modern worldview*. That is why the tenets of the *Manifesto* seemed so obviously correct to my friend and now also to me.

But to someone who is beginning or who has only partly worked through the struggles from a traditional Christian upbringing to an informed modern worldview, the statements of the *Manifesto* are too great a "leap of faith" from traditional Christianity. One simply cannot get from the former to the latter by reading the *Manifesto*. There is little or no logical connection.

The story is told of an urban man who wished to visit a village in a backwoods area that had relatively few roads, most of which were neither well-mapped nor well-marked. However, the man was confident of his own navigational skills and felt he could find the village on his own. After traveling for some time in the backwoods and realizing that he was completely lost, he came upon a native who was walking along the road. He stopped to ask the native if he knew where the village was and how he could get to the village. The native replied, "Yes, I know where that village is, but you can't get there from here."

From an objective perspective, the native was not correct. If the village was somewhere in the vicinity, one could have traveled by some means to get to the village. But from his perspective at the place where the visitor from the city asked him, the local native concluded that "you can't get there from here."

To people who are *here* – indoctrinated and firmly integrated into traditional Christianity, it seems impossible, at least in any simple and direct way, to get *there* – situated and oriented in a thoroughly modern worldview. From my own experience, I can appreciate and understand that the journey from *here* to *there* occurs through a gradual process in which informed reasoning moves us step by step from *here* to *there*. People who have not made that journey (or perhaps have made it in their distant past) may find it impossible to appreciate and to accept the difficulty of making the journey from *here* to *there*. Moreover, in a person's life the longer one has lived *here*, the more difficult it is to get *there*.

Unfortunately, too often the attitudes of people who are already *there* towards people who are still *here* are characterized by belittlement, ridicule and condescension, often implying a lack of intelligence and reasoning capacity by people who are *here*. In the realm of human relations, such attitudes almost never serve to win people over to a new way of thinking – no matter how valid, reliable and desirable that new perspective might be. Much more productive is respectfully engaging people in a way that invites them to undertake that journey. To be sure, many will not want to take that journey because it is simply too threatening for them. Others who have already been asking themselves serious questions about the validity of their traditional religion may be curious and even eager to proceed on that journey. For those persons, the willingness of a *there* person to walk step by step with them

through that journey is invaluable. The journey is ultimately traveled when through informed reasoning the *here* person convinces him/herself to give up one by one those tenets of traditional Christianity no longer credible and to replace them with worldview elements that are helpful in orienting a person in the modern world. When that process is well under way, a bridge from *here* to *there* will have been constructed.

It is my hope that this book can assist people in traveling step by step the journey from traditional Christianity (and other ancient religions) to a worldview that embraces tenets such as those included in the *American Humanist Manifesto*. For those of us who are *there*, it seems important and necessary that the process of informed reasoning become the norm for planning and ordering our lives, in order for individuals and nations in our global community to find ways to live together peaceably and to use and to share our planet's resources responsibly and sustainably. Indeed, both human survival and our planet's survival depend upon it.

Citations and References

Introduction

Marshall, George N. and Poling, David. *Schweitzer: A Biography*. Baltimore, Maryland: Johns Hopkins Paperbacks. 2000, p. 205.

Chapter 2

Gould, Stephen Jay, "Nonoverlapping Magisteria." *Natural History* 106:16-22, March 1997.

Kipling, Rudyard, "If," from *A Complete Collection of Poems by Rudyard Kipling*. http://www.poetryloverspage.com/poets/kipling/kipling_ind.html.

Chapters 7, 8, 9 and 10

Achtemeier, Paul J., Ed. *Harper Collins Bible Dictionary*. San Francisco: Harper. 1996, 1256 pp.

Buttrick, George Arthur, Ed. *The Interpreter's Dictionary of the Bible*. Nashville: Abingdon Press. 1991, Five Volumes.

Darwin, Charles. *The Origin of Species*. 1859.

Darwin, Charles. *The Descent of Man*. 1871.

Dowley, Tim, Ed. *Eerdmans' Handbook to the History of Christianity*. Grand Rapids, MI: Wm. B. Eerdmans Publishing Co. 1977, 640 pp.

Harris, Stephen L. The *New Testament: A Student's Introduction*. Fourth Edition. McGraw-Hill. 2002, 480 pp.

Jacobson, Diane L. and Kysar, Robert. *A Beginner's Guide to the Books of the Bible*. Minneapolis, MN: Augsburg. 1991, 125 pp.

Lutheran Book of Worship. Minneapolis, MN: Augsburg Publishing House. 1978.

Metzger, Bruce M. and Murphy, Roland E. *The New Oxford Annotated Bible: New Revised Standard Version*. New York: Oxford University Press. 1991.

Mills, Watson E., Ed. *Mercer Dictionary of the Bible*. Macon, Georgia: Mercer University Press. 1991, 993 pp.

Occasional Services: A Companion to Lutheran Book of Worship. Minneapolis, MN: Augsburg Publishing House. 1982, 316 pp.

The Random House College Dictionary. Revised Edition. New York: Random House, Inc. 1980, 1568 pp.

Selvidge, Marla J. *Exploring the New Testament*. Second Edition. Upper Saddle River, NJ: Pearson-Prentice Hall. 2002, 424 pp.

Tappert, Theodore G., in collaboration with Pelikan, Jaroslav, Fischer, Robert H. and Piepkorn, Arthur C. *The Book of Concord: The Confessions of the Evangelical Lutheran Church*. Philadelphia, PA: Fortress Press. 1959, 717 pp.

Tullock, John H. and McEntire, Mark. *The Old Testament Story*. NJ: Upper Saddle River: Pearson-Prentice Hall. 8th ed., 2009. 433 pp.

The New Interpreter's Bible: General Articles and Introduction, Commentary, and Reflections for Each Book of the Bible Including the Apocryphal/Deuterocanonical Books in Twelve Volumes. Nashville: Abingdon Press. 1994.

http://www.google.com/search?hl=en&lr=&oi=defmore&q=define:authority.

Chapter 11

Diamond, Jared. *The Third Chimpanzee: The Evolution and Future of the Human Animal*. New York: Harper Perennial. 1992, 407 pp.

Gould, Stephen Jay, "Nonoverlapping Magisteria." *Natural History* 106:16-22, March 1997.

http://atheisme.free.fr/Religion/What-is-religion-1.htm.

Lewis, Ricki. *Human Genetics: Concepts and Applications*. 8th ed., New York: McGraw-Hill, 2008, 442 pp.

Metzger, Bruce M. and Murphy, Roland E. *The New Oxford Annotated Bible: New Revised Standard Version*. New York: Oxford University Press. 1991.

Chapter 12

Briggs, John and Peat, F. David. *Turbulent Mirror: An Illustrated Guide to Chaos Theory and the Science of Wholeness*. New York: Harper and Row. 1990, 222 pp.

Complexity\definecomplexity - Google Search.mht.

Definition of knowledge - Merriam-Webster Online Dictionary.mht.

Diamond, Jared. *The Third Chimpanzee: The Evolution and Future of the Human Animal*. New York: Harper Perennial. 1992, 407 pp.

EXPLORING CHRISTIANITY: Four major worldviews.mht.

Free Online Dictionary, - worldview.htm.

Gleick, James. *Chaos: Making a New Science*. New York: Penguin Group. 1987, 352 pp.

Gould, Stephen Jay, "Nonoverlapping Magisteria." *Natural History* 106:16-22, March 1997.

Hawking, Stephen and Mlodinow, Leonard. *The Grand Design*. New York: Bantam, 2010, 208 pp.

http://en.wikipedia.org/wiki/M-theory.

http://en.wikipedia.org/wiki/Dark_Matter.

http://en.wikipedia.org/wiki/Knowledge#Defining_knowledge_.28philosophy.29.

Kaufman, Gordon D. *God the Problem*. Cambridge, MA: Harvard University Press. 1972, 276 pp.

Kaufman, Gordon D. *In Face of Mystery: A Constructive Theology*. Cambridge, MA: Harvard University Press. 1993, 507 pp.

Kauffman, Stuart A. *The Origins of Order: Self-organization and Selection in Evolution*. New York: Oxford University Press, 1993, 709 pp.

Knowledge\defineknowledge - Google Search.mht.

Knowledge - definition of knowledge by the Free Online Dictionary, Thesaurus and Encyclopedia.htm.

Merriam-Webster Online Dictionary.mht. Definition of weltanschauung.

Nicolis, Grégoire, and Prigogine, Ilya. *Exploring Complexity: An Introduction*. New York: W. H. Freeman and Company. 1989, 313 pp.

String Theory\Wikipedia String Theory.mht.

Website: Chaos Theory and Fractals.

Wilson, Edward O. *Consilience: The Unity of Knowledge*. New York: Vintage Books. 1998, 367 pp.

Worldview Materials\What is a world view.mht.

Worldview Materials\Worldview - Web definitions.mht.

Chapter 13

Crosby, Donald. *A Religion of Nature*. Albany, NY: State University of New York Press. 2002, 200 pp.

Haught, John F. *God after Darwin: A Theology of Evolution*. Boulder, CO: Westview Press. 2000, 221 pp.

Haught, John F. *Deeper than Darwin: The Prospect for Religion in the Age of Evolution*. Boulder, CO: Westview Press. 2003, 214 pp.

Kaufman, Gordon D. *In Face of Mystery: A Constructive Theology*. Cambridge, MA: Harvard University Press. 1993, 507 pp.

Metzger, Bruce M. and Murphy, Roland E. *The New Oxford Annotated Bible: New Revised Standard Version*. New York: Oxford University Press. 1991.

Shaw, George Bernard. *Everybody's Political What's What*. London, England: nConstable. 1944, ch. 19.

Chapter 14

Diamond, Jared. *Collapse: How Societies Choose to Fail or Succeed*. New York: Penguin Group. 2005, 575 pp.

Gore, Al. *The Assault on Reason*. New York: The Penguin Press. 2007, 308 pp.

Hecht, Jennifer Michael. *Doubt: A History: The Great Doubters and Their Legacy of Innovation from Socrates and Jesus to Thomas Jefferson and Emily Dickinson*. San Francisco, CA: Harper. 2003, 551 pp.

Metzger, Bruce M. and Murphy, Roland E. *The New Oxford Annotated Bible: New Revised Standard Version*. New York: Oxford University Press. 1991.

Stein, Jess, Ed. *The Random House College Dictionary: Revised Edition*. New York: Random House. 1973, 1,568 pp.

Chapter 15

Hannay, Alastair, *Soren Kierkegaard: Papers and Journals: A Selection. 1840-1945: Berlin and the First Round*. New York: Penguin Books USA Inc. 1996. (43 IV A 164).

Hardel, Dick. "The Power of a Father's Blessing." Video presentation at August 1999 ELCA Lutheran Men in Mission Conference at Breckenridge, CO.

Hecht, Jennifer Michael. *Doubt: A History: The Great Doubters and Their Legacy of Innovation from Socrates and Jesus to Thomas Jefferson and Emily Dickinson*. San Francisco, CA: Harper. 2003, 551 pp.

Ilardi, Stephen S. *The Depression Cure: The 6-Step Program to Beat Depression without Drugs*. Cambridge, MA: Da Capo Press. 2009, 289 pp.

Lewis, C. S. *Surprised by Joy*. Orlando, FL: Harcourt Brace and Company, 1955, 238 pp.

Luther, Martin. "On the Jews and Their Lies." 1543. Translated by Martin H. Bertram. Web address: Martin Luther - On the Jews and Their Lies.mht.

Peck, M. Scott. *The Road Less Traveled: A New Psychology of Love, Traditional Values and Spiritual Growth*. New York: Simon & Schuster. 1978, 316 pp.

Epilog

Einstein, Albert. Letter to a friend in 1901. http://www.whale.to/vaccine/quotes4.htm

http://www.americanhumanist.org/Who_We_Are/About_Humanism/Humanist_Manifesto_I.

http://www.americanhumanist.org/Who_We_Are/About_Humanism/Humanist_Manifesto_II.

http://www.americanhumanist.org/Who_We_Are/About_Humanism/Humanist_Manifesto_III.

223828LV00003B/1/P